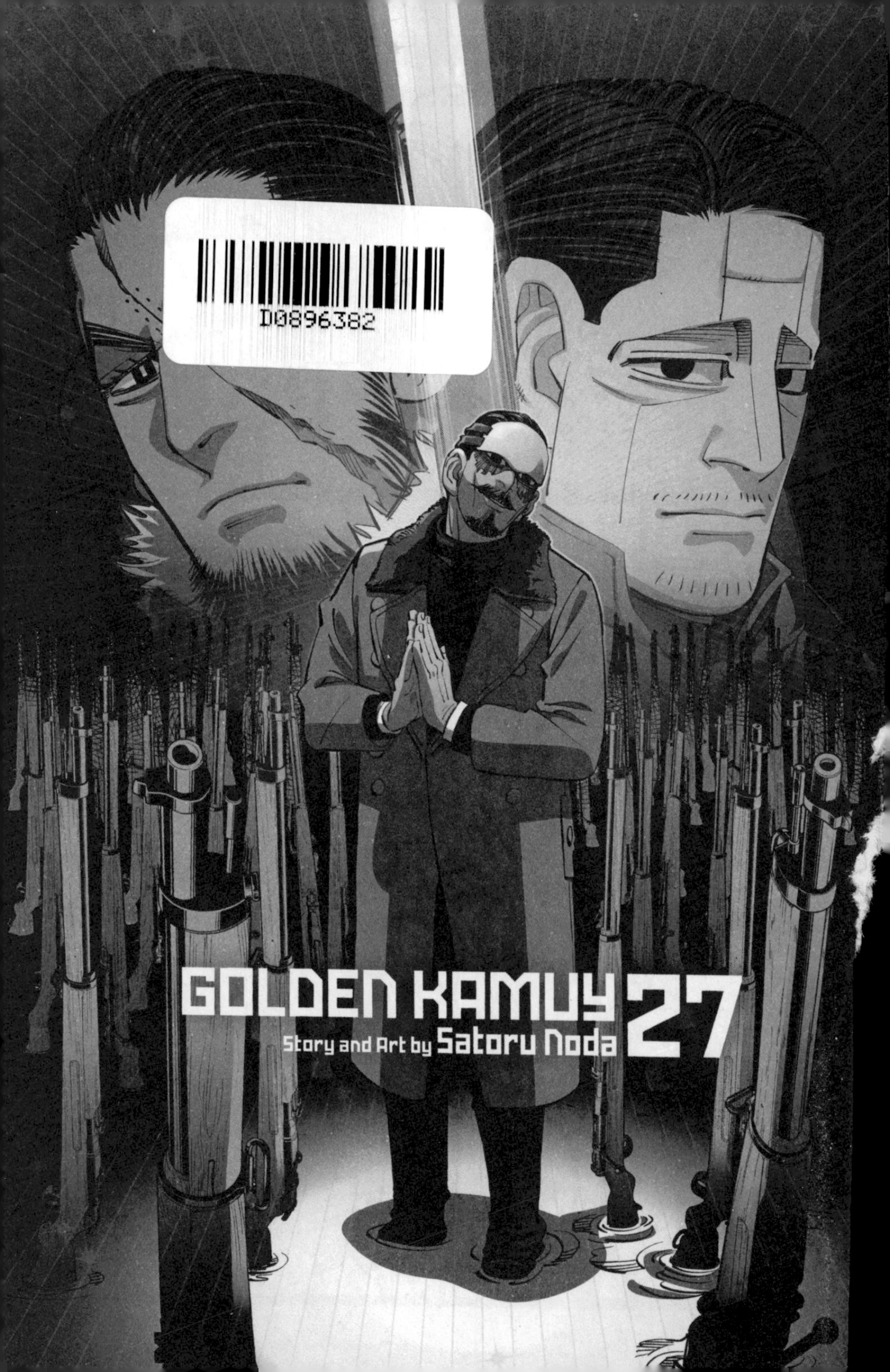
GOLDEN KAMUY 27
Story and Art by Satoru Noda

The Story So Far

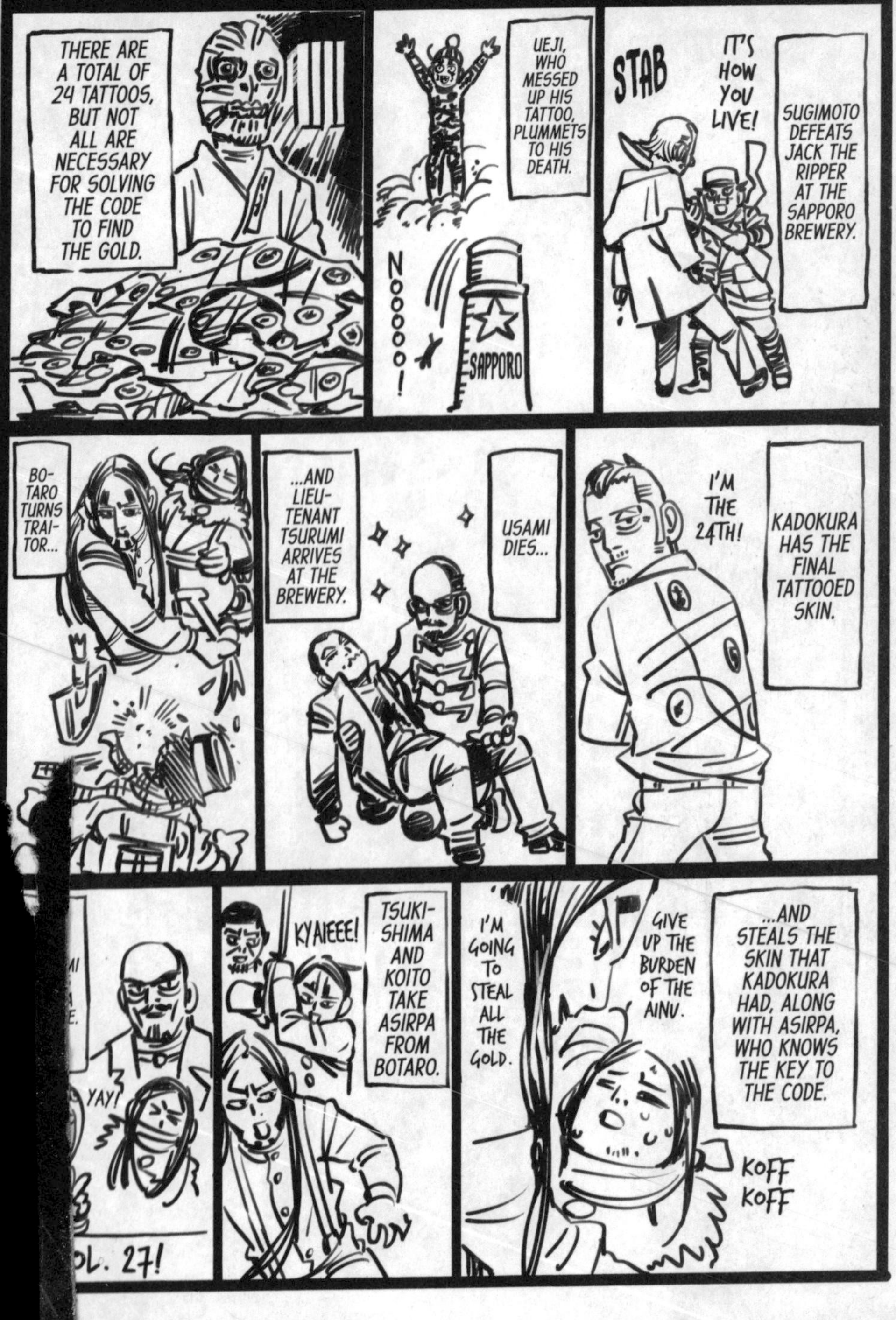
SUGIMOTO DEFEATS JACK THE RIPPER AT THE SAPPORO BREWERY.
IT'S HOW YOU LIVE!
STAB
UEJI, WHO MESSED UP HIS TATTOO, PLUMMETS TO HIS DEATH.
NOOOOO!
SAPPORO
THERE ARE A TOTAL OF 24 TATTOOS, BUT NOT ALL ARE NECESSARY FOR SOLVING THE CODE TO FIND THE GOLD.
KADOKURA HAS THE FINAL TATTOOED SKIN.
I'M THE 24TH!
USAMI DIES...
...AND LIEUTENANT TSURUMI ARRIVES AT THE BREWERY.
BOTARO TURNS TRAITOR...
...AND STEALS THE SKIN THAT KADOKURA HAD, ALONG WITH ASIRPA, WHO KNOWS THE KEY TO THE CODE.
GIVE UP THE BURDEN OF THE AINU.
I'M GOING TO STEAL ALL THE GOLD.
KOFF KOFF
TSUKISHIMA AND KOITO TAKE ASIRPA FROM BOTARO.
KYAIEEE!
YAY!

GOLDEN KAMUY

Story and Art by **Satoru Noda**

27

CONTENTS

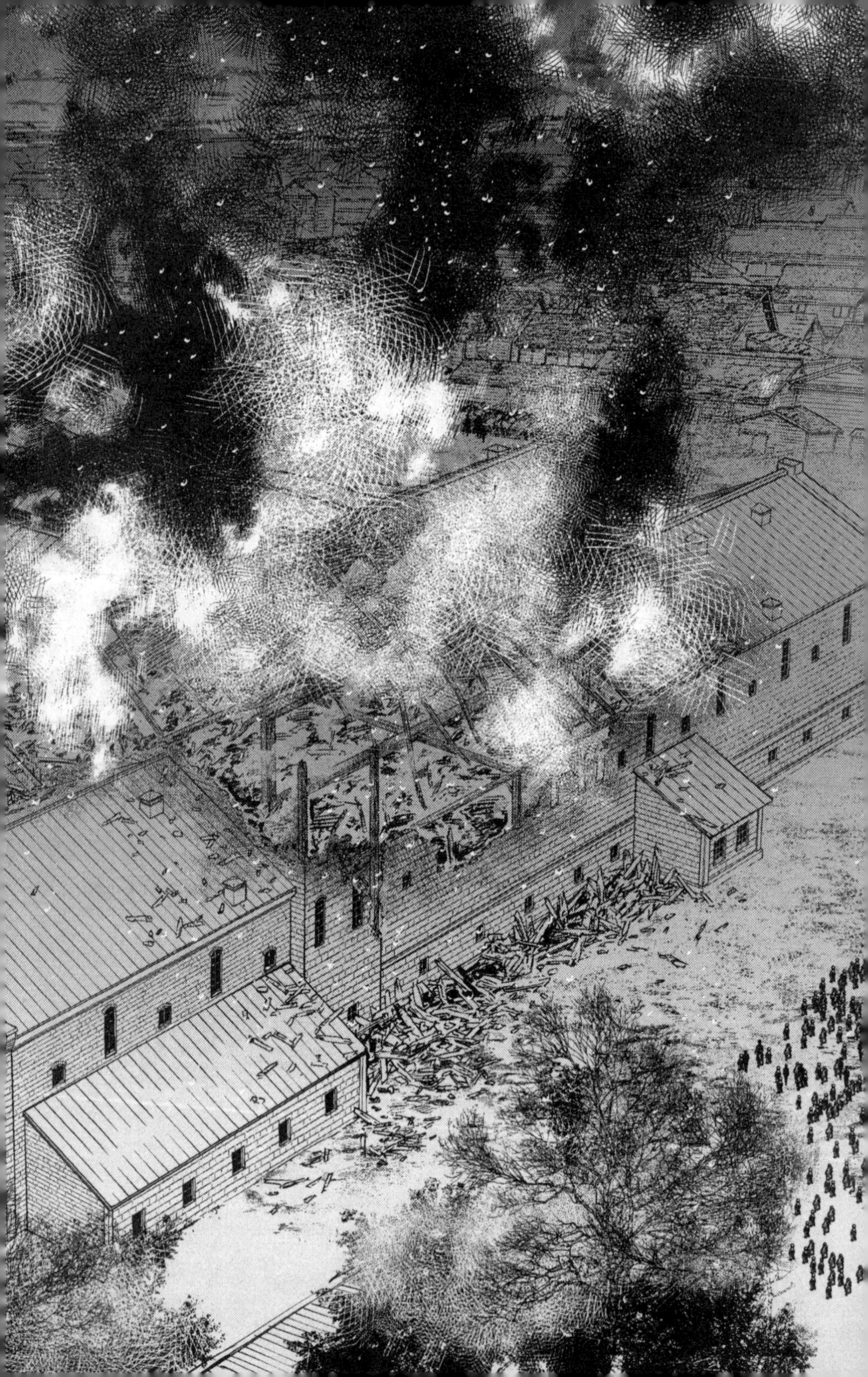

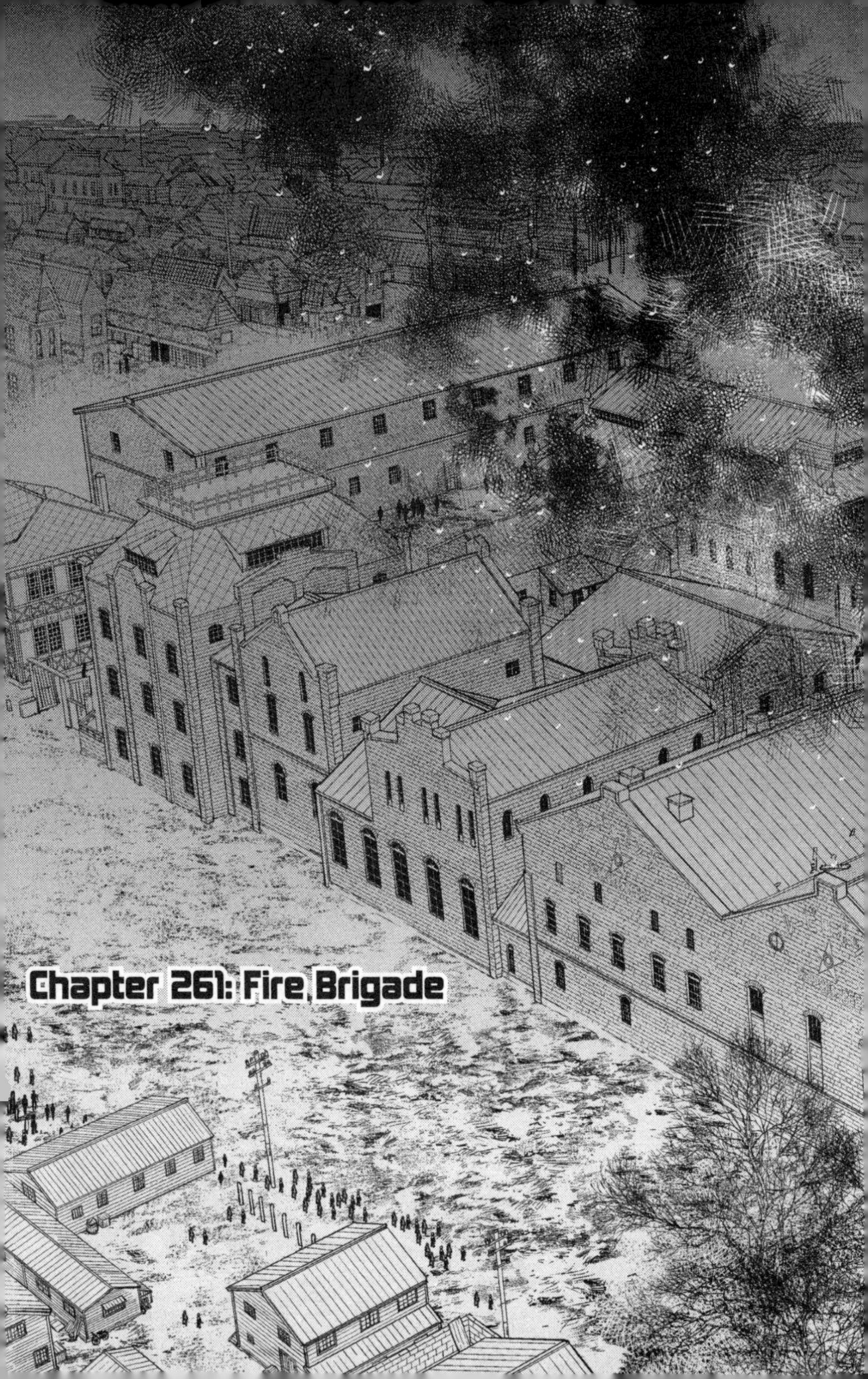
Chapter 261: Fire Brigade

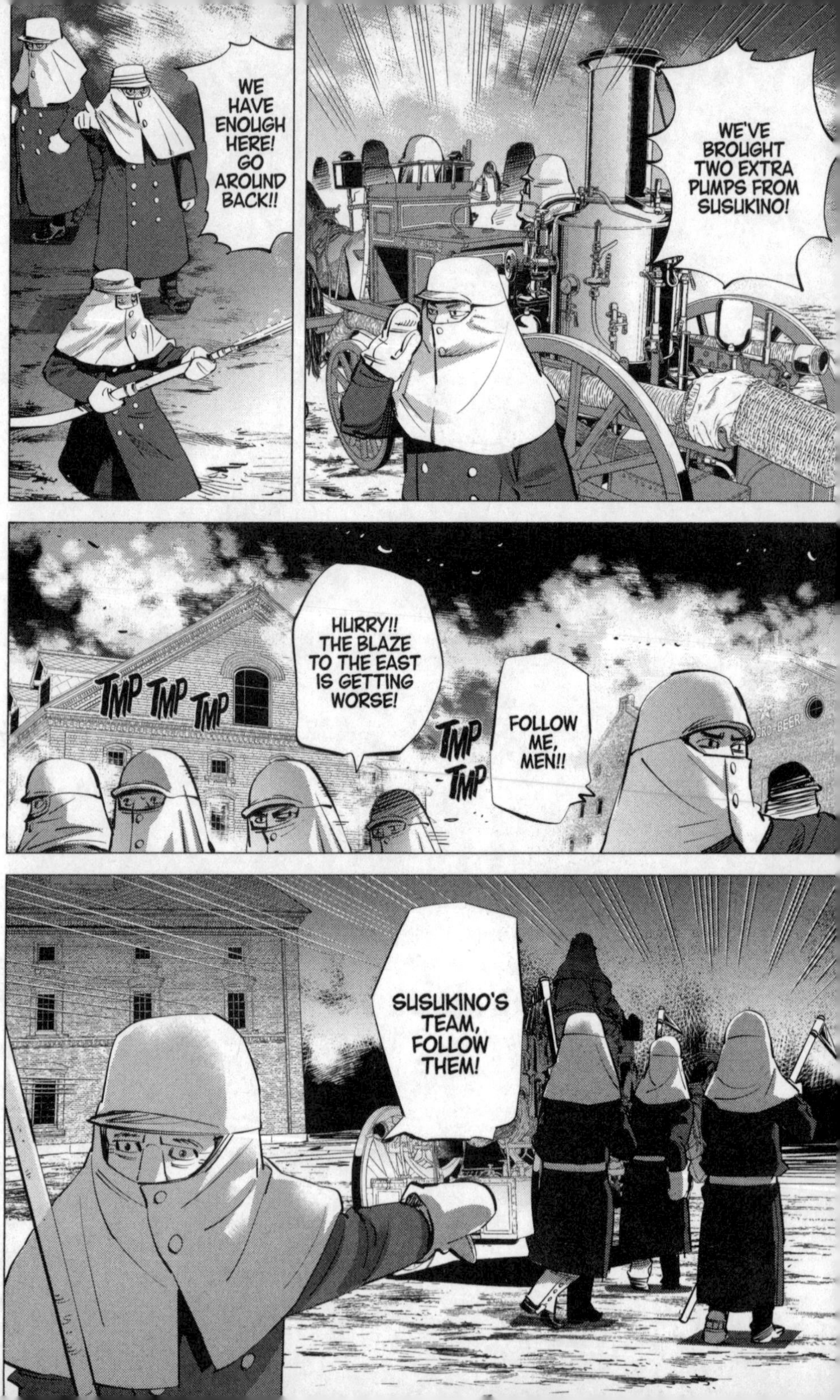
WE'VE BROUGHT TWO EXTRA PUMPS FROM SUSUKINO!
WE HAVE ENOUGH HERE! GO AROUND BACK!!
HURRY!! THE BLAZE TO THE EAST IS GETTING WORSE!
FOLLOW ME, MEN!!
TMP TMP
TMP TMP TMP
SUSUKINO'S TEAM, FOLLOW THEM!

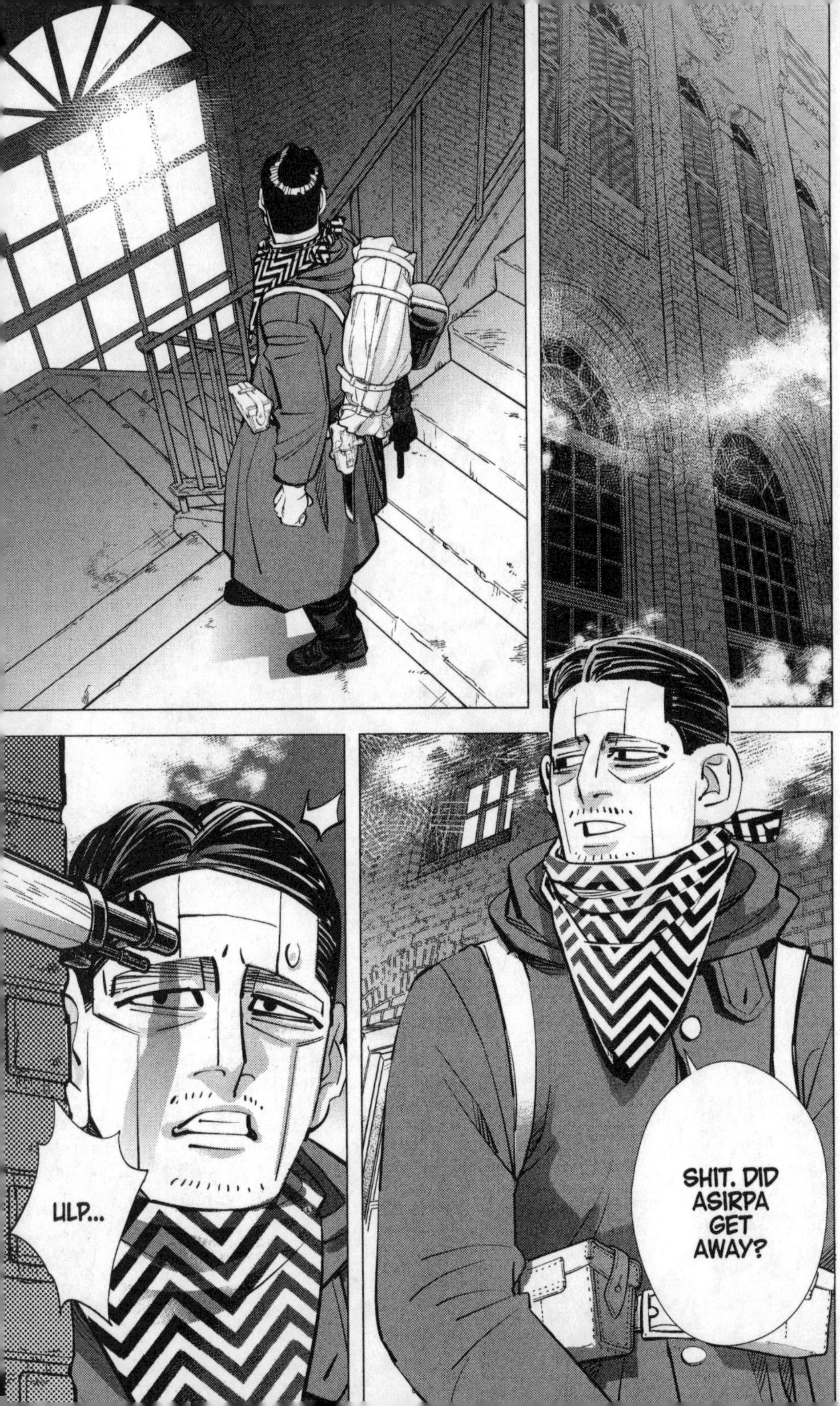
SHIT. DID ASIRPA GET AWAY?
ULP...

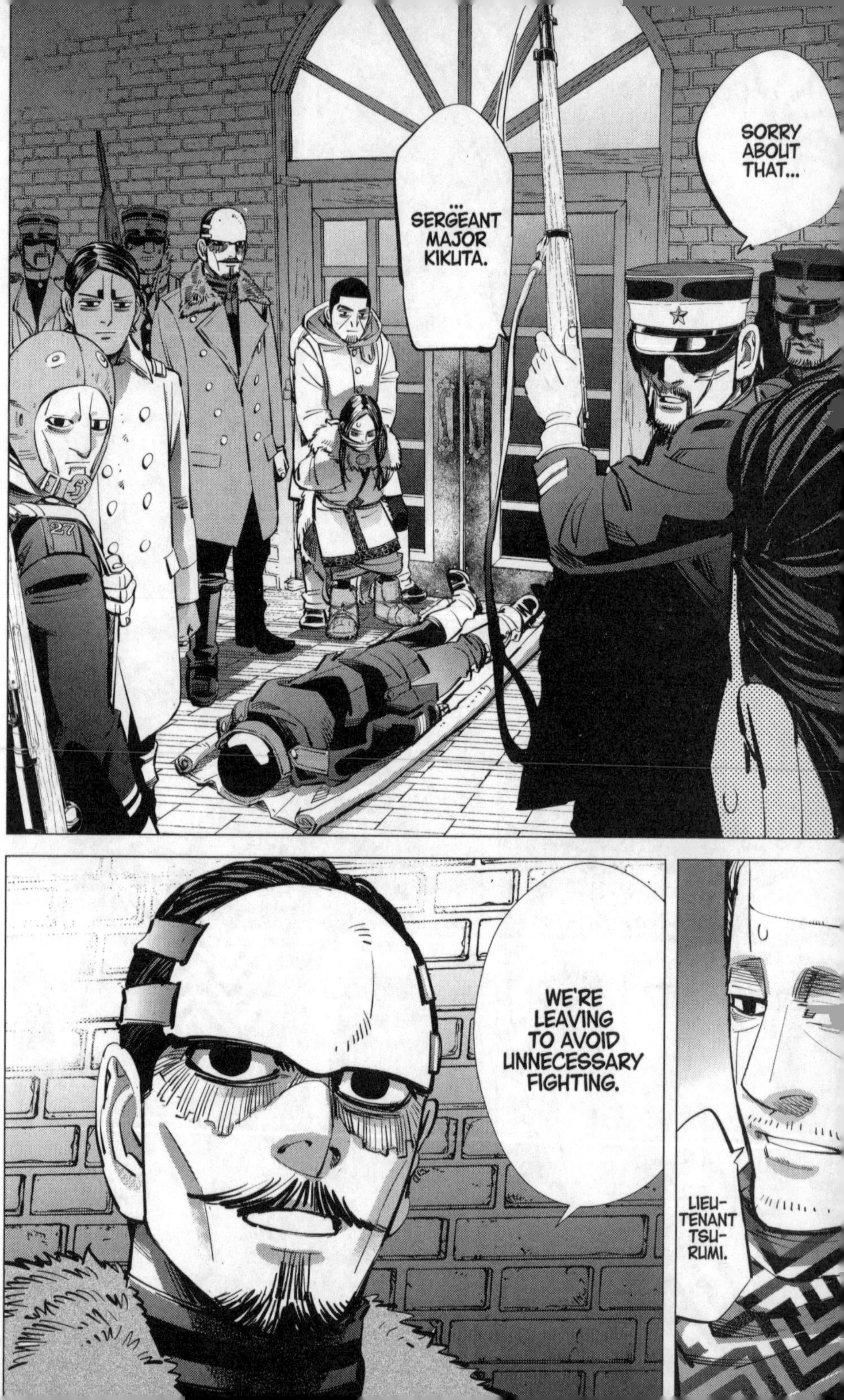
SORRY ABOUT THAT...
...SERGEANT MAJOR KIKUTA.
LIEU-TENANT TSU-RUMI.
WE'RE LEAVING TO AVOID UNNECESSARY FIGHTING.

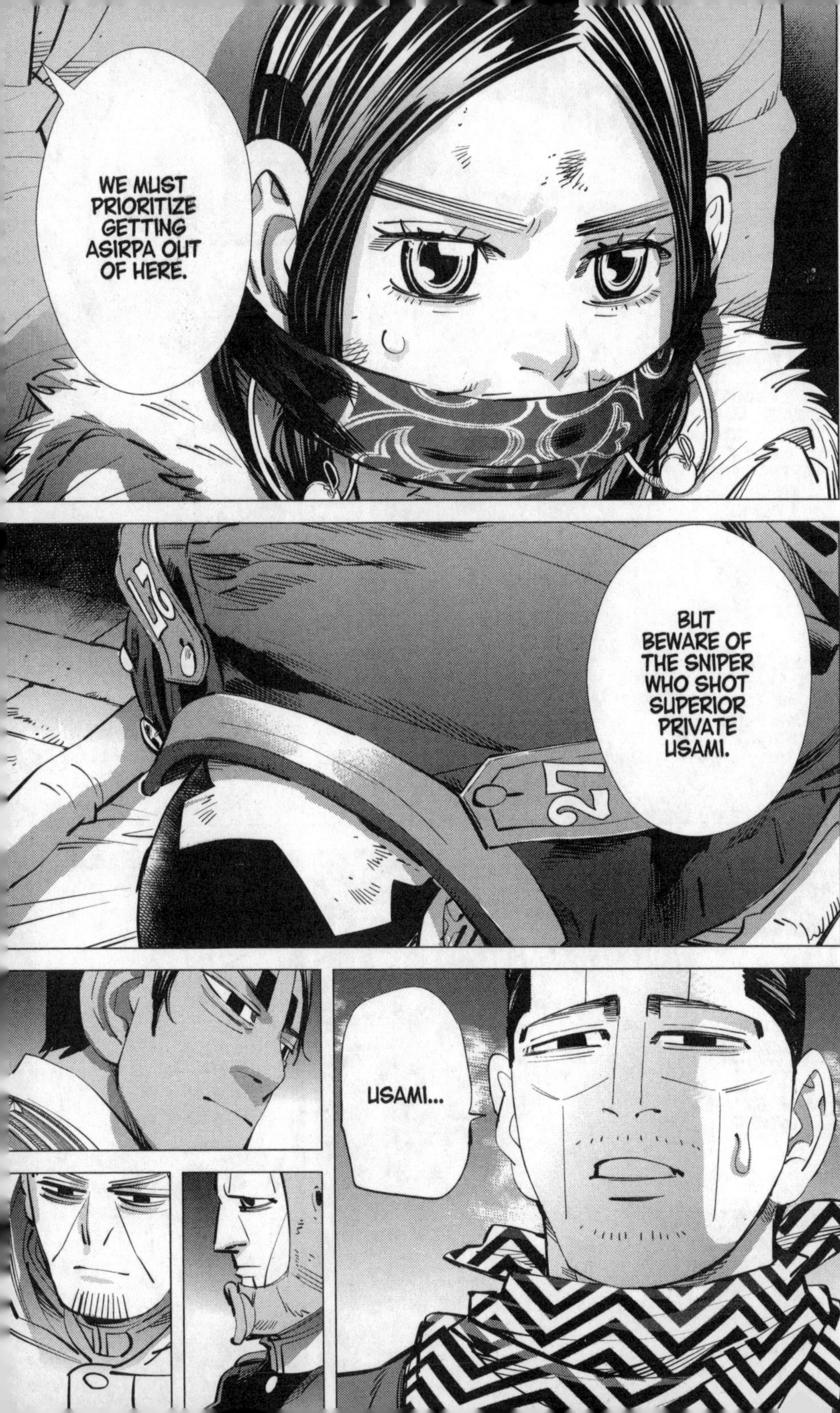
WE MUST PRIORITIZE GETTING ASIRPA OUT OF HERE.
BUT BEWARE OF THE SNIPER WHO SHOT SUPERIOR PRIVATE USAMI.
USAMI...

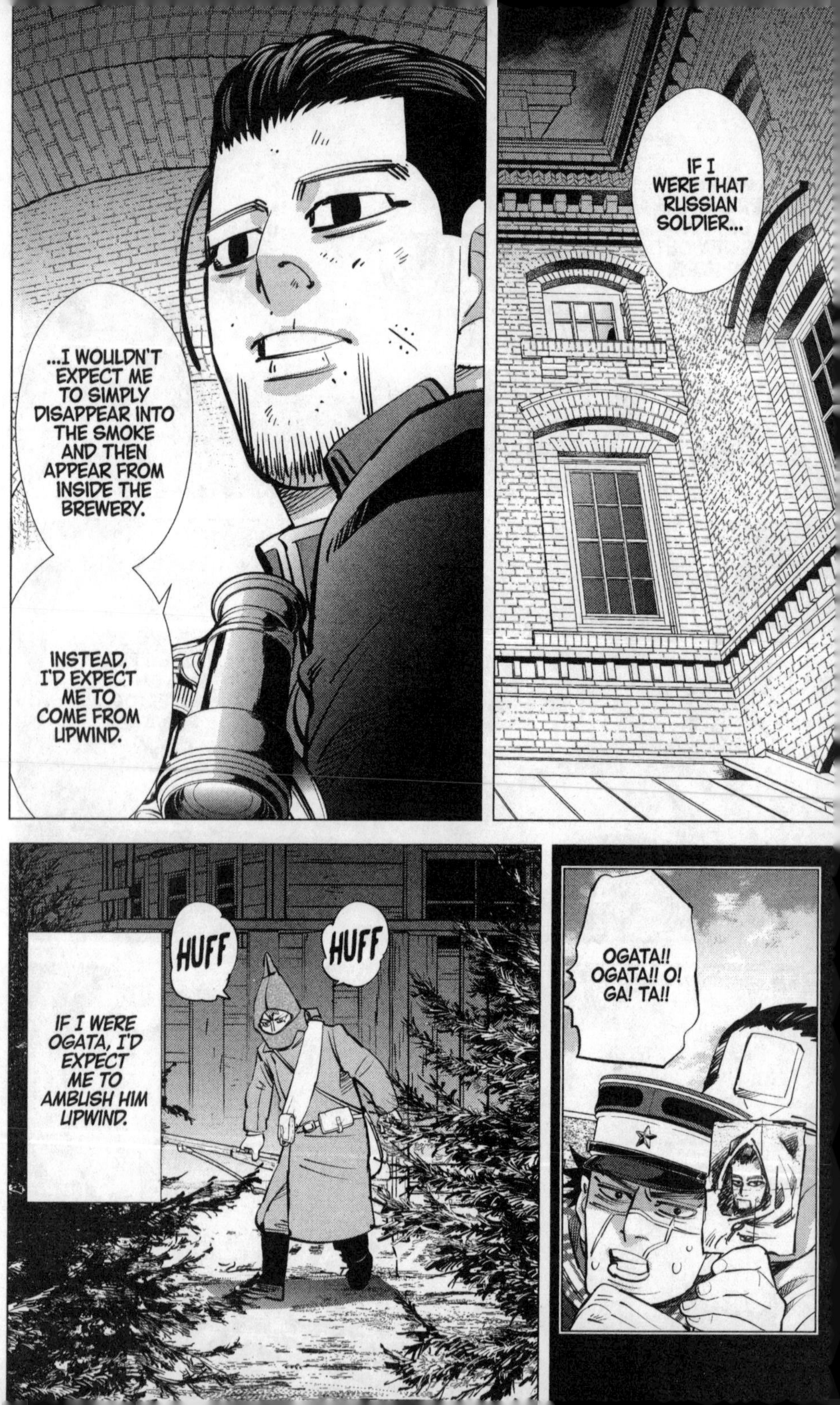
IF I WERE THAT RUSSIAN SOLDIER...
...I WOULDN'T EXPECT ME TO SIMPLY DISAPPEAR INTO THE SMOKE AND THEN APPEAR FROM INSIDE THE BREWERY.
INSTEAD, I'D EXPECT ME TO COME FROM UPWIND.
OGATA!! OGATA!! O! GA! TA!!
HUFF
HUFF
IF I WERE OGATA, I'D EXPECT ME TO AMBUSH HIM UPWIND.

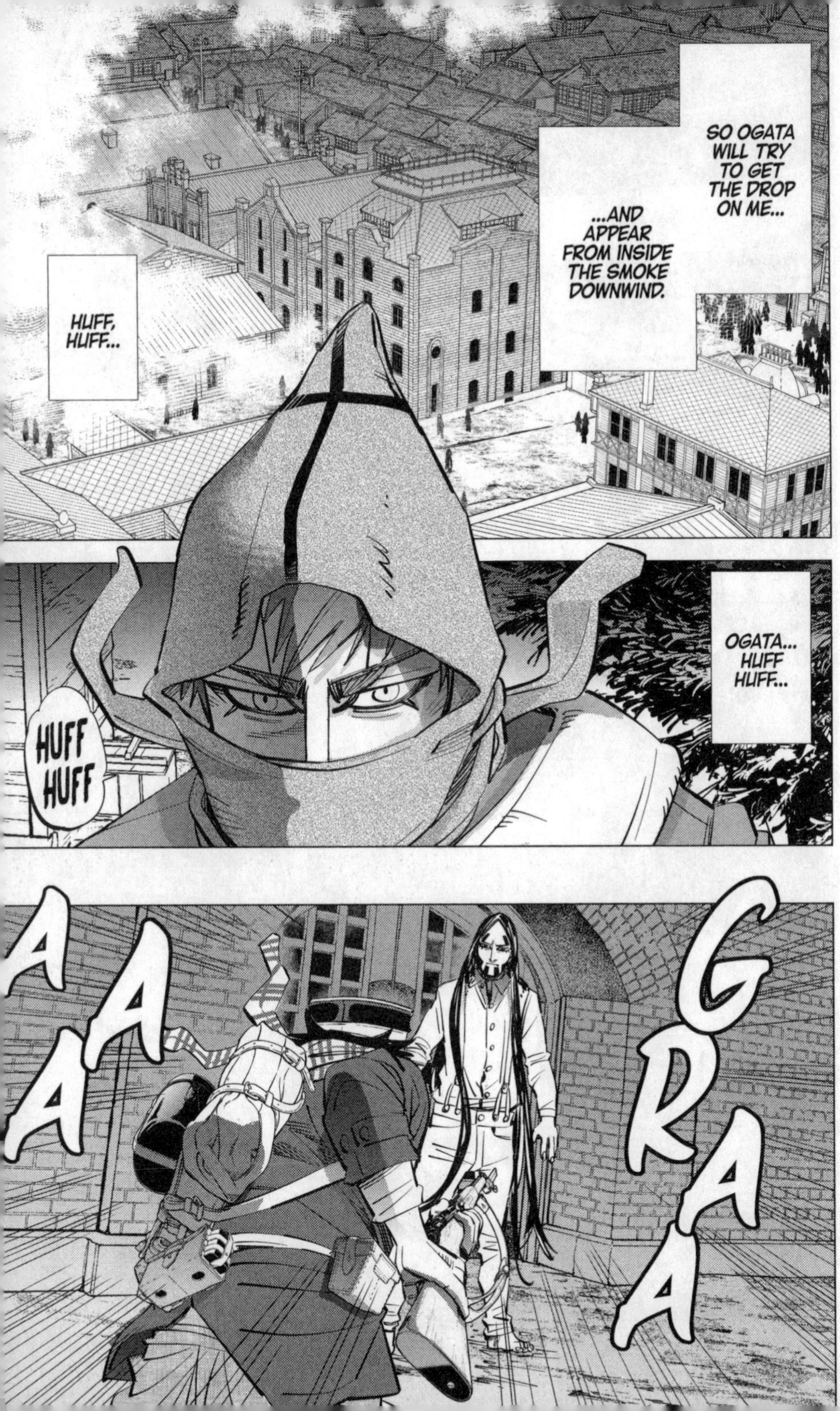
SO OGATA WILL TRY TO GET THE DROP ON ME...
...AND APPEAR FROM INSIDE THE SMOKE DOWNWIND.
HUFF, HUFF...
OGATA... HUFF HUFF...
HUFF HUFF
GRAA
AAA

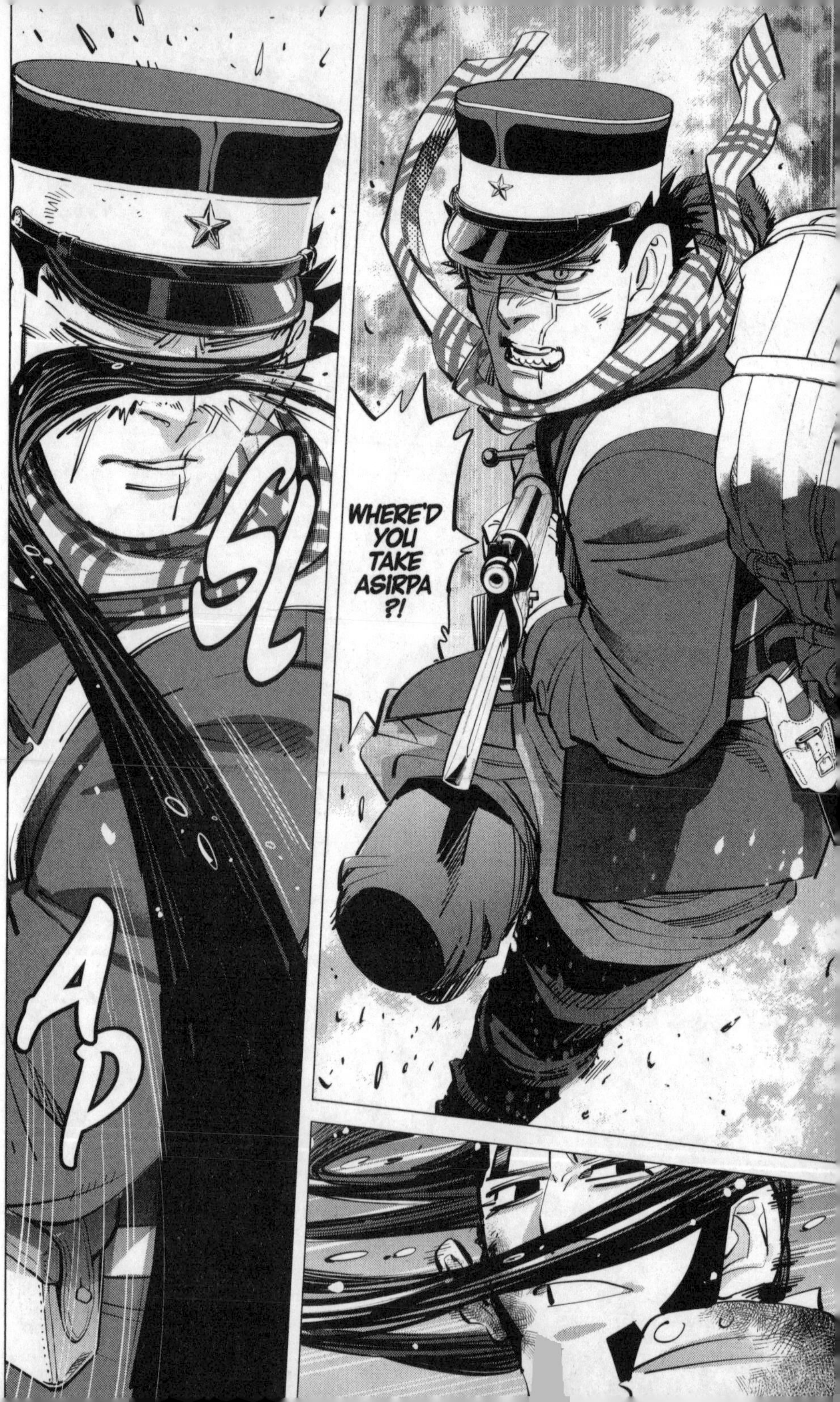
WHERE'D YOU TAKE ASIRPA ?!
SL
AP

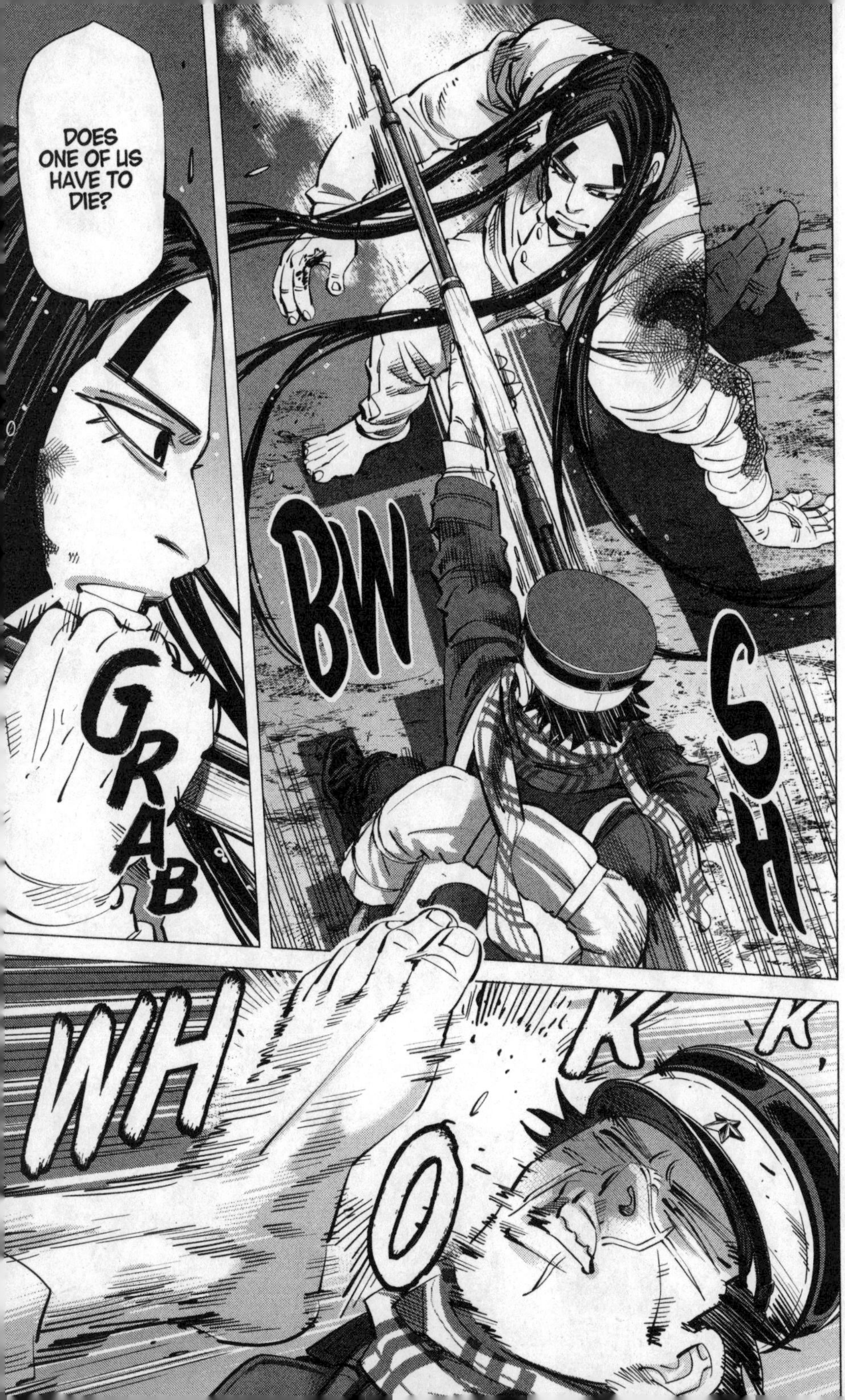
BW
SH
DOES ONE OF US HAVE TO DIE?
GRAB
WHOKK

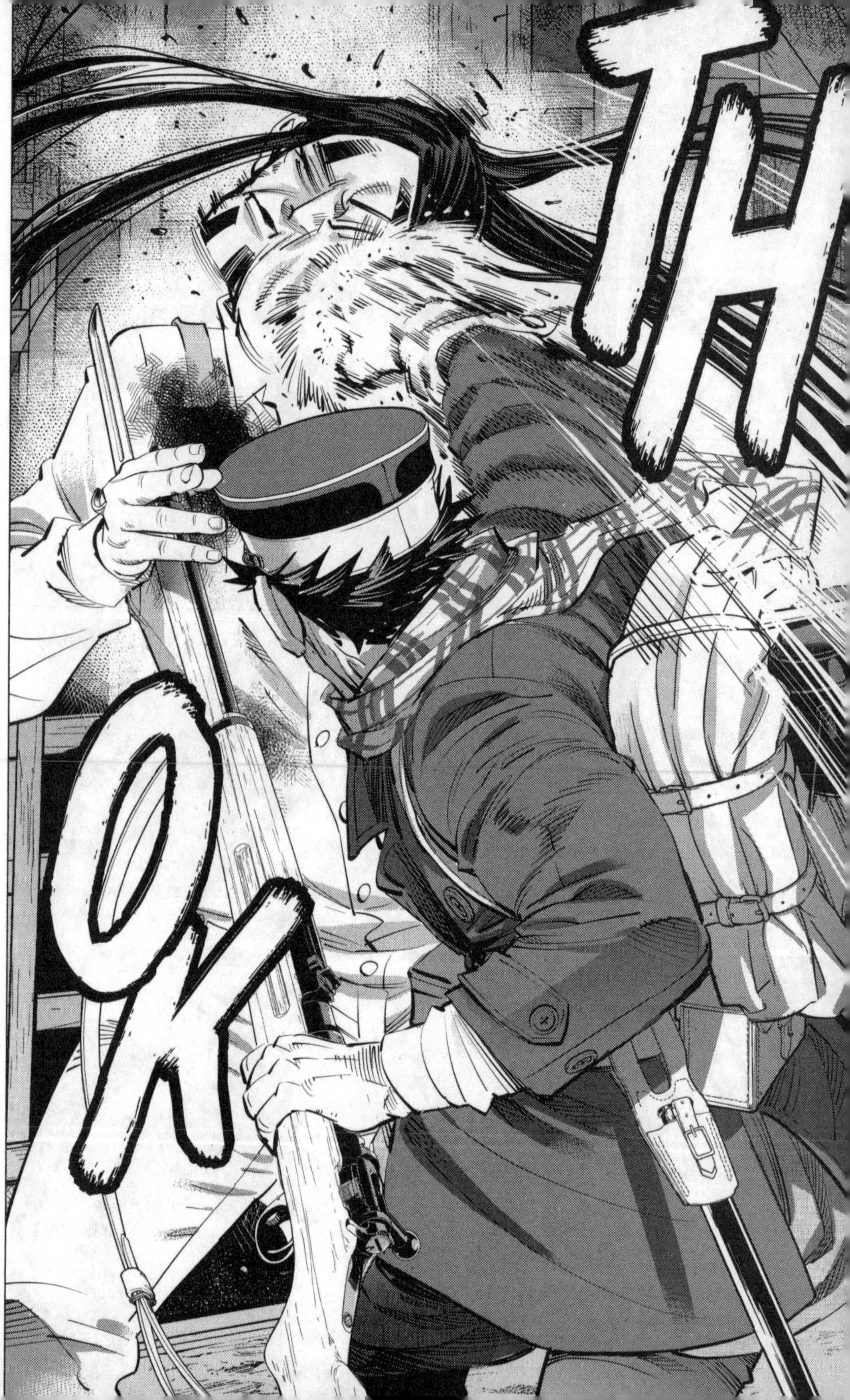
THOK

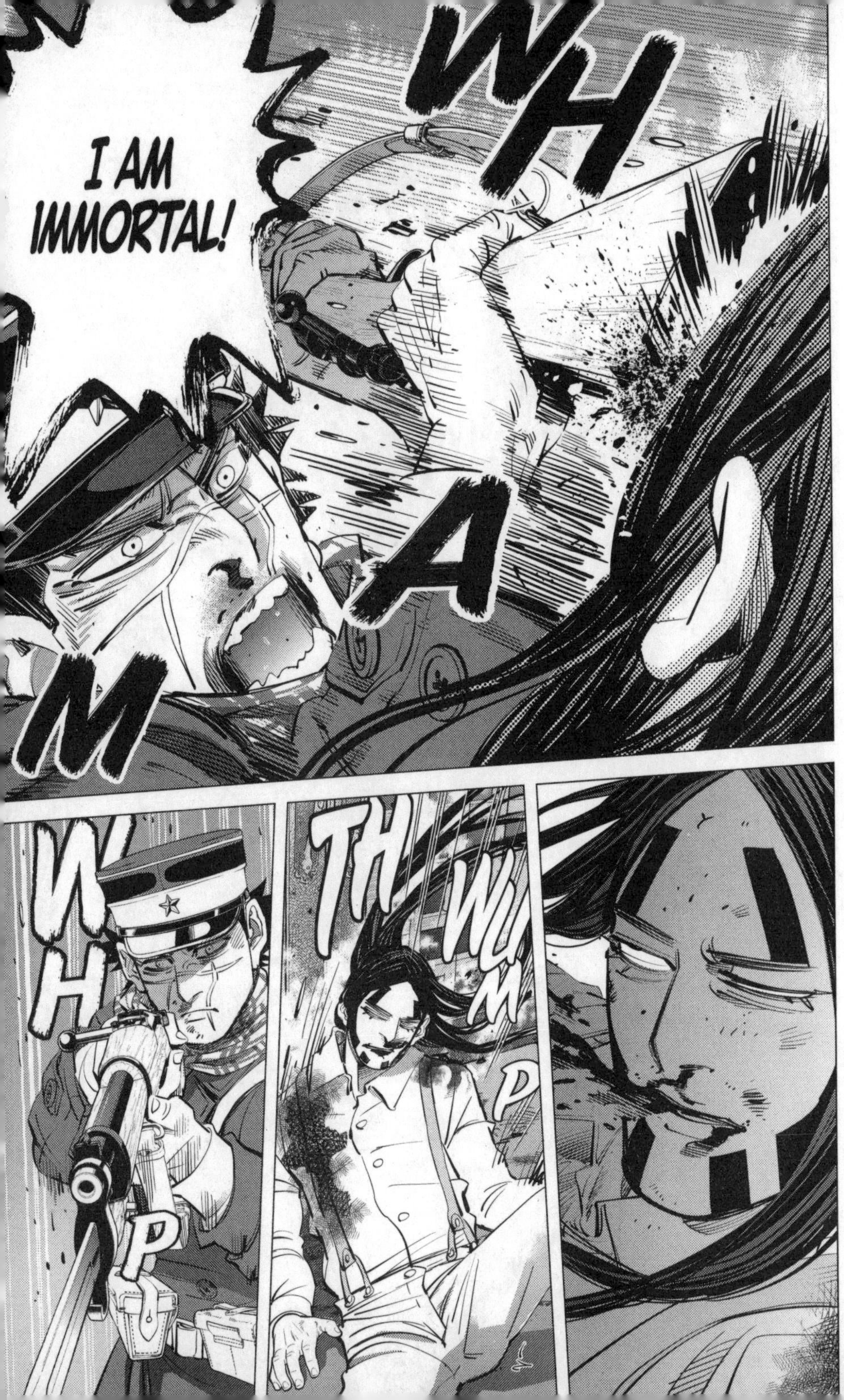
WHAM
I AM IMMORTAL!
THWUMP

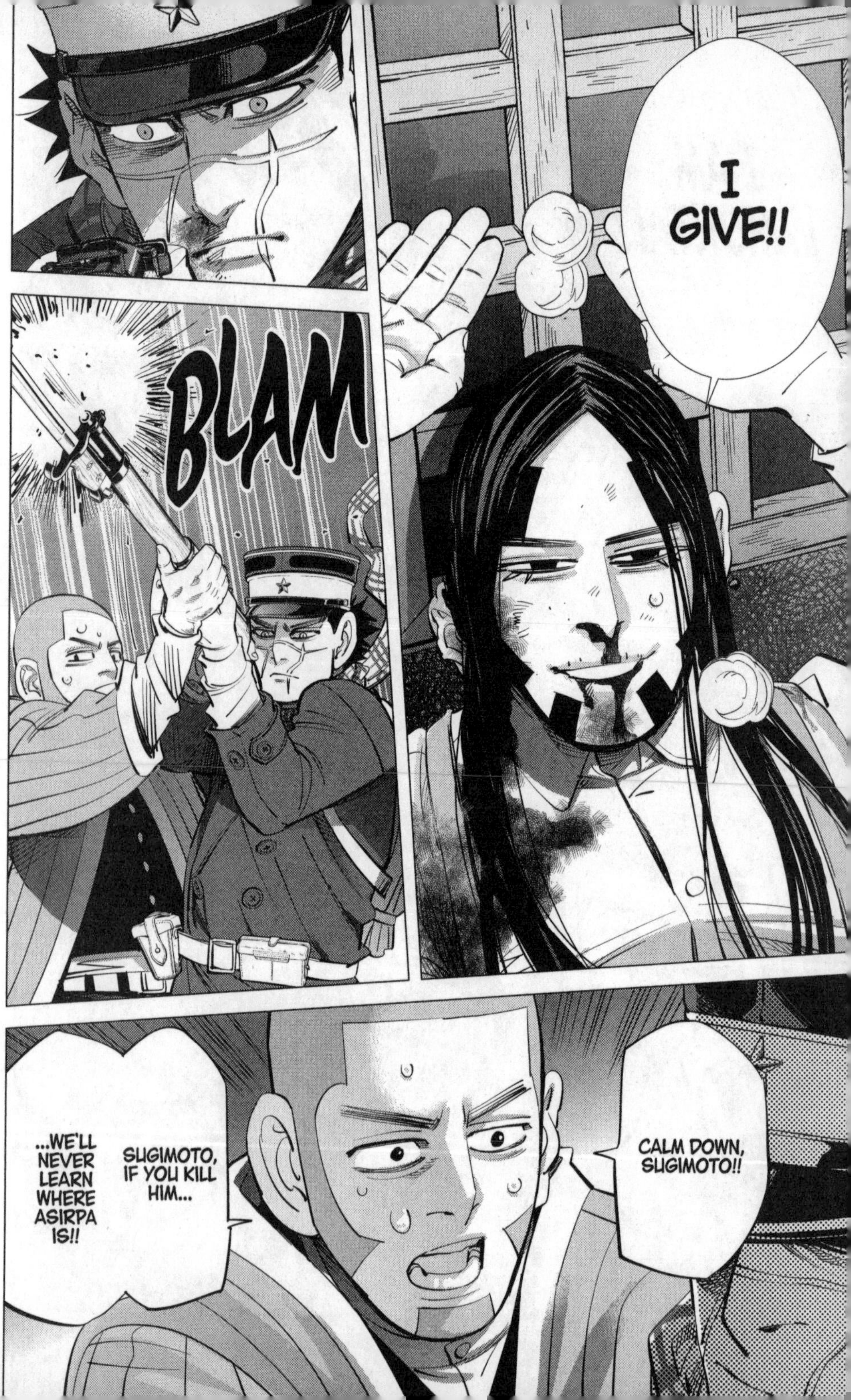
I GIVE!!
BLAM
CALM DOWN, SUGIMOTO!!
SUGIMOTO, IF YOU KILL HIM...
...WE'LL NEVER LEARN WHERE ASIRPA IS!!

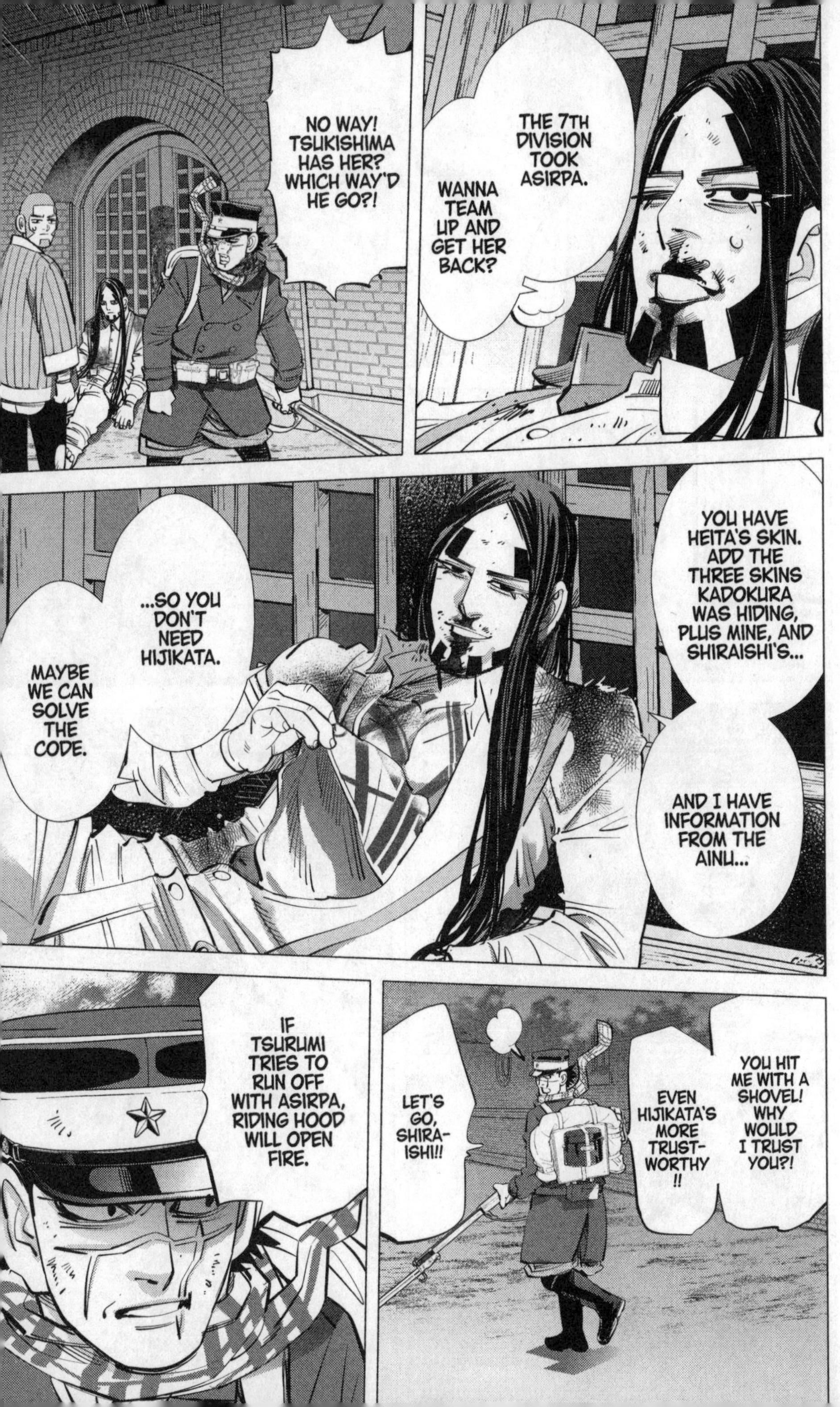
THE 7TH DIVISION TOOK ASIRPA.
WANNA TEAM UP AND GET HER BACK?
NO WAY! TSUKISHIMA HAS HER? WHICH WAY'D HE GO?!
YOU HAVE HEITA'S SKIN. ADD THE THREE SKINS KADOKURA WAS HIDING, PLUS MINE, AND SHIRAISHI'S...
AND I HAVE INFORMATION FROM THE AINU...
...SO YOU DON'T NEED HIJIKATA.
MAYBE WE CAN SOLVE THE CODE.
YOU HIT ME WITH A SHOVEL! WHY WOULD I TRUST YOU?!
EVEN HIJIKATA'S MORE TRUST-WORTHY !!
LET'S GO, SHIRA-ISHI!!
IF TSURUMI TRIES TO RUN OFF WITH ASIRPA, RIDING HOOD WILL OPEN FIRE.

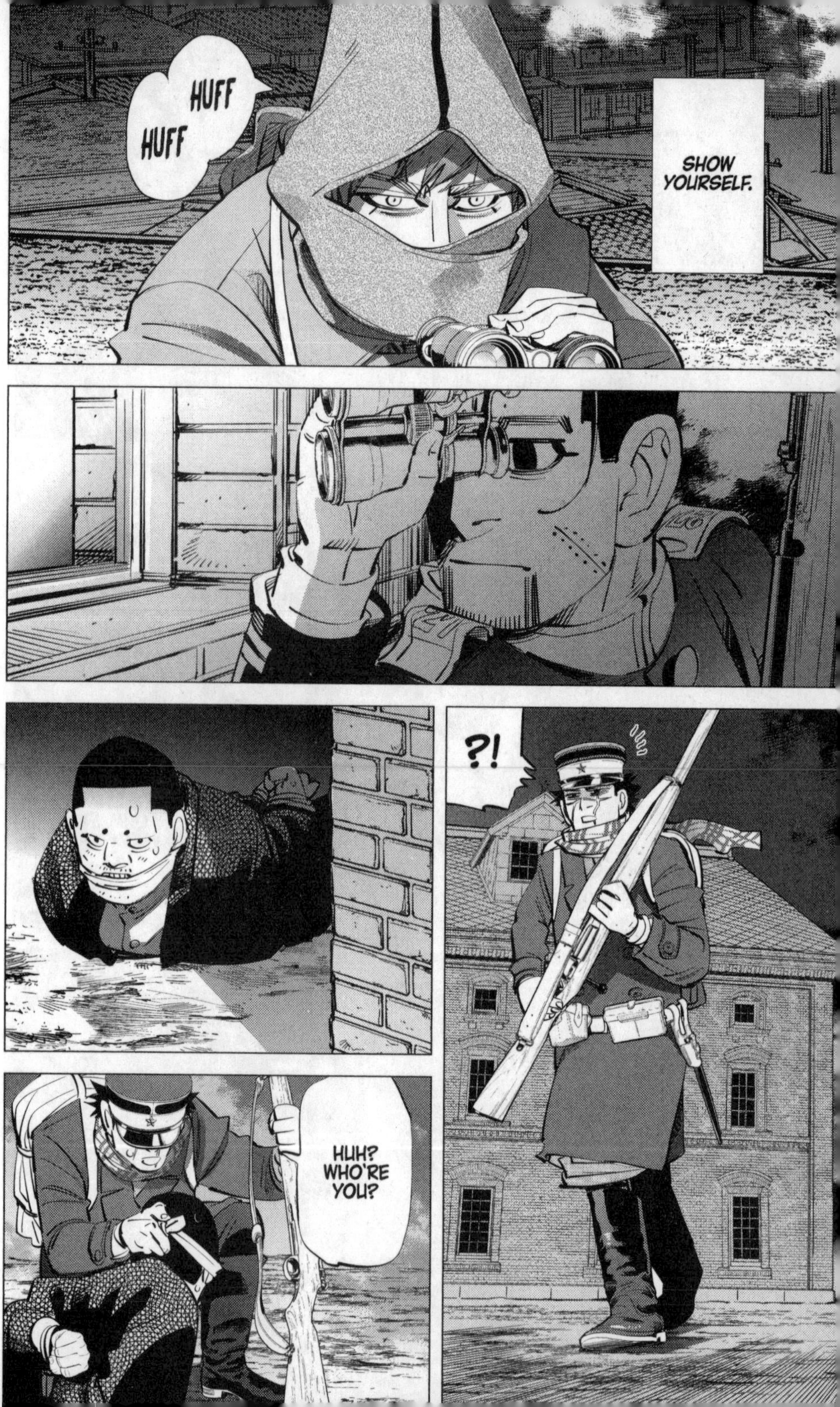
SHOW YOURSELF.
HUFF
HUFF
?!
HUH? WHO'RE YOU?

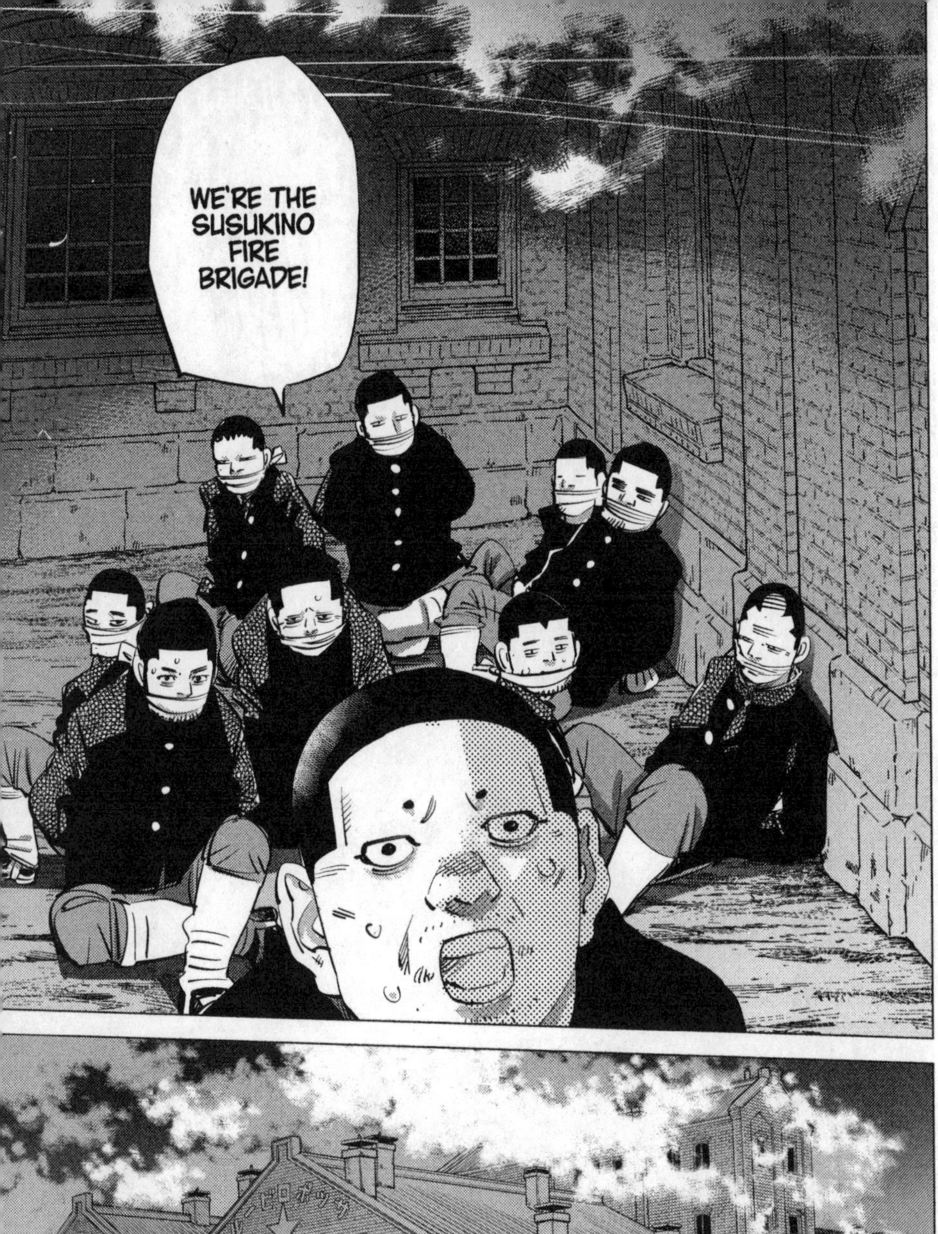
WE'RE THE SUSUKINO FIRE BRIGADE!

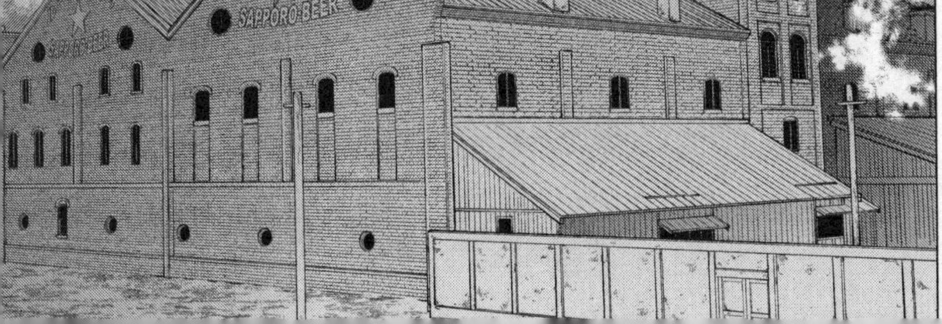
SAPPORO BEER

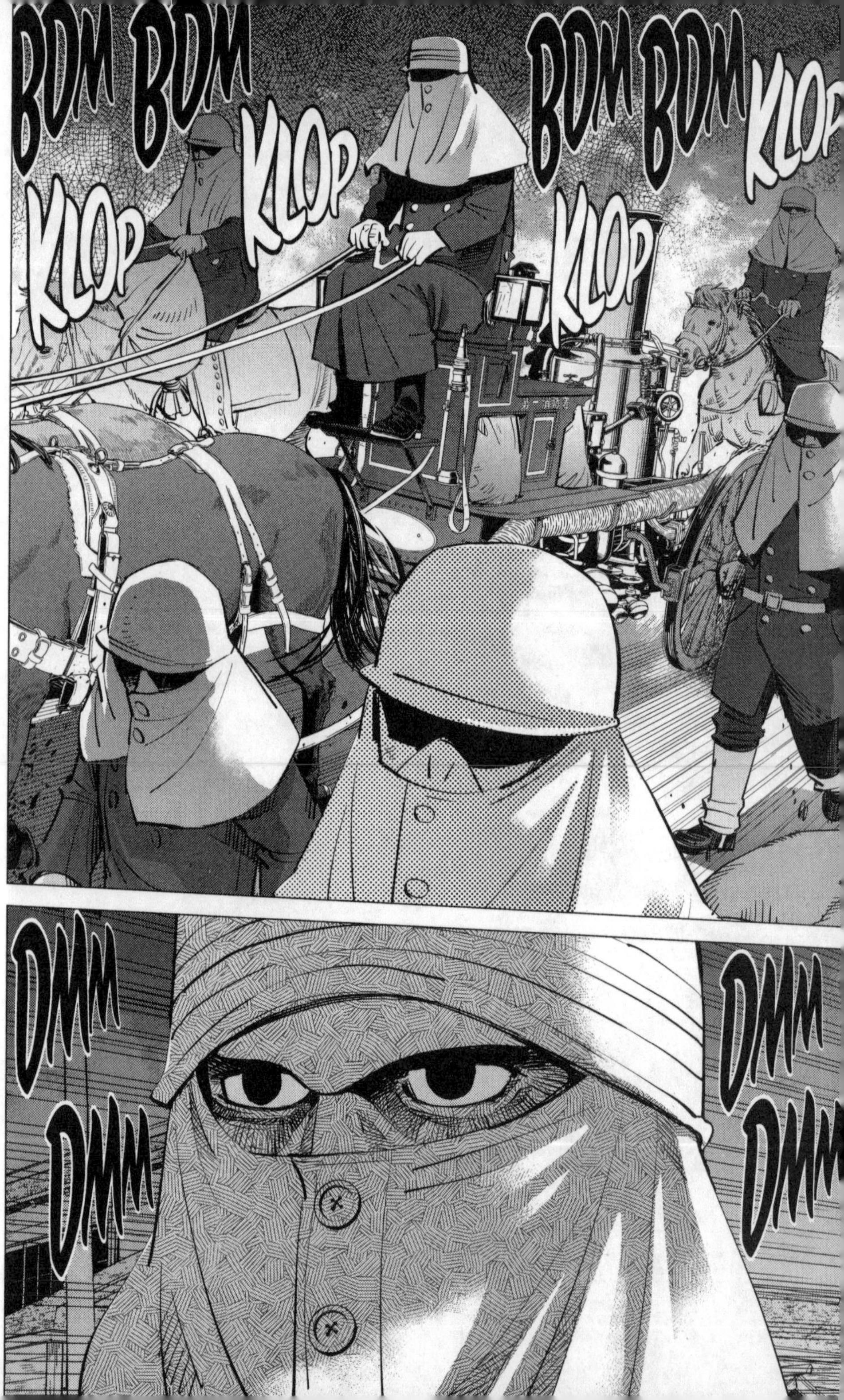
KLOP
BDM BDM
KLOP
KLOP
BDM BDM
KLOP
DMM
DMM
DMM
DMM

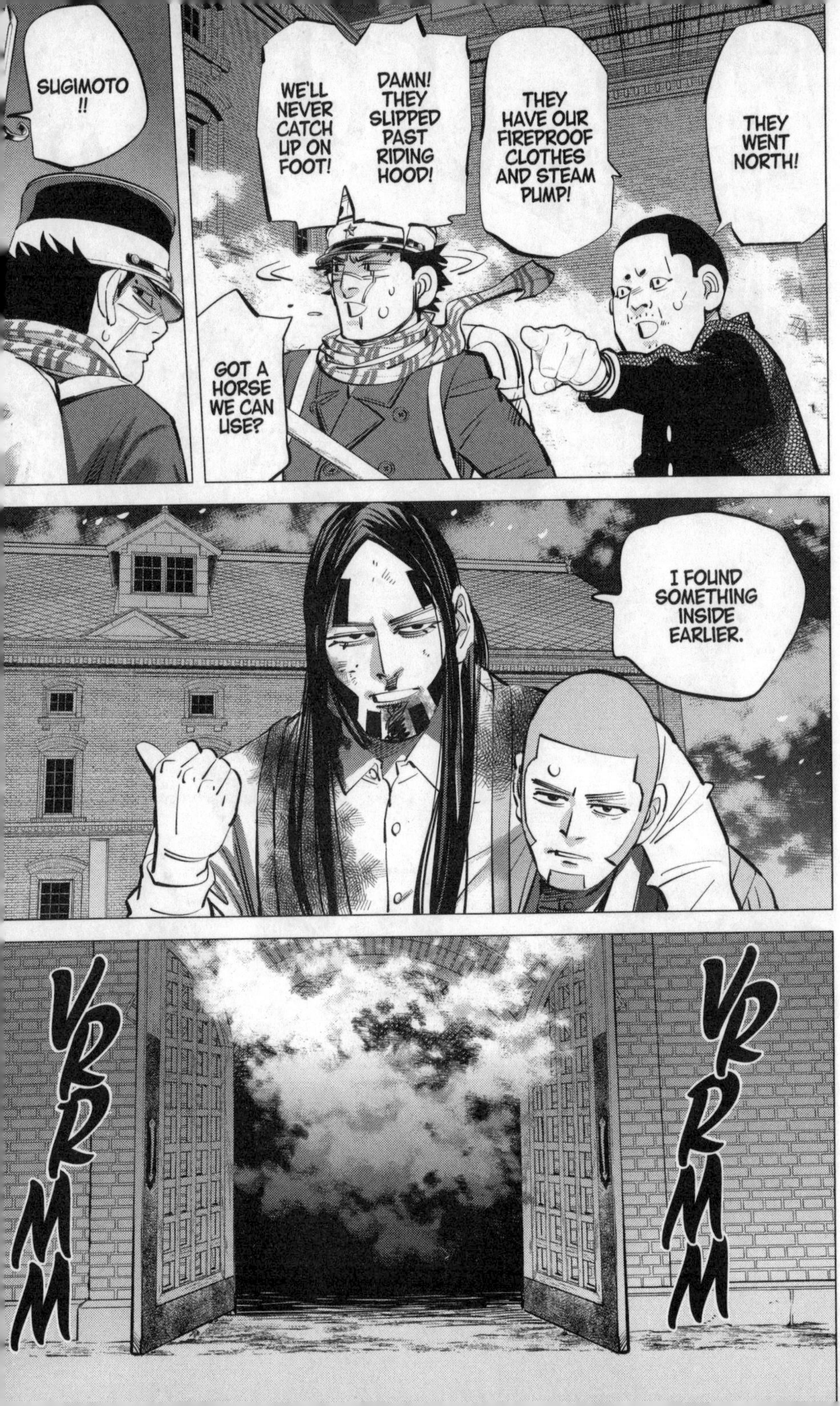
THEY WENT NORTH!
THEY HAVE OUR FIREPROOF CLOTHES AND STEAM PUMP!
DAMN! THEY SLIPPED PAST RIDING HOOD!
WE'LL NEVER CATCH UP ON FOOT!
GOT A HORSE WE CAN USE?
SUGIMOTO !!
I FOUND SOMETHING INSIDE EARLIER.
VRRMM
VRRMM

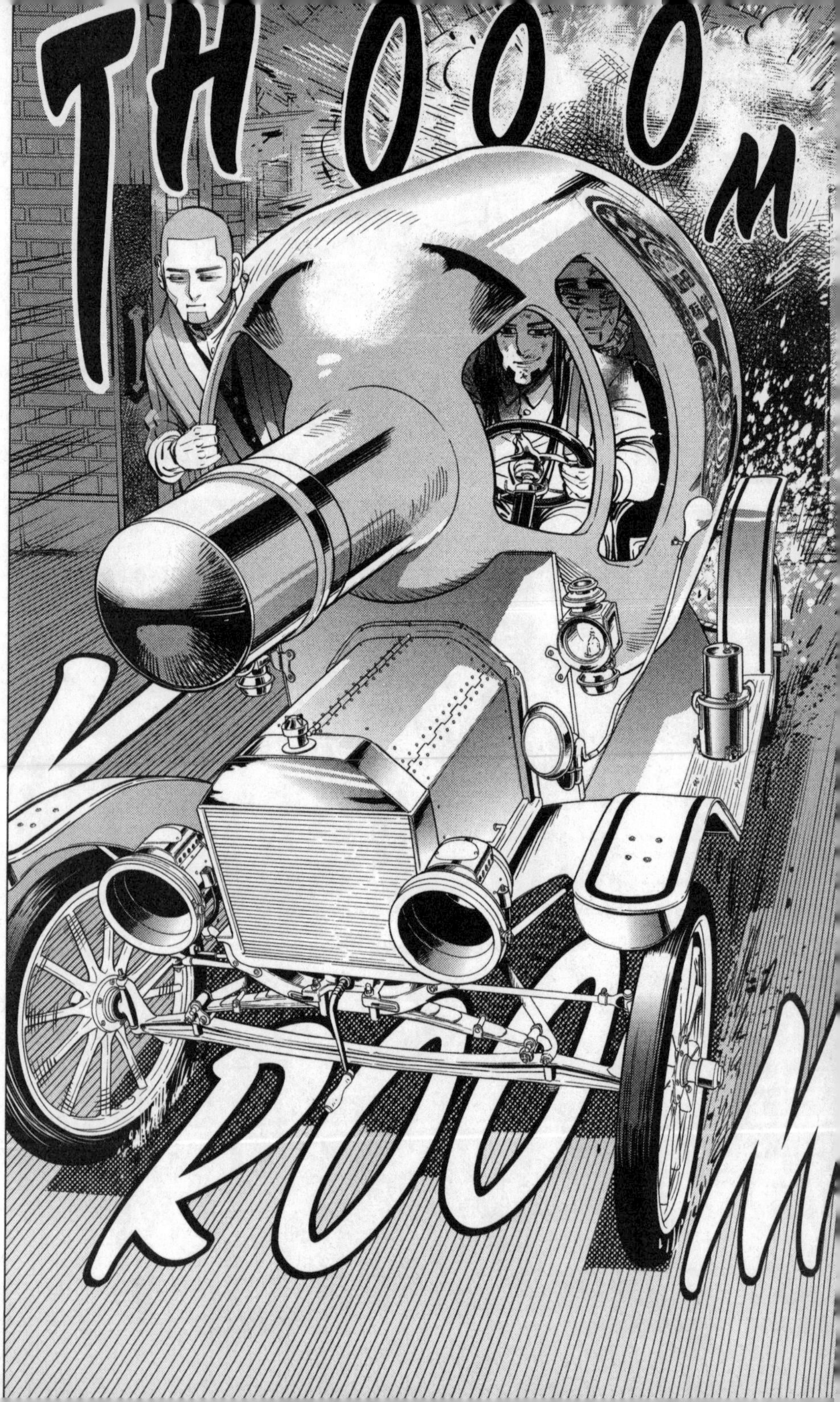
THOOOM
VROOOM

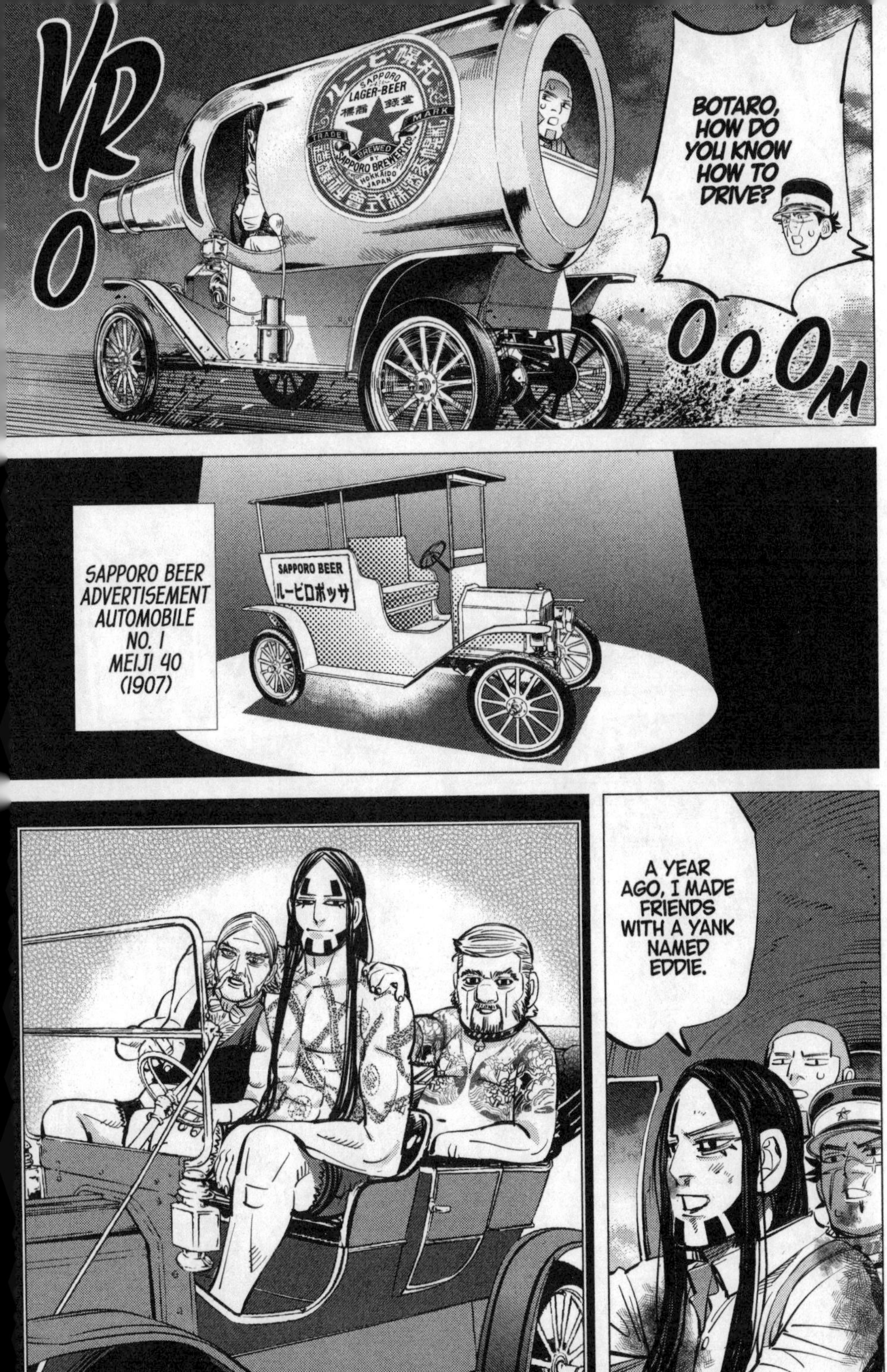
BOTARO, HOW DO YOU KNOW HOW TO DRIVE?
VROOOOM
SAPPORO LAGER-BEER
SAPPORO BEER
ルービロボッサ
SAPPORO BEER ADVERTISEMENT AUTOMOBILE NO. 1 MEIJI 40 (1907)
A YEAR AGO, I MADE FRIENDS WITH A YANK NAMED EDDIE.

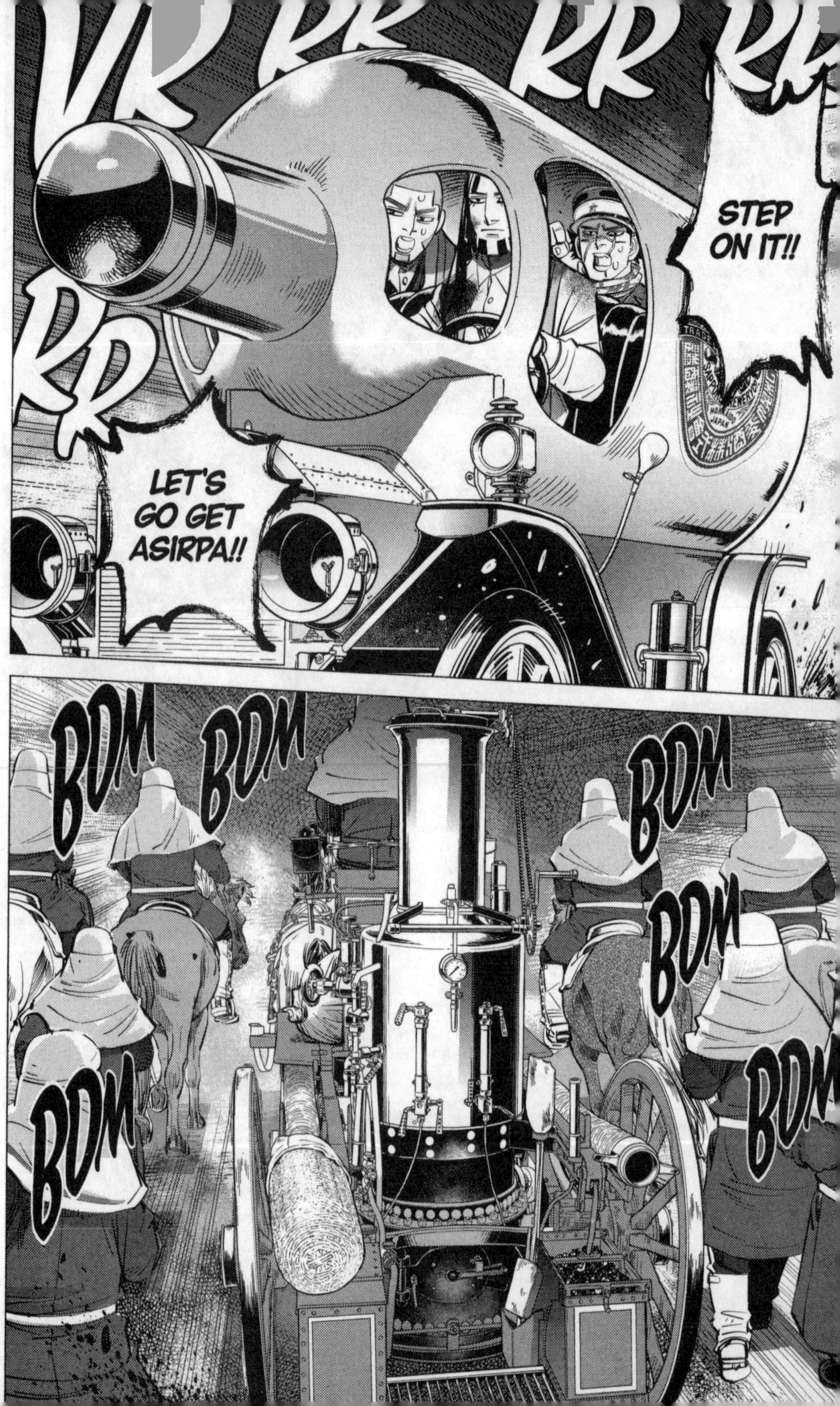
STEP ON IT!!
LET'S GO GET ASIRPA!!
BOM
BOM
BOM
BOM
BOM
BOM

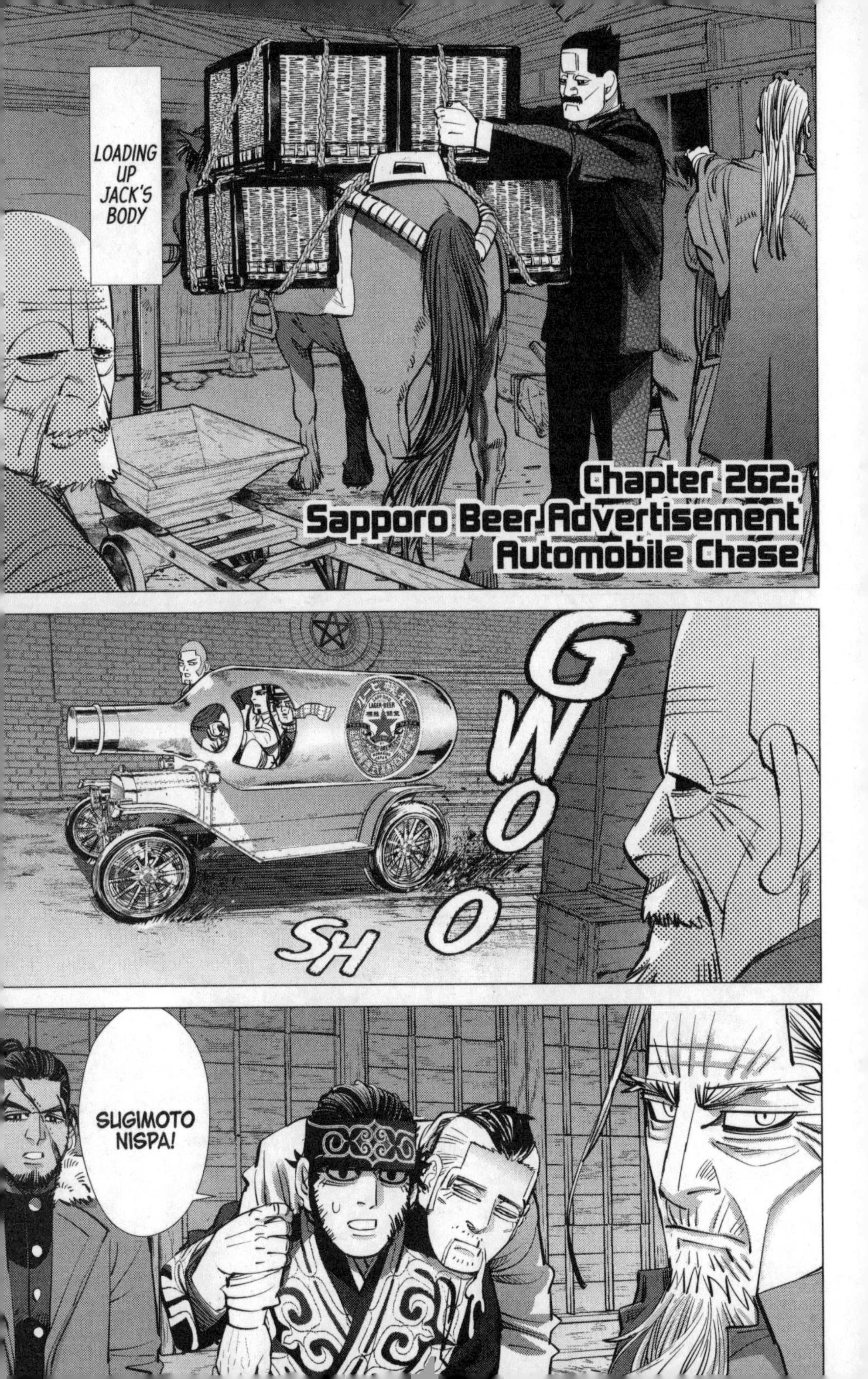
LOADING UP JACK'S BODY
Chapter 262: Sapporo Beer Advertisement Automobile Chase
GWOOOSH
SUGIMOTO NISPA!

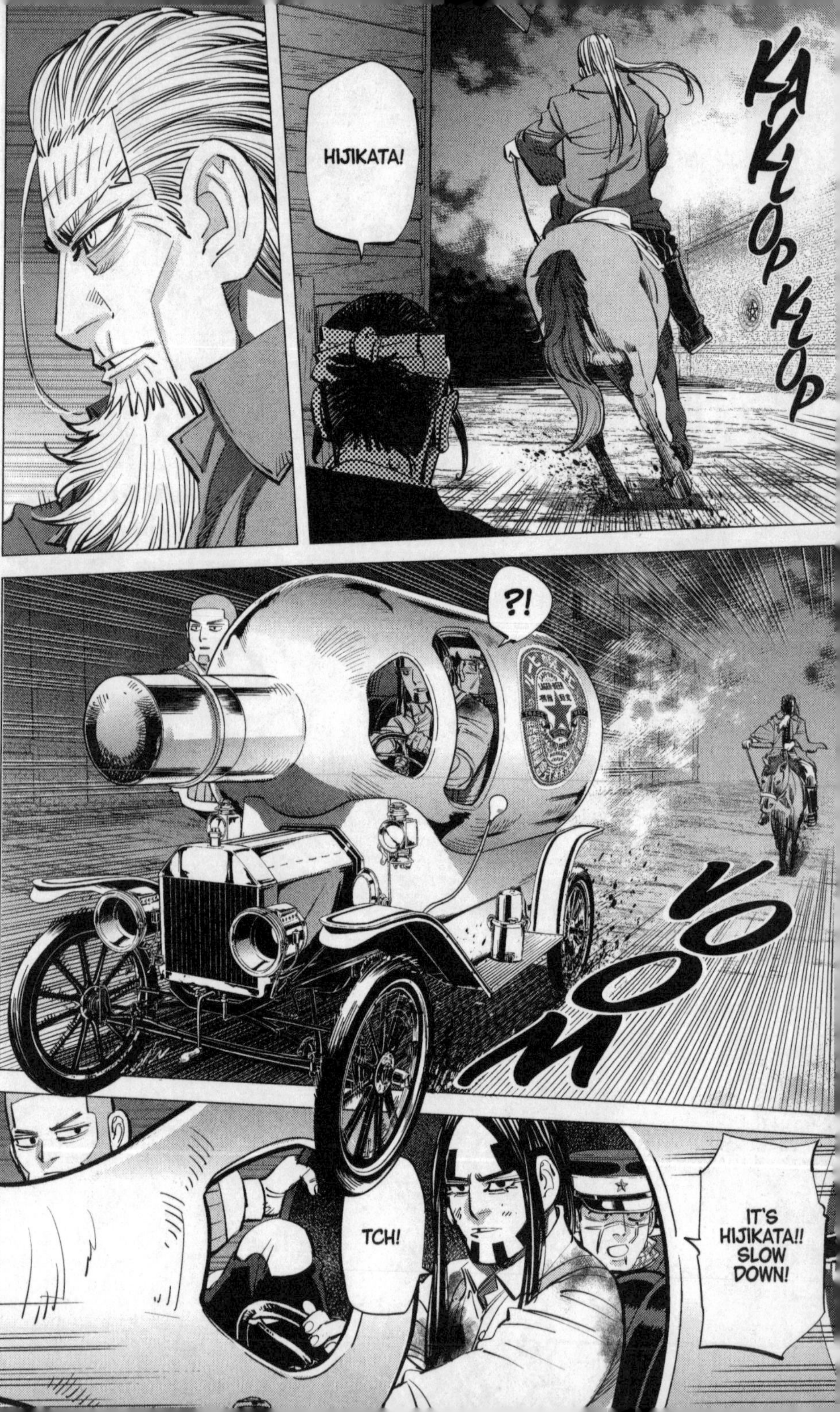
KAKLOP KLOP KLOP
HIJIKATA!
?!
VOOM
IT'S HIJIKATA!! SLOW DOWN!
TCH!

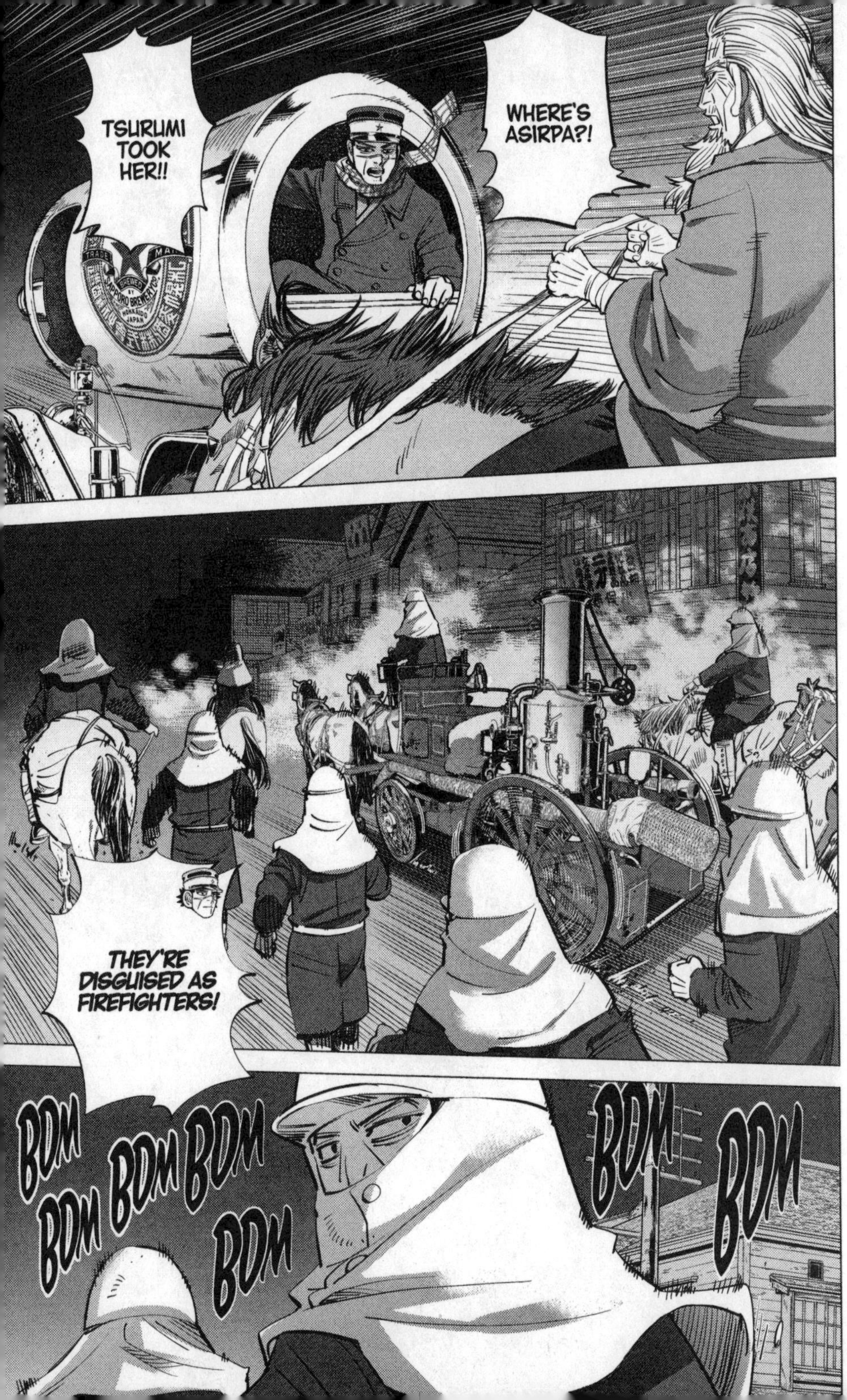
WHERE'S ASIRPA?!
TSURUMI TOOK HER!!
THEY'RE DISGUISED AS FIREFIGHTERS!
BDM BDM
BDM BDM
BDM BDM BDM BDM BDM BDM

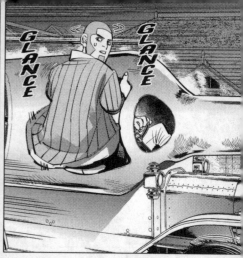

GLANCE GLANCE

THERE THEY ARE!!

SKR EE

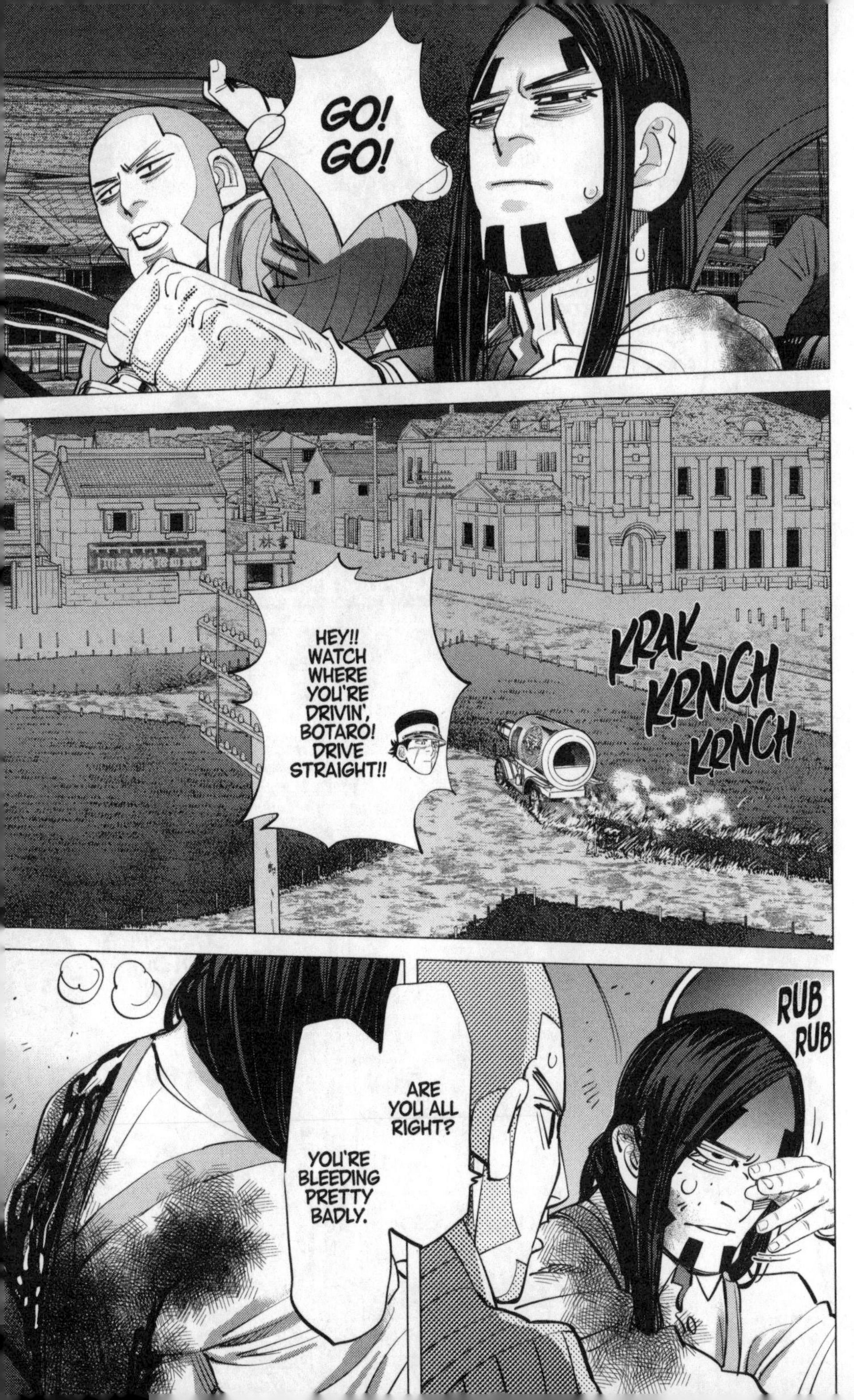
GO! GO!
KRAK KRNCH KRNCH
HEY!! WATCH WHERE YOU'RE DRIVIN', BOTARO! DRIVE STRAIGHT!!
RUB RUB
ARE YOU ALL RIGHT?
YOU'RE BLEEDING PRETTY BADLY.

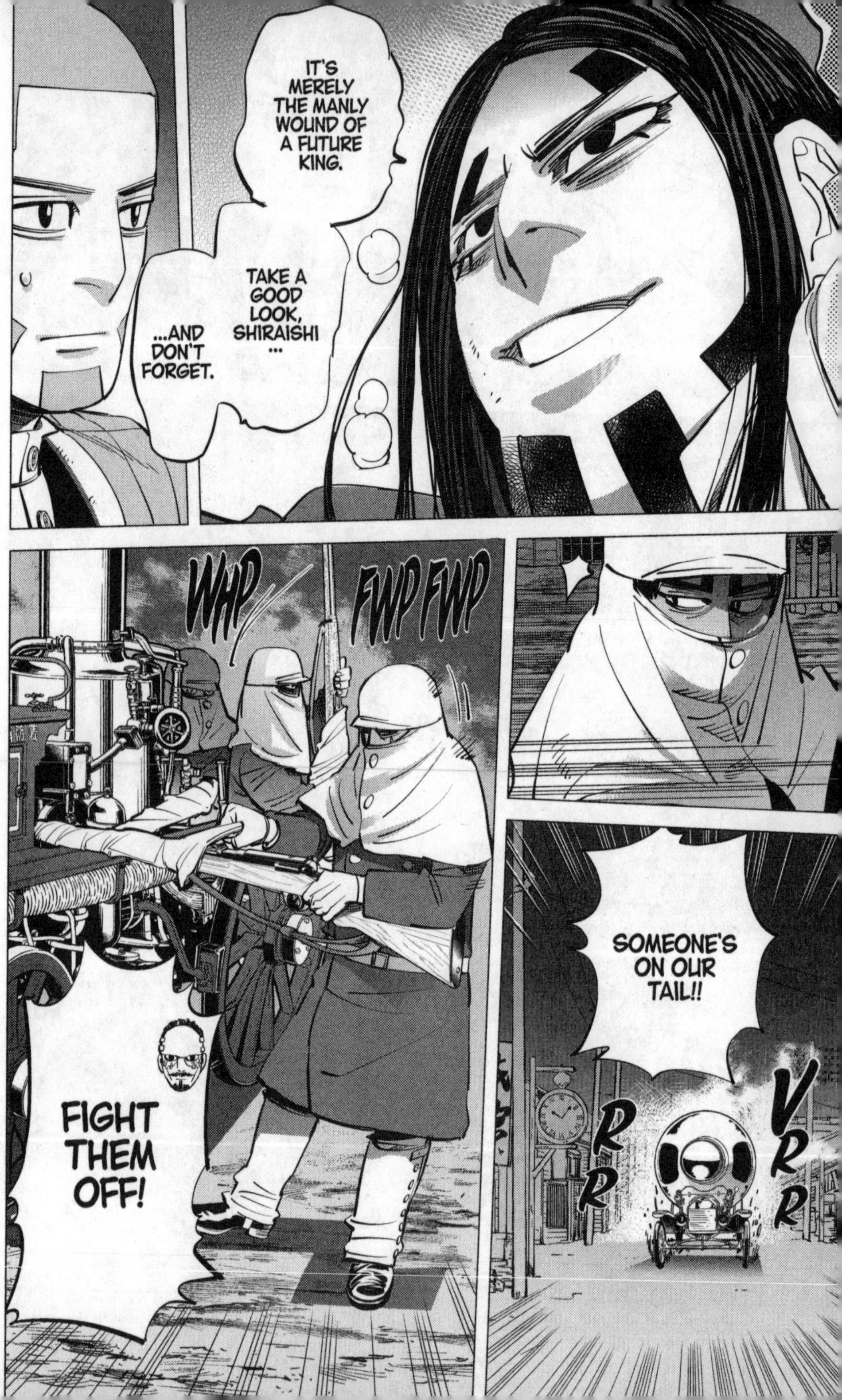
IT'S MERELY THE MANLY WOUND OF A FUTURE KING.
TAKE A GOOD LOOK, SHIRAISHI...
...AND DON'T FORGET.
SOMEONE'S ON OUR TAIL!!
VRR
RR
FWP FWP
WHP
FIGHT THEM OFF!

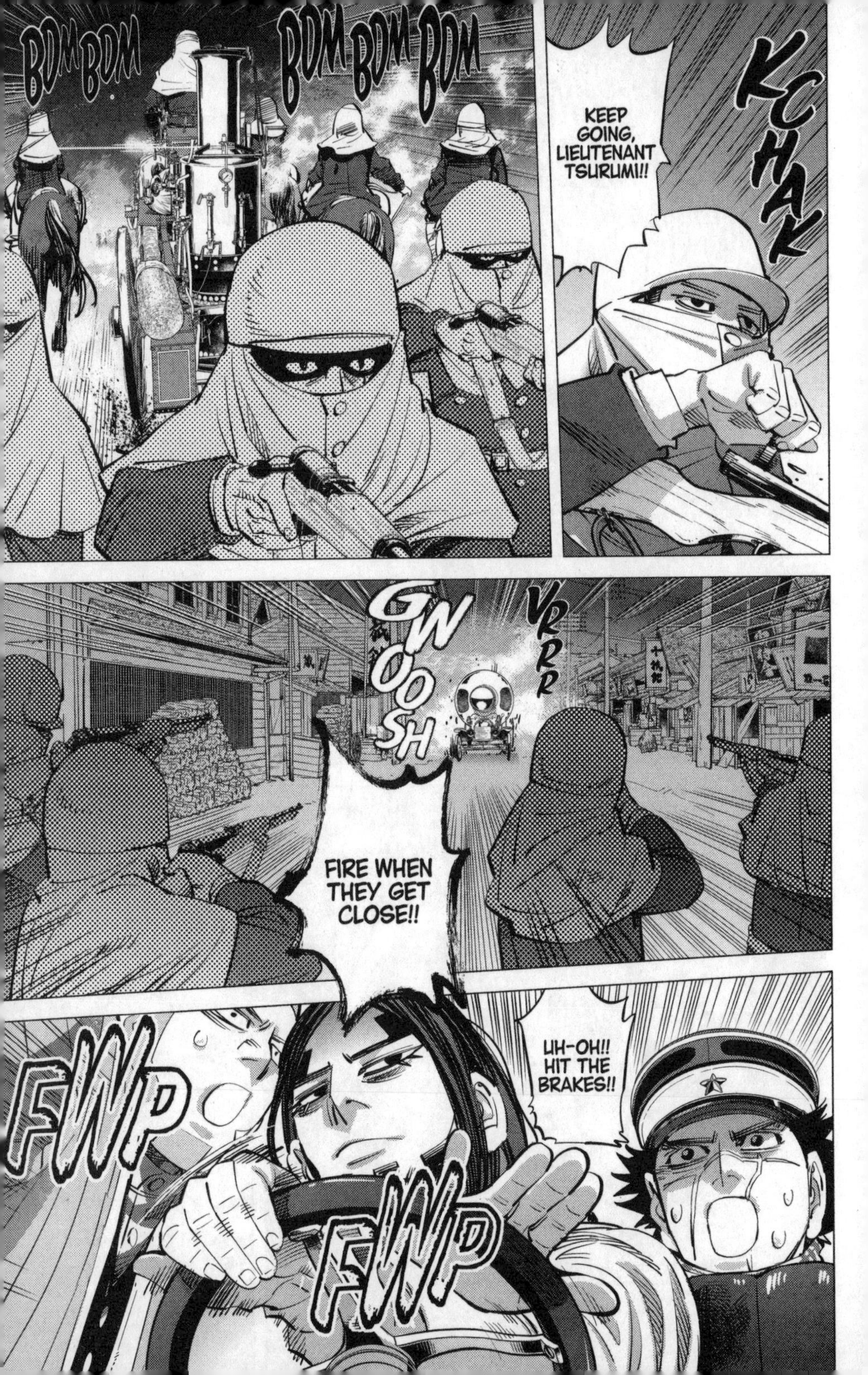
KCHAK
KEEP GOING, LIEUTENANT TSURUMI!!
BDM BDM BDM
BDM BDM
VRRR
GWOOOSH
FIRE WHEN THEY GET CLOSE!!
UH-OH!! HIT THE BRAKES!!
FWP
FWP

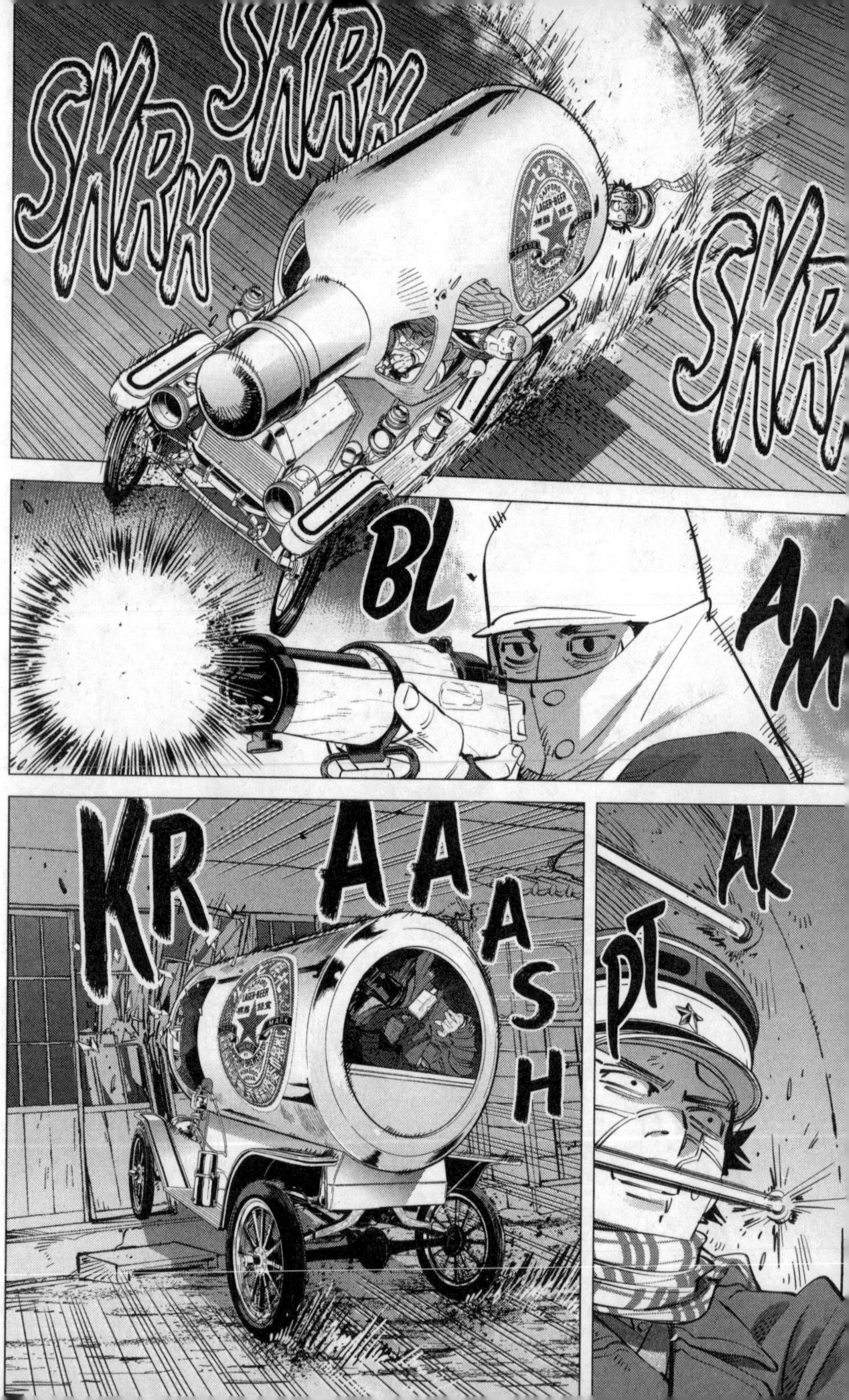
SHR
SHRK
SHRK
BLAM
PT AK
KRAAASH

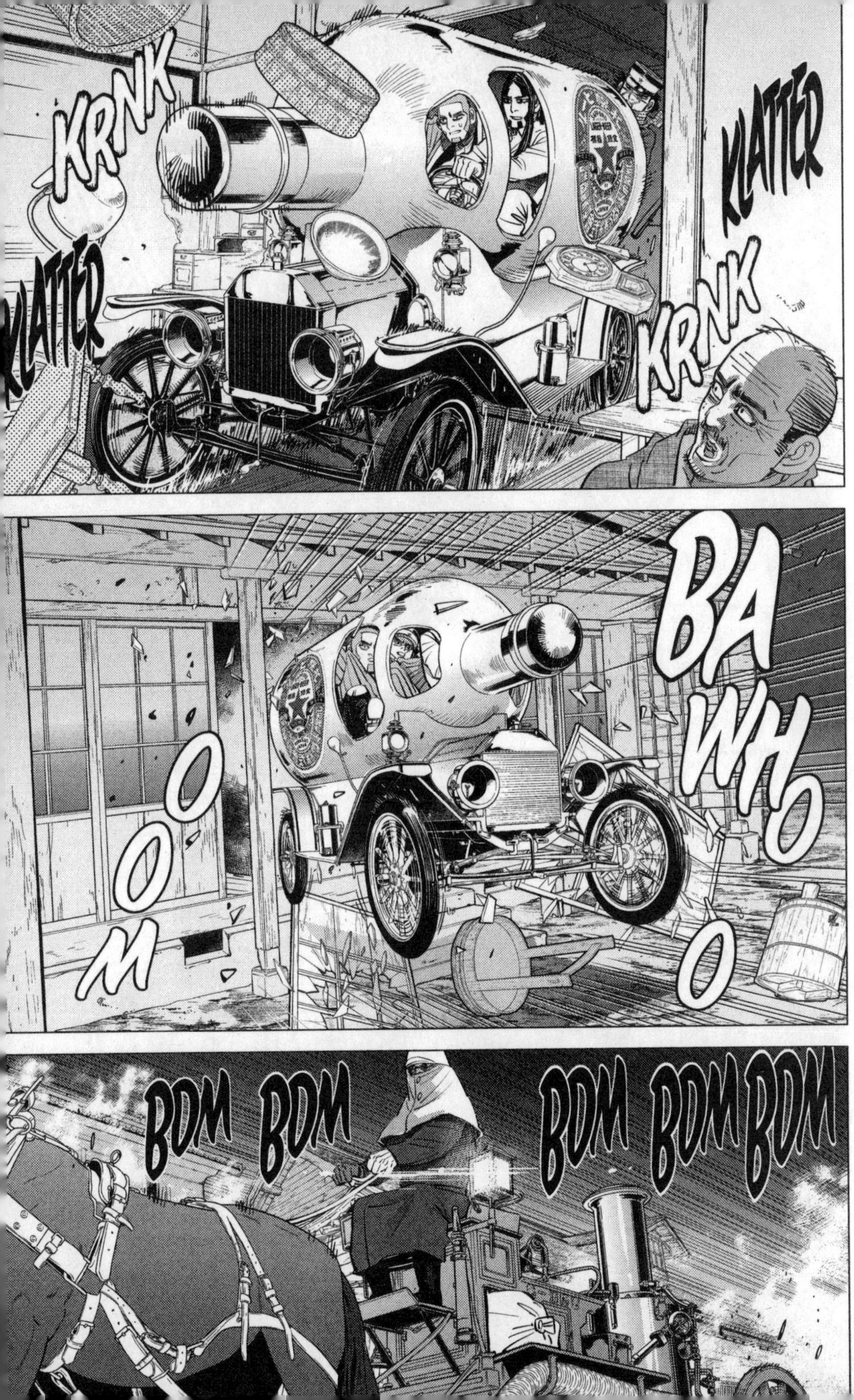
KLATTER
KRNK
KRNK
KLATTER
BAWHOOOOOM
BDM BDM BDM
BDM BDM

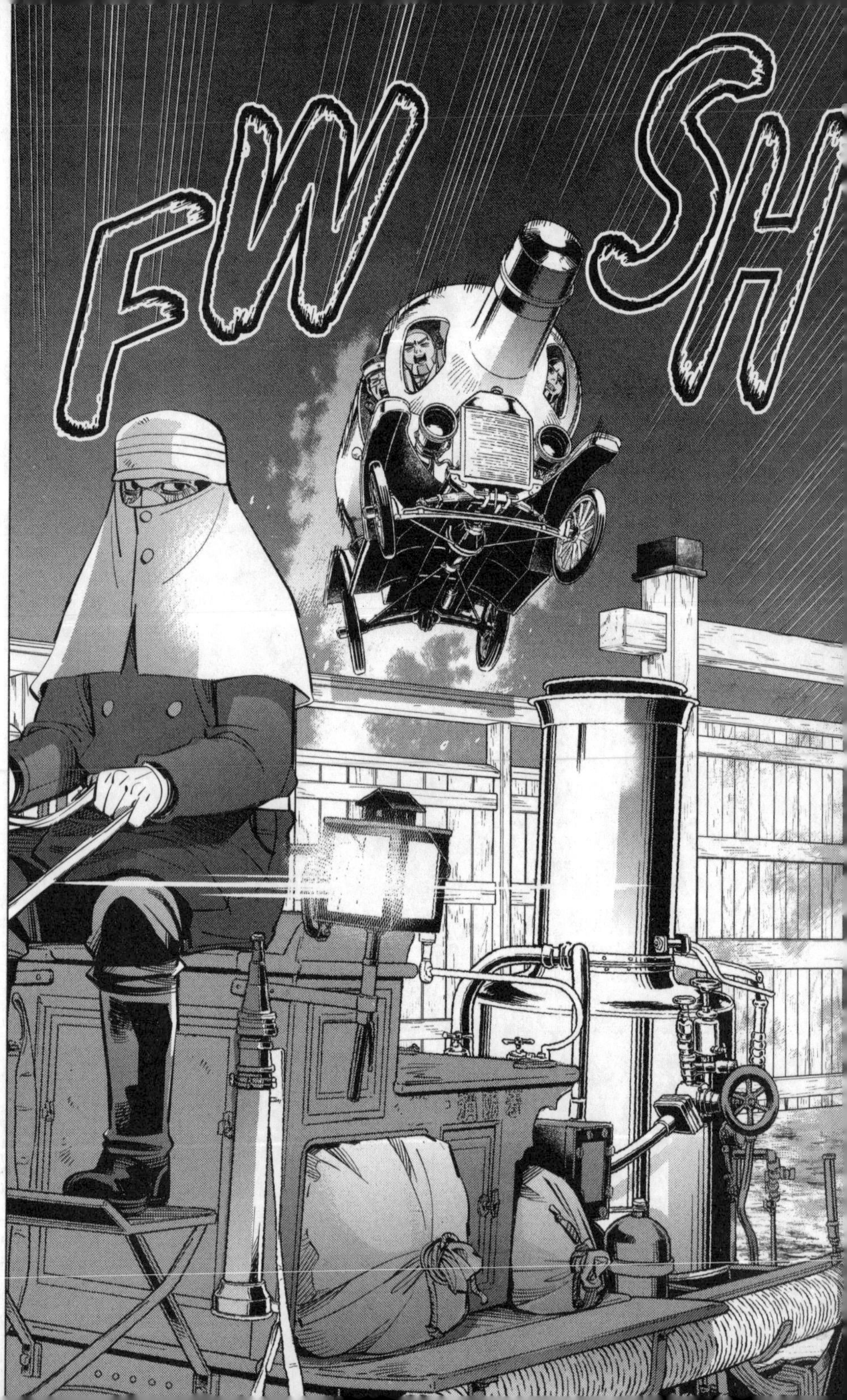
FWSH

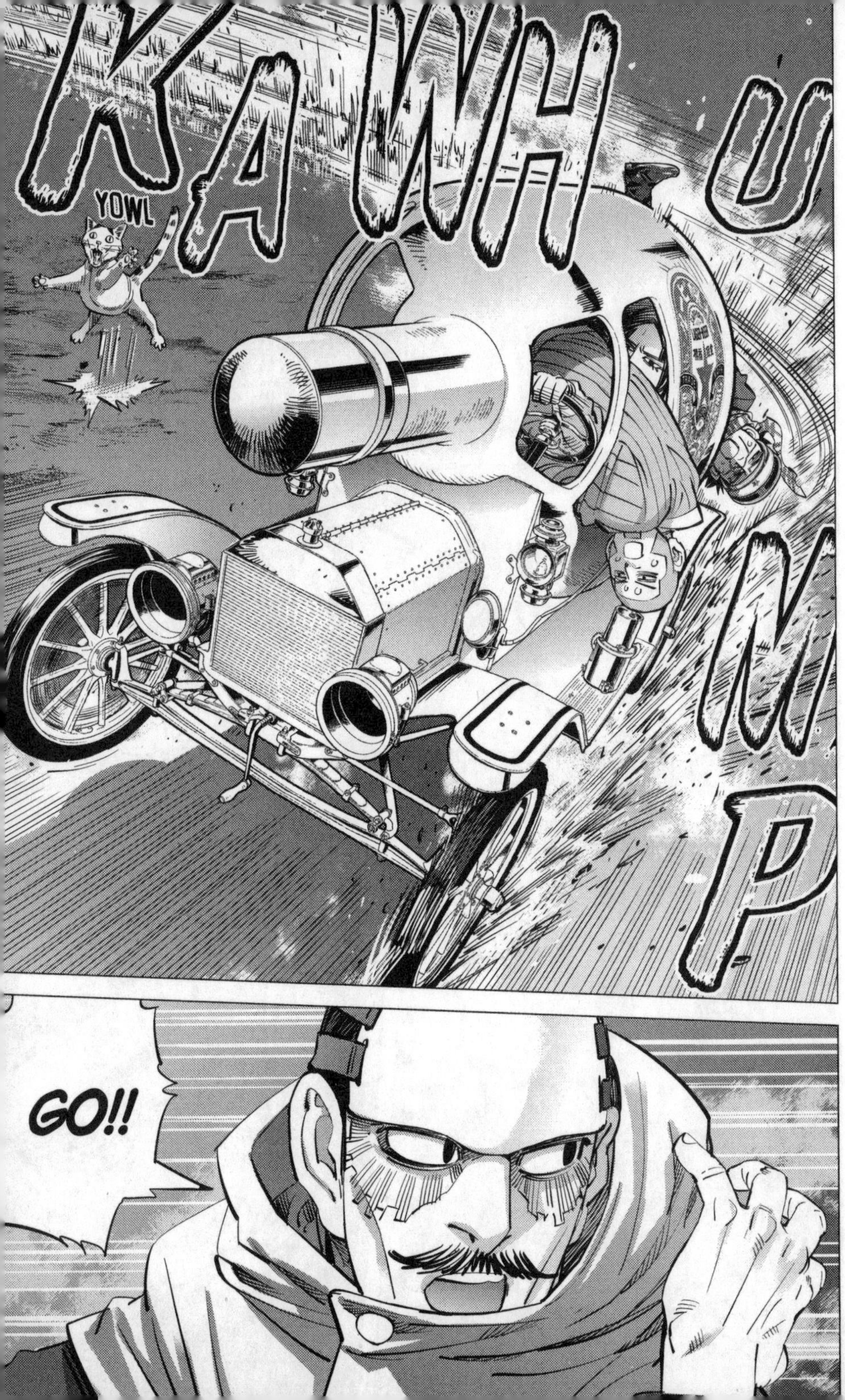
KAWHUMP
YOWL
GO!!

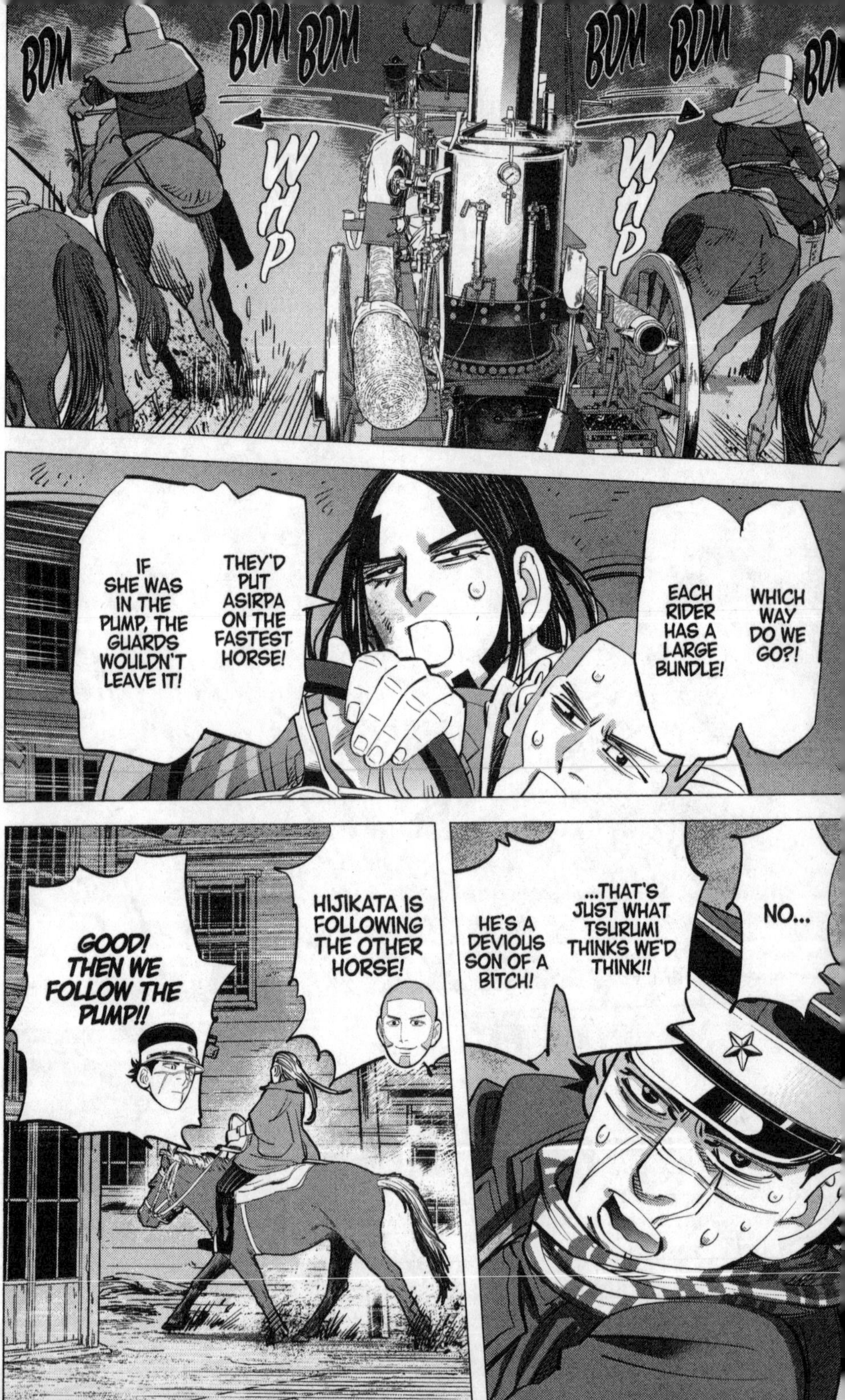
BDM BDM
WHP
WHP
BDM BDM
BDM
WHICH WAY DO WE GO?!
EACH RIDER HAS A LARGE BUNDLE!
THEY'D PUT ASIRPA ON THE FASTEST HORSE!
IF SHE WAS IN THE PUMP, THE GUARDS WOULDN'T LEAVE IT!
NO...
...THAT'S JUST WHAT TSURUMI THINKS WE'D THINK!!
HE'S A DEVIOUS SON OF A BITCH!
HIJIKATA IS FOLLOWING THE OTHER HORSE!
GOOD! THEN WE FOLLOW THE PUMP!!

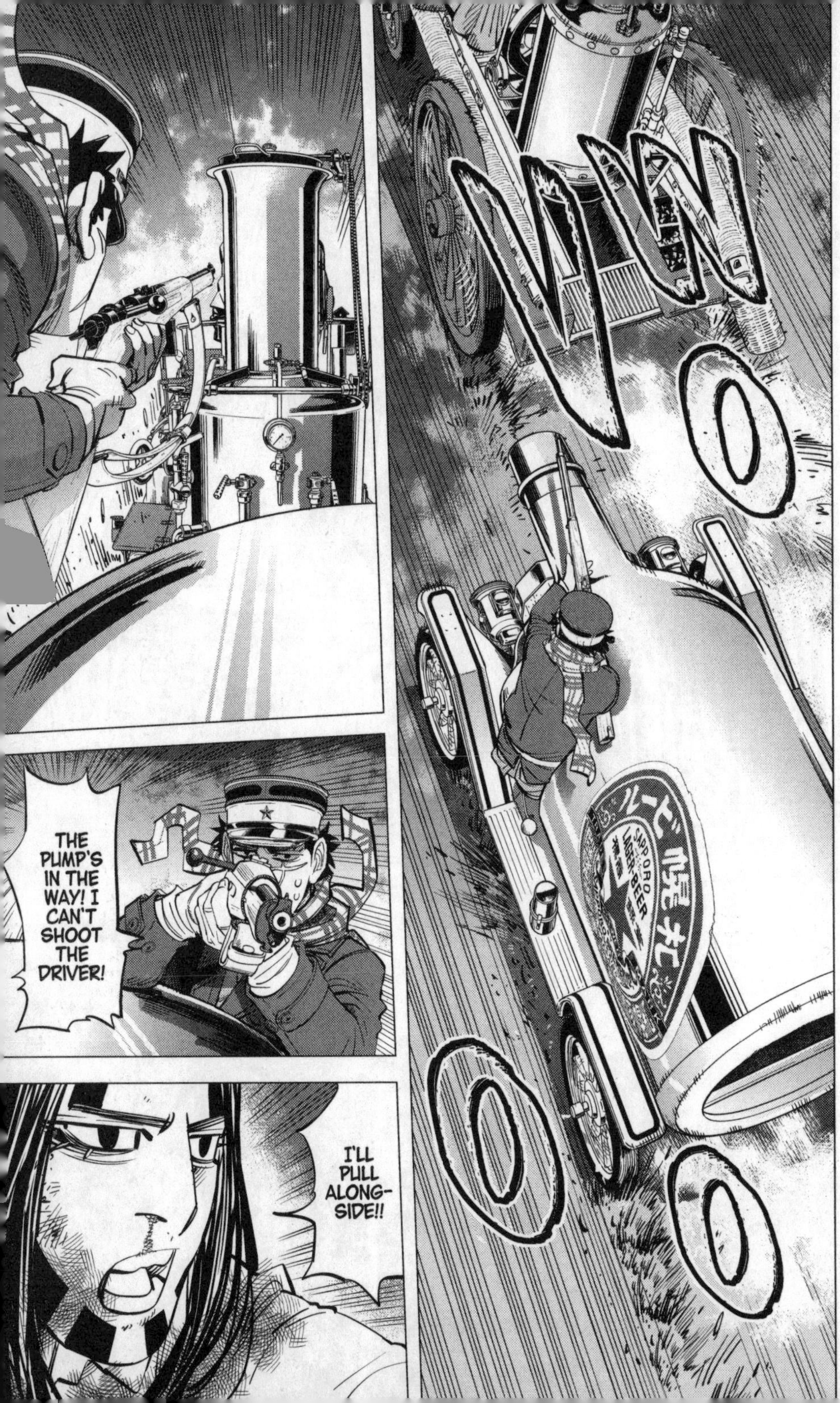
SAPPORO LAGER BEER
THE PUMP'S IN THE WAY! I CAN'T SHOOT THE DRIVER!
I'LL PULL ALONG-SIDE!!

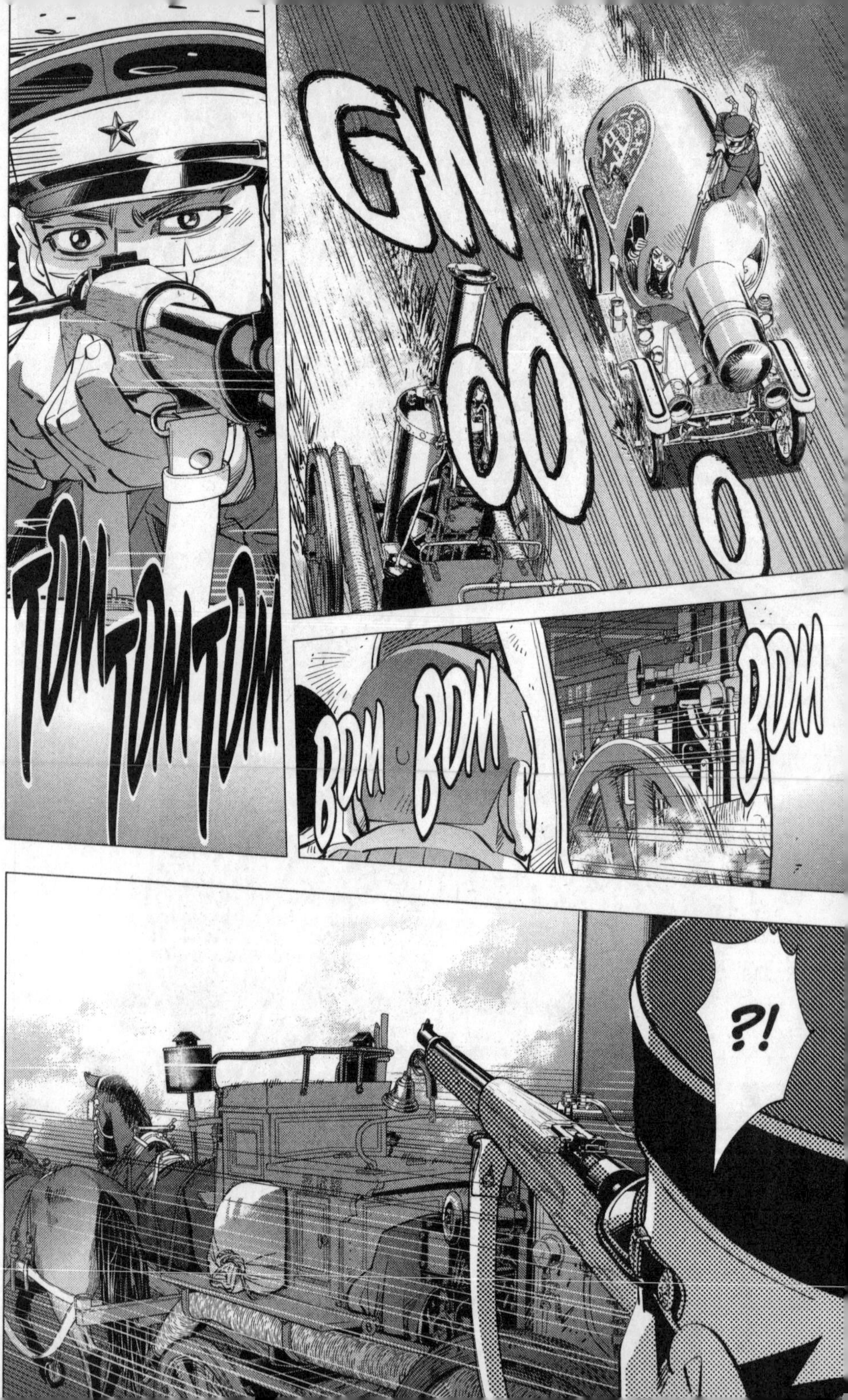
GWOOO
BDM BDM BDM
TOM TOM TOM
?!

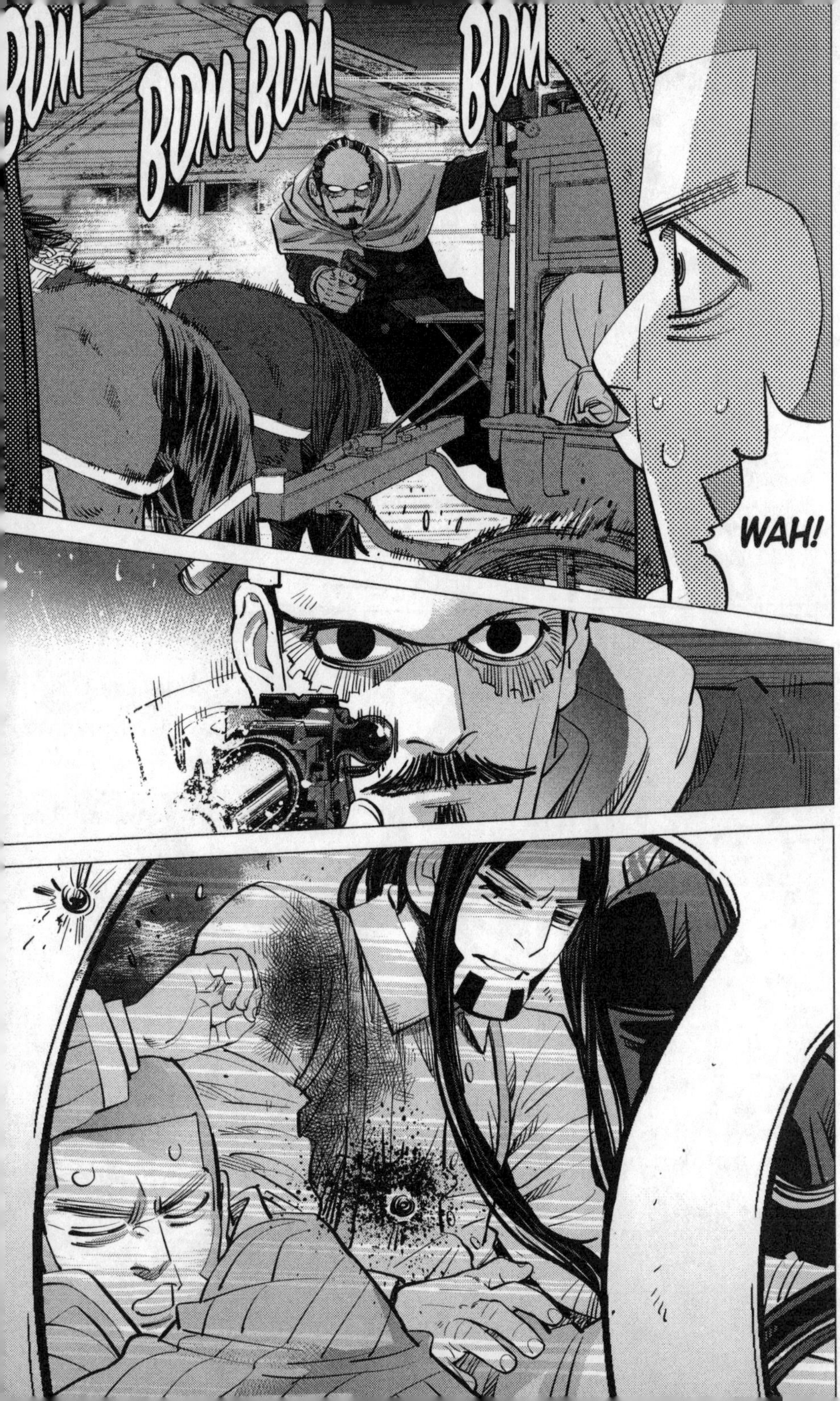
BDM
BDM BDM
BDM
WAH!

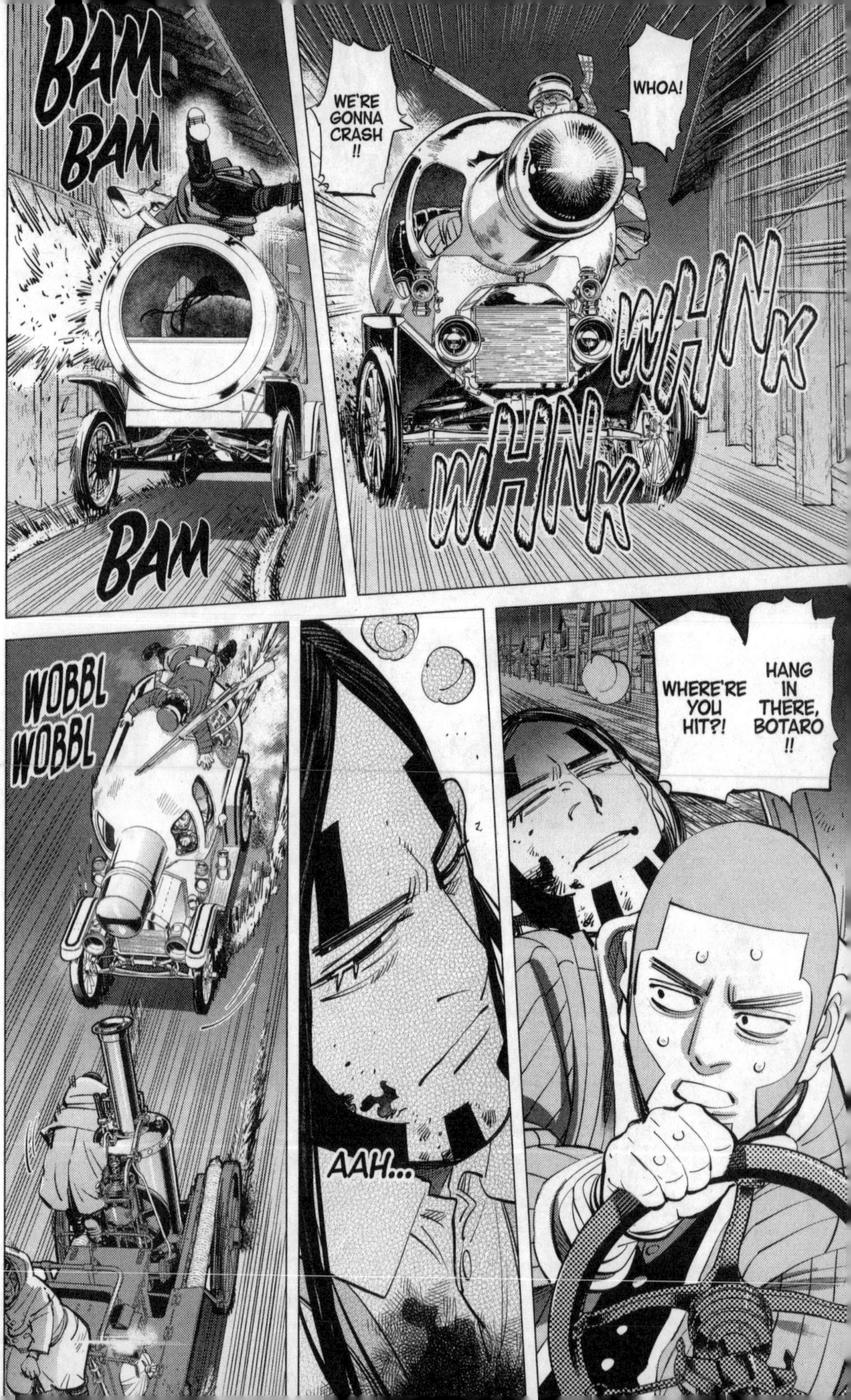
WHOA!
WE'RE GONNA CRASH!!
WHNK
WHNK
BAM BAM
BAM
HANG IN THERE, BOTARO!!
WHERE'RE YOU HIT?!
AAH...
WOBBL WOBBL

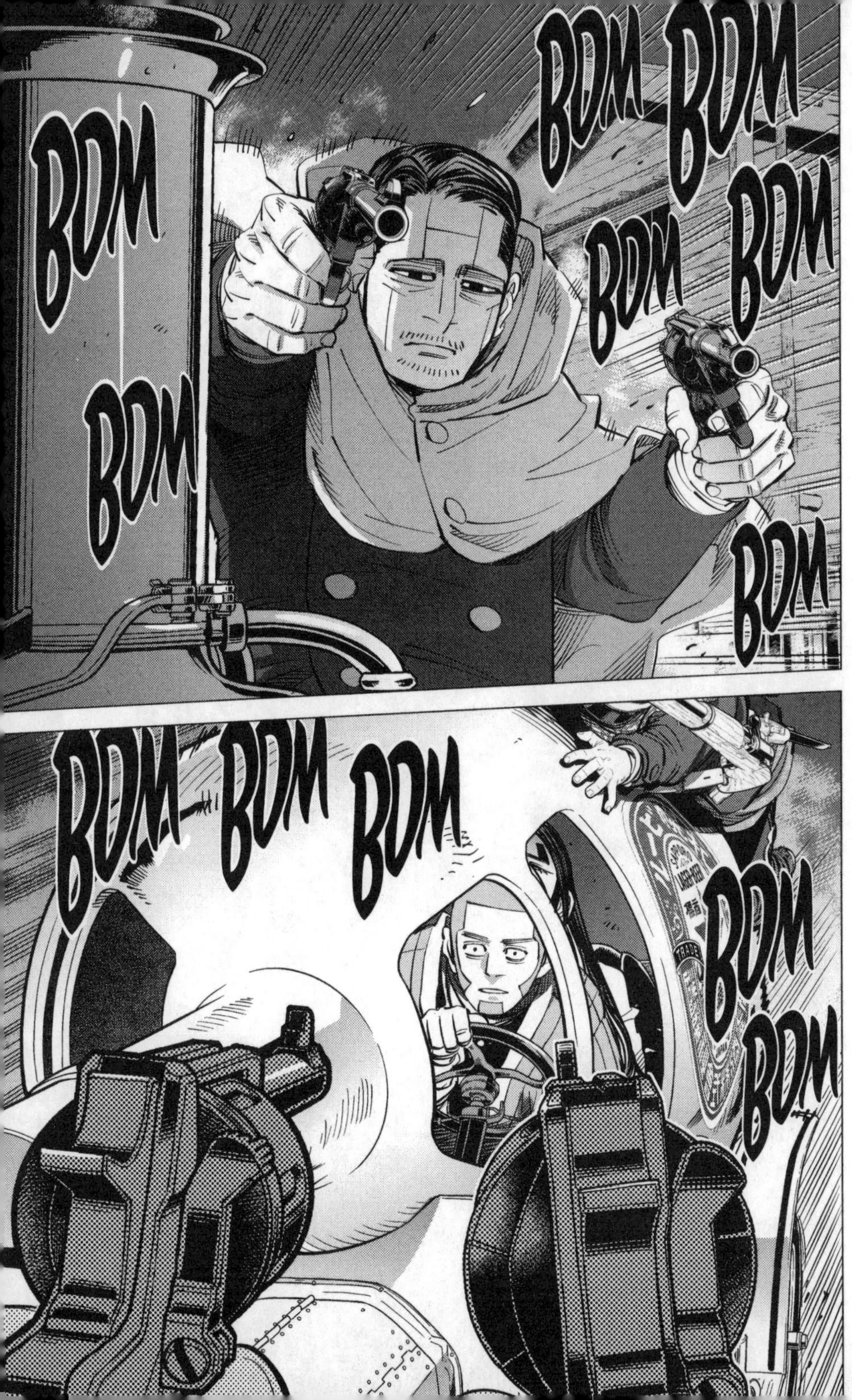
BDM BDM
BDM BDM
BDM
BDM
BDM
BDM BDM
BDM BDM BDM

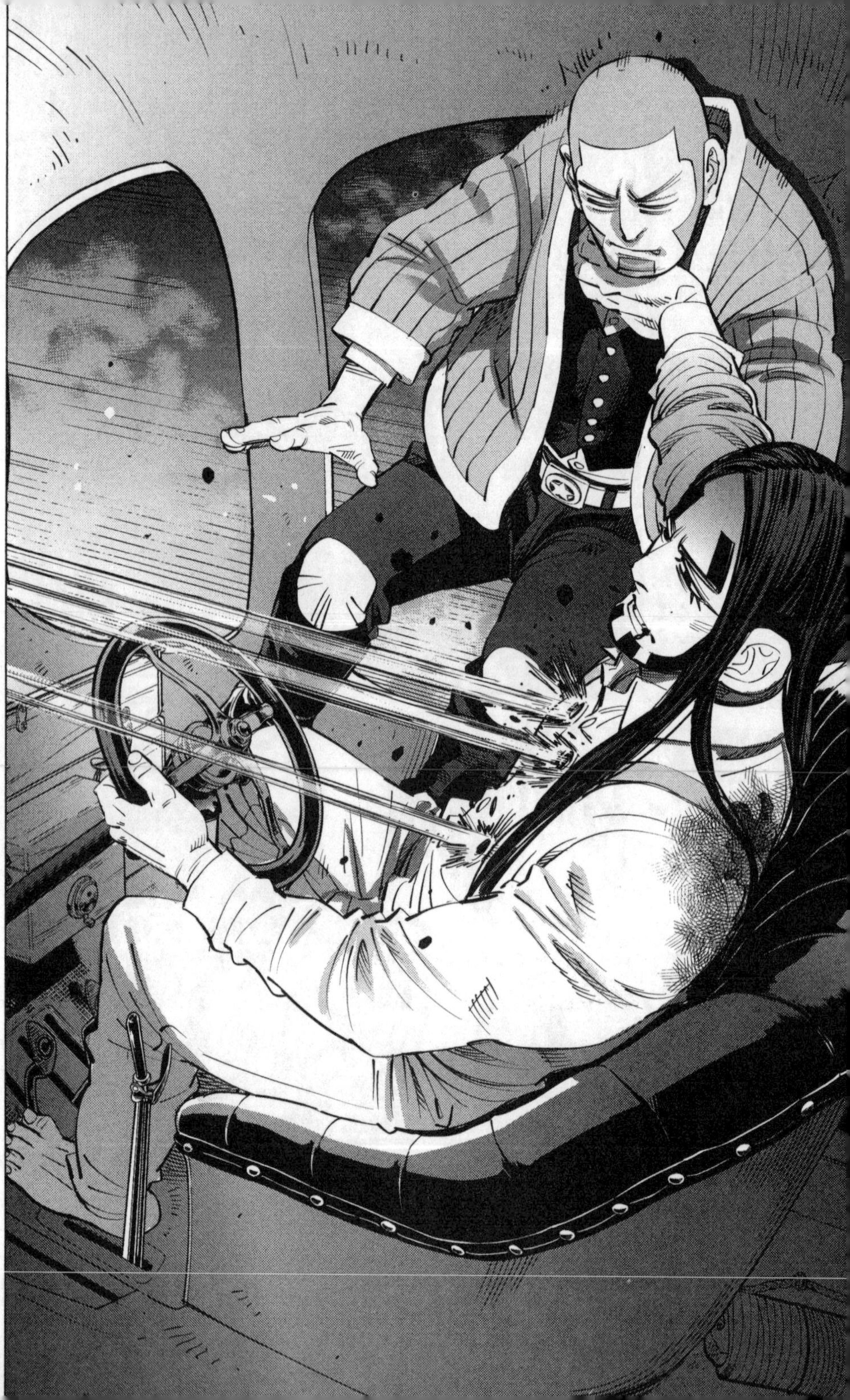

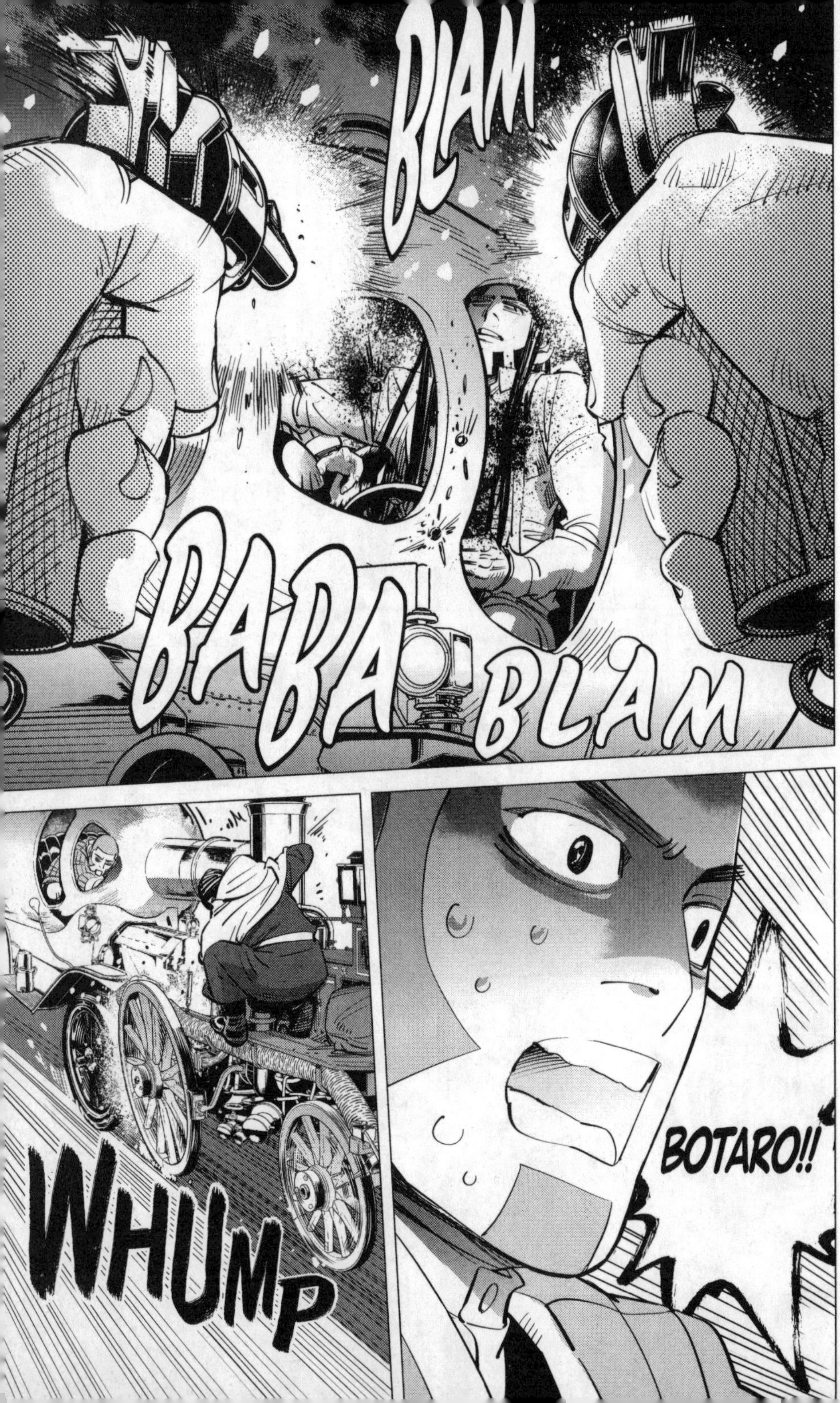
BLAM
BABA BLAM
BOTARO!!
WHUMP

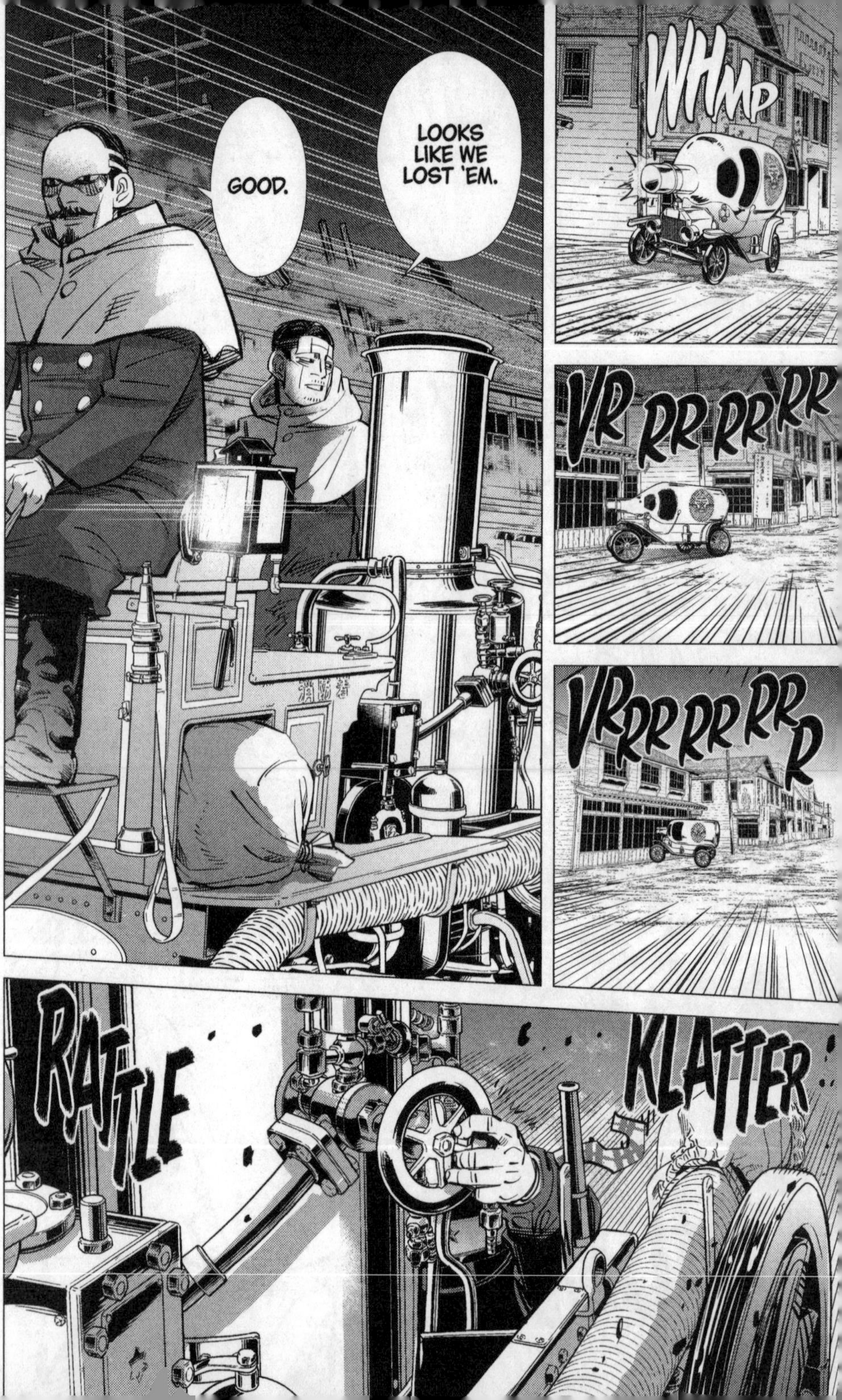
WHMP
VR RR RR RR
VRRR RR RR R
LOOKS LIKE WE LOST 'EM.
GOOD.
KLATTER
RATTLE

Chapter 263: Fusataro Osawa, a.k.a. Botaro the Pirate

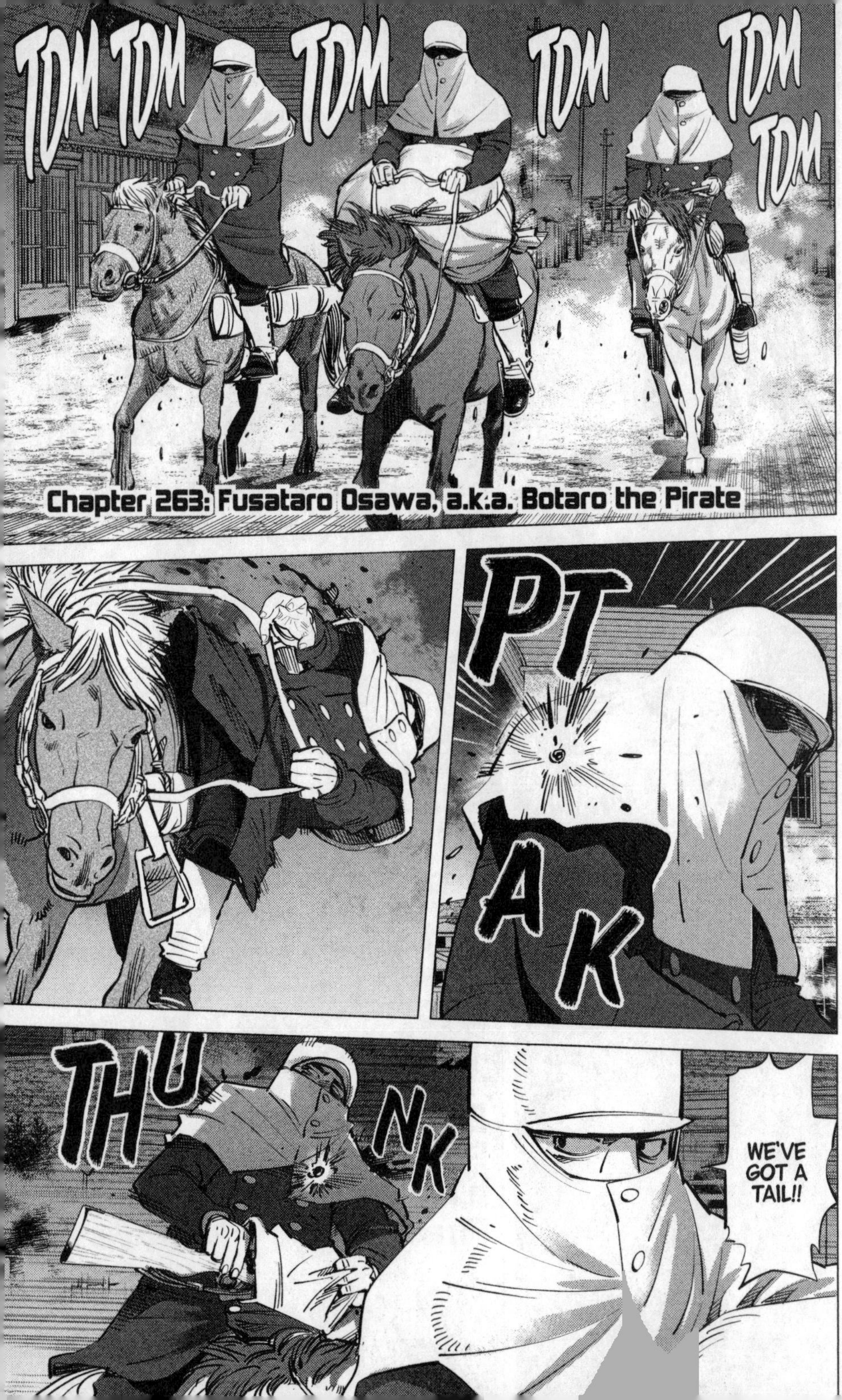
TOM
TOM
TOM
TOM
TOM
TOM
TOM
PTAK
WE'VE GOT A TAIL!!
THUNK

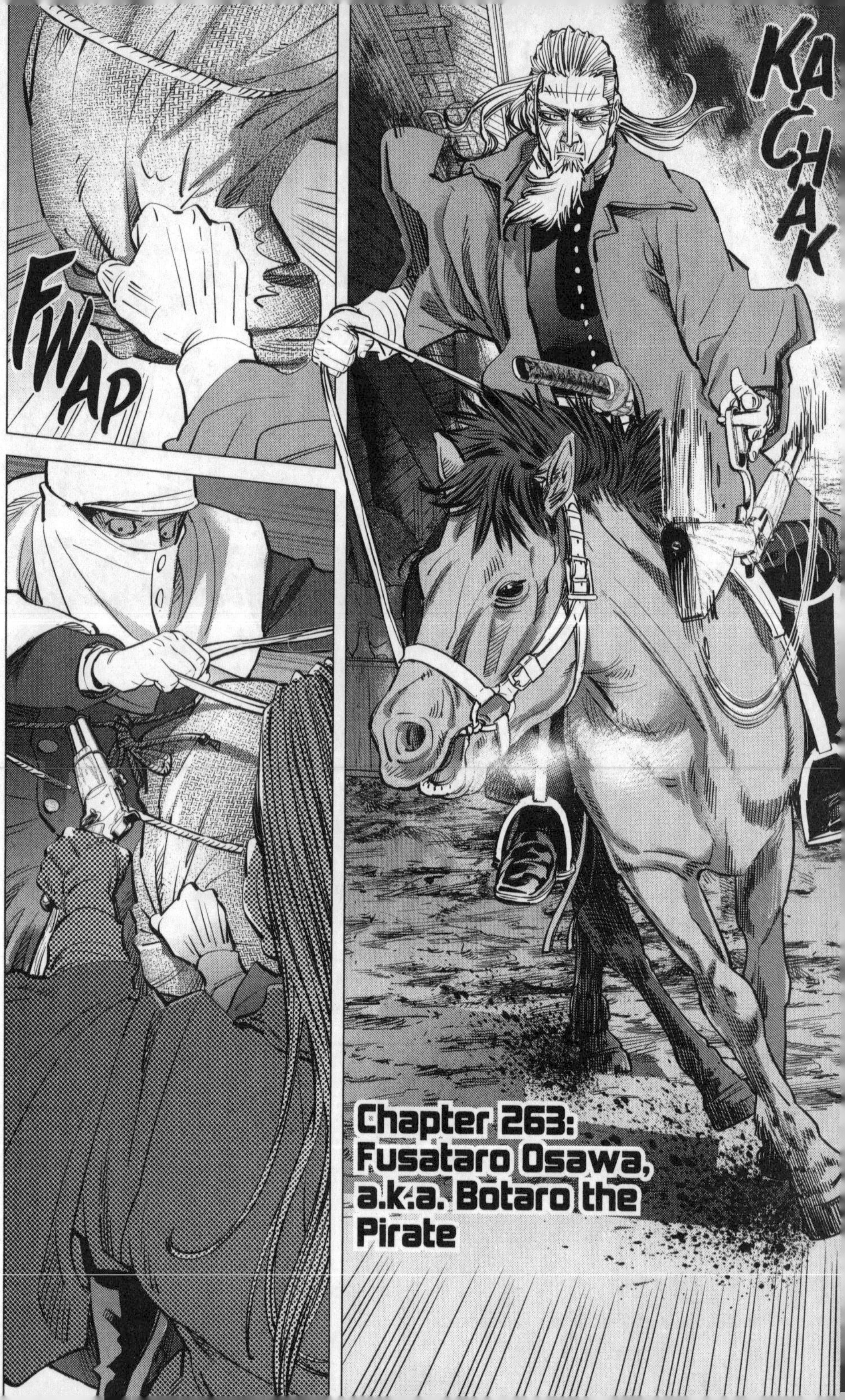
KA CHAK
Chapter 263: Fusataro Osawa, a.k.a. Botaro the Pirate
FWAP

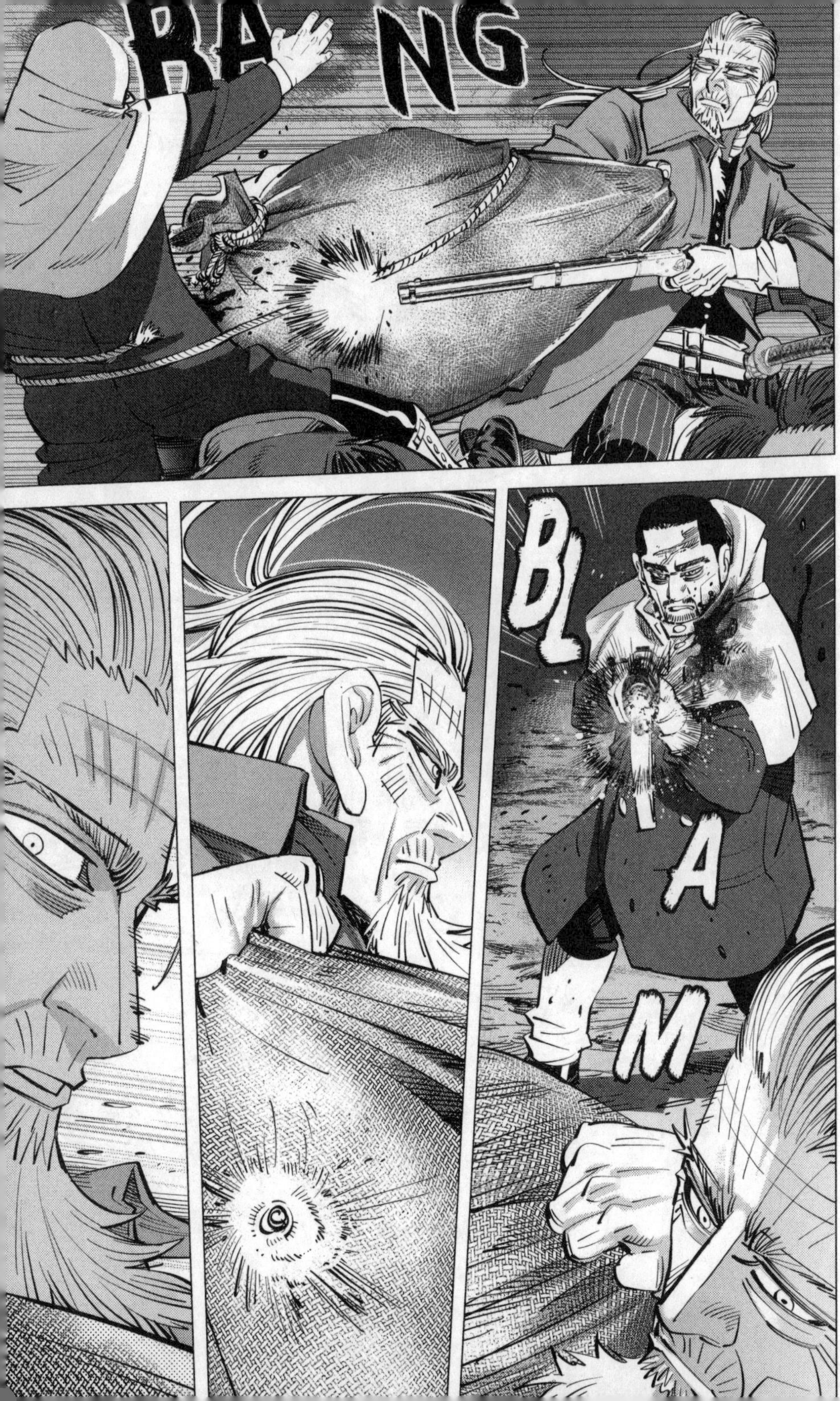
BANG
BLAM

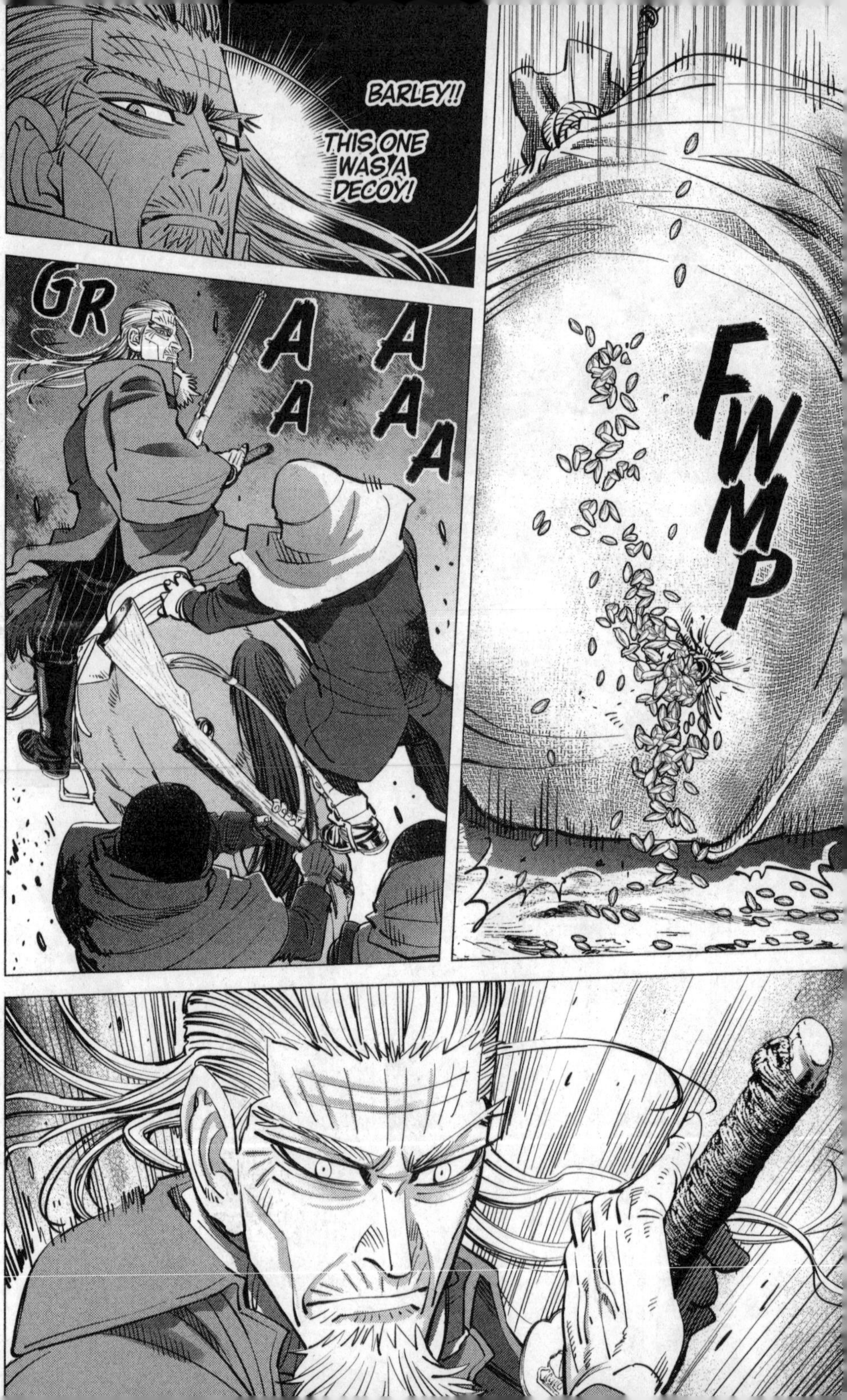
FWMP
BARLEY!!
THIS ONE WAS A DECOY!
GRAAAAA

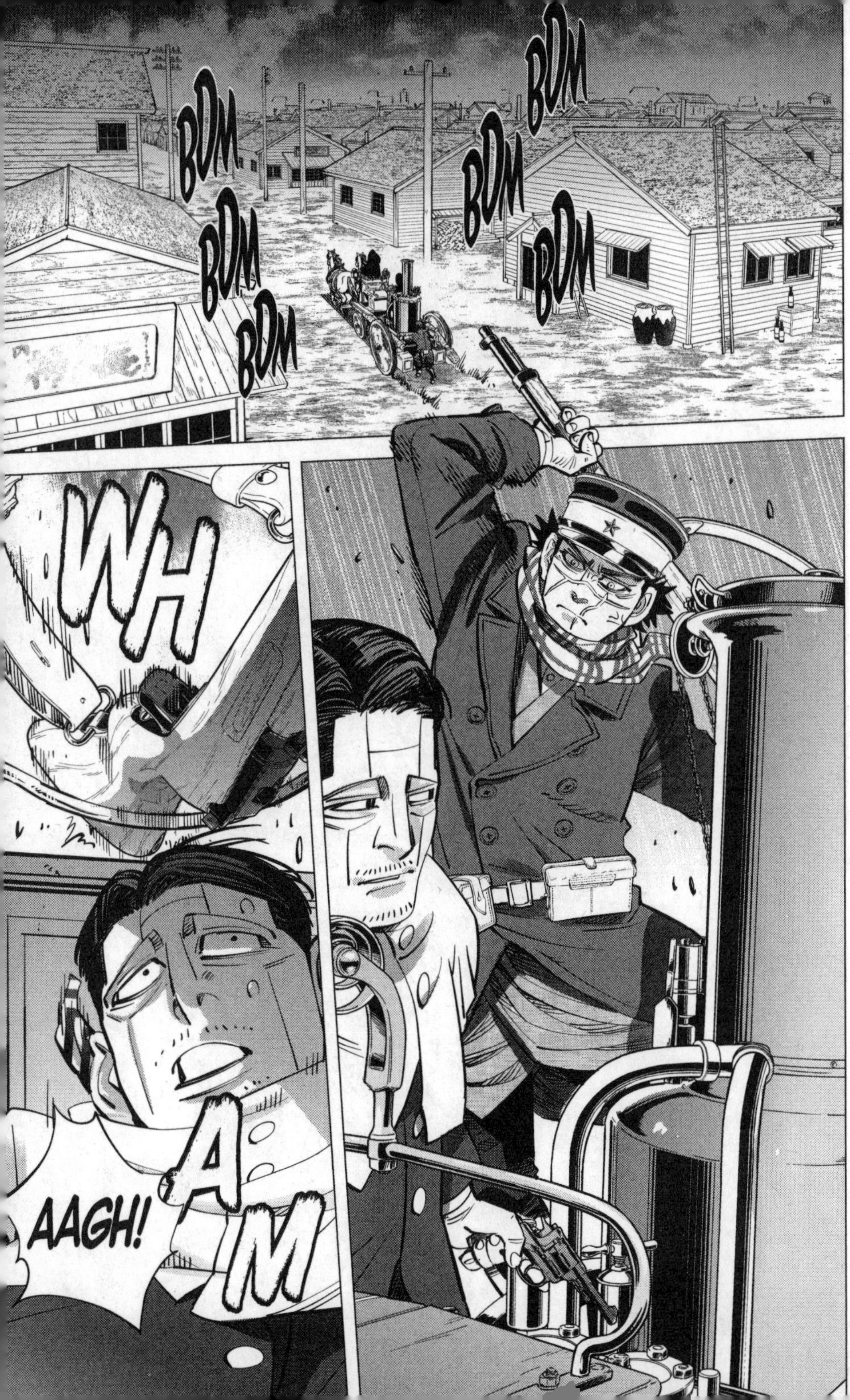
BDM
BDM
BDM
BDM
BDM
BDM
BDM
BDM
WH
AM
AAGH!

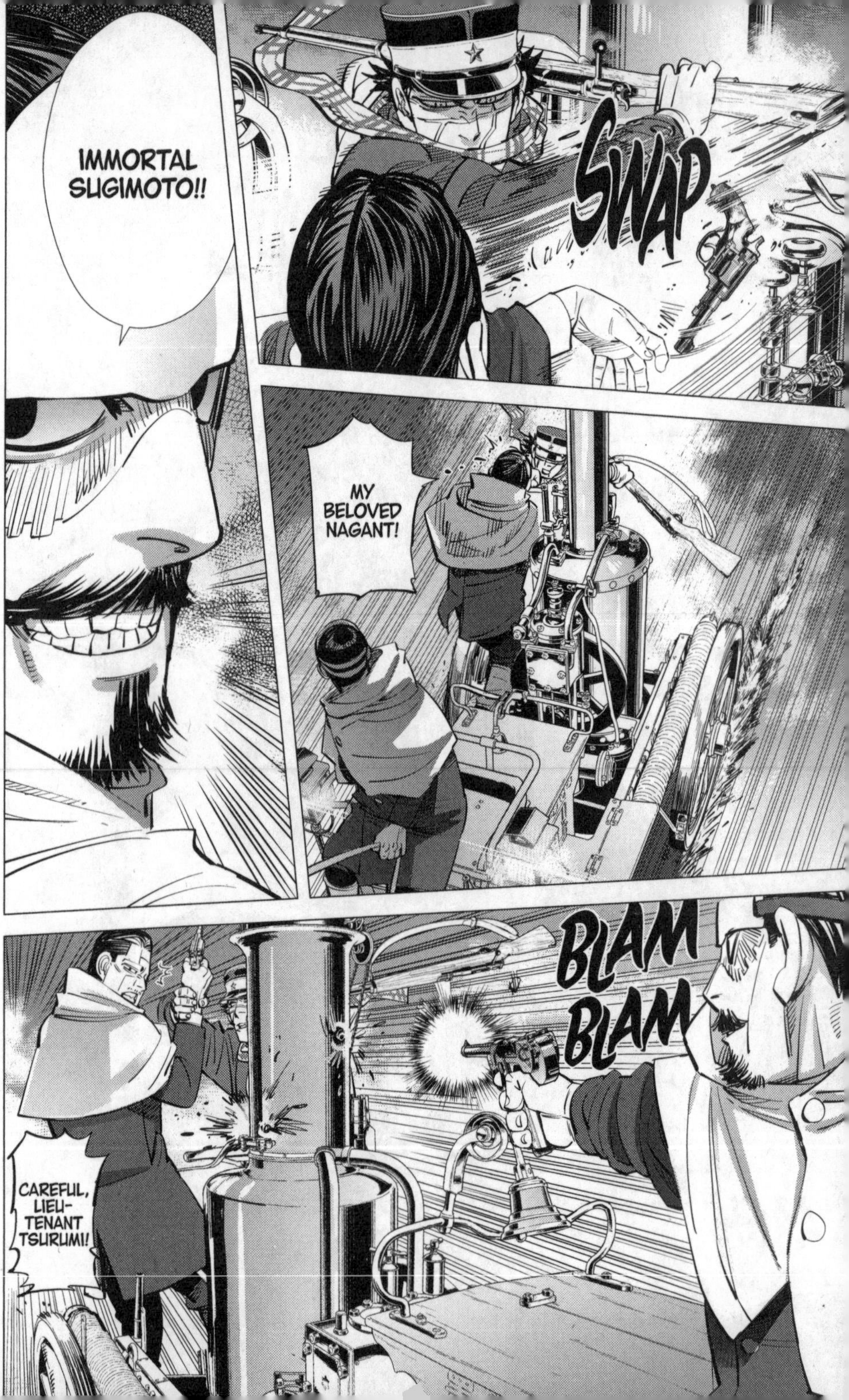
SWAP
MY BELOVED NAGANT!
IMMORTAL SUGIMOTO!!
BLAM BLAM
CAREFUL, LIEU-TENANT TSURUMI!

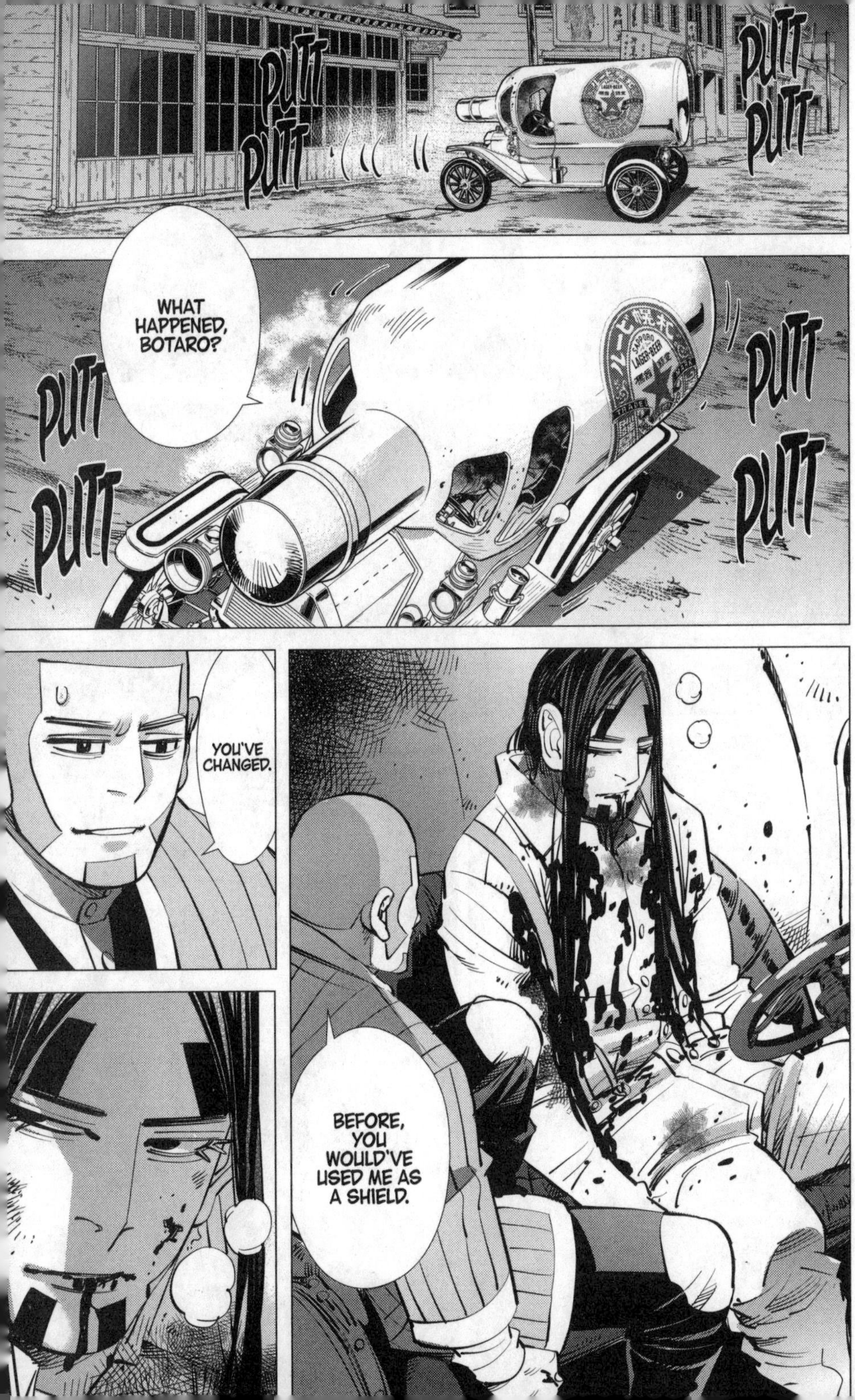
PUTT PUTT
PUTT PUTT
PUTT PUTT
WHAT HAPPENED, BOTARO?
PUTT PUTT
BEFORE, YOU WOULD'VE USED ME AS A SHIELD.
YOU'VE CHANGED.

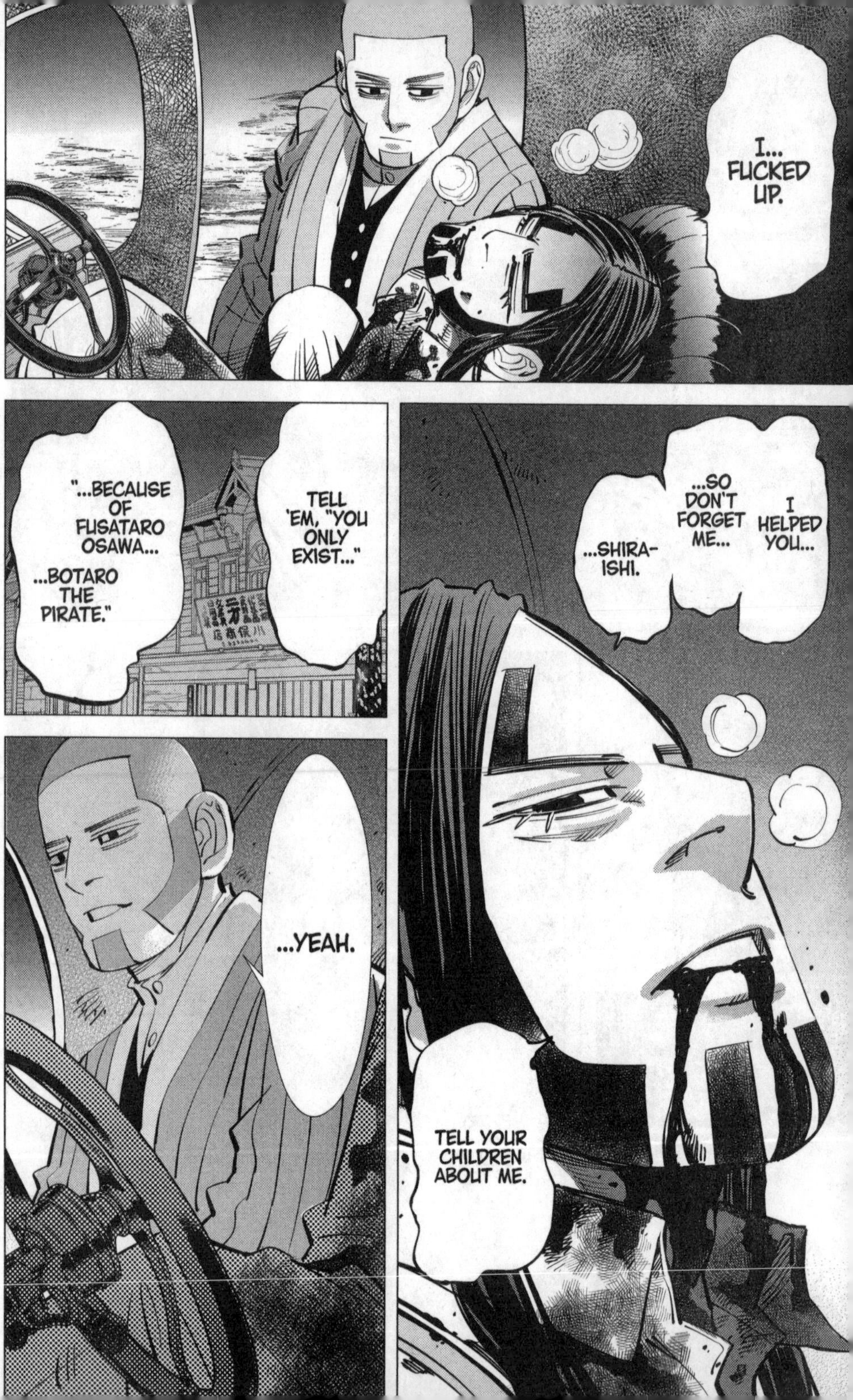
I... FUCKED UP.
I HELPED YOU...
...SO DON'T FORGET ME...
...SHIRA-ISHI.
TELL YOUR CHILDREN ABOUT ME.
TELL 'EM, "YOU ONLY EXIST..."
"...BECAUSE OF FUSATARO OSAWA... ...BOTARO THE PIRATE."
...YEAH.

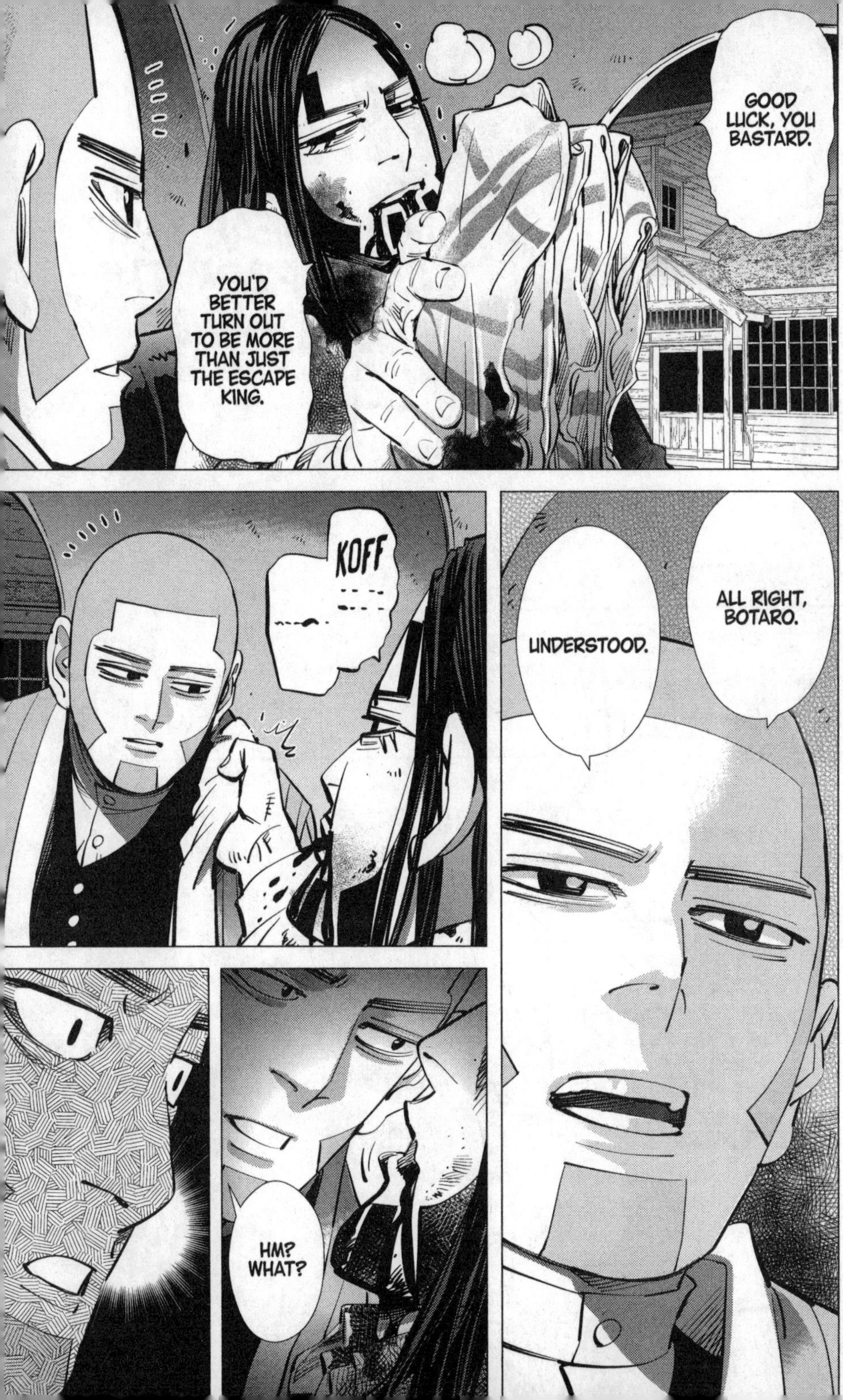
GOOD LUCK, YOU BASTARD.
YOU'D BETTER TURN OUT TO BE MORE THAN JUST THE ESCAPE KING.
ALL RIGHT, BOTARO.
UNDERSTOOD.
KOFF
HM? WHAT?

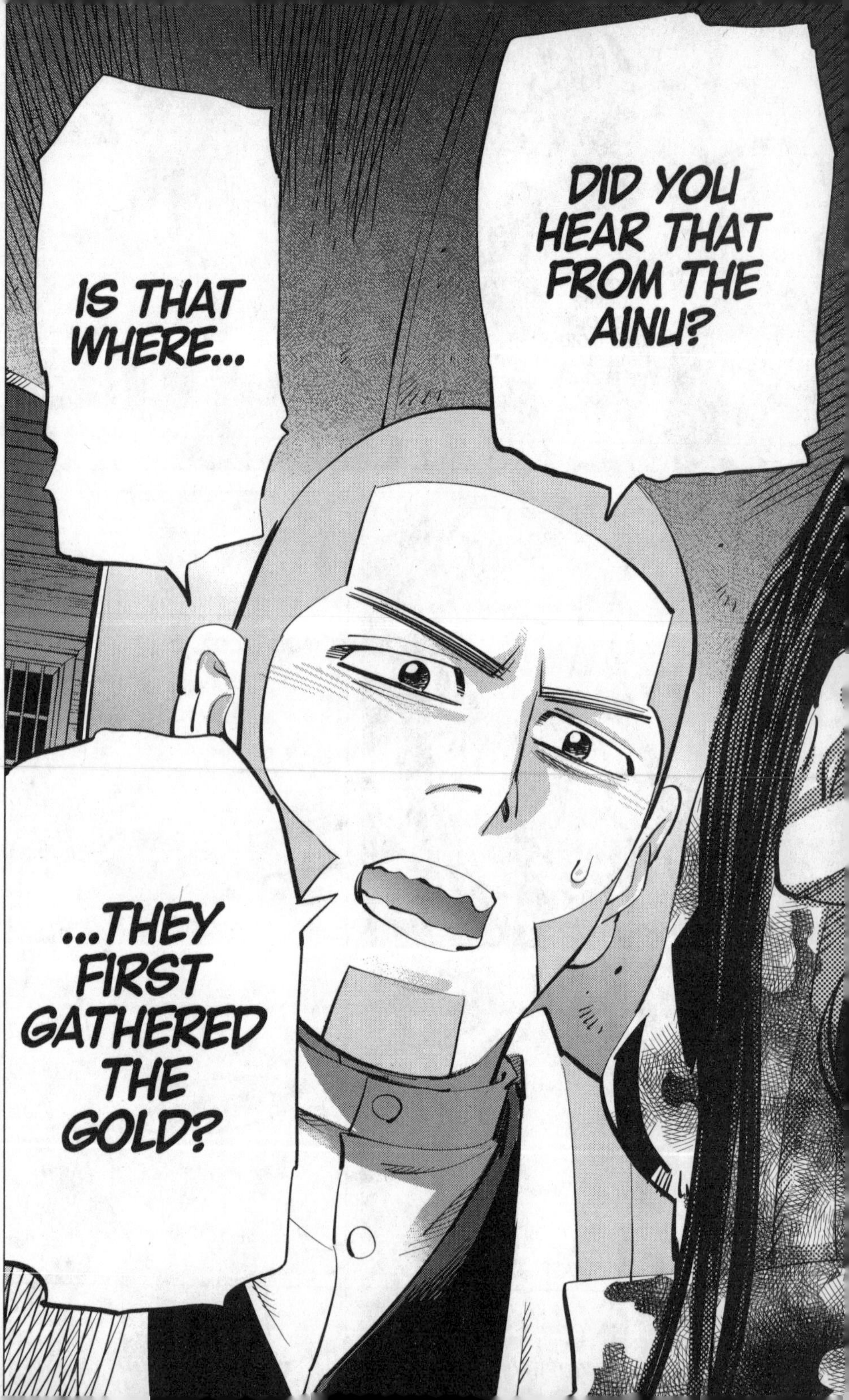
DID YOU HEAR THAT FROM THE AINU?
IS THAT WHERE...
...THEY FIRST GATHERED THE GOLD?

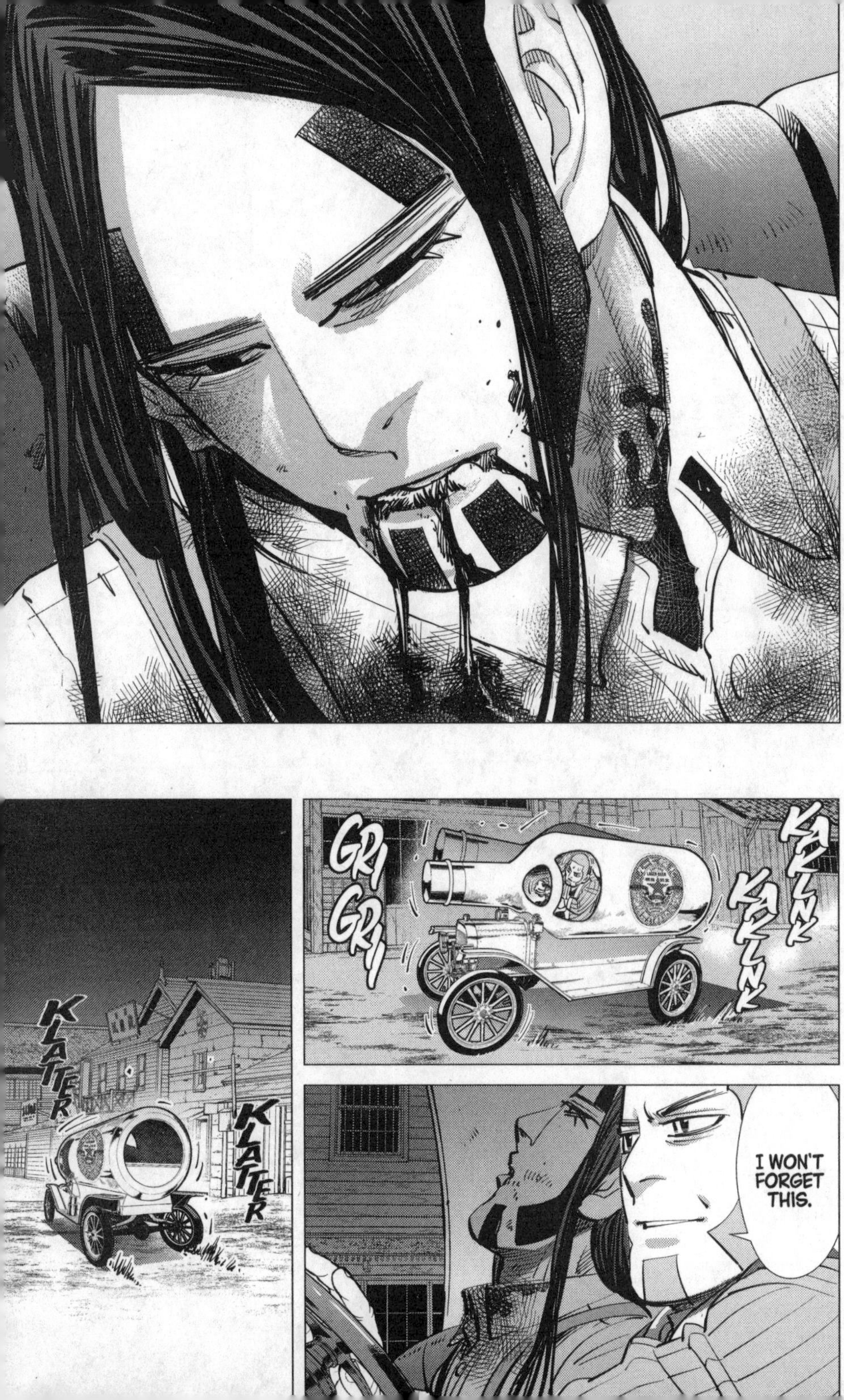
KAKLNK
KAKLNK
GRI GRI
I WON'T FORGET THIS.
KLATTER
KLATTER

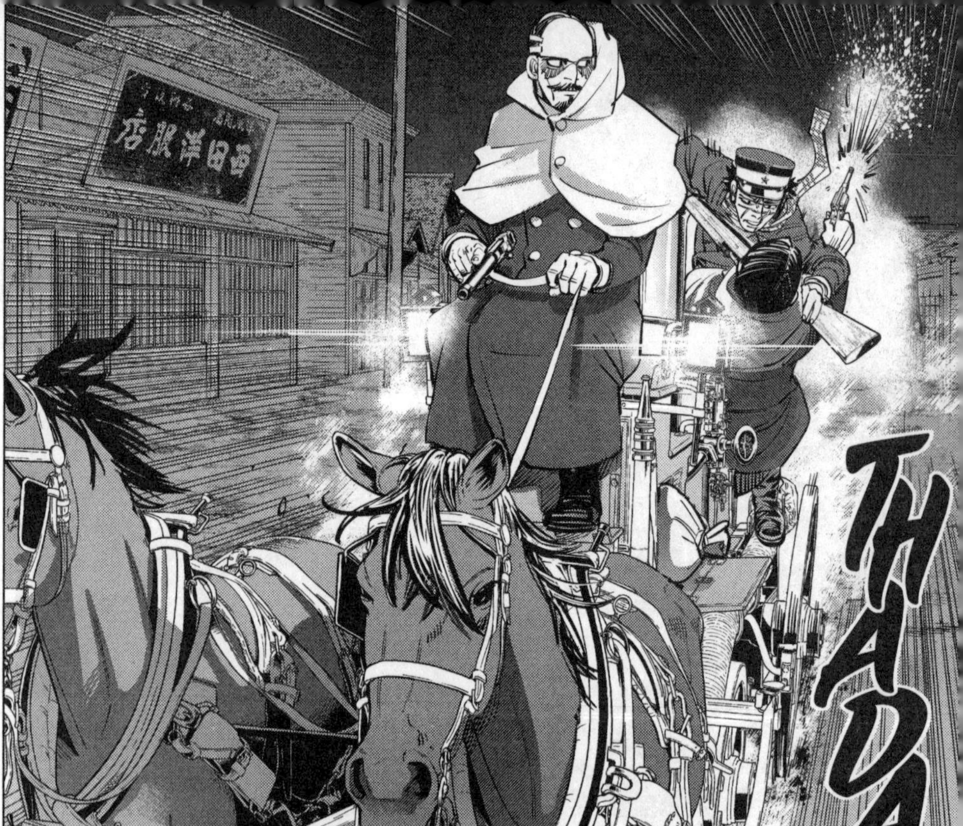
西田洋服店
THADADUM

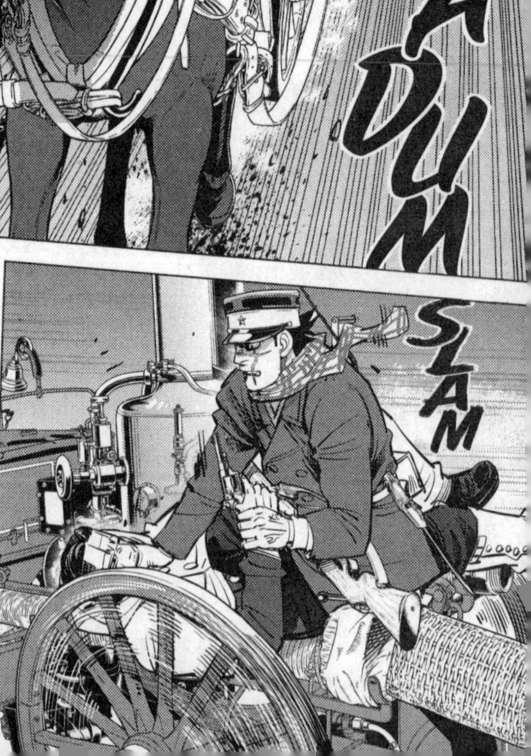
SLAM

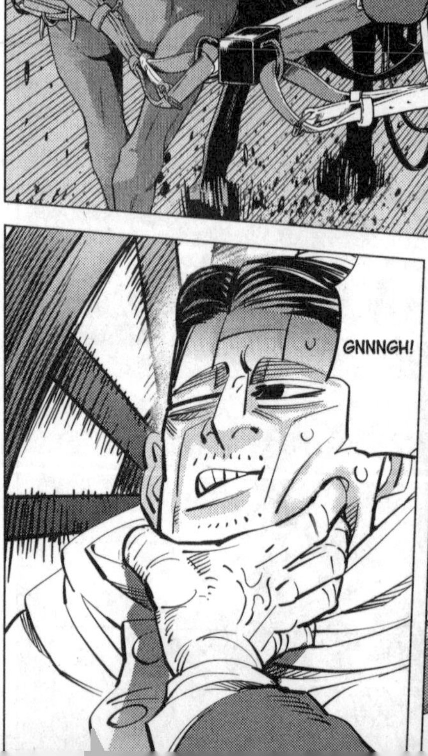
GNNNGH!

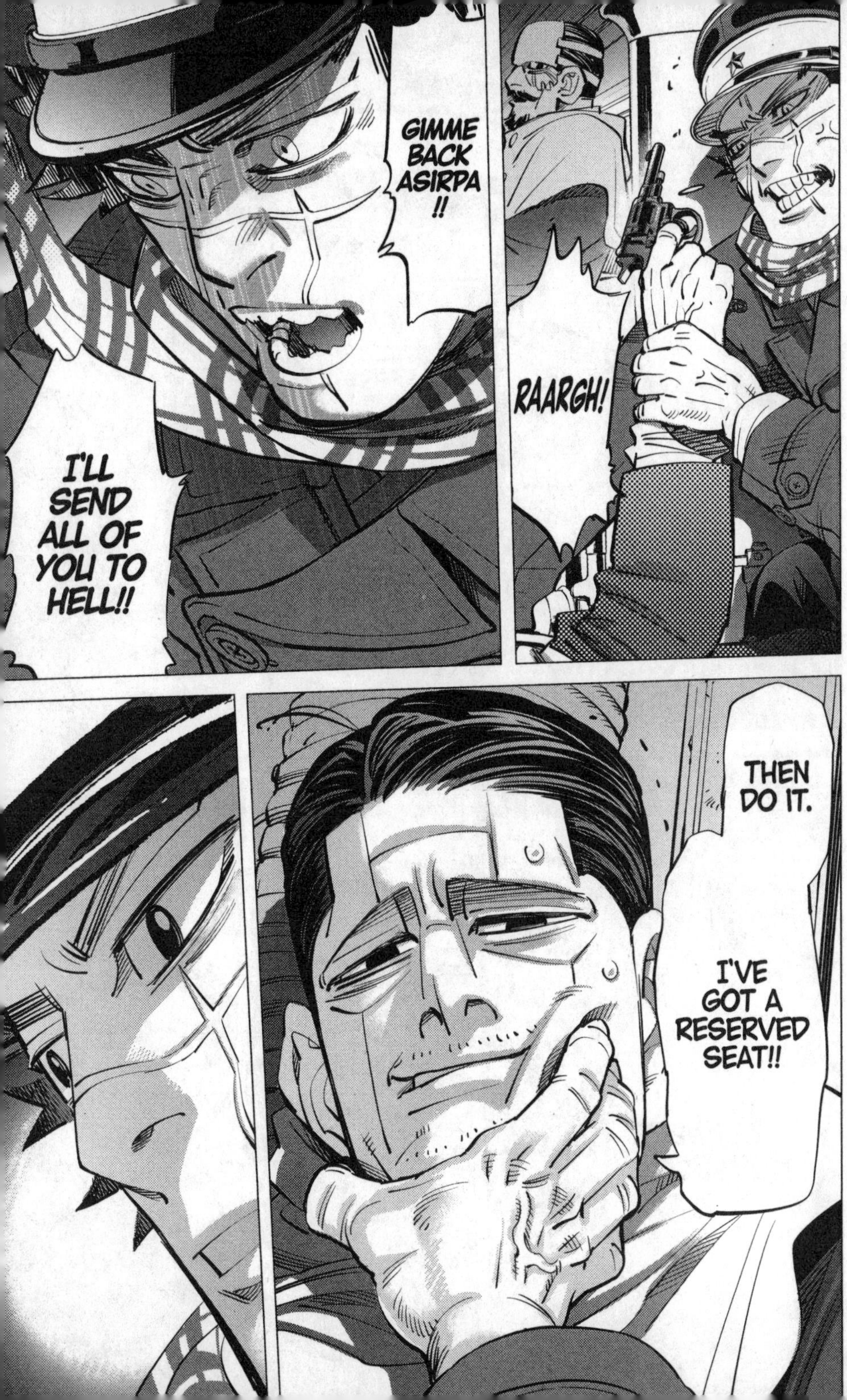
RAARGH!
GIMME BACK ASIRPA !!
I'LL SEND ALL OF YOU TO HELL!!
THEN DO IT.
I'VE GOT A RESERVED SEAT!!

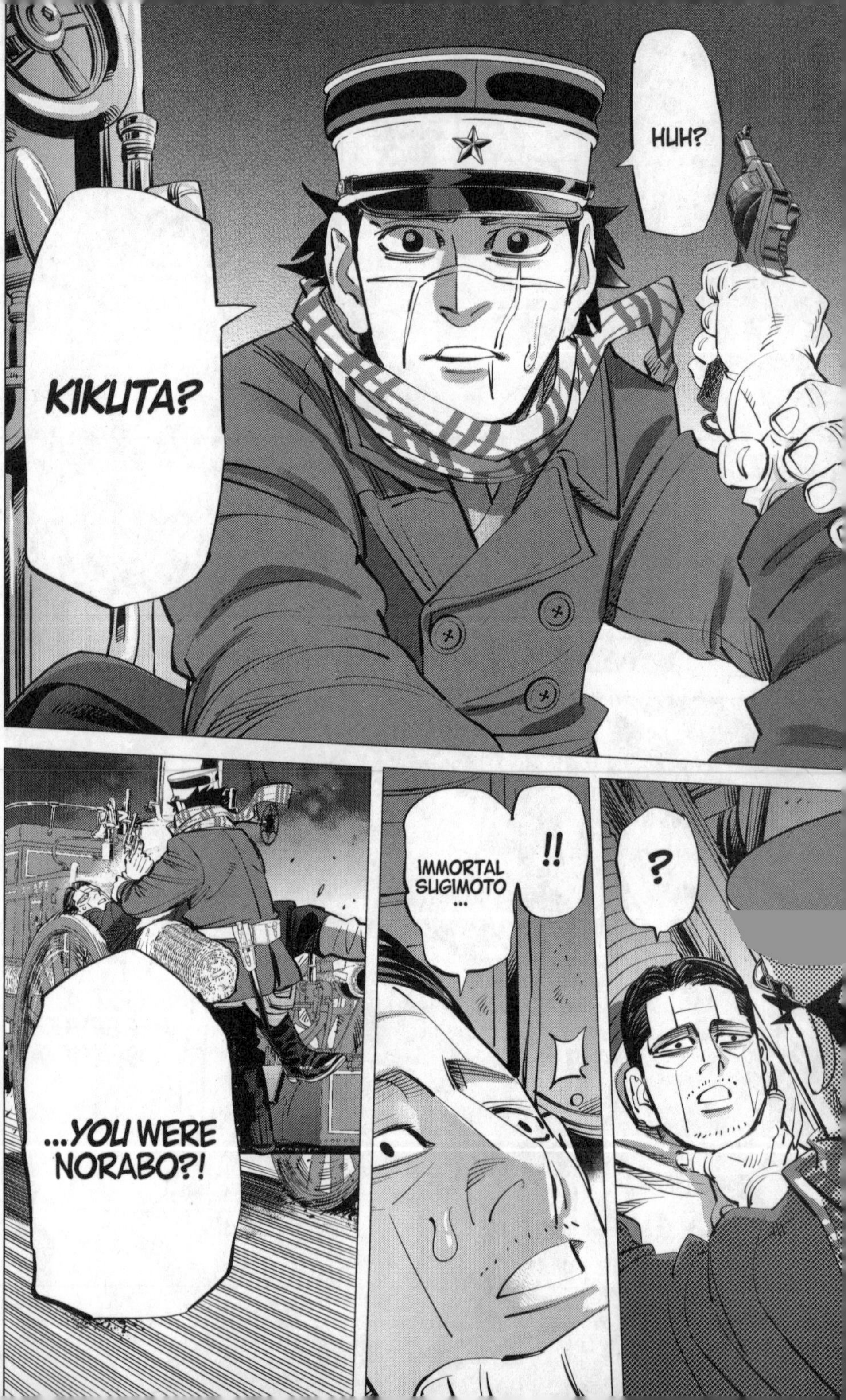
HUH?
KIKUTA?
?
!!
IMMORTAL SUGIMOTO ...
...YOU WERE NORABO?!

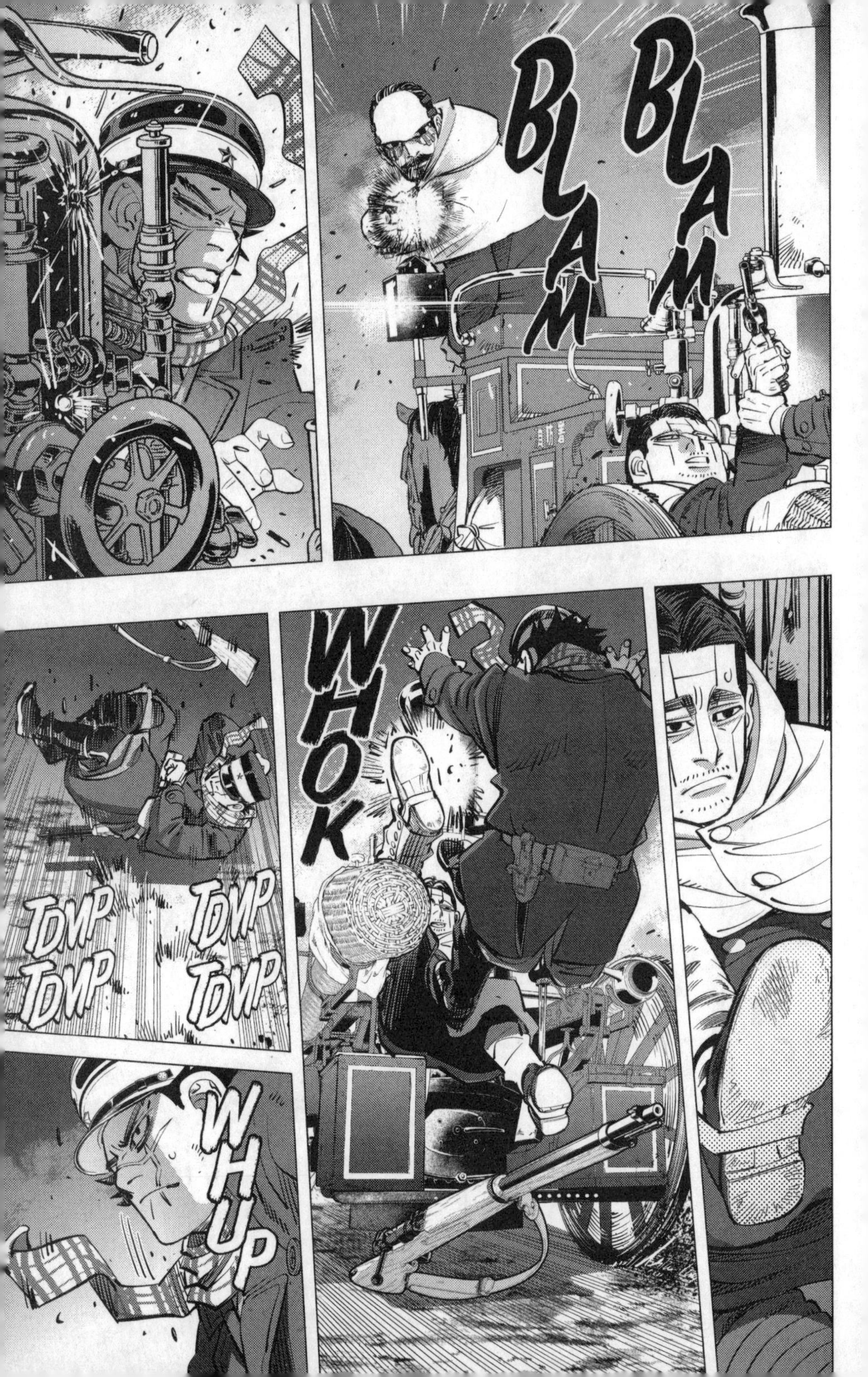
BLAM
BLAM
WHOK
TOMP
TOMP
TOMP
TOMP
WHUP

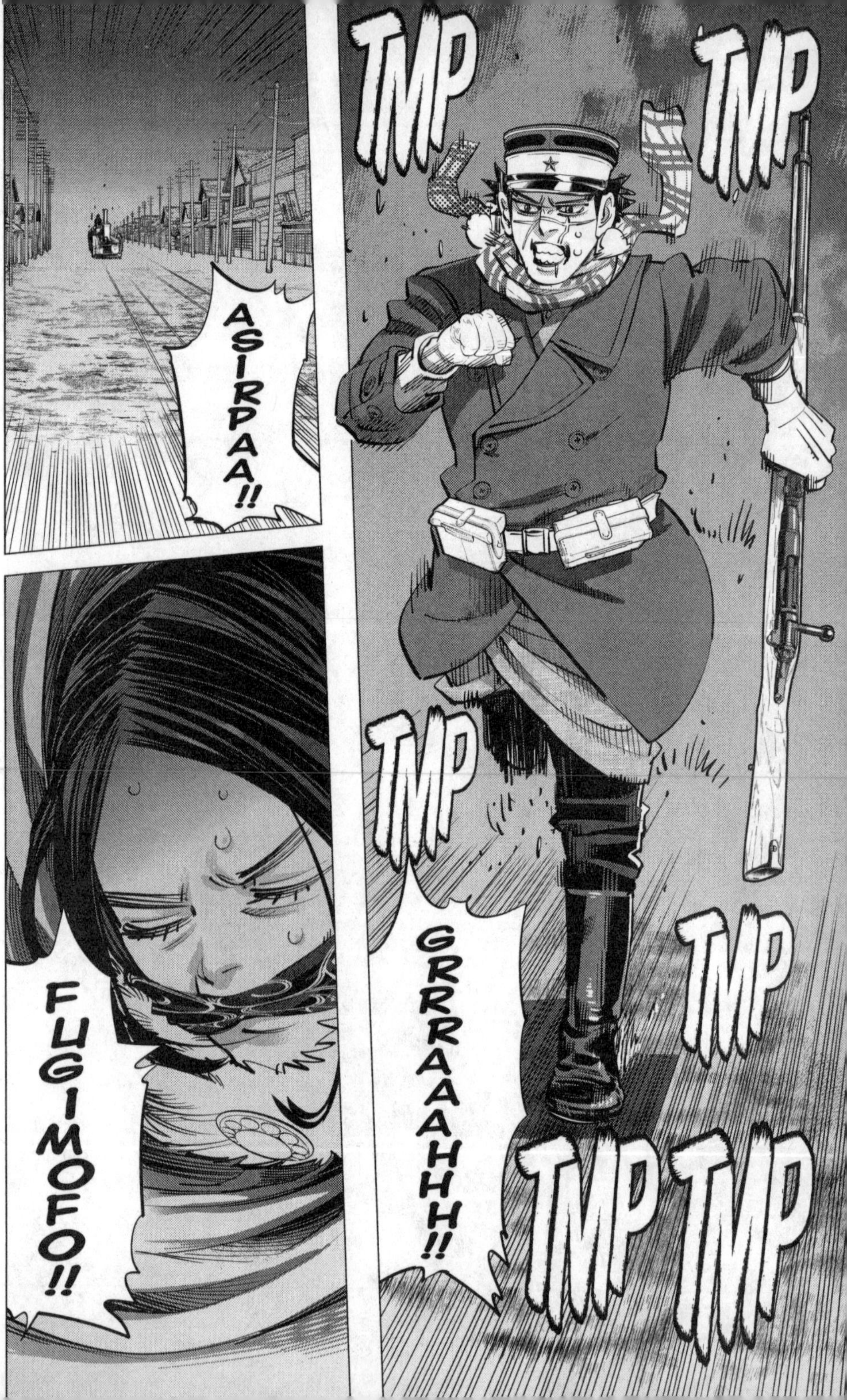
TMP
TMP
TMP
TMP
GRRRAAAHHH!!
TMP TMP
ASIRPAA!!
FUGIMOFO!!

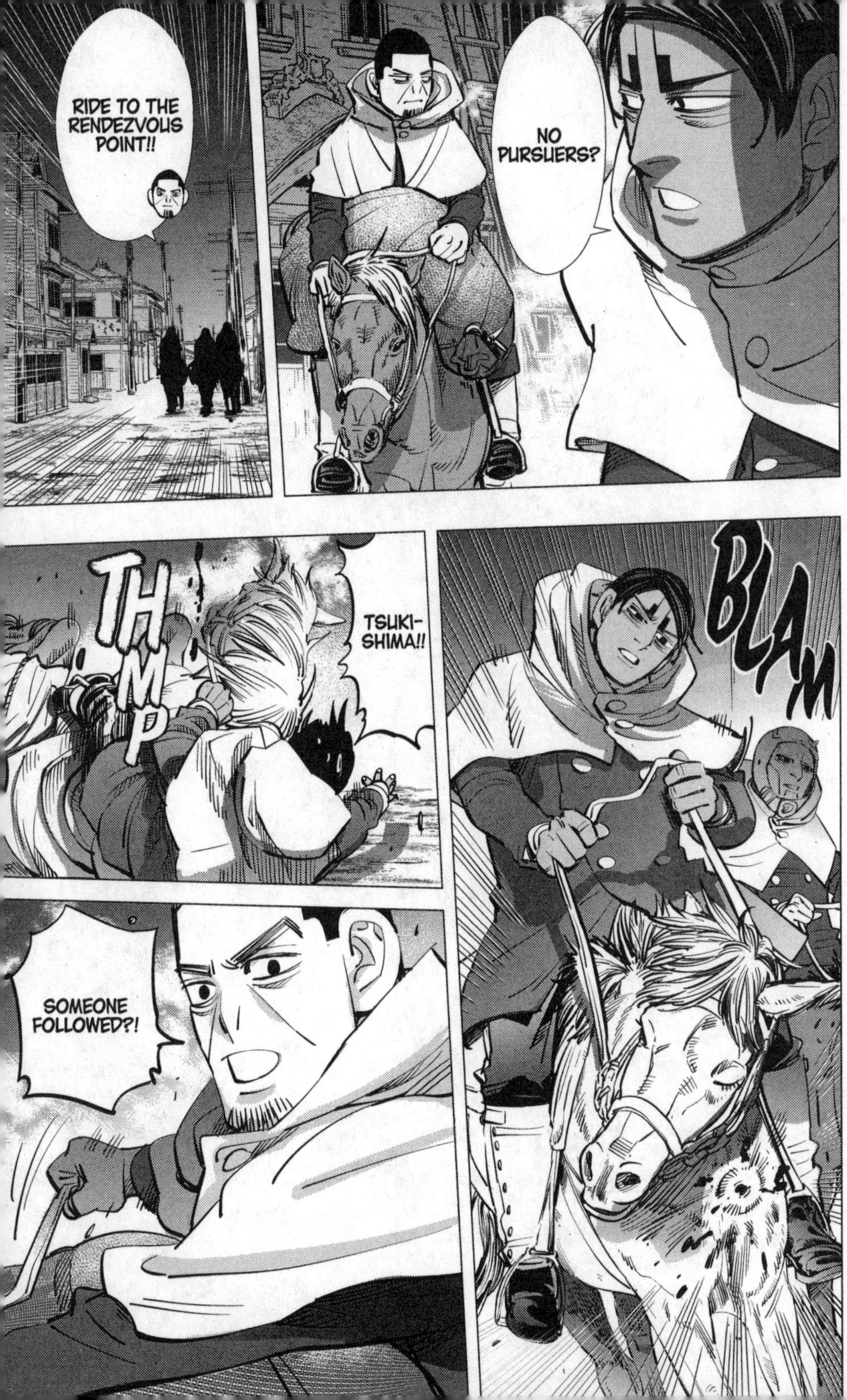
NO PURSUERS?
RIDE TO THE RENDEZVOUS POINT!!
BLAM
TSUKI-SHIMA!!
THMP
SOMEONE FOLLOWED?!

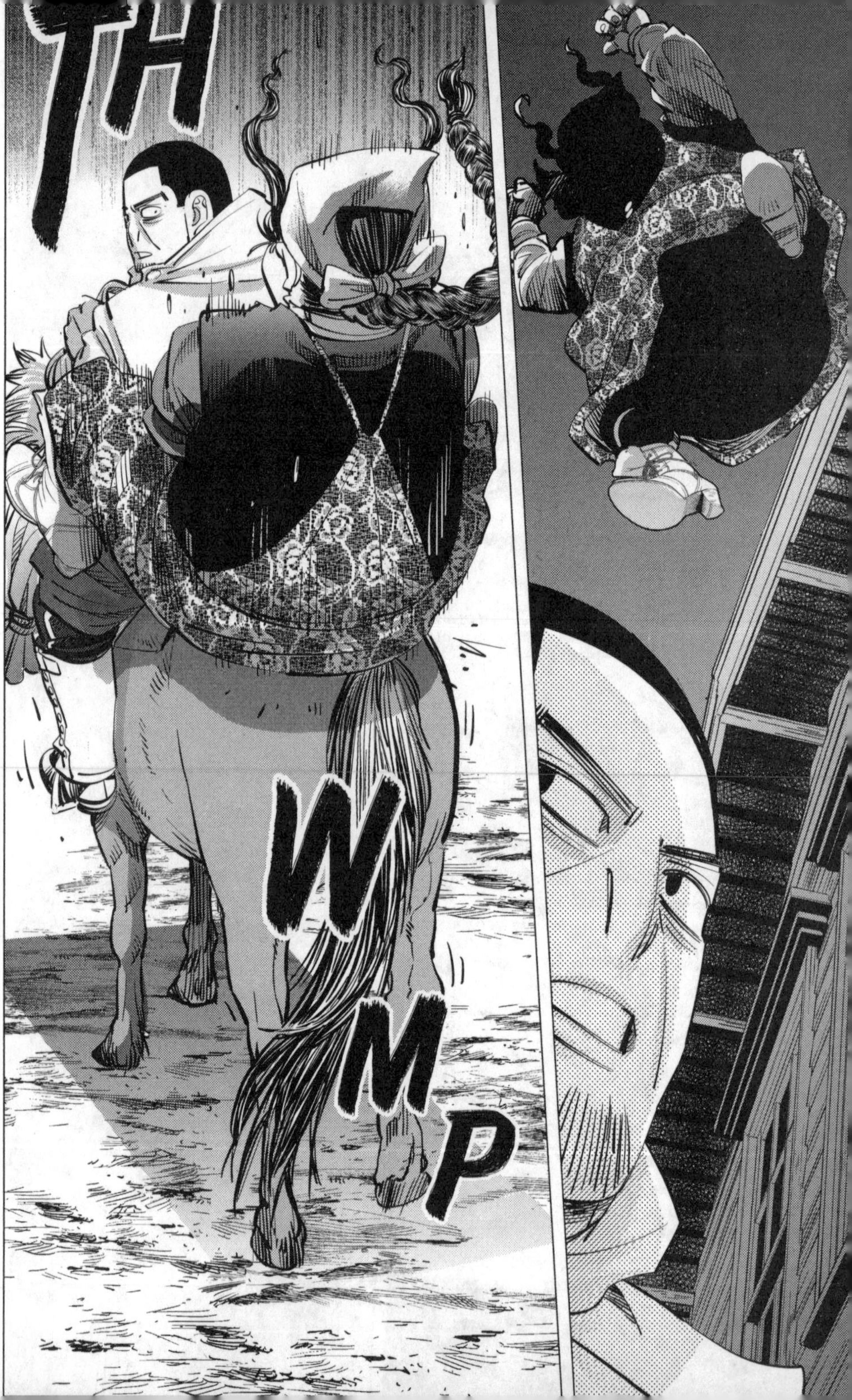
THWMP

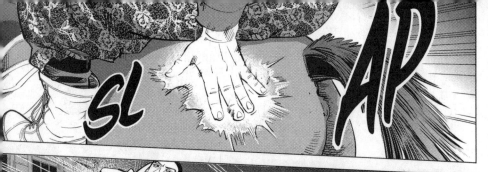

Chapter 264: The Woman at the Hospital in Otaru

KHOROSHO!

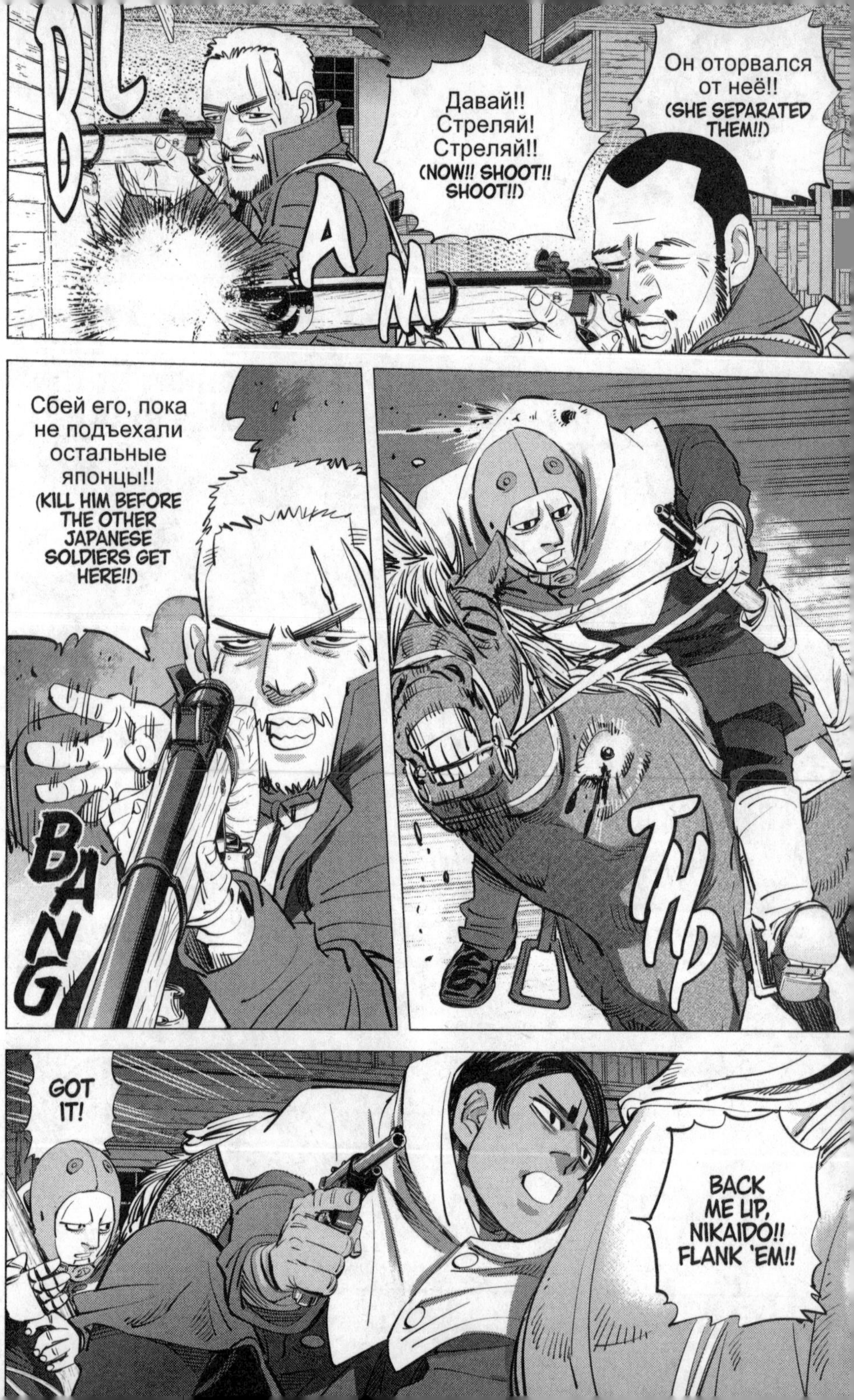
Он оторвался от неё!!
(SHE SEPARATED THEM!!)
Давай!! Стреляй! Стреляй!!
(NOW!! SHOOT!! SHOOT!!)
BLAM
THD
Сбей его, пока не подъехали остальные японцы!!
(KILL HIM BEFORE THE OTHER JAPANESE SOLDIERS GET HERE!!)
BANG
BACK ME UP, NIKAIDO!! FLANK 'EM!!
GOT IT!

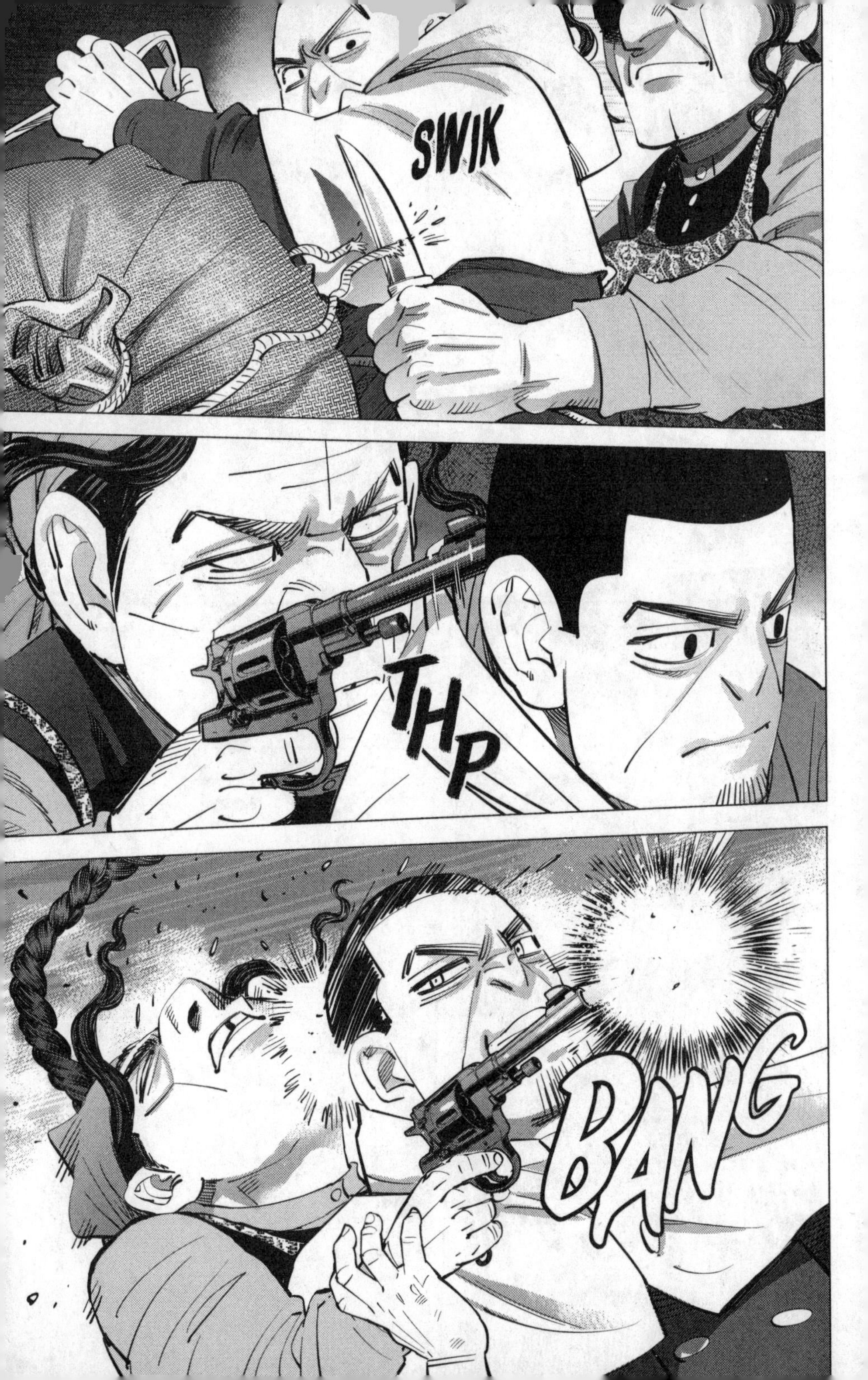
SWIK
THP
BANG

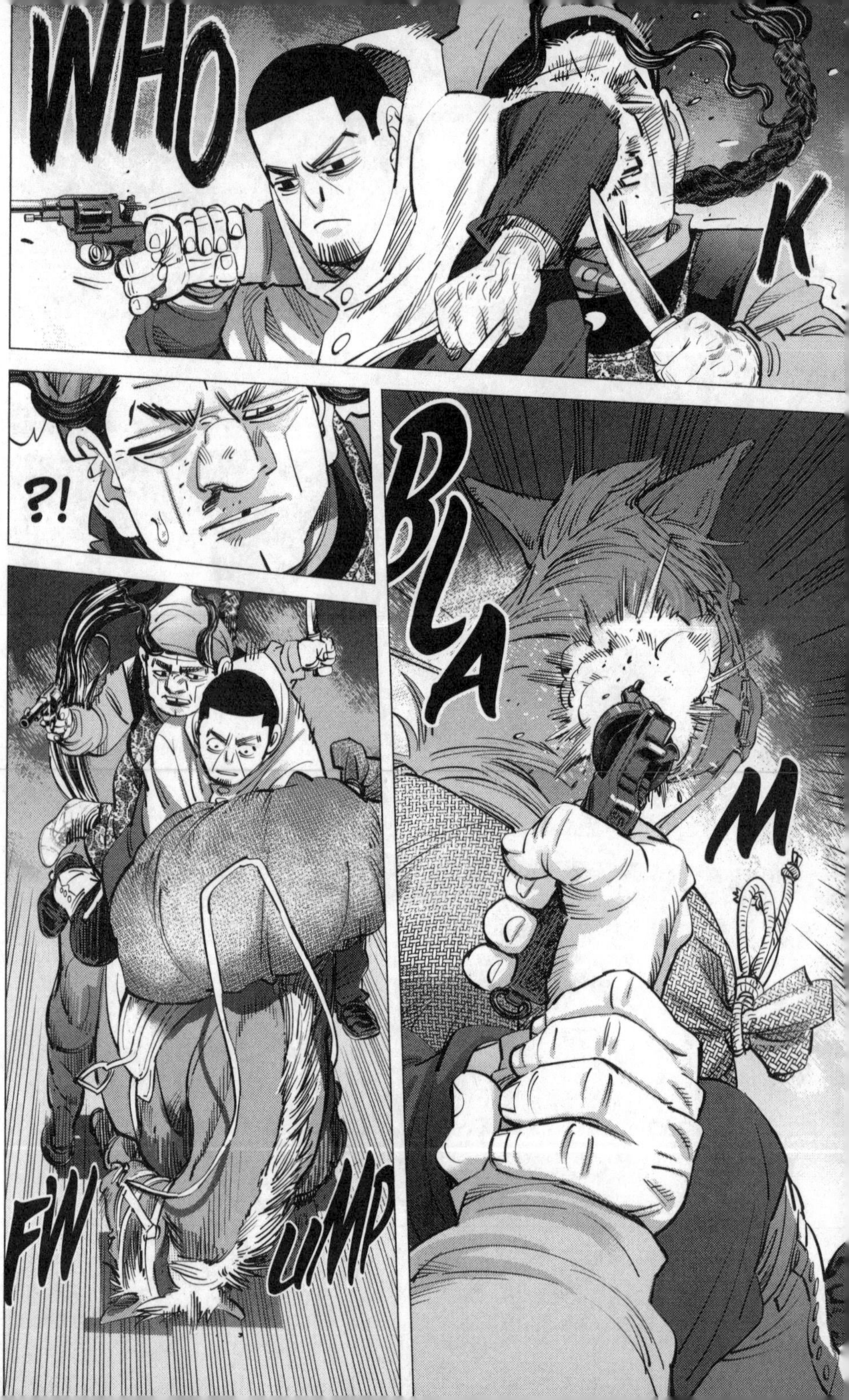
WHOK
BLAM
?!
FWUMP

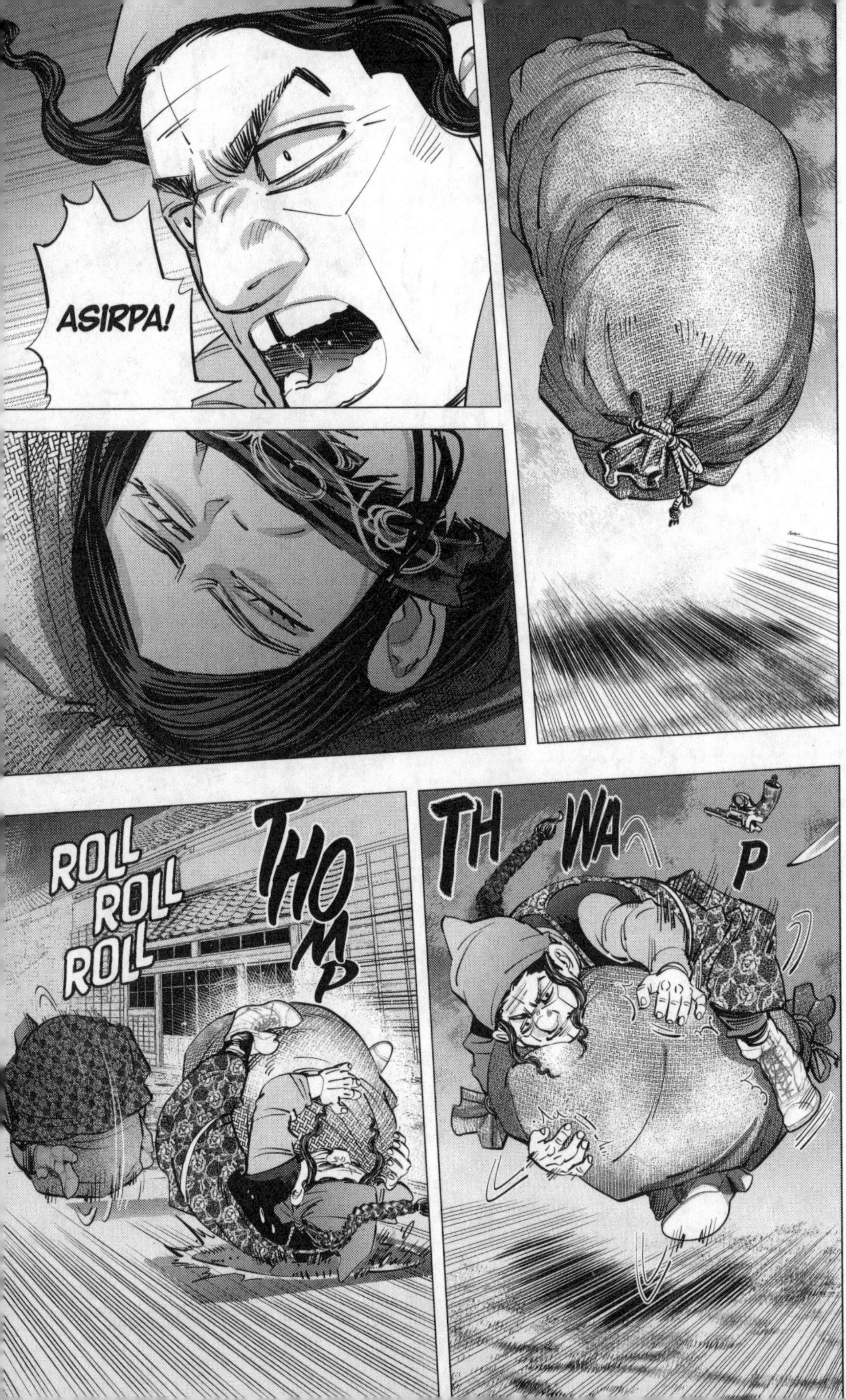
ASIRPA!
THWAP
ROLL ROLL ROLL
THOMP

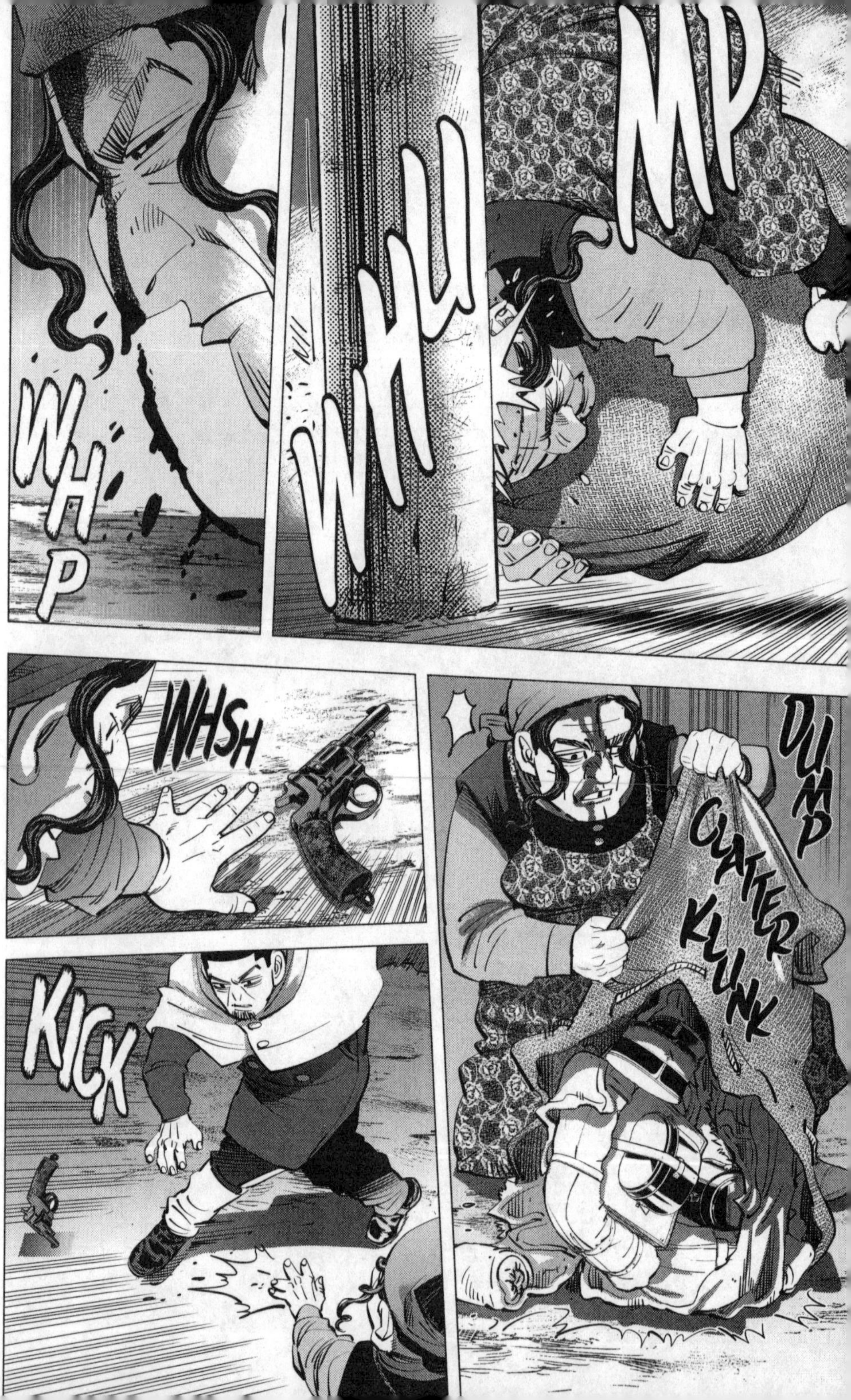
WHUMP
WHP
DUMP
CLATTER
KLUNK
WHSH
KICK

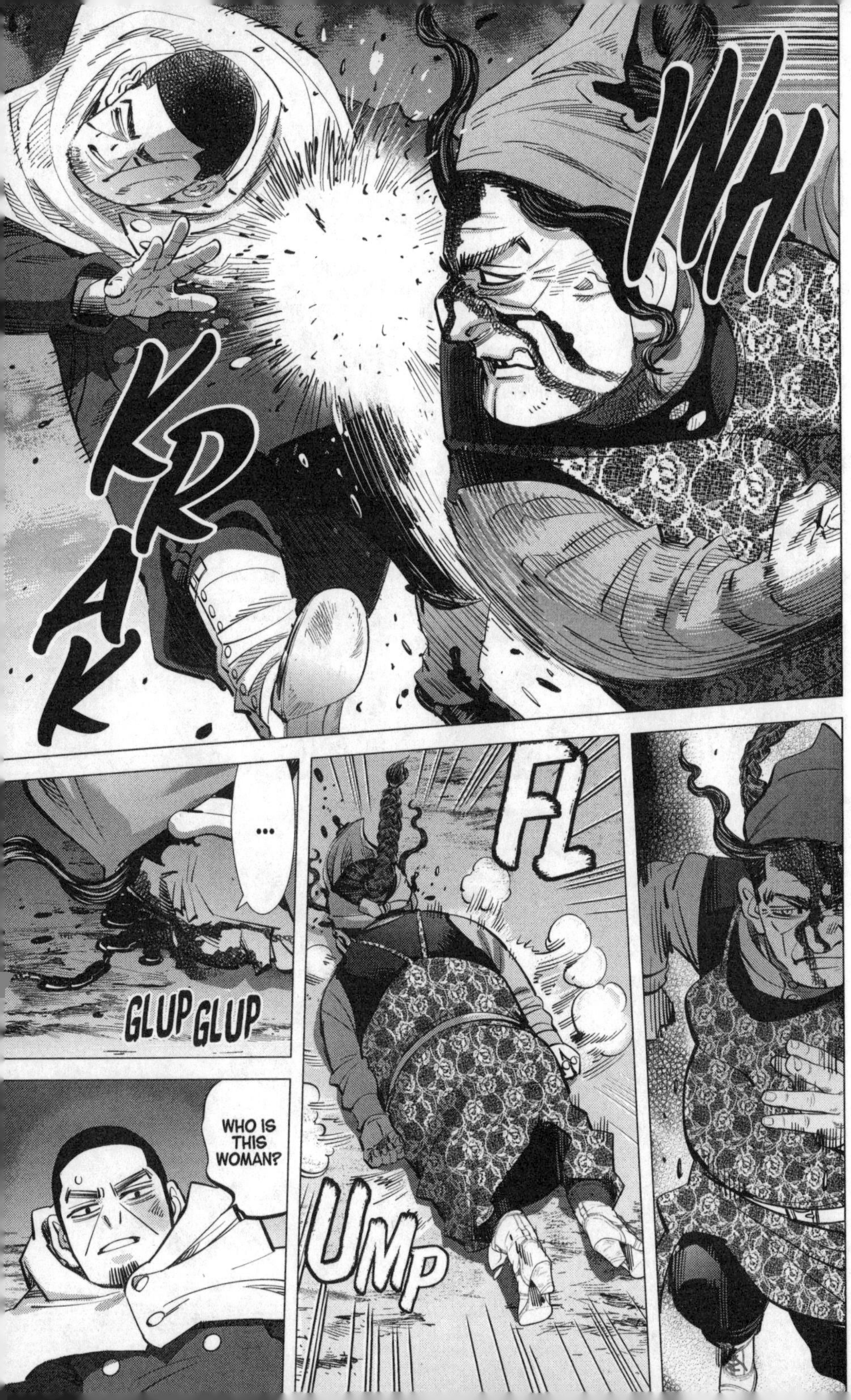
WH
KRAK
FL
UMP
...
GLUP GLUP
WHO IS THIS WOMAN?

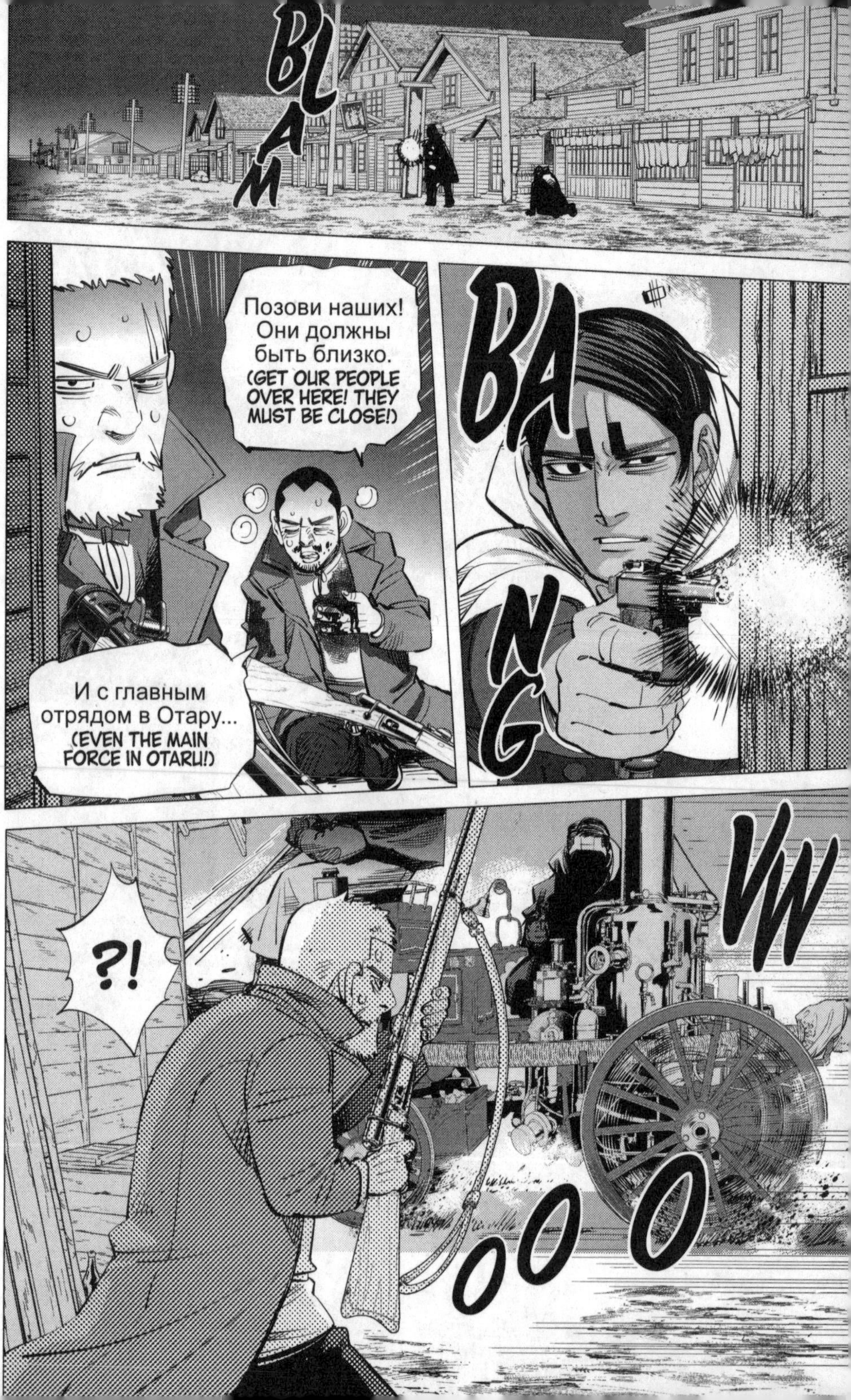
BLAM
BANG
Позови наших! Они должны быть близко.
(GET OUR PEOPLE OVER HERE! THEY MUST BE CLOSE!)
И с главным отрядом в Отару...
(EVEN THE MAIN FORCE IN OTARU!)
VW
?!
OOOO

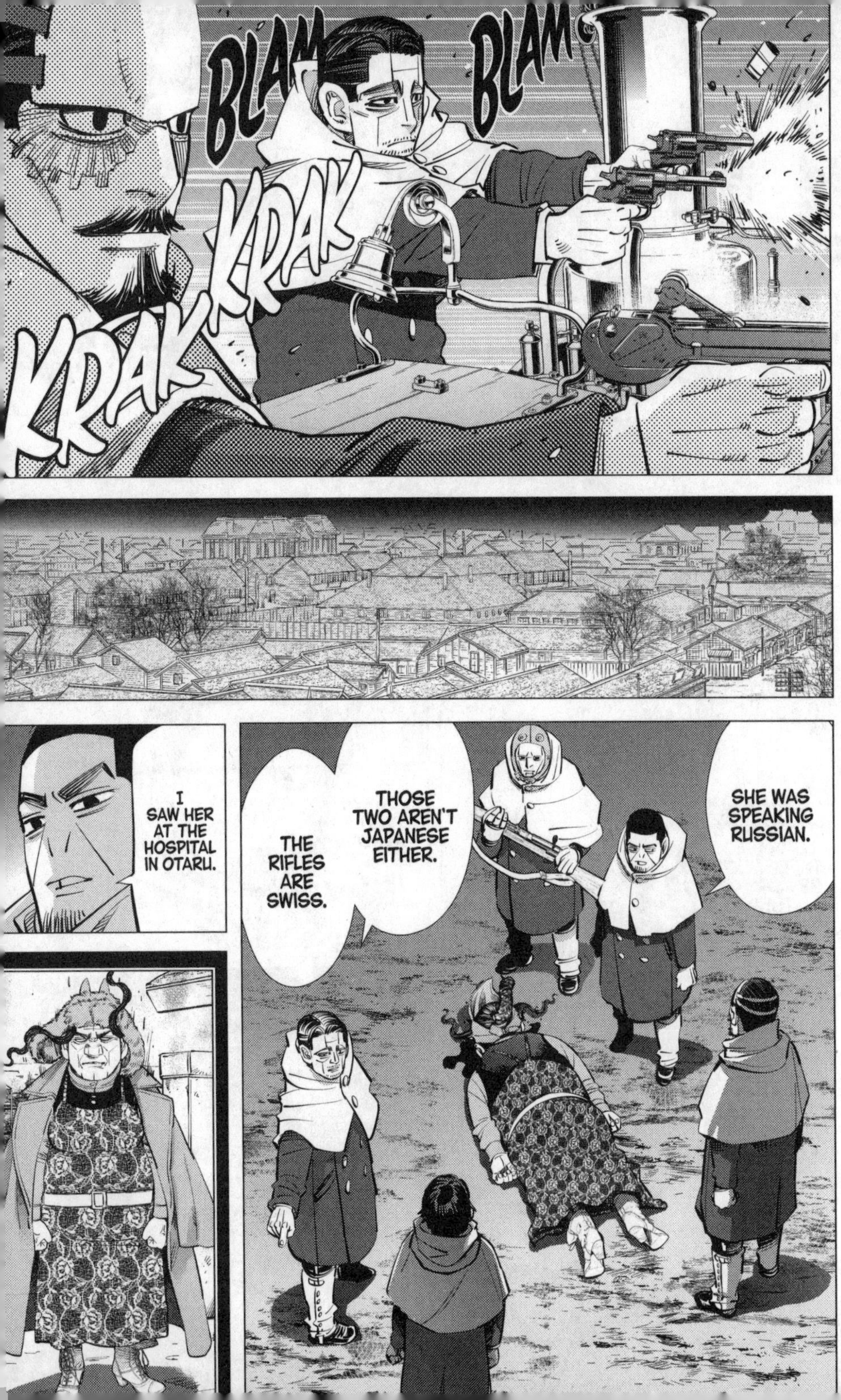
BLAM
BLAM
KRAK
KRAK
SHE WAS SPEAKING RUSSIAN.
THOSE TWO AREN'T JAPANESE EITHER.
THE RIFLES ARE SWISS.
I SAW HER AT THE HOSPITAL IN OTARU.

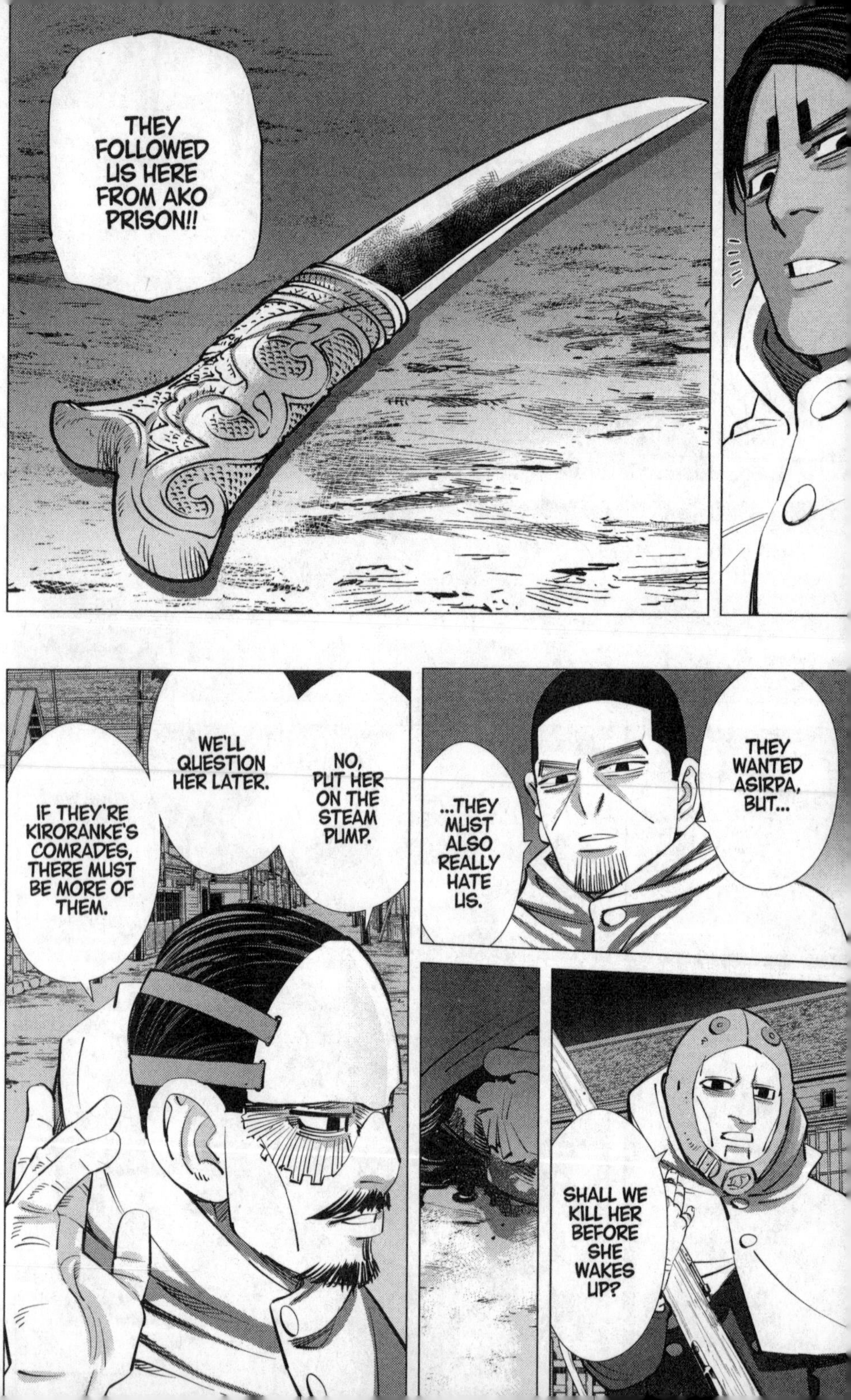
THEY FOLLOWED US HERE FROM AKO PRISON!!
THEY WANTED ASIRPA, BUT...
...THEY MUST ALSO REALLY HATE US.
SHALL WE KILL HER BEFORE SHE WAKES UP?
NO, PUT HER ON THE STEAM PUMP.
WE'LL QUESTION HER LATER.
IF THEY'RE KIRORANKE'S COMRADES, THERE MUST BE MORE OF THEM.

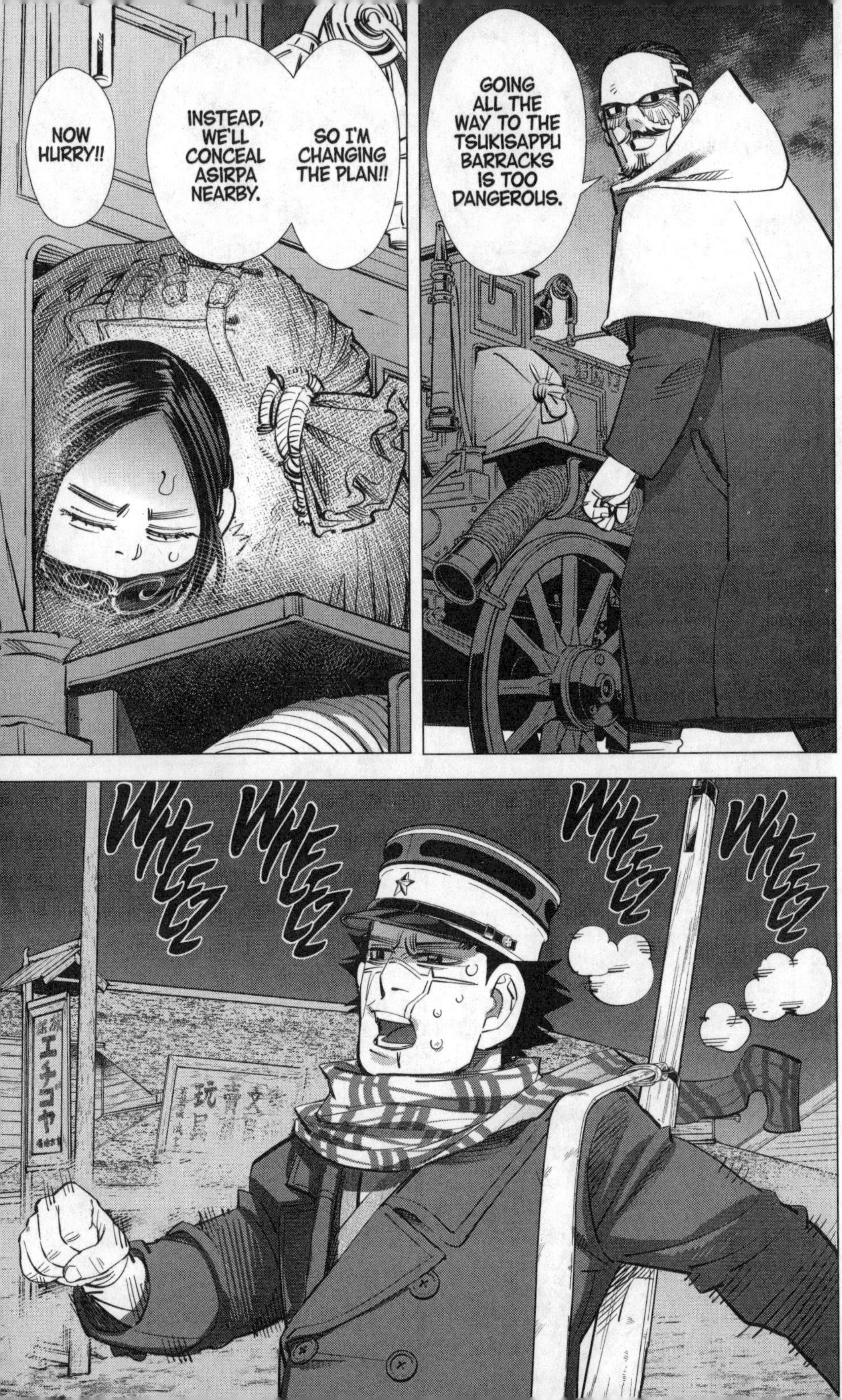
GOING ALL THE WAY TO THE TSUKISAPPU BARRACKS IS TOO DANGEROUS.
SO I'M CHANGING THE PLAN!!
INSTEAD, WE'LL CONCEAL ASIRPA NEARBY.
NOW HURRY!!
WHEEZ
WHEEZ
WHEEZ
WHEEZ
エチゴヤ

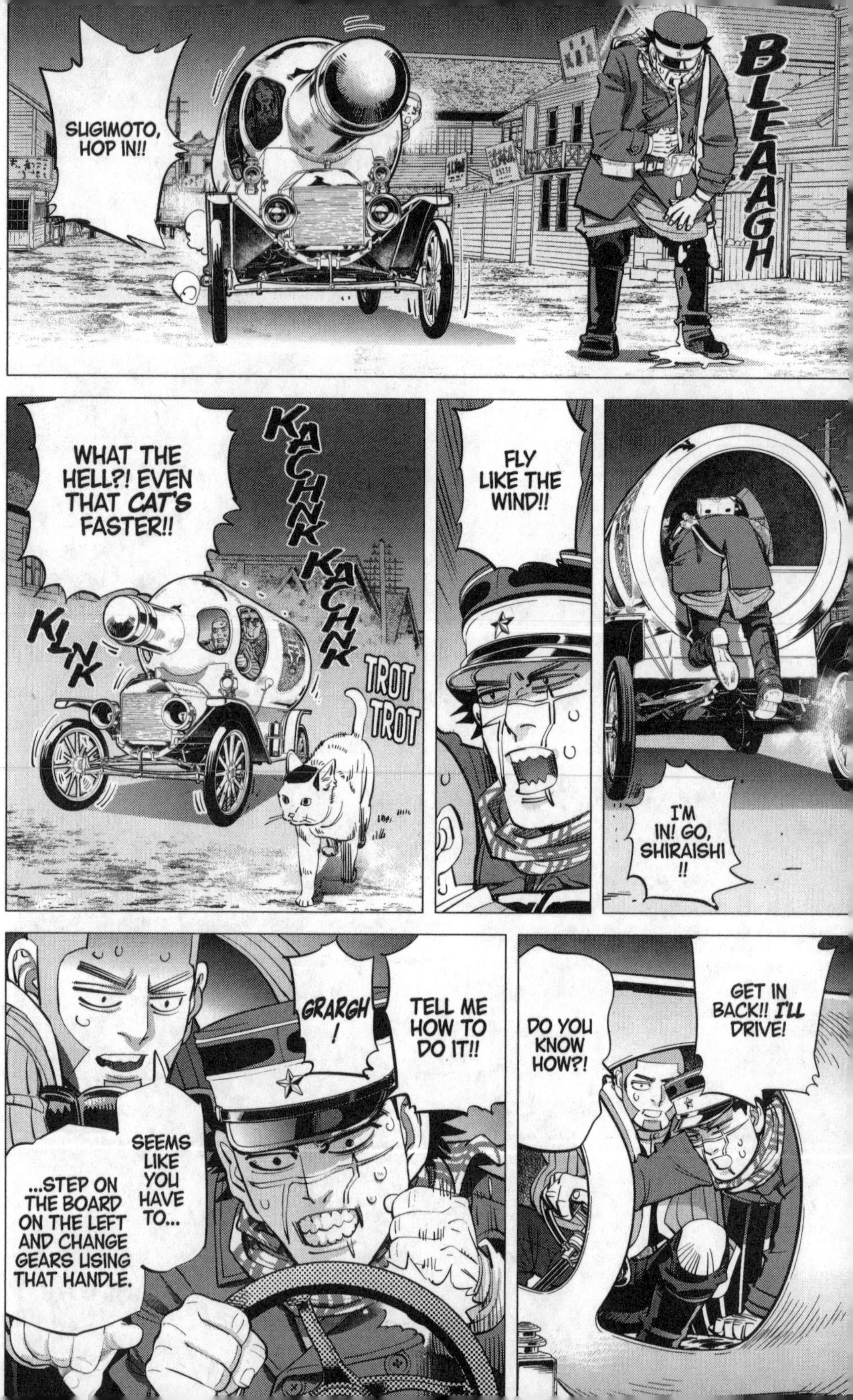
BLEAAGH
SUGIMOTO, HOP IN!!
I'M IN! GO, SHIRAISHI!!
FLY LIKE THE WIND!!
KACHNK KACHNK
WHAT THE HELL?! EVEN THAT CAT'S FASTER!!
TROT TROT
KLNK
GET IN BACK!! I'LL DRIVE!
DO YOU KNOW HOW?!
TELL ME HOW TO DO IT!!
GRARGH!
SEEMS LIKE YOU HAVE TO...
...STEP ON THE BOARD ON THE LEFT AND CHANGE GEARS USING THAT HANDLE.

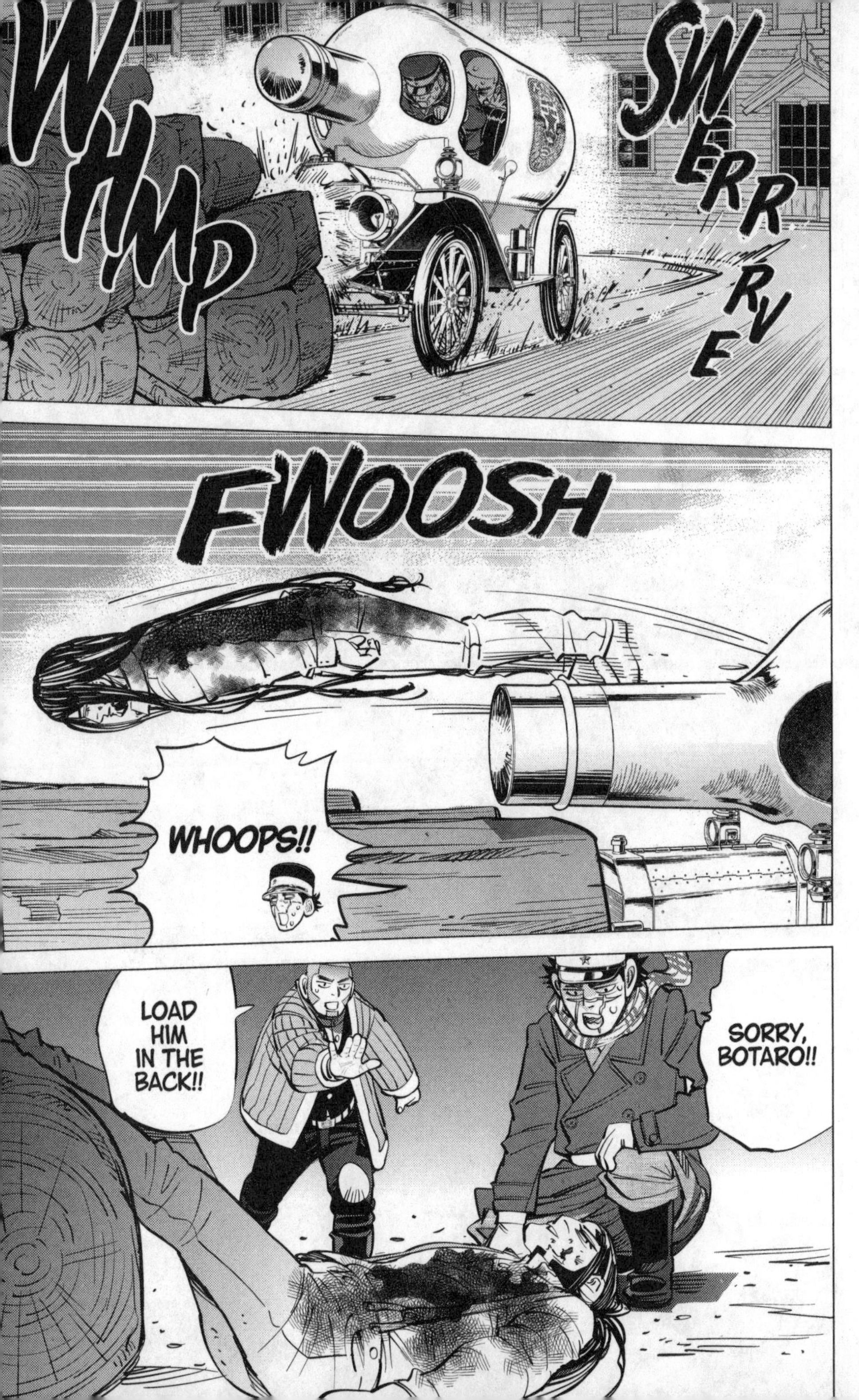
SWERRRVE
WHMP
FWOOSH
WHOOPS!!
SORRY, BOTARO!!
LOAD HIM IN THE BACK!!

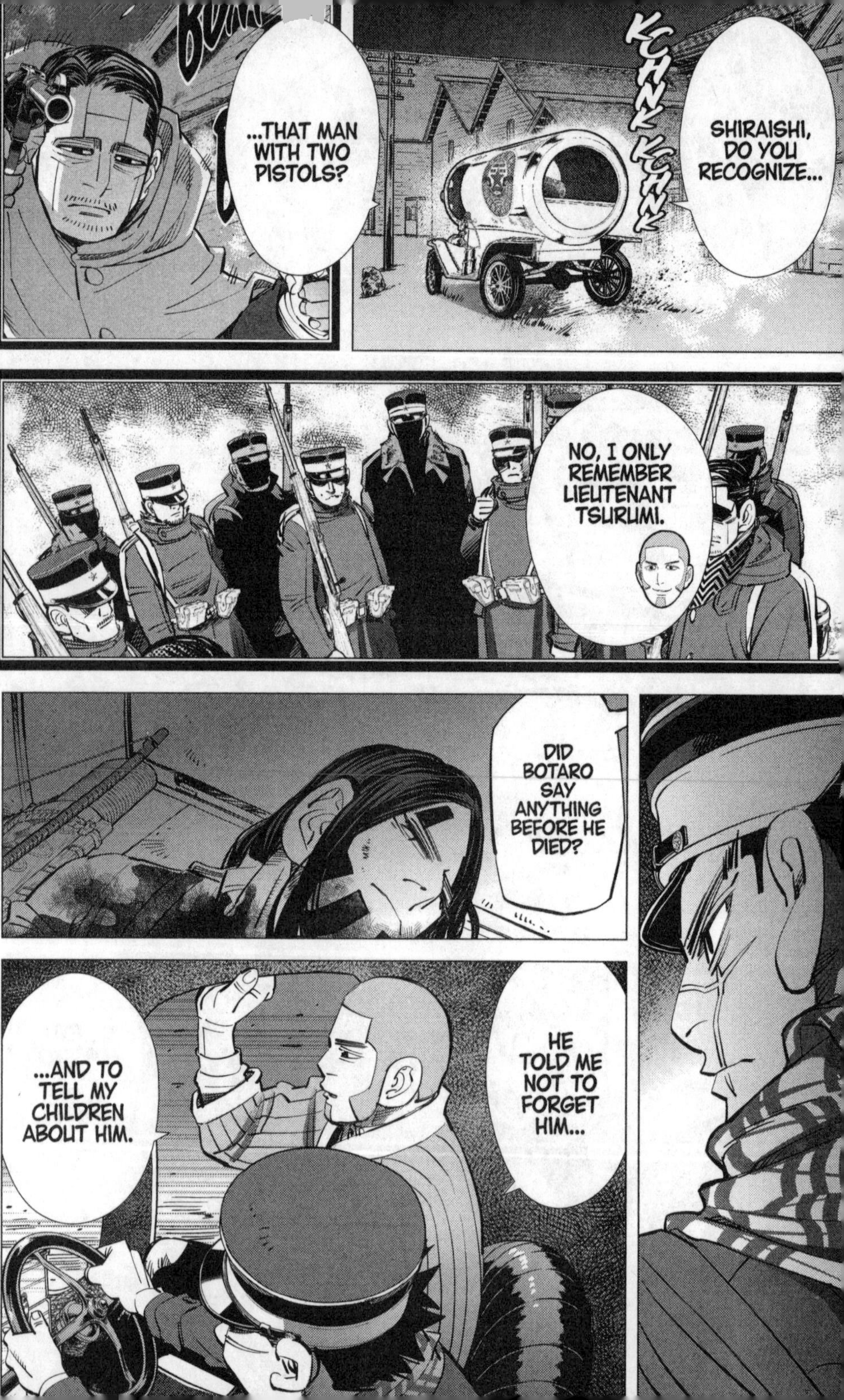
KCHNK KCHNK KCHNK
SHIRAISHI, DO YOU RECOGNIZE...
...THAT MAN WITH TWO PISTOLS?
NO, I ONLY REMEMBER LIEUTENANT TSURUMI.
DID BOTARO SAY ANYTHING BEFORE HE DIED?
HE TOLD ME NOT TO FORGET HIM...
...AND TO TELL MY CHILDREN ABOUT HIM.

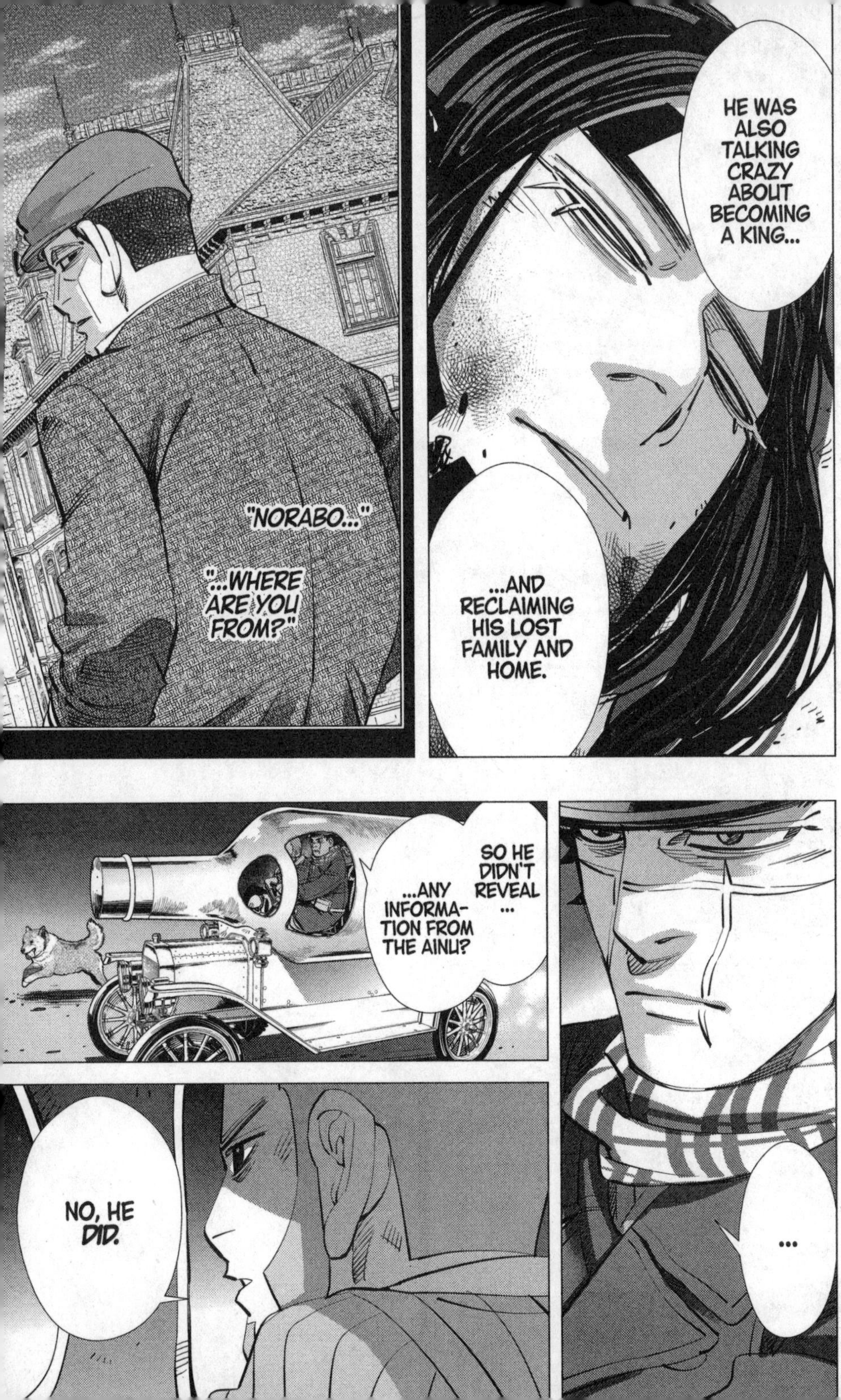
HE WAS ALSO TALKING CRAZY ABOUT BECOMING A KING...
...AND RECLAIMING HIS LOST FAMILY AND HOME.
"NORABO..."
"...WHERE ARE YOU FROM?"
...
SO HE DIDN'T REVEAL ...
...ANY INFORMATION FROM THE AINU?
NO, HE DID.

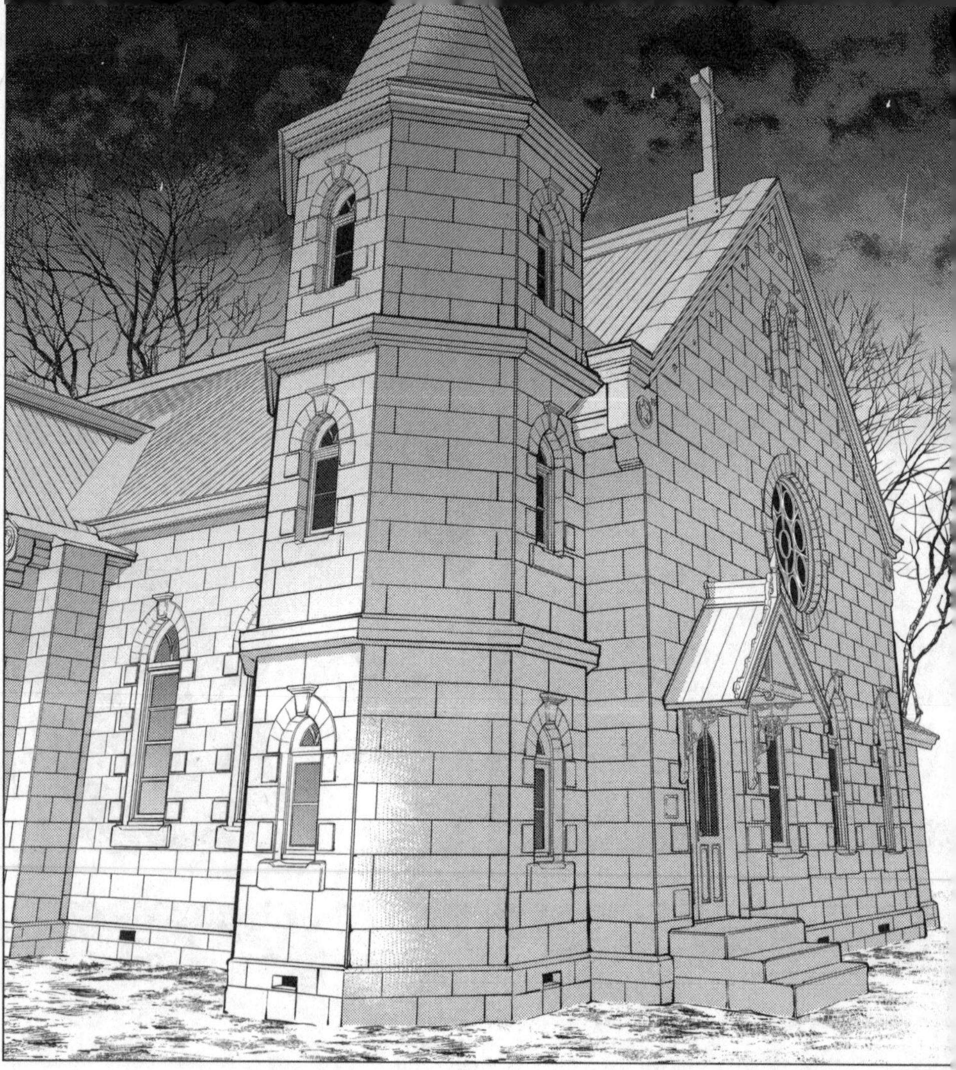
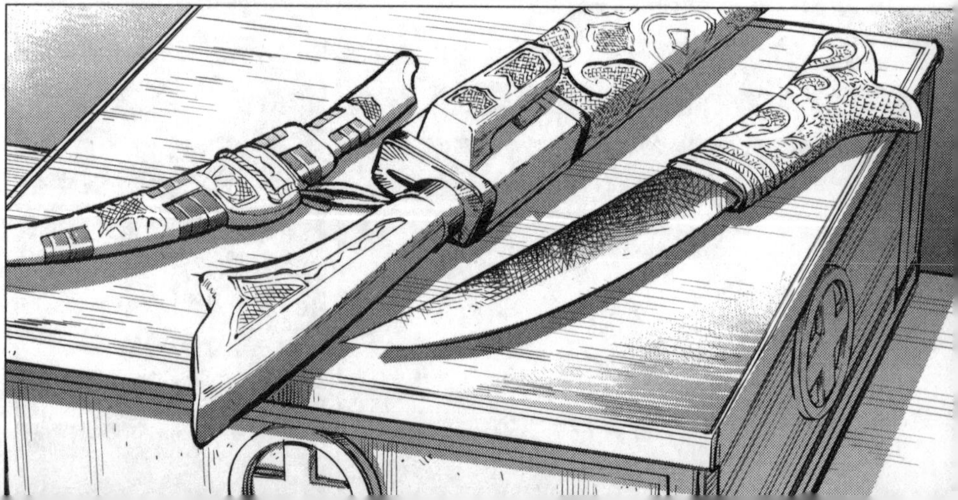

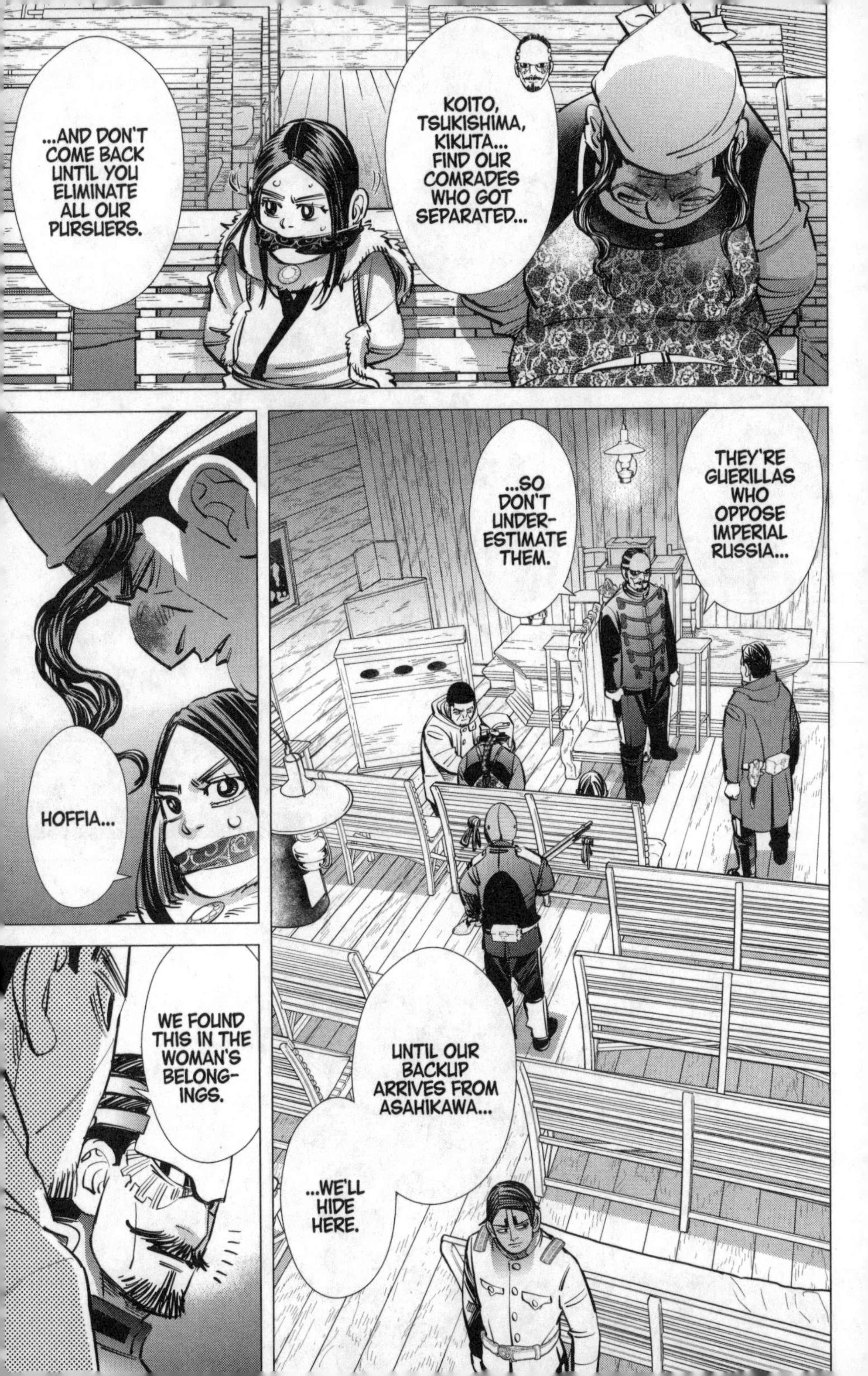
KOITO, TSUKISHIMA, KIKUTA... FIND OUR COMRADES WHO GOT SEPARATED...
...AND DON'T COME BACK UNTIL YOU ELIMINATE ALL OUR PURSUERS.
THEY'RE GUERILLAS WHO OPPOSE IMPERIAL RUSSIA...
...SO DON'T UNDER-ESTIMATE THEM.
UNTIL OUR BACKUP ARRIVES FROM ASAHIKAWA...
...WE'LL HIDE HERE.
HOFFIA...
WE FOUND THIS IN THE WOMAN'S BELONG-INGS.

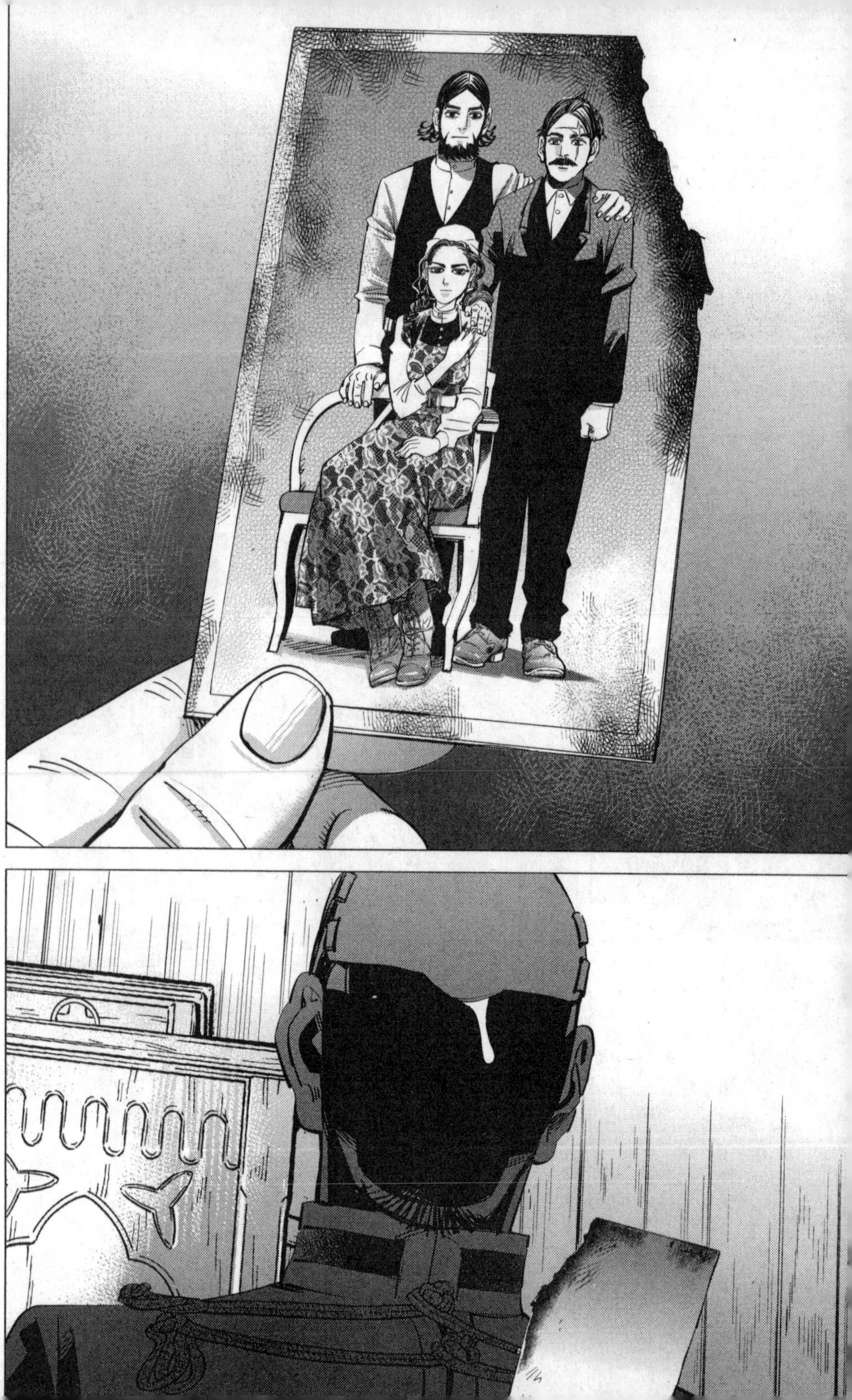

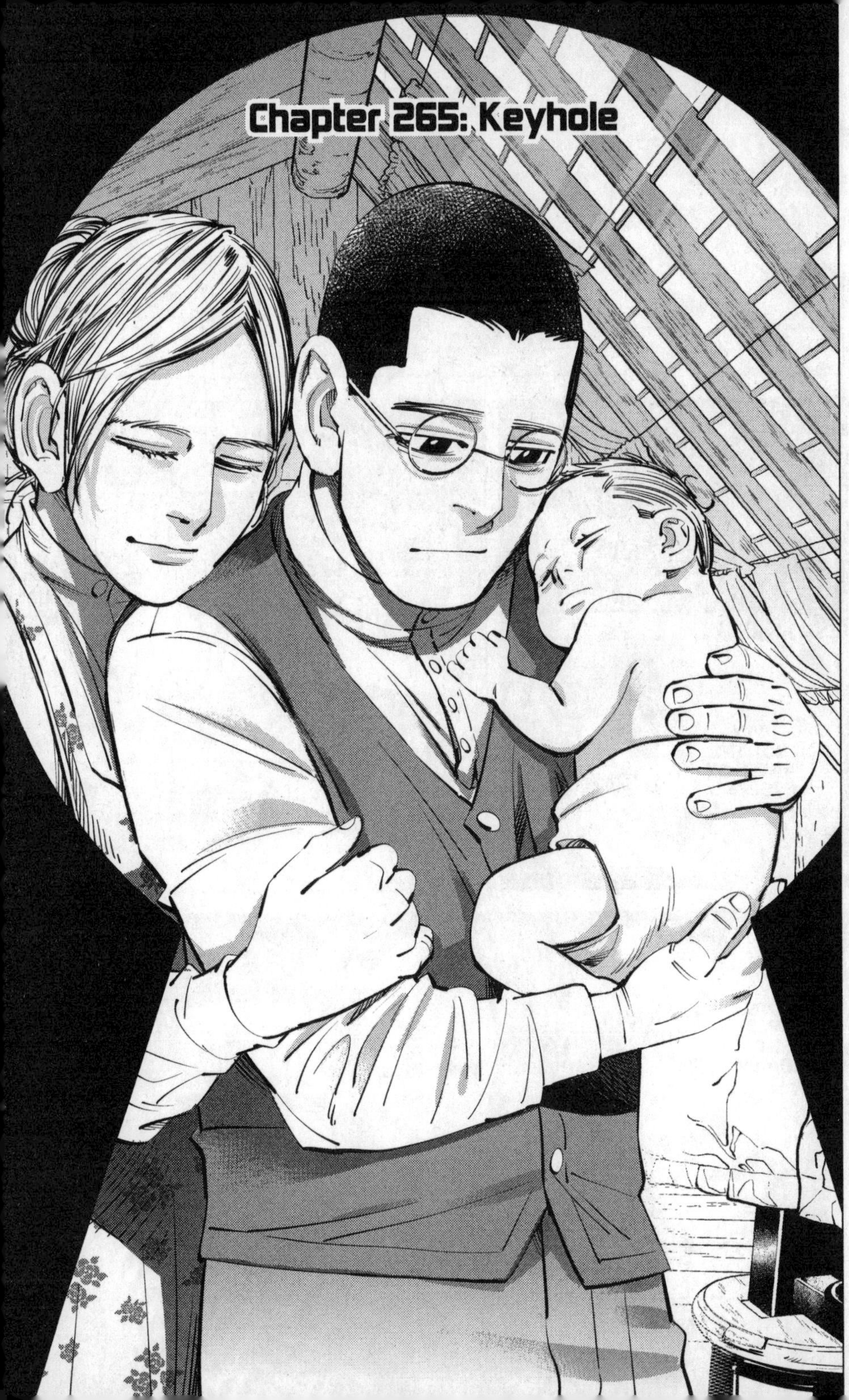
Chapter 265: Keyhole

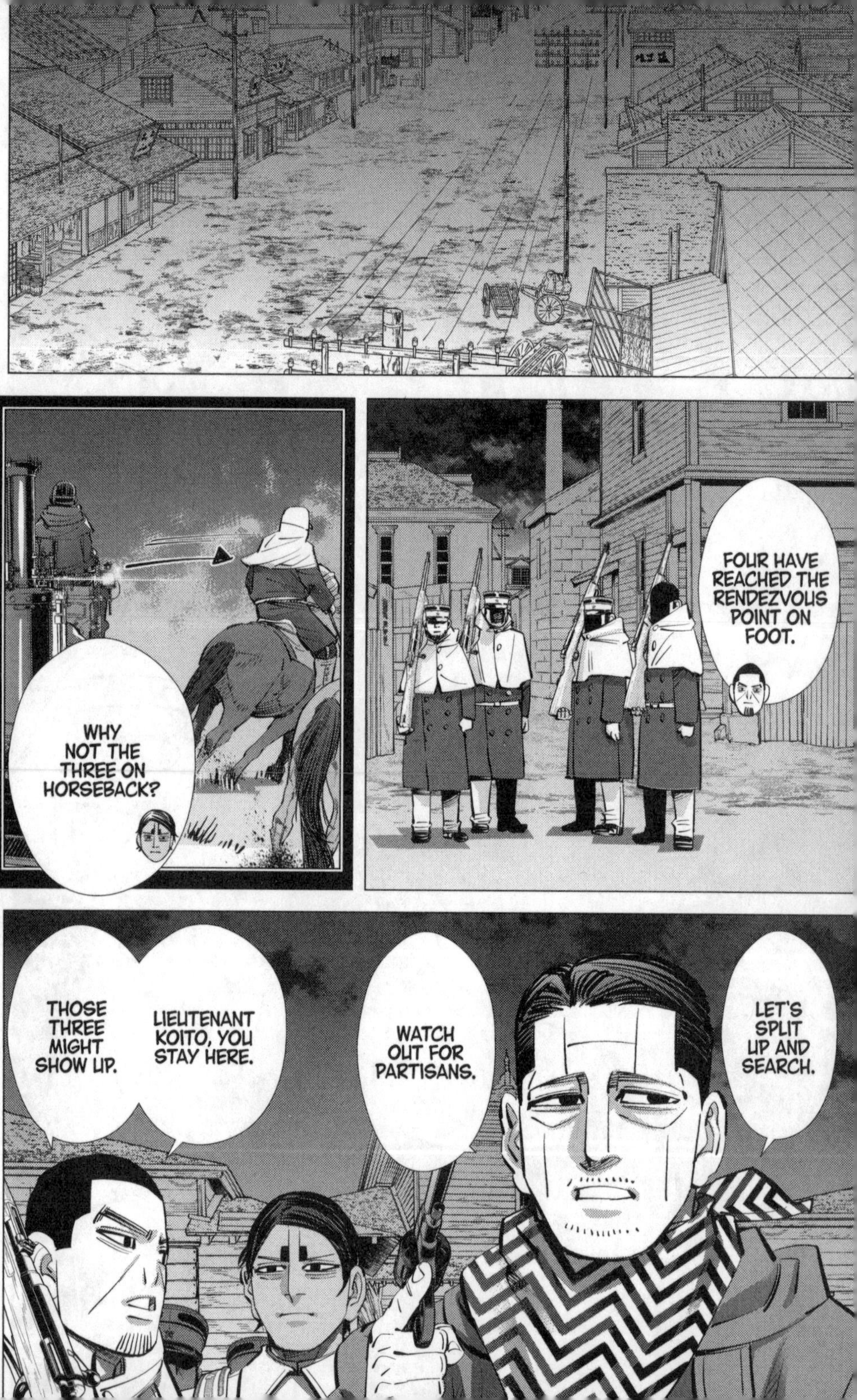
FOUR HAVE REACHED THE RENDEZVOUS POINT ON FOOT.
WHY NOT THE THREE ON HORSEBACK?
LET'S SPLIT UP AND SEARCH.
WATCH OUT FOR PARTISANS.
LIEUTENANT KOITO, YOU STAY HERE.
THOSE THREE MIGHT SHOW UP.

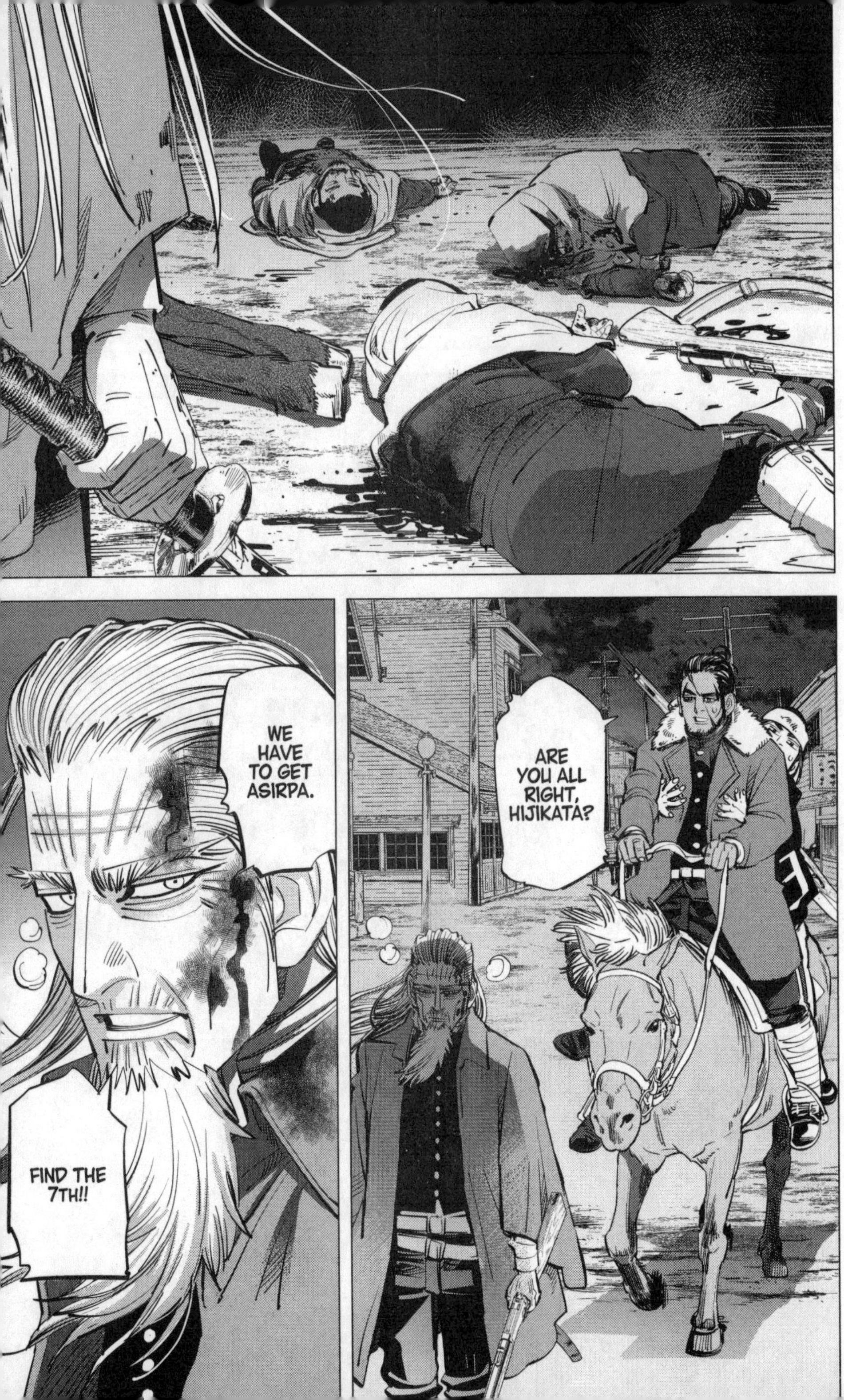
ARE YOU ALL RIGHT, HIJIKATA?
WE HAVE TO GET ASIRPA.
FIND THE 7TH!!

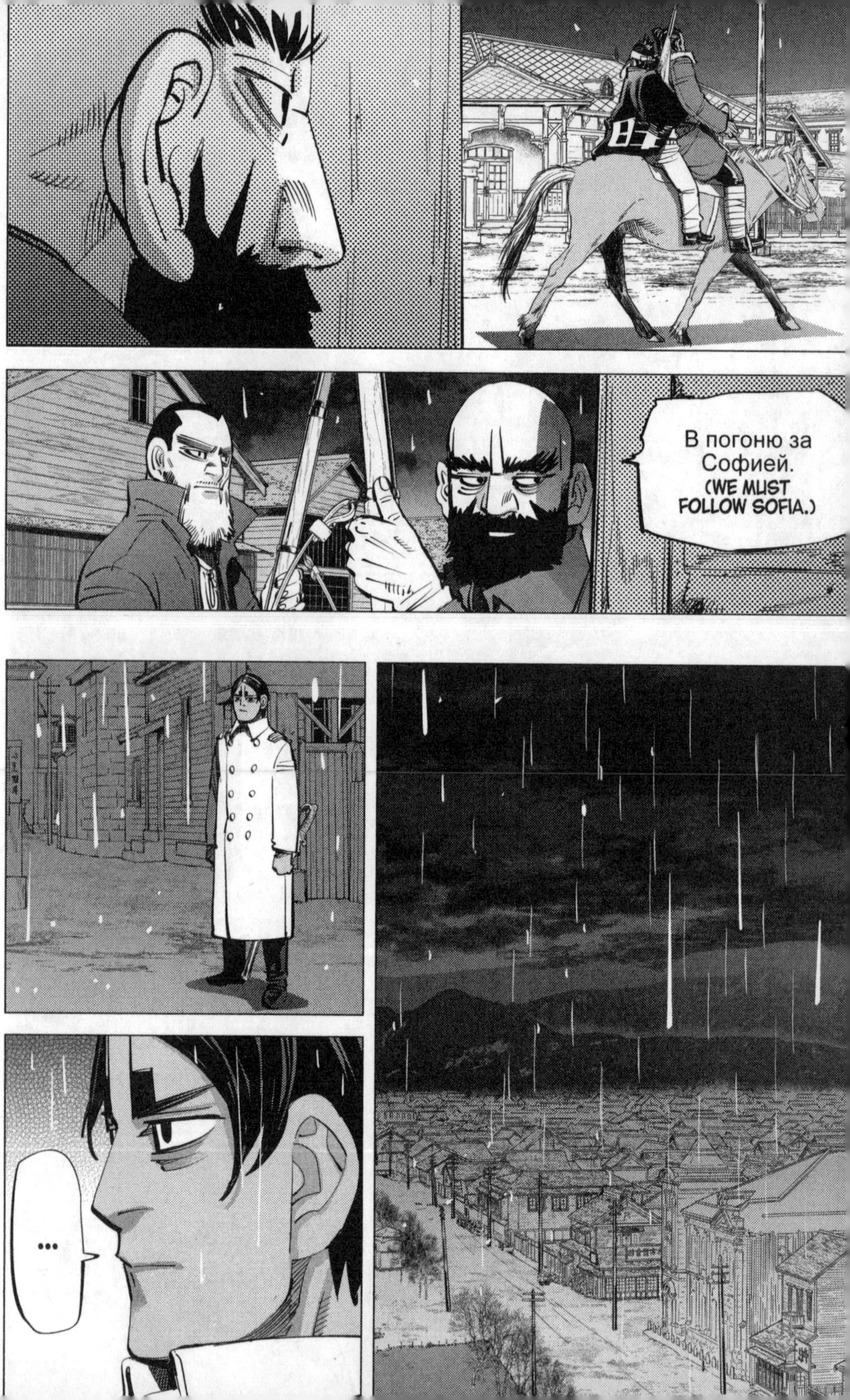
В погоню за Софией.
(WE MUST FOLLOW SOFIA.)
...

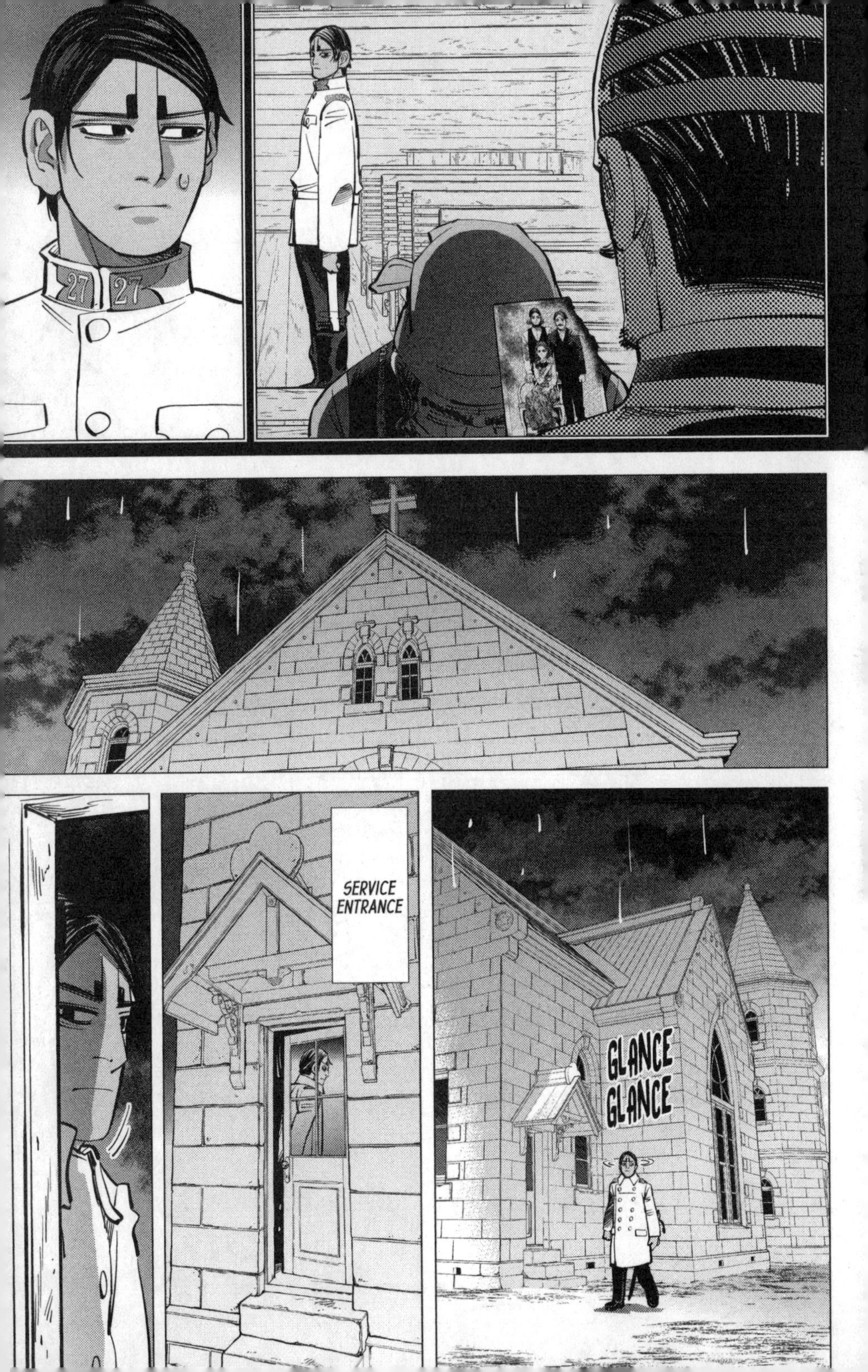
SERVICE ENTRANCE
GLANCE GLANCE

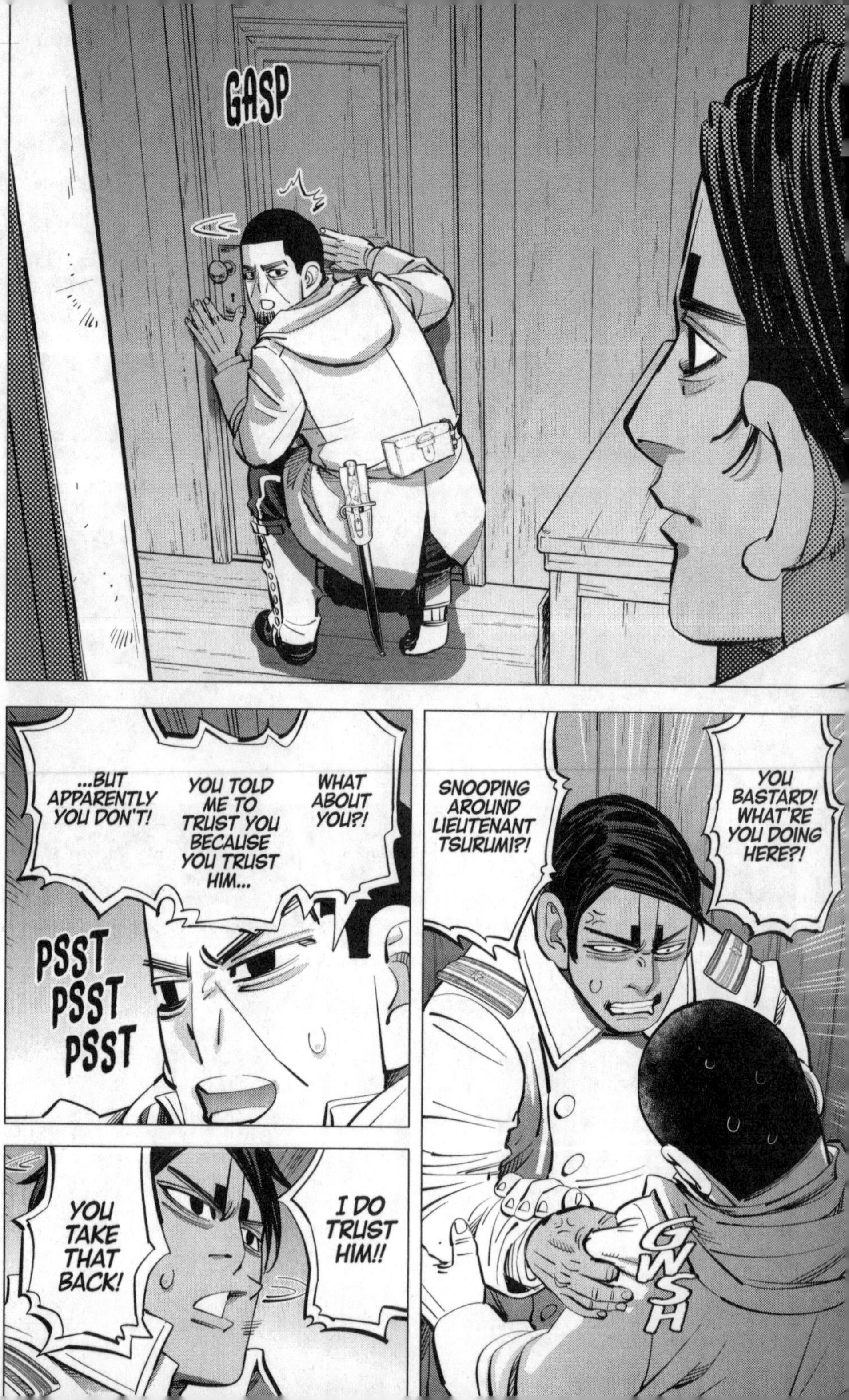
GASP
YOU BASTARD! WHAT'RE YOU DOING HERE?!
SNOOPING AROUND LIEUTENANT TSURUMI?!
GWSH
WHAT ABOUT YOU?!
YOU TOLD ME TO TRUST YOU BECAUSE YOU TRUST HIM...
...BUT APPARENTLY YOU DON'T!
PSST PSST PSST
I DO TRUST HIM!!
YOU TAKE THAT BACK!

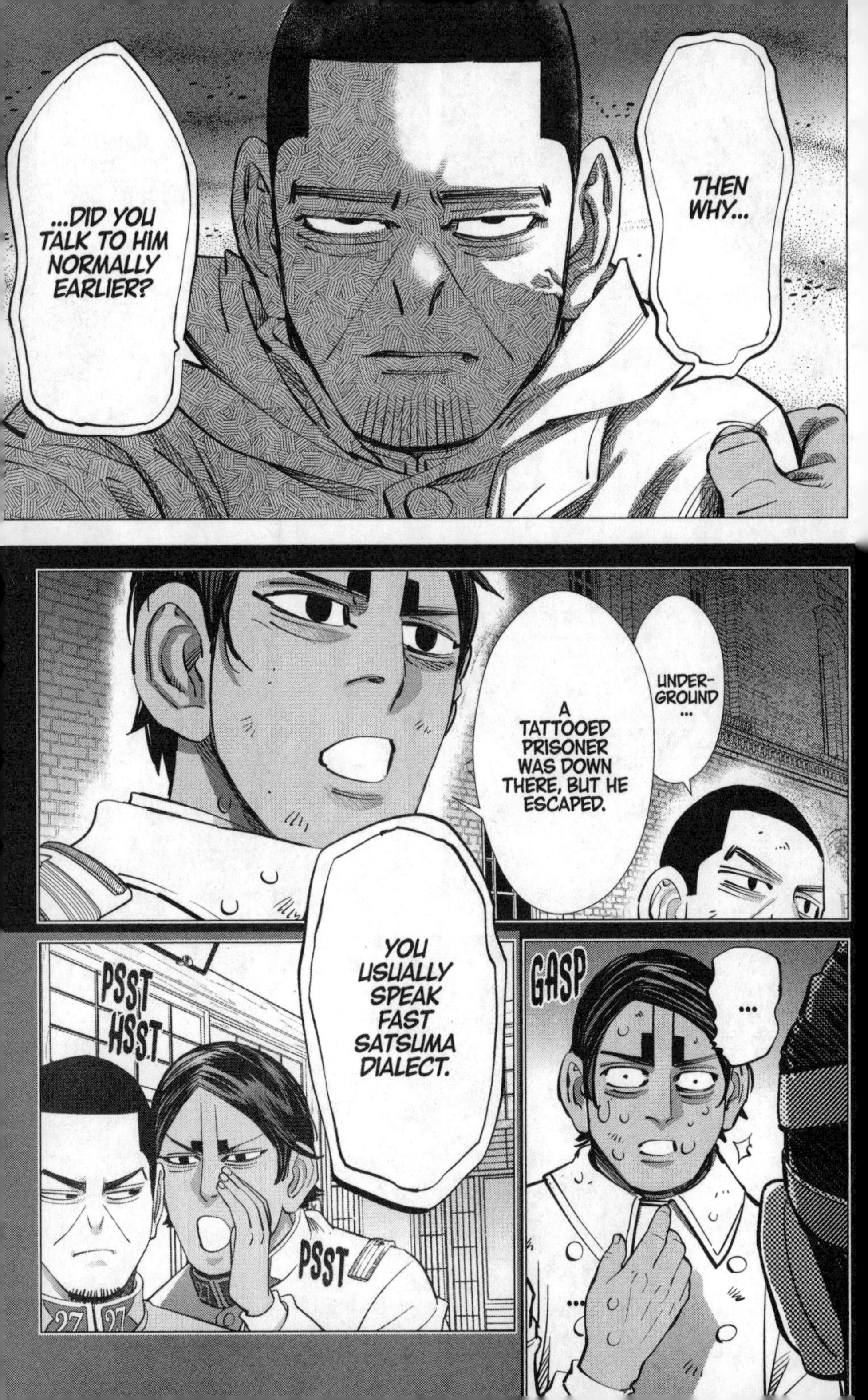
THEN WHY...
...DID YOU TALK TO HIM NORMALLY EARLIER?
UNDER-GROUND ...
A TATTOOED PRISONER WAS DOWN THERE, BUT HE ESCAPED.
GASP
...
...
PSST HSS.T
YOU USUALLY SPEAK FAST SATSUMA DIALECT.
PSST

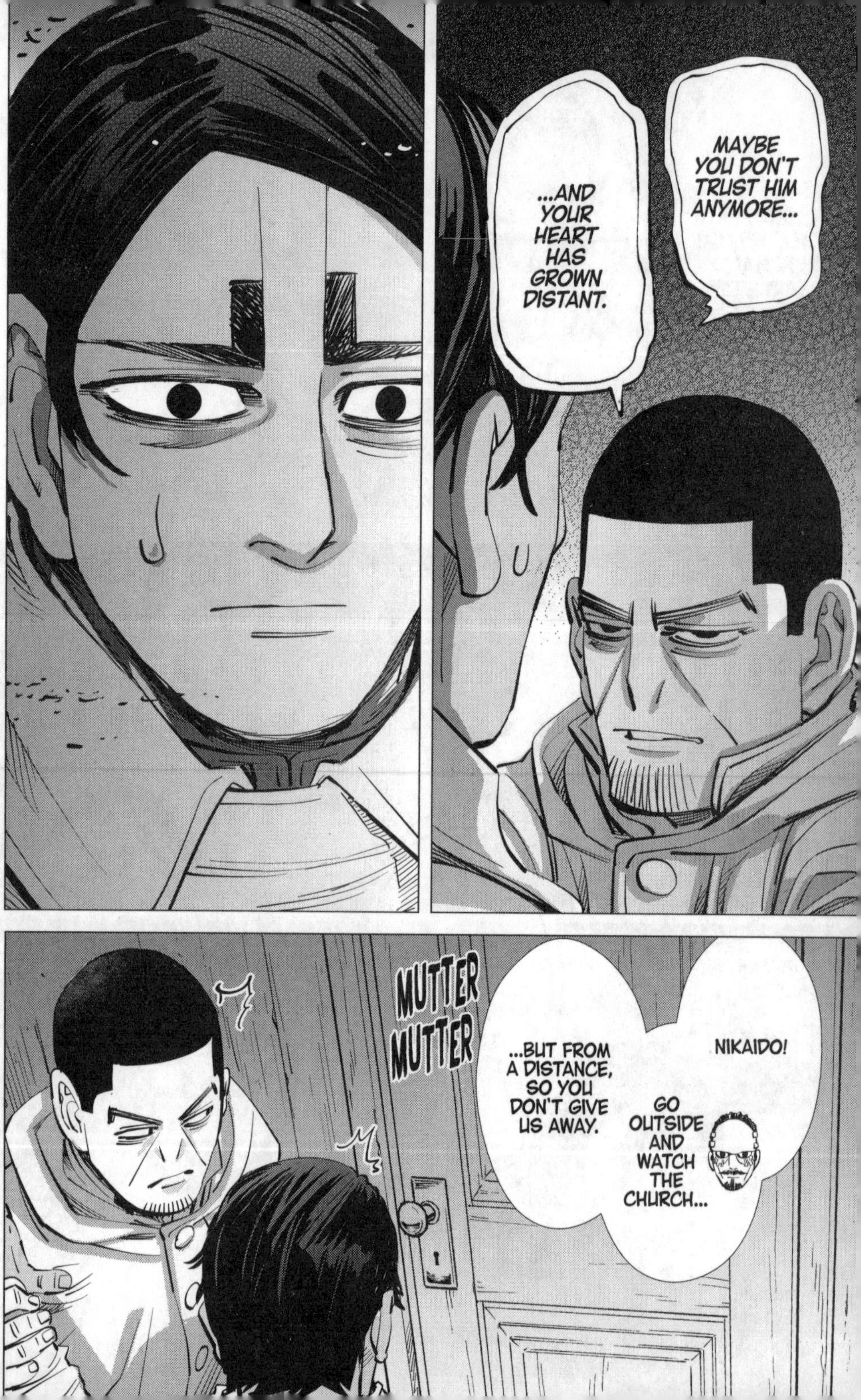
MAYBE YOU DON'T TRUST HIM ANYMORE...
...AND YOUR HEART HAS GROWN DISTANT.
NIKAIDO!
GO OUTSIDE AND WATCH THE CHURCH...
...BUT FROM A DISTANCE, SO YOU DON'T GIVE US AWAY.
MUTTER MUTTER

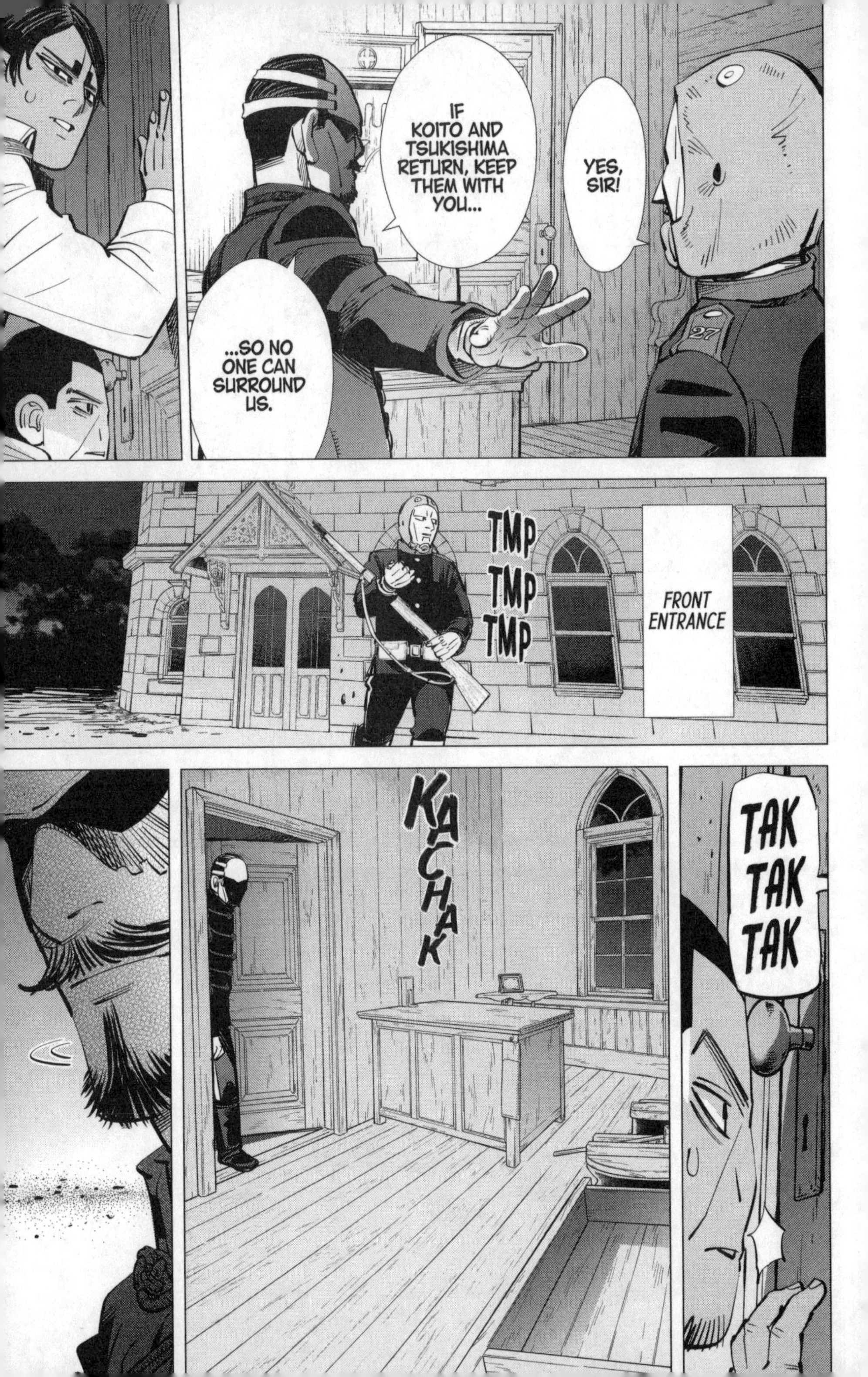
IF KOITO AND TSUKISHIMA RETURN, KEEP THEM WITH YOU...
...SO NO ONE CAN SURROUND US.
YES, SIR!
FRONT ENTRANCE
TMP TMP TMP
TAK TAK TAK
KACHAK

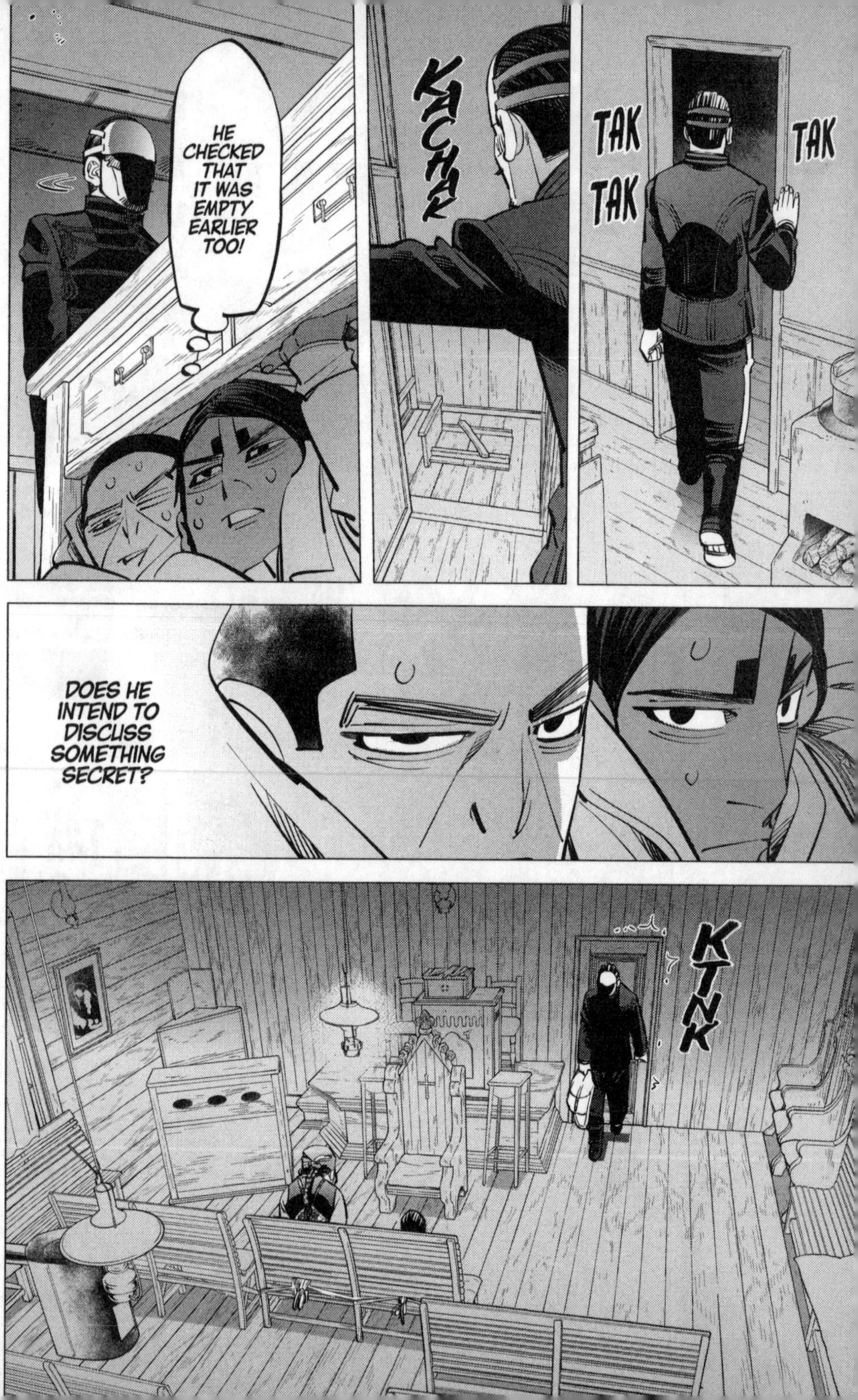
TAK
TAK
TAK
KACHAK
HE CHECKED THAT IT WAS EMPTY EARLIER TOO!
DOES HE INTEND TO DISCUSS SOMETHING SECRET?
KTNK

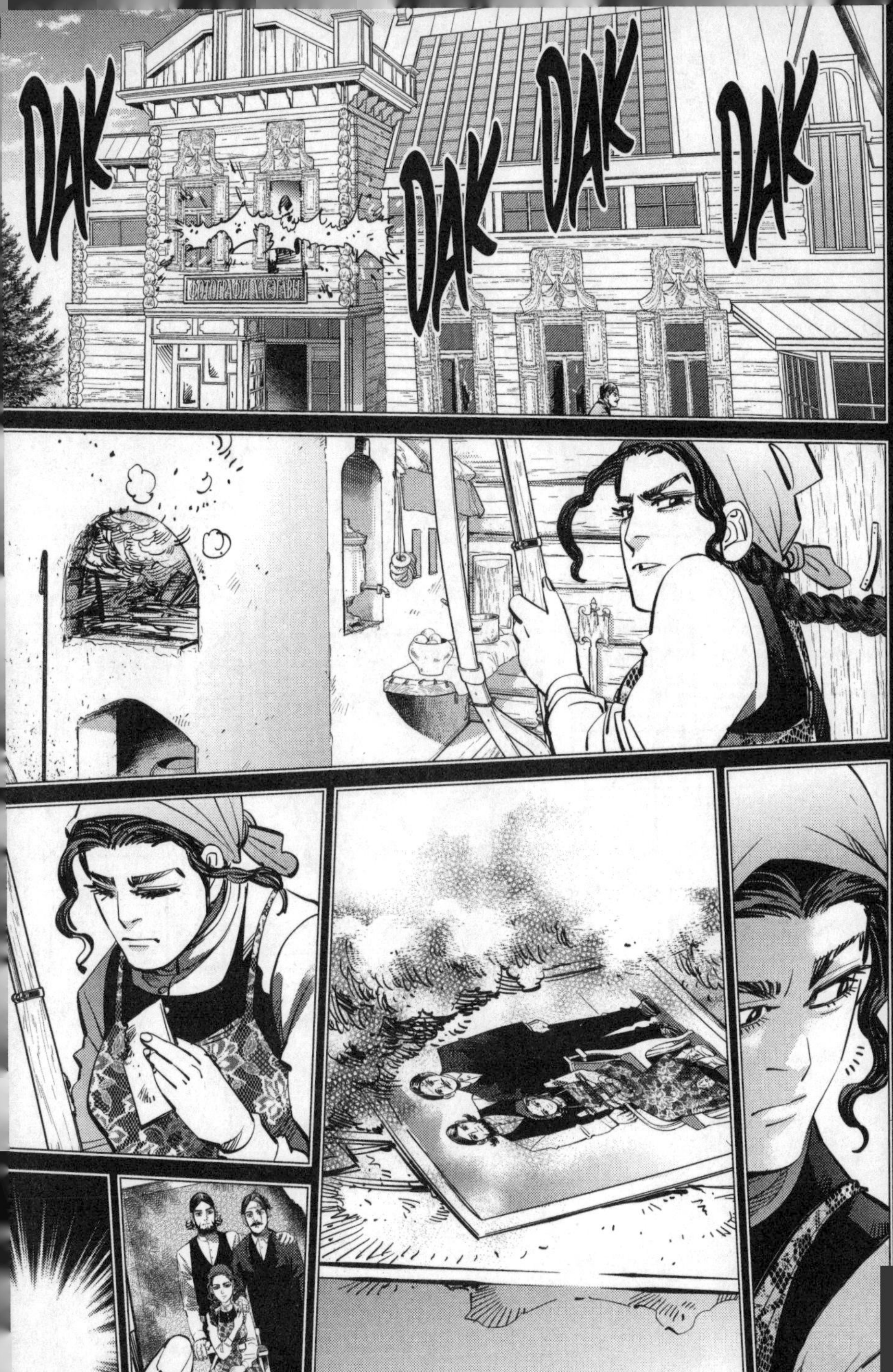
DAK
DAK
DAK
DAK
ФОТОГРАФIЯ ХАСЭГАВЫ

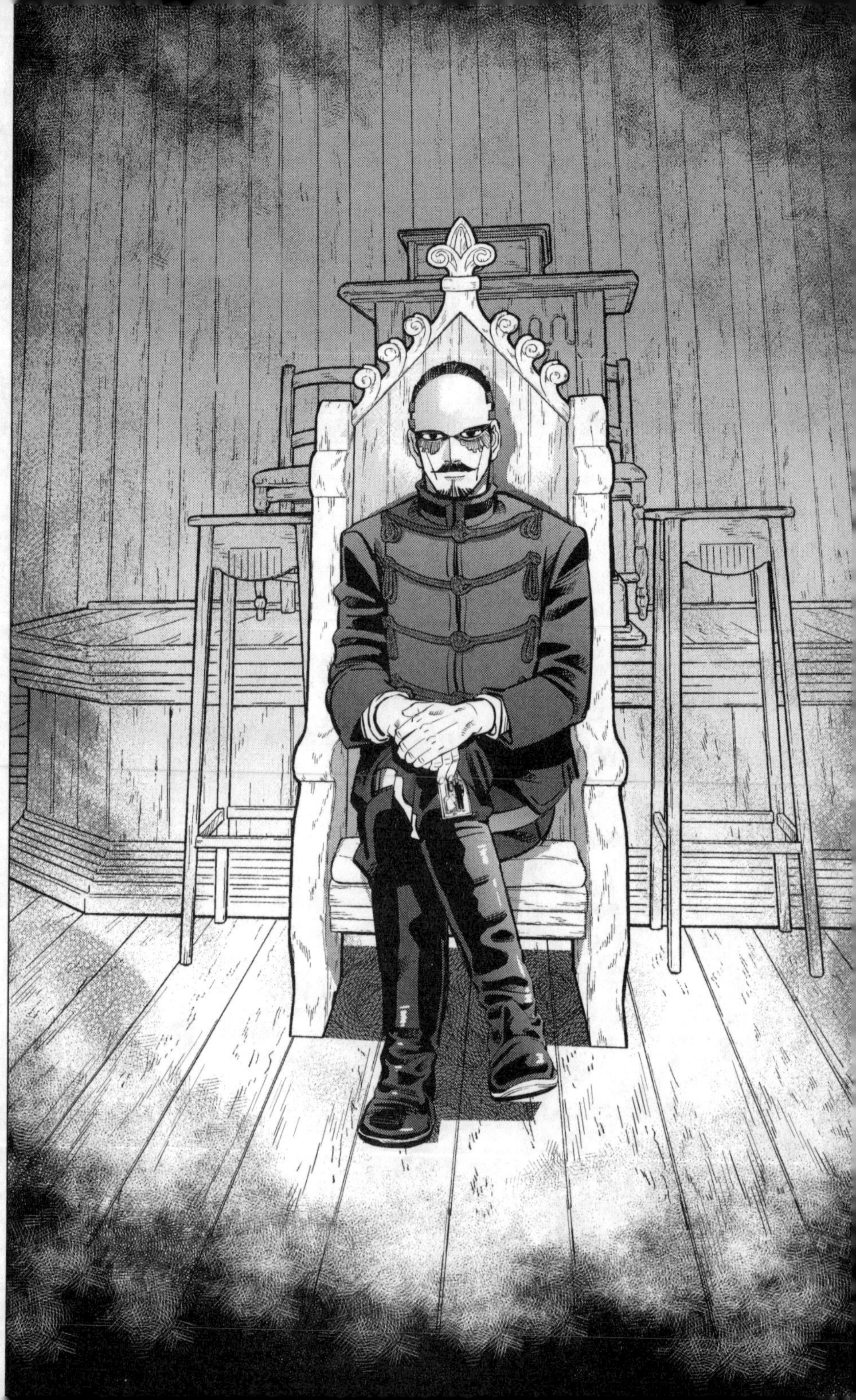

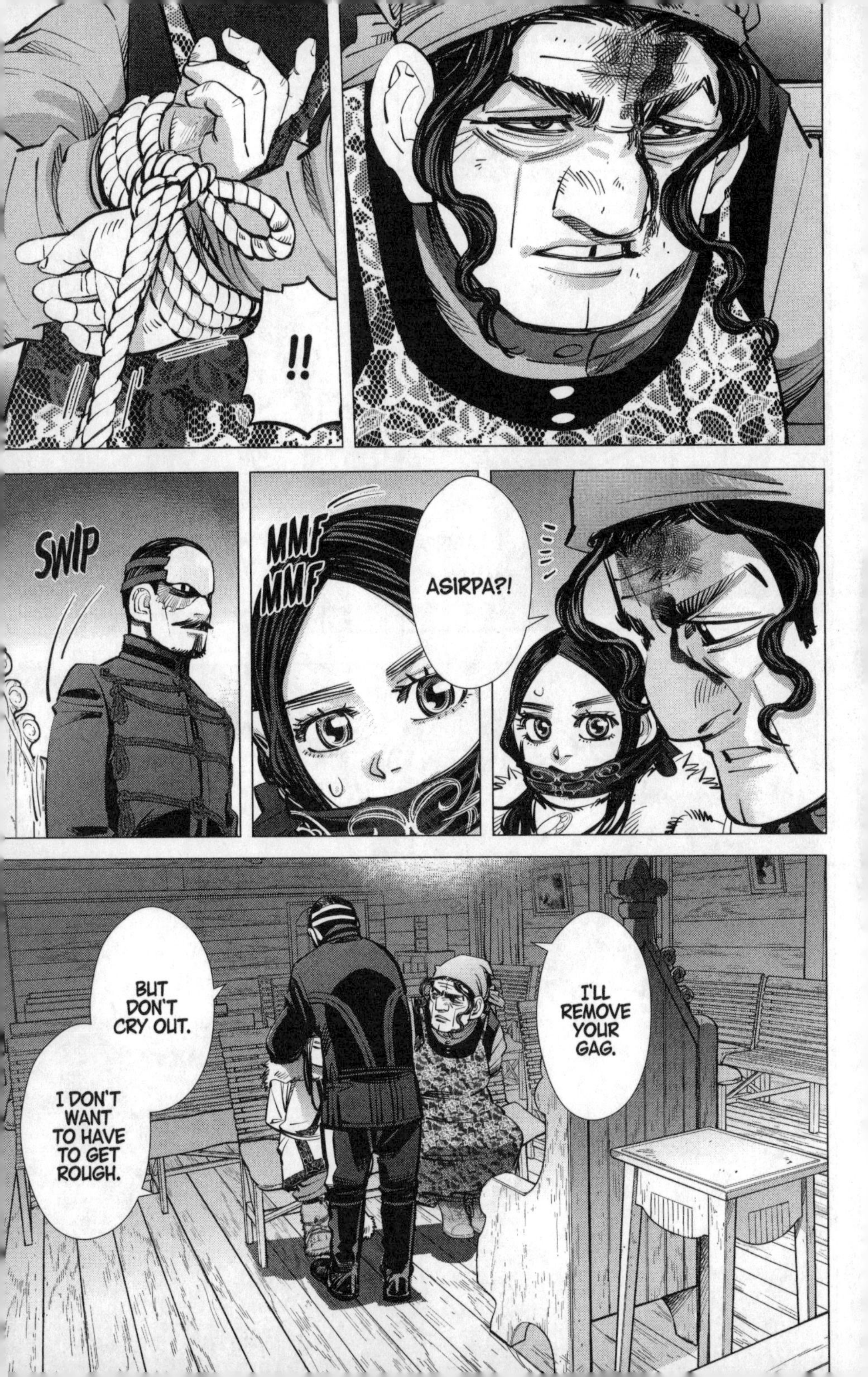
!!
ASIRPA?!
MMF MMF
SWIP
I'LL REMOVE YOUR GAG.
BUT DON'T CRY OUT.
I DON'T WANT TO HAVE TO GET ROUGH.

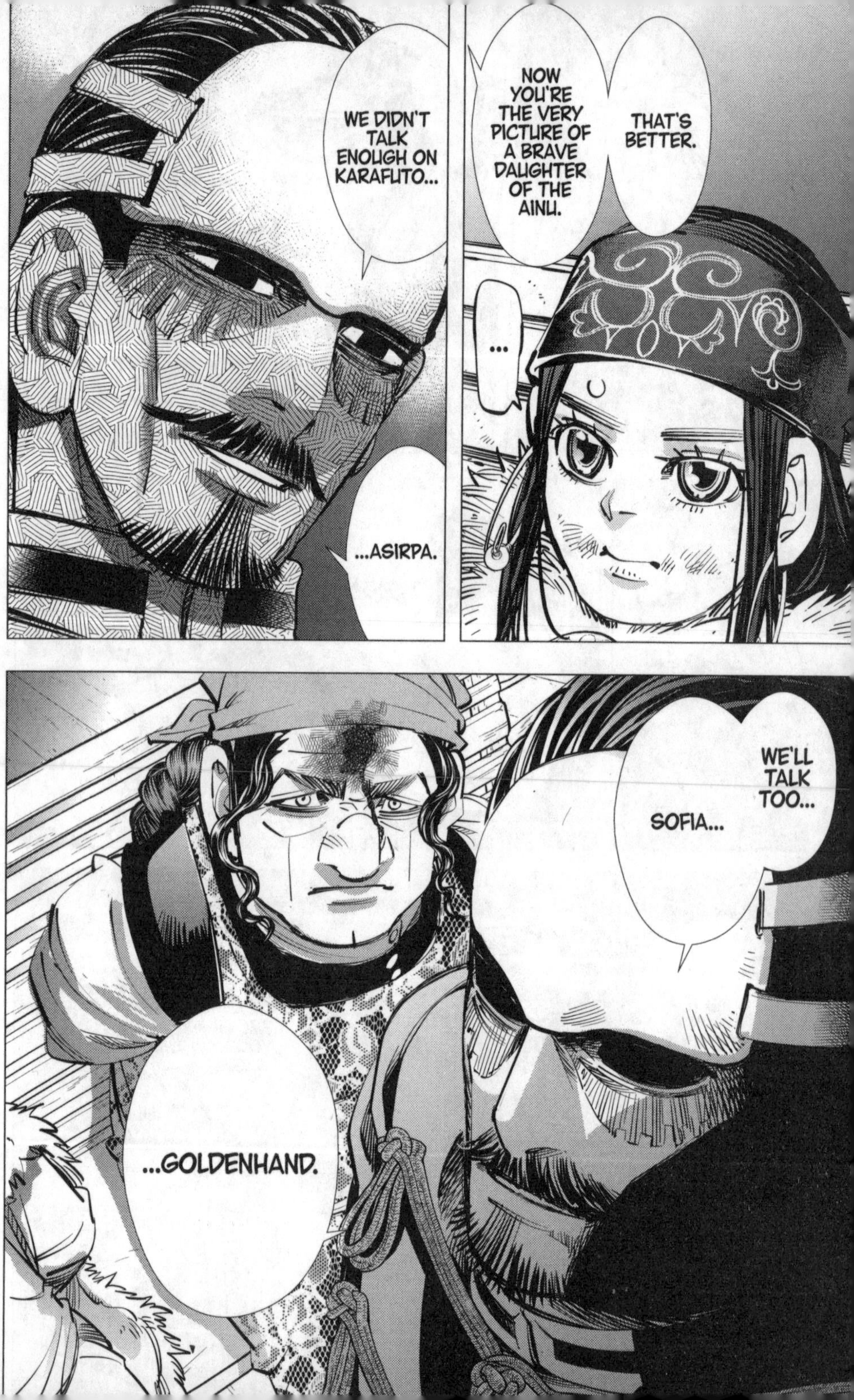
THAT'S BETTER.
NOW YOU'RE THE VERY PICTURE OF A BRAVE DAUGHTER OF THE AINU.
...
WE DIDN'T TALK ENOUGH ON KARAFUTO...
...ASIRPA.
WE'LL TALK TOO...
SOFIA...
...GOLDENHAND.

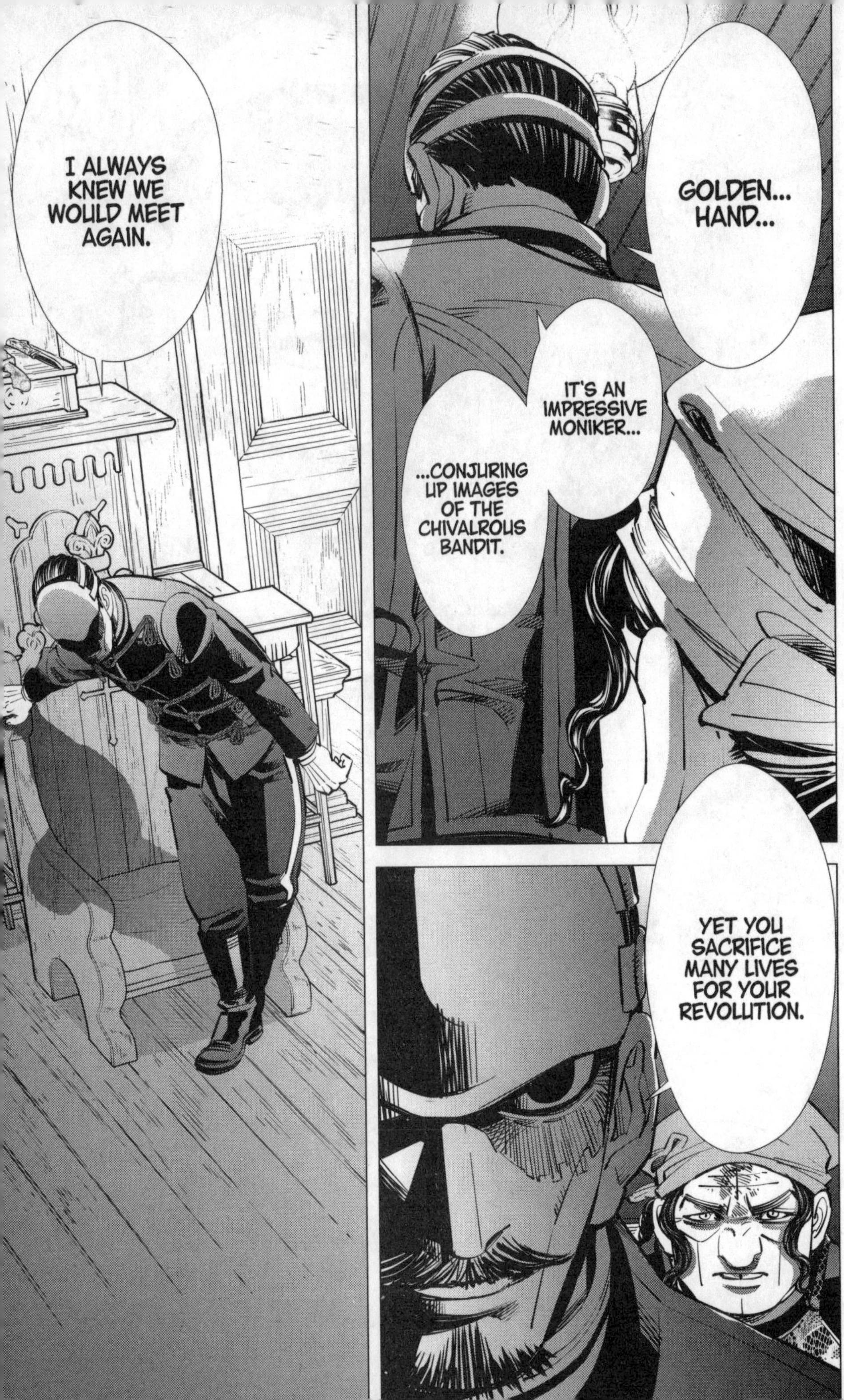
GOLDEN... HAND...
IT'S AN IMPRESSIVE MONIKER...
...CONJURING UP IMAGES OF THE CHIVALROUS BANDIT.
YET YOU SACRIFICE MANY LIVES FOR YOUR REVOLUTION.
I ALWAYS KNEW WE WOULD MEET AGAIN.

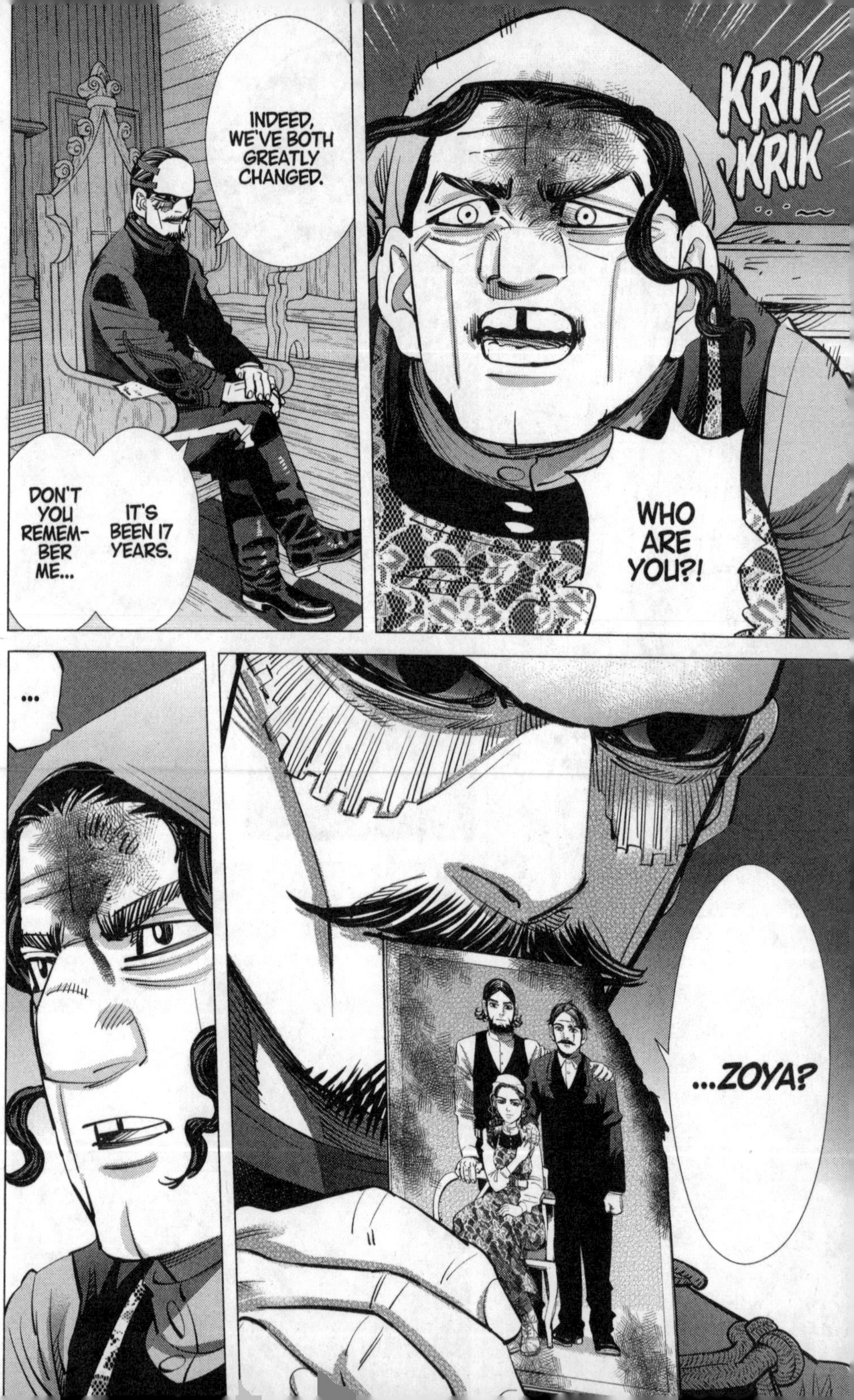
KRIK KRIK
WHO ARE YOU?!
INDEED, WE'VE BOTH GREATLY CHANGED.
IT'S BEEN 17 YEARS.
DON'T YOU REMEM-BER ME...
...ZOYA?
...

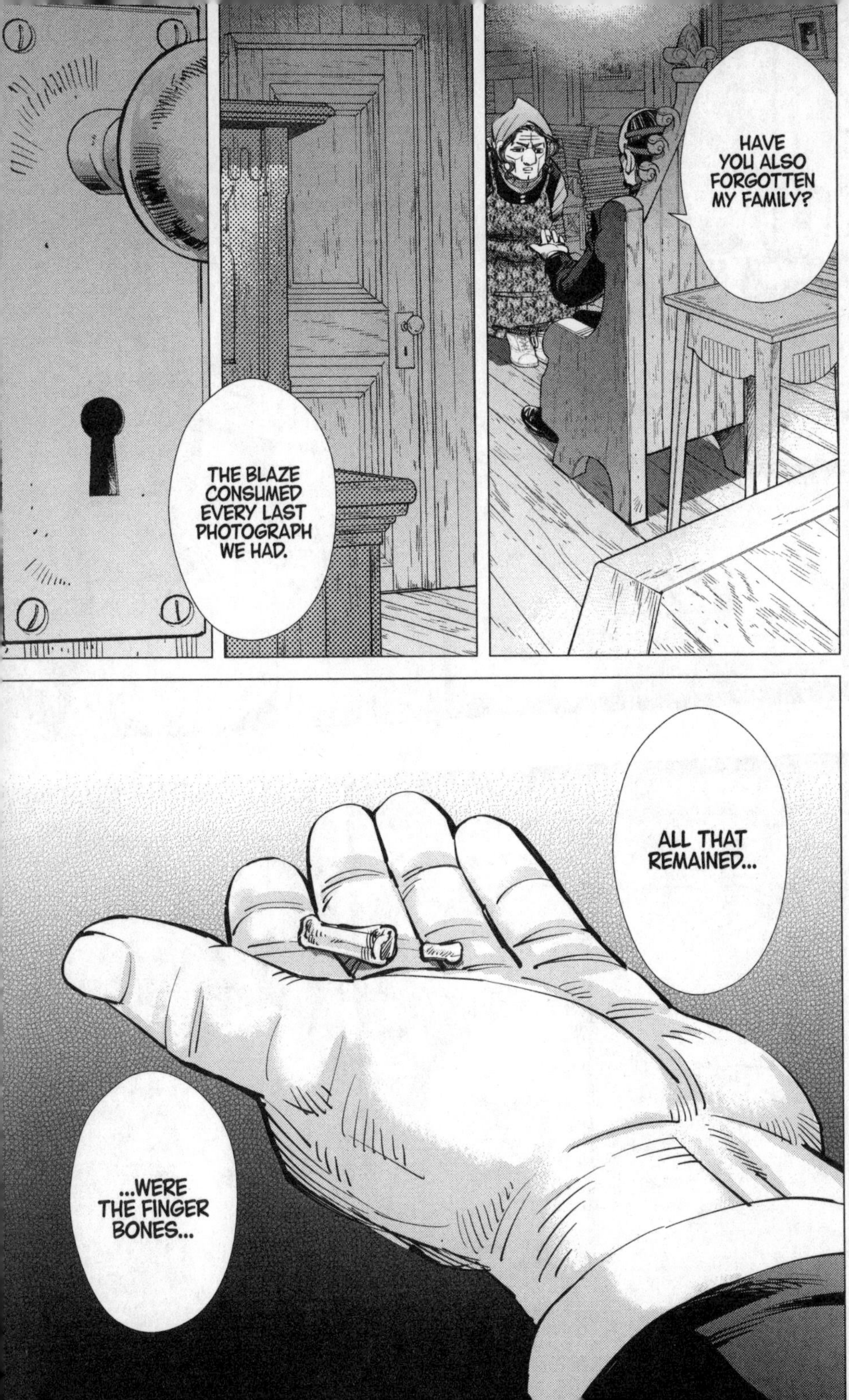
HAVE YOU ALSO FORGOTTEN MY FAMILY?
THE BLAZE CONSUMED EVERY LAST PHOTOGRAPH WE HAD.
ALL THAT REMAINED...
...WERE THE FINGER BONES...

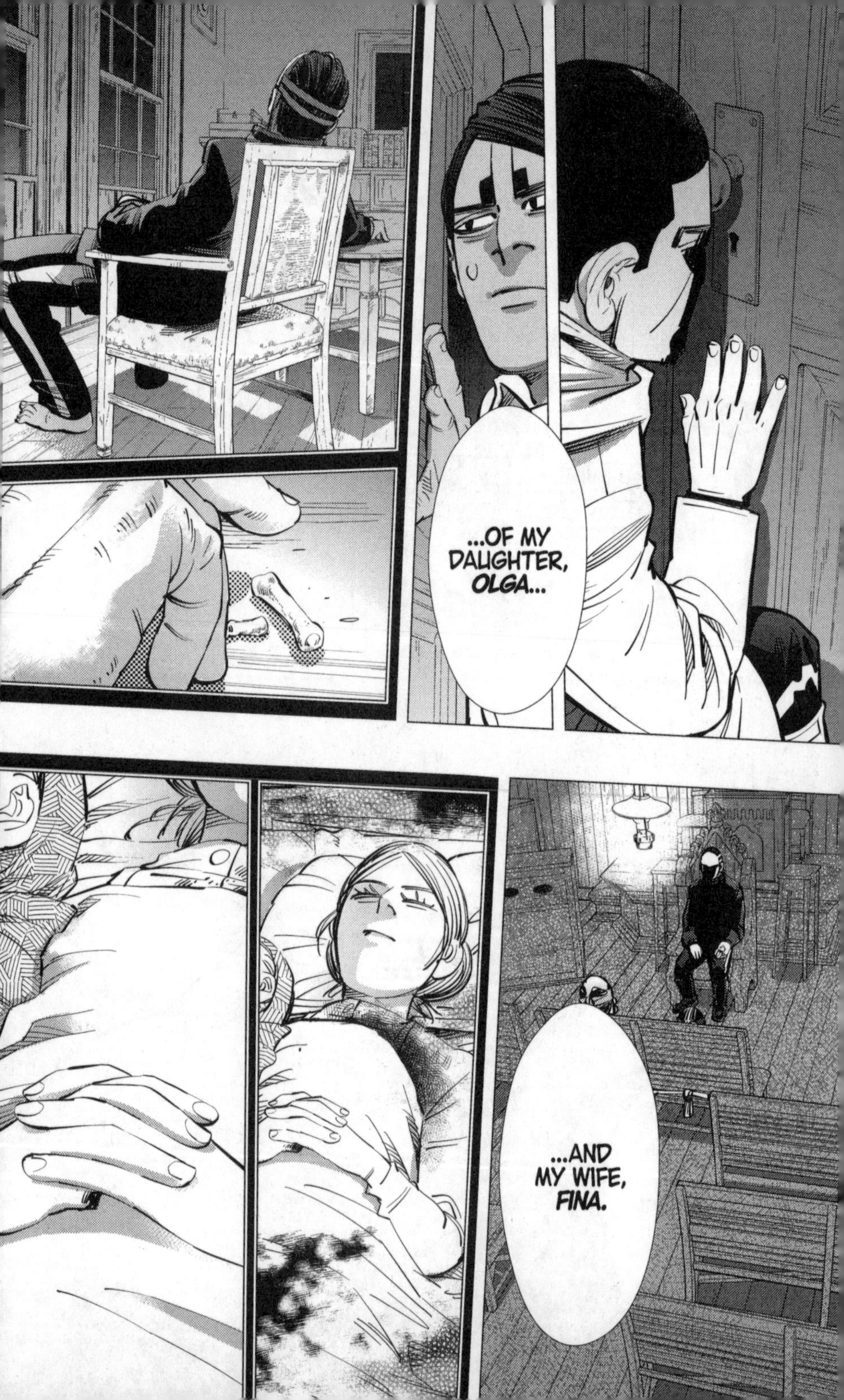
...OF MY DAUGHTER, OLGA...
...AND MY WIFE, FINA.

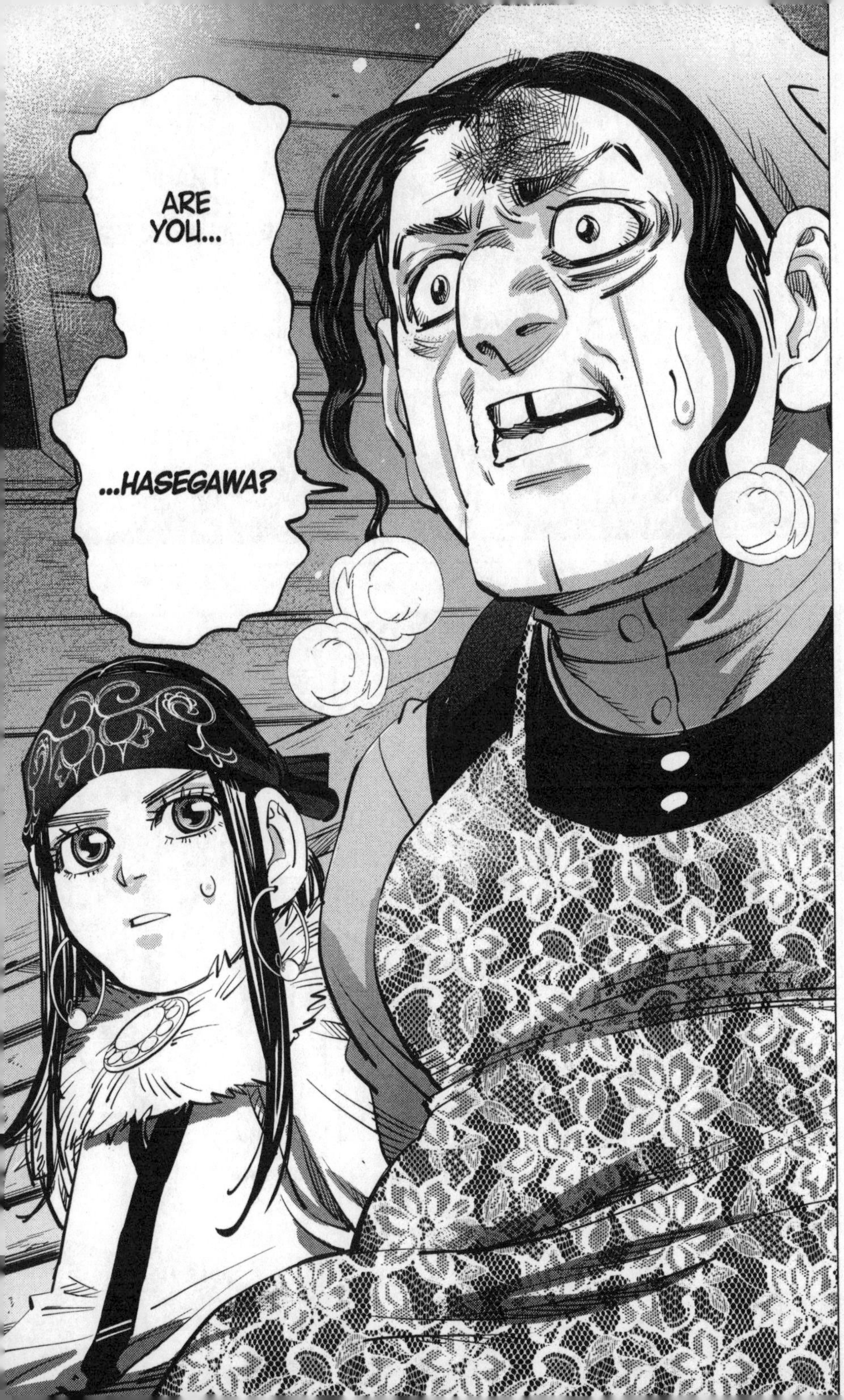
ARE YOU...
...HASEGAWA?

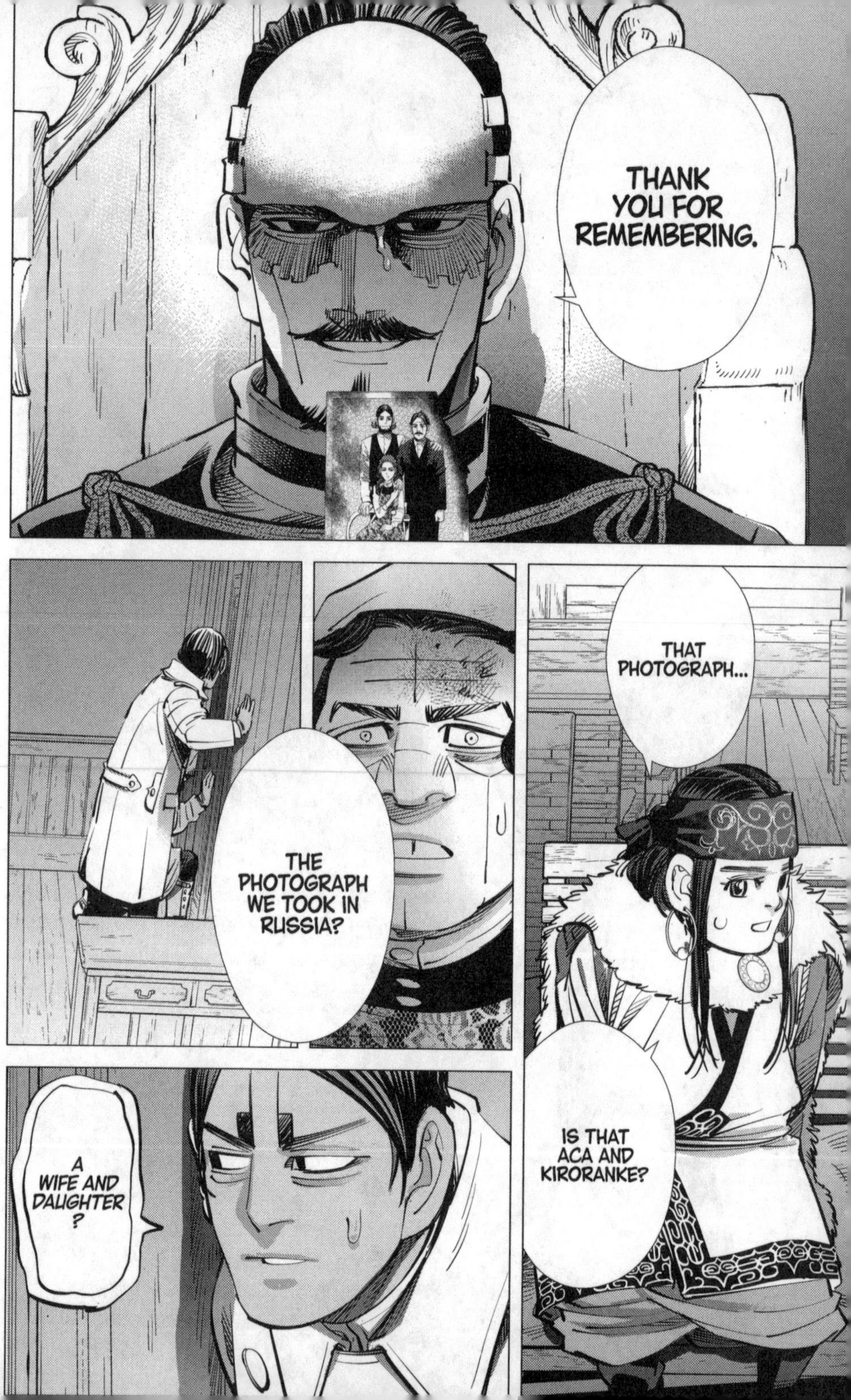
THANK YOU FOR REMEMBERING.
THAT PHOTOGRAPH...
IS THAT ACA AND KIRORANKE?
THE PHOTOGRAPH WE TOOK IN RUSSIA?
A WIFE AND DAUGHTER?

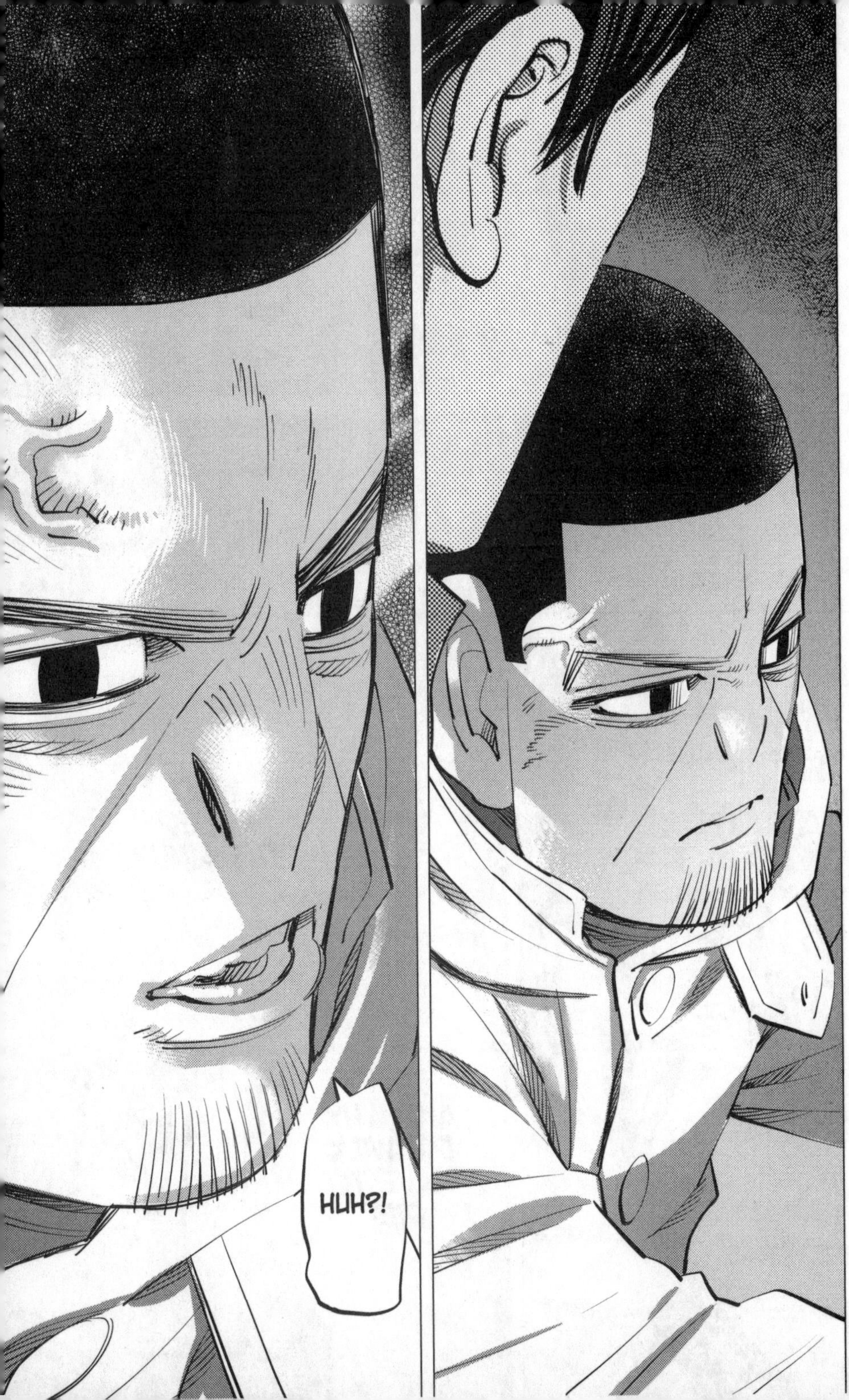
HUH?!

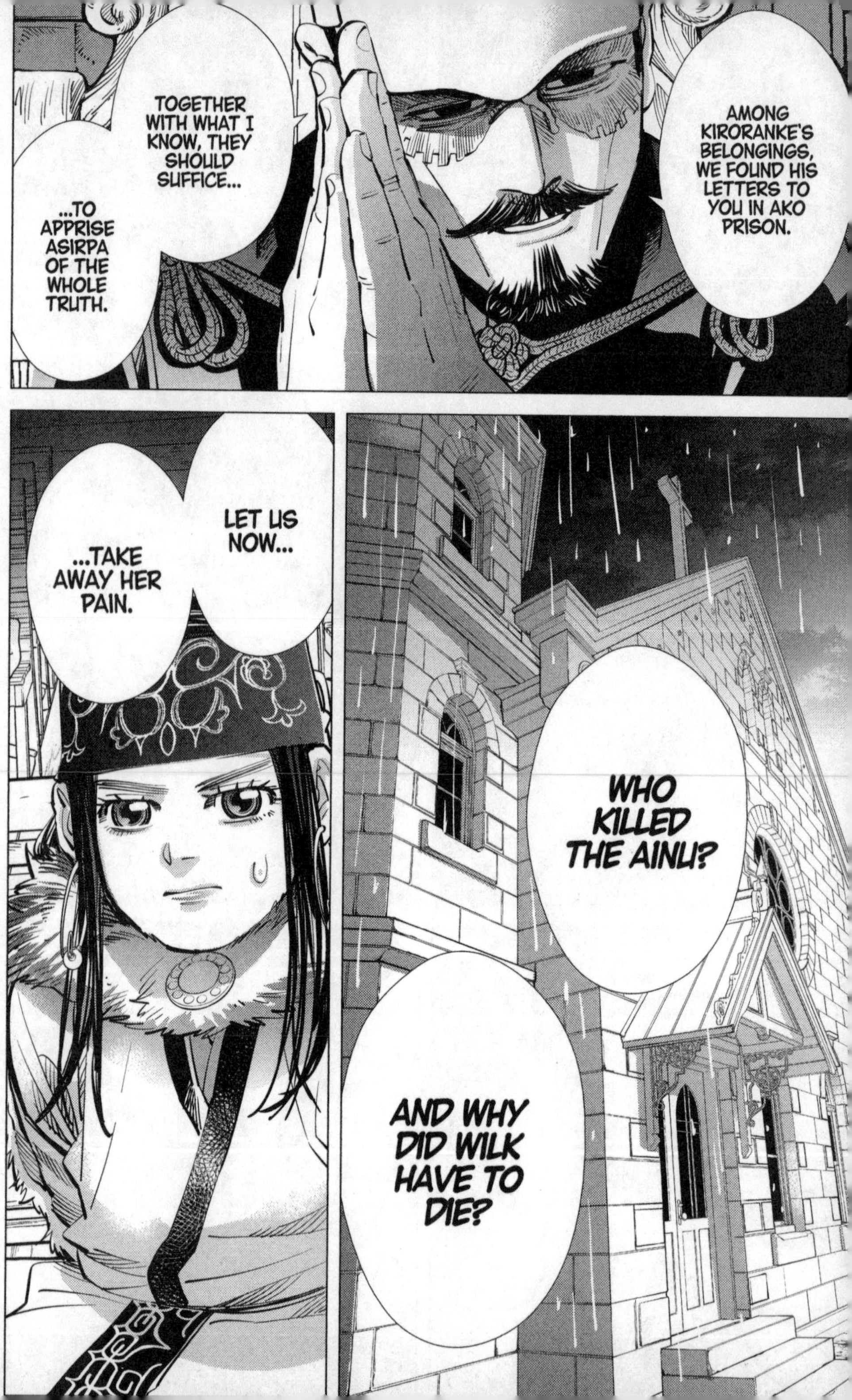
AMONG KIRORANKE'S BELONGINGS, WE FOUND HIS LETTERS TO YOU IN AKO PRISON.
TOGETHER WITH WHAT I KNOW, THEY SHOULD SUFFICE...
...TO APPRISE ASIRPA OF THE WHOLE TRUTH.
WHO KILLED THE AINU?
AND WHY DID WILK HAVE TO DIE?
LET US NOW...
...TAKE AWAY HER PAIN.

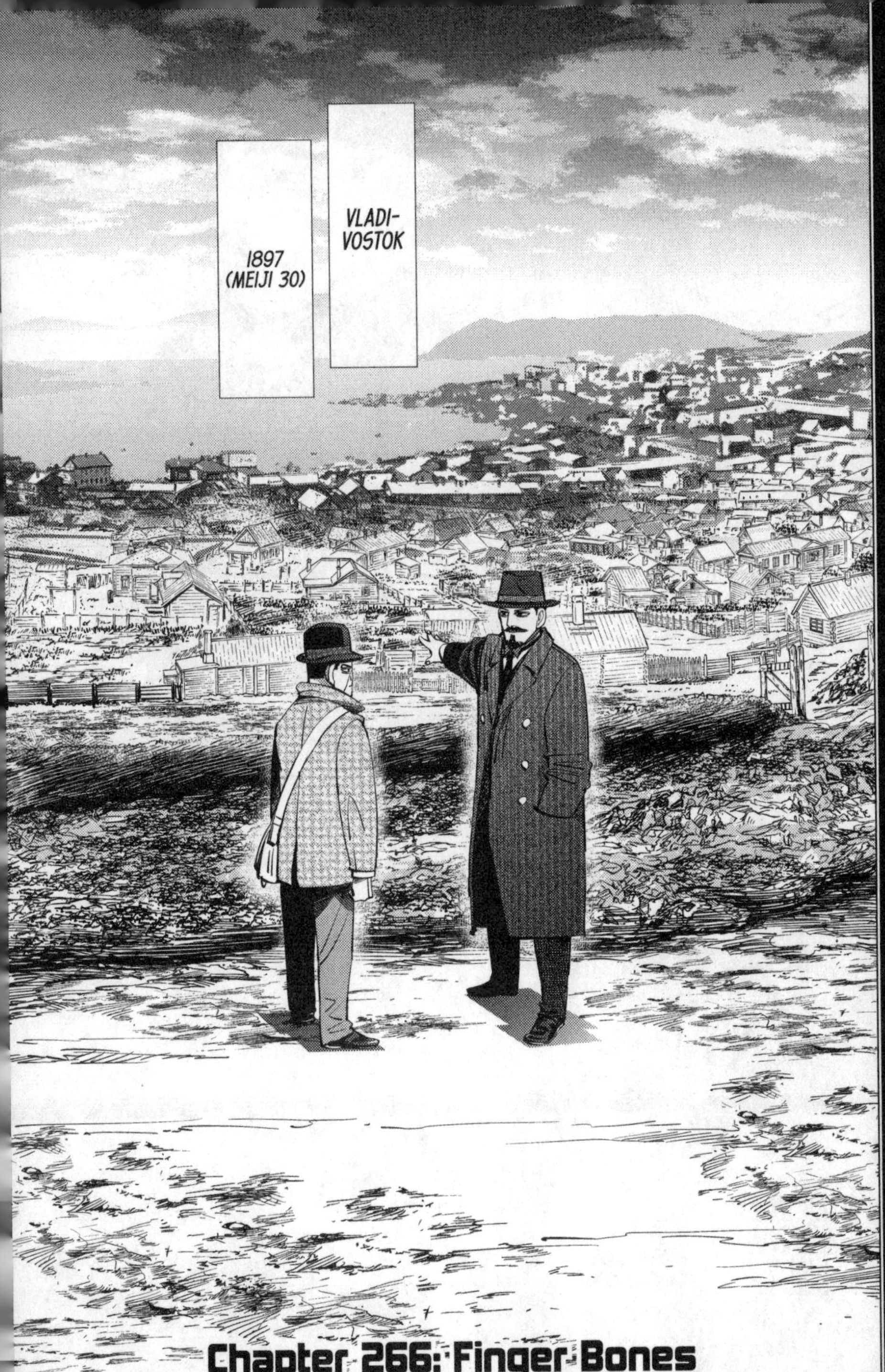
VLADI-
VOSTOK
1897
(MEIJI 30)
Chapter 266: Finger Bones

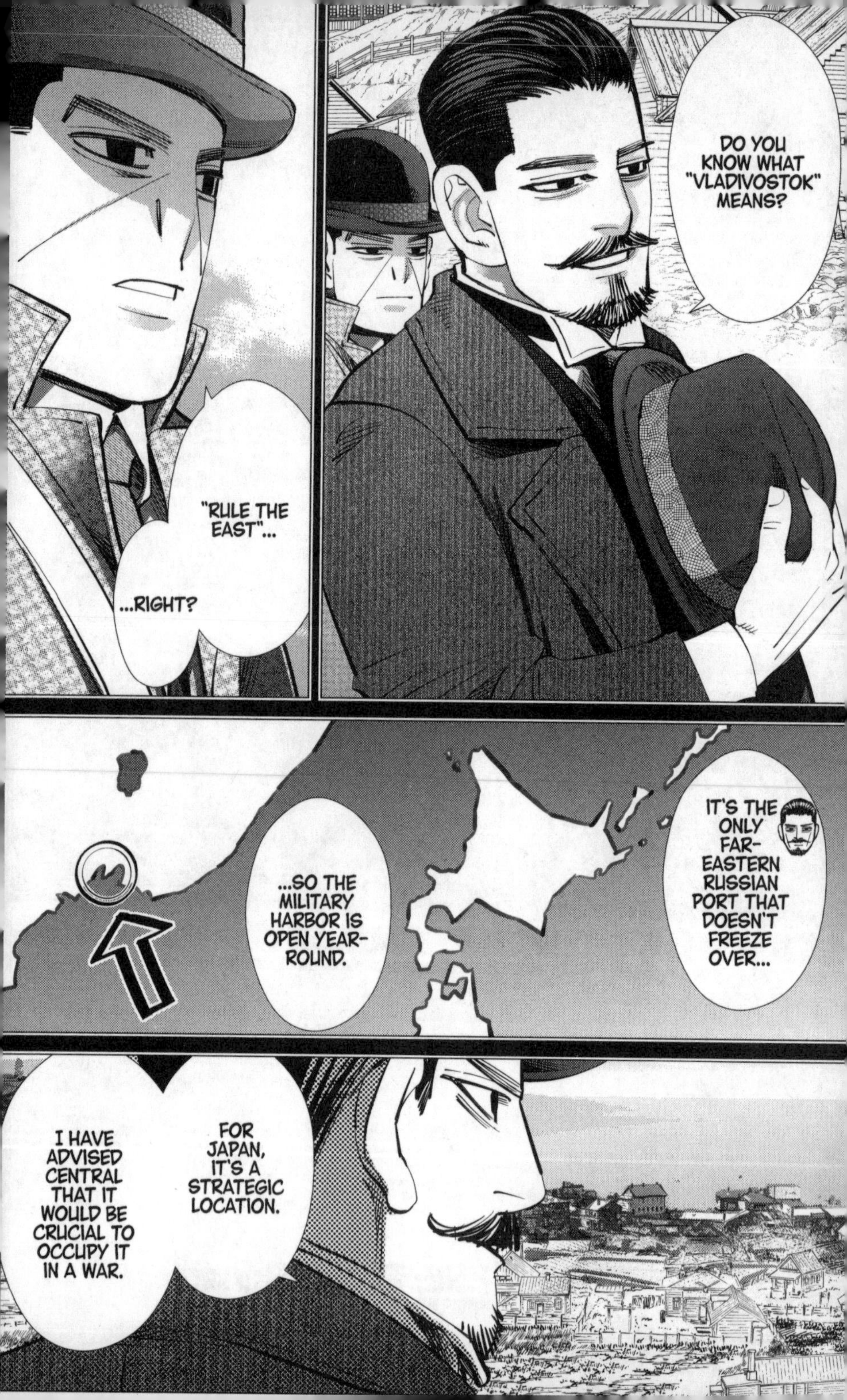
DO YOU KNOW WHAT "VLADIVOSTOK" MEANS?
"RULE THE EAST"...
...RIGHT?
IT'S THE ONLY FAR-EASTERN RUSSIAN PORT THAT DOESN'T FREEZE OVER...
...SO THE MILITARY HARBOR IS OPEN YEAR-ROUND.
FOR JAPAN, IT'S A STRATEGIC LOCATION.
I HAVE ADVISED CENTRAL THAT IT WOULD BE CRUCIAL TO OCCUPY IT IN A WAR.

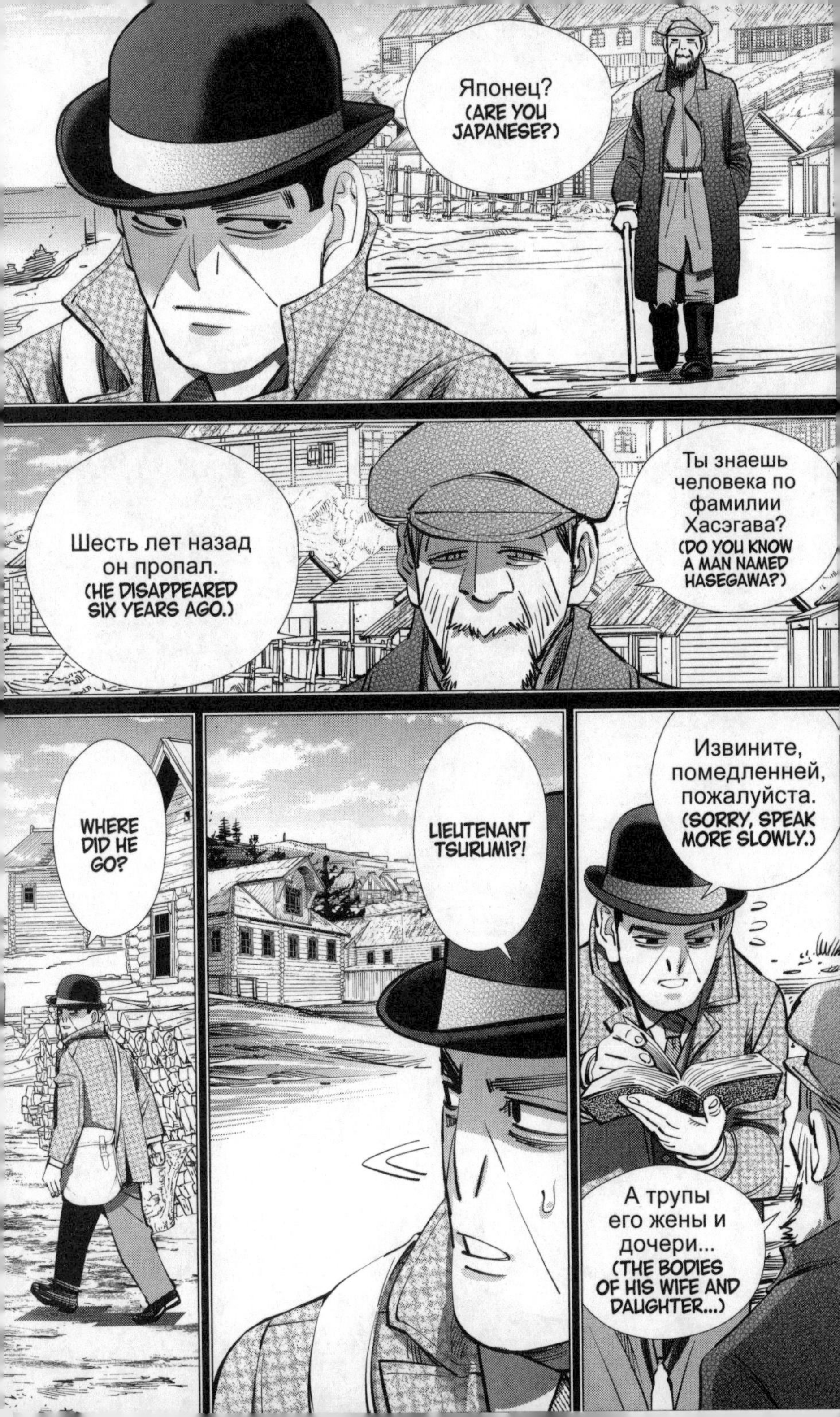
Японец? (ARE YOU JAPANESE?)
Ты знаешь человека по фамилии Хасэгава? (DO YOU KNOW A MAN NAMED HASEGAWA?)
Шесть лет назад он пропал. (HE DISAPPEARED SIX YEARS AGO.)
Извините, помедленней, пожалуйста. (SORRY, SPEAK MORE SLOWLY.)
А трупы его жены и дочери... (THE BODIES OF HIS WIFE AND DAUGHTER...)
LIEUTENANT TSURUMI?!
WHERE DID HE GO?

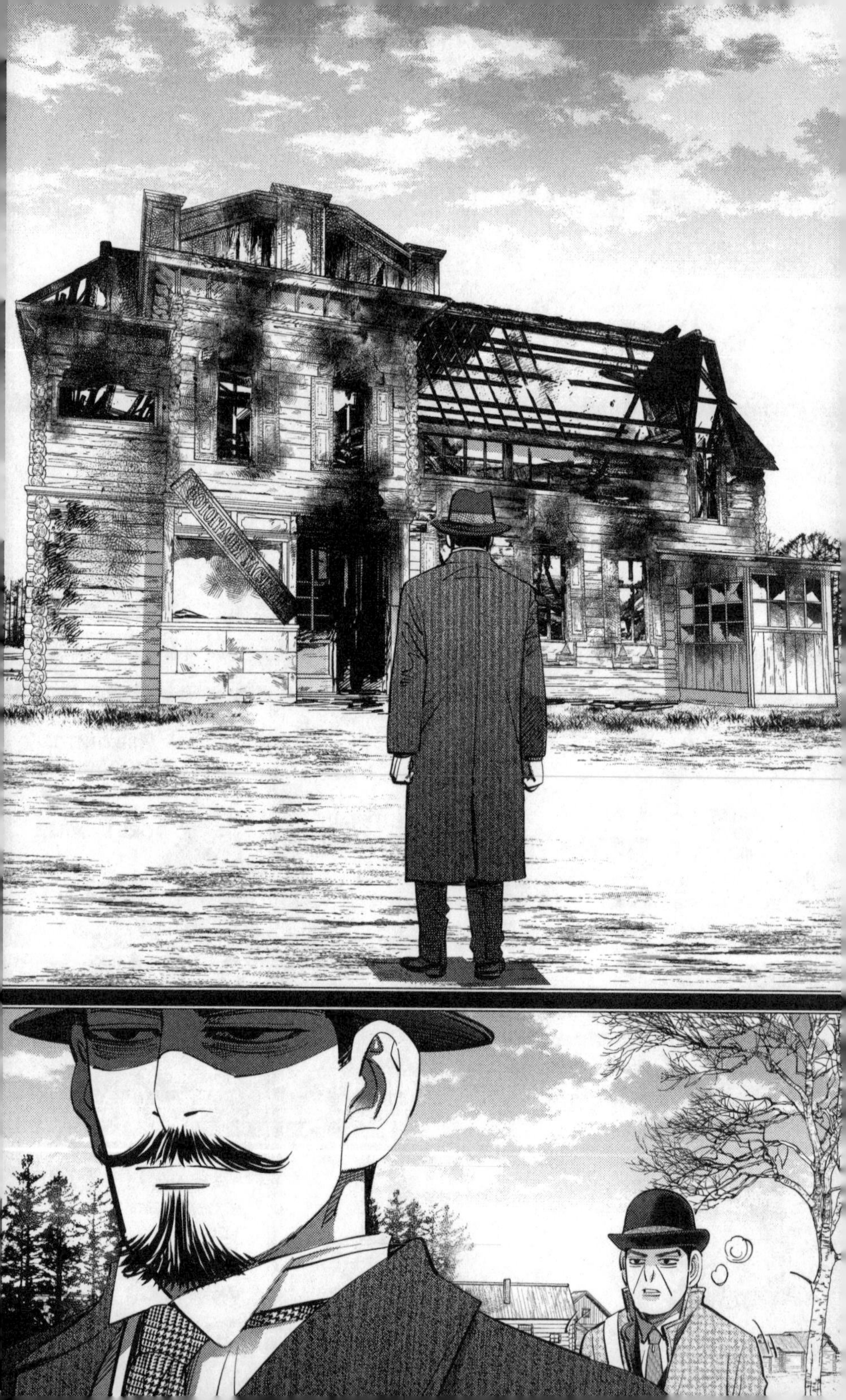

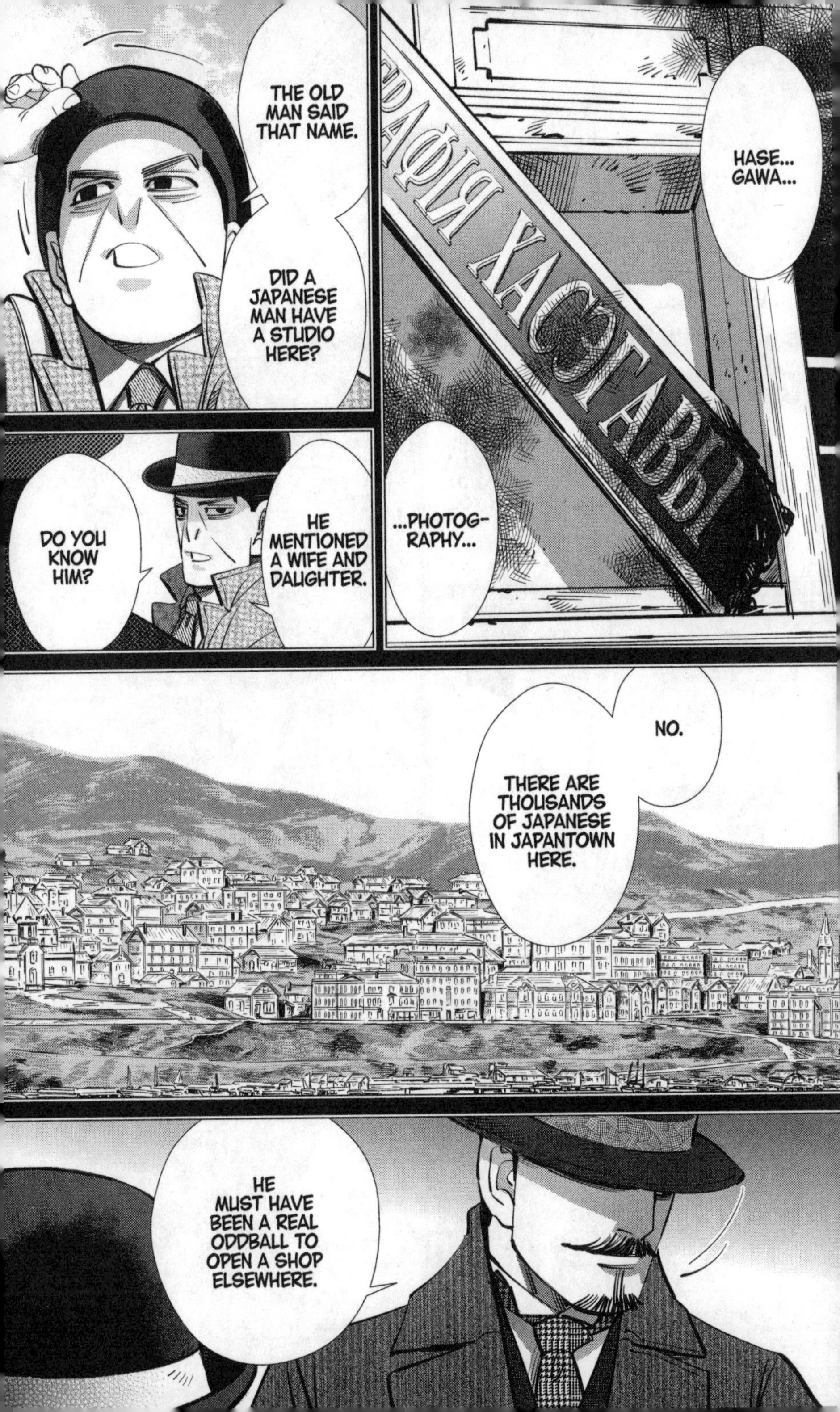
HASE... GAWA...
...PHOTOG-RAPHY...
THE OLD MAN SAID THAT NAME.
DID A JAPANESE MAN HAVE A STUDIO HERE?
HE MENTIONED A WIFE AND DAUGHTER.
DO YOU KNOW HIM?
NO.
THERE ARE THOUSANDS OF JAPANESE IN JAPANTOWN HERE.
HE MUST HAVE BEEN A REAL ODDBALL TO OPEN A SHOP ELSEWHERE.

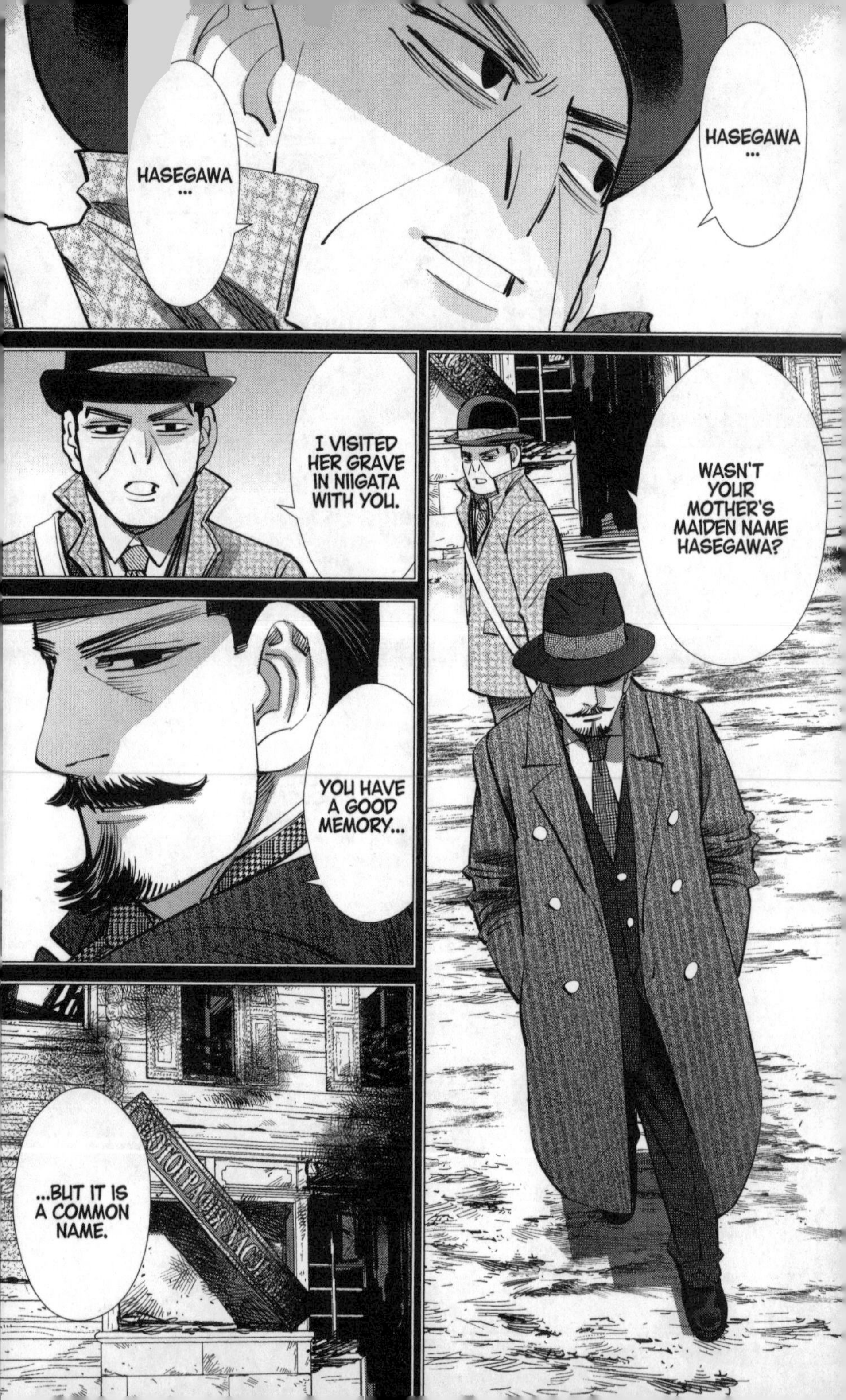

HASEGAWA ...
HASEGAWA ...
WASN'T YOUR MOTHER'S MAIDEN NAME HASEGAWA?
I VISITED HER GRAVE IN NIIGATA WITH YOU.
YOU HAVE A GOOD MEMORY...
...BUT IT IS A COMMON NAME.

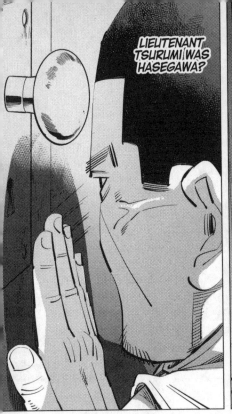

LIEUTENANT TSURUMI WAS HASEGAWA?

ABOUT 50 YEARS AGO...

...SOME RADICAL AINU HAD PLANS FOR USING THE GOLD.

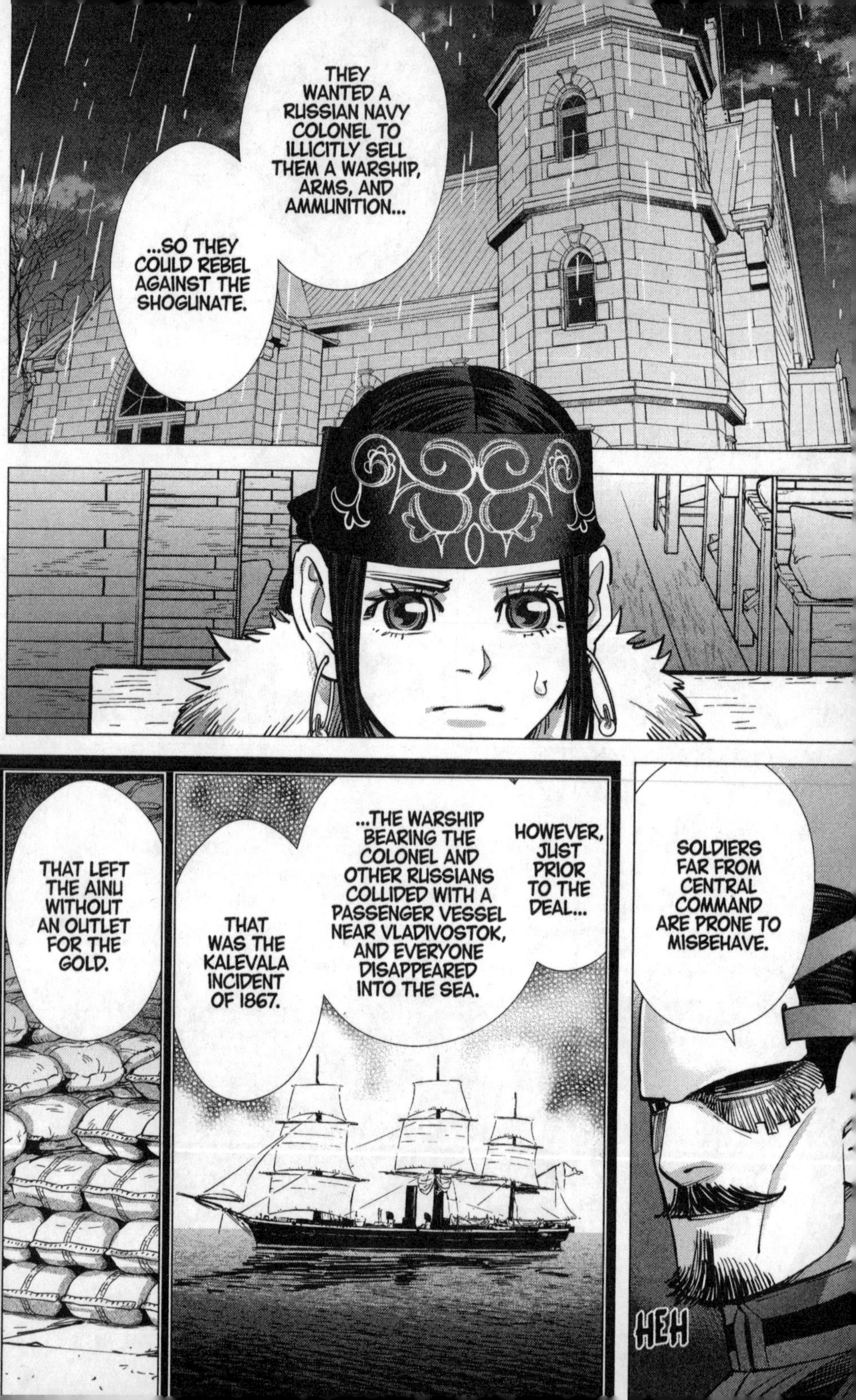
THEY WANTED A RUSSIAN NAVY COLONEL TO ILLICITLY SELL THEM A WARSHIP, ARMS, AND AMMUNITION...
...SO THEY COULD REBEL AGAINST THE SHOGUNATE.
SOLDIERS FAR FROM CENTRAL COMMAND ARE PRONE TO MISBEHAVE.
HEH
HOWEVER, JUST PRIOR TO THE DEAL...
...THE WARSHIP BEARING THE COLONEL AND OTHER RUSSIANS COLLIDED WITH A PASSENGER VESSEL NEAR VLADIVOSTOK, AND EVERYONE DISAPPEARED INTO THE SEA.
THAT WAS THE KALEVALA INCIDENT OF 1867.
THAT LEFT THE AINU WITHOUT AN OUTLET FOR THE GOLD.

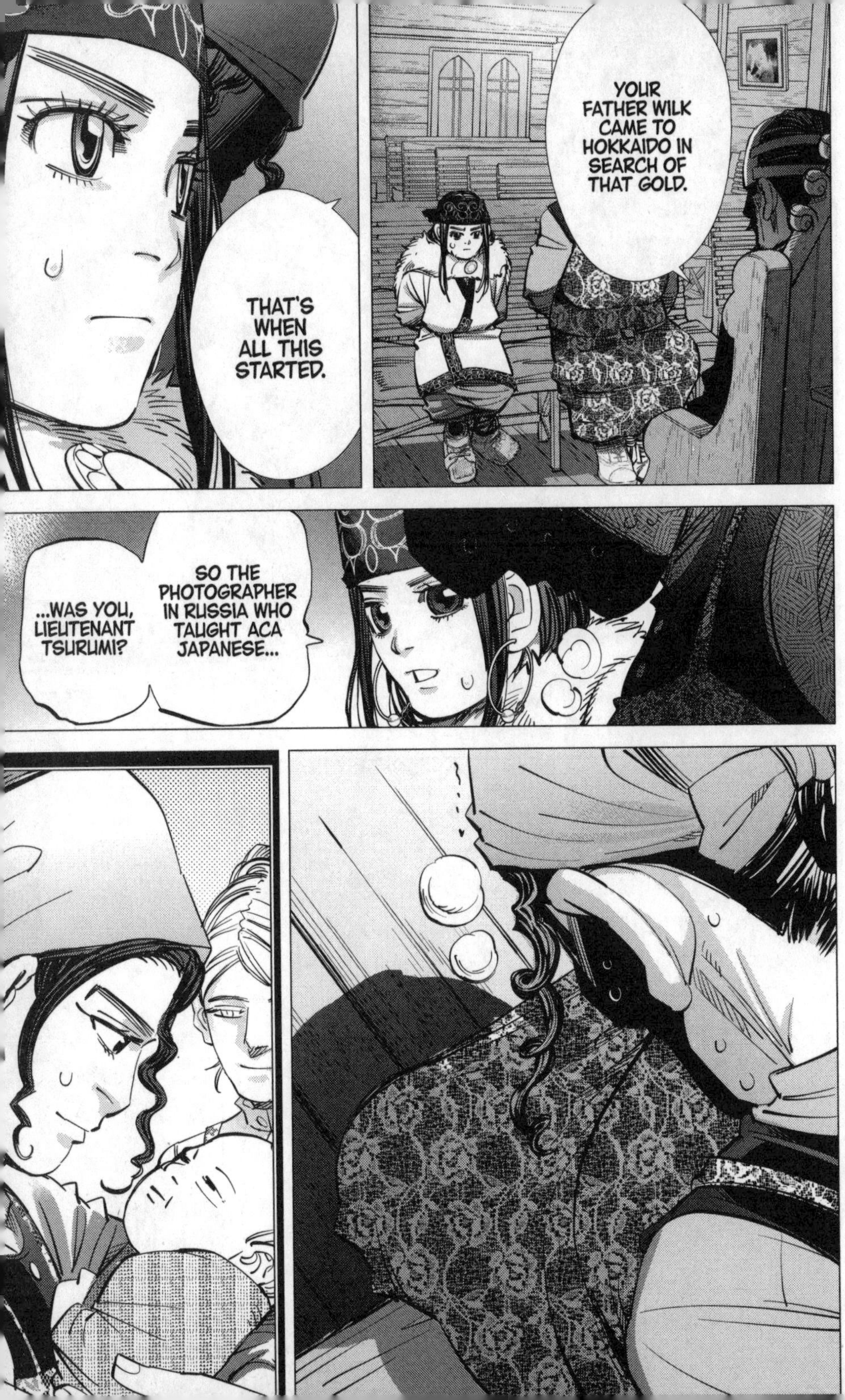
YOUR FATHER WILK CAME TO HOKKAIDO IN SEARCH OF THAT GOLD.
THAT'S WHEN ALL THIS STARTED.
SO THE PHOTOGRAPHER IN RUSSIA WHO TAUGHT ACA JAPANESE...
...WAS YOU, LIEUTENANT TSURUMI?
...

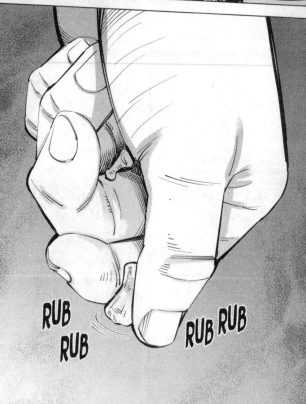

RUB
RUB

RUB RUB

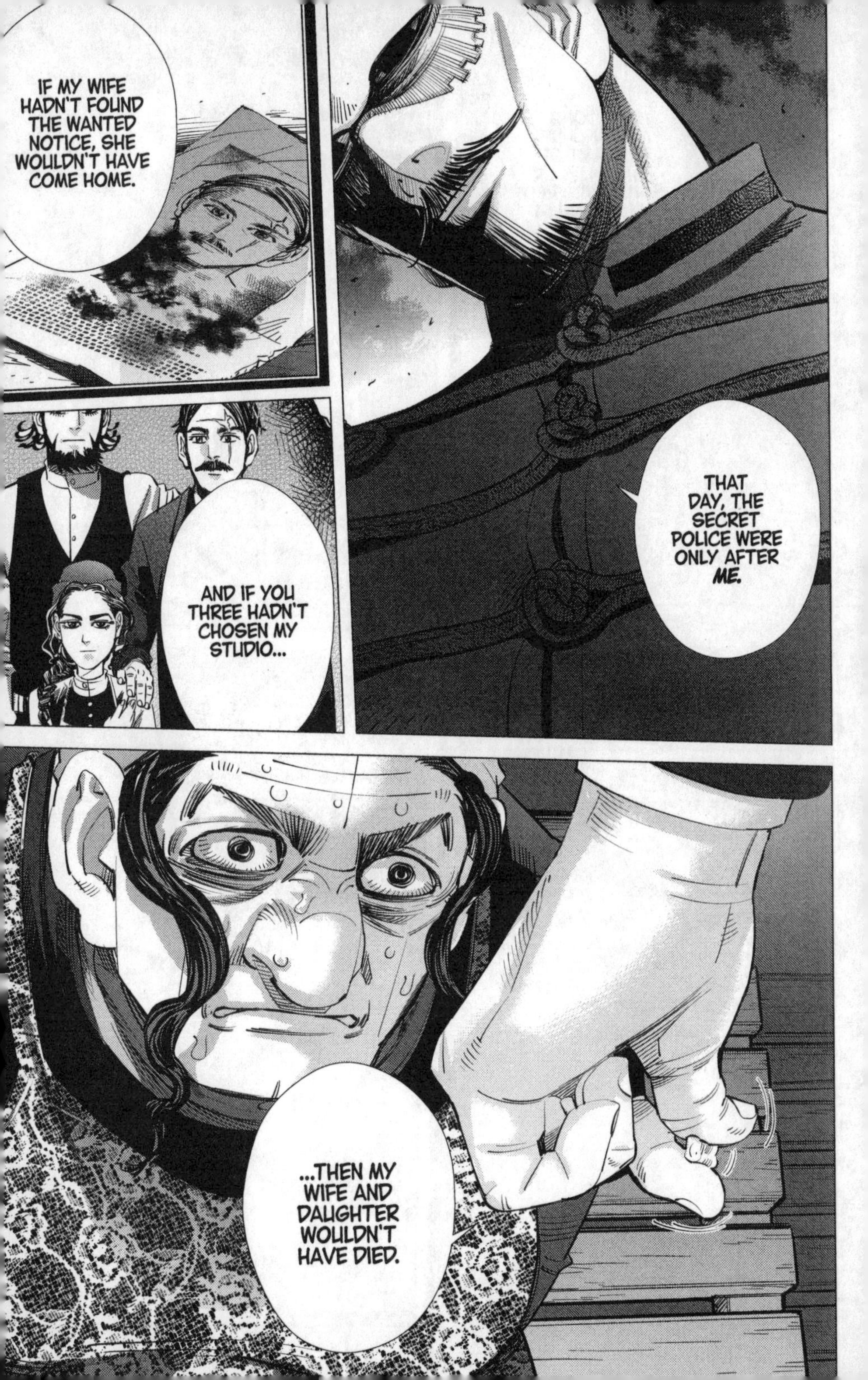
THAT DAY, THE SECRET POLICE WERE ONLY AFTER *ME.*
IF MY WIFE HADN'T FOUND THE WANTED NOTICE, SHE WOULDN'T HAVE COME HOME.
AND IF YOU THREE HADN'T CHOSEN MY STUDIO...
...THEN MY WIFE AND DAUGHTER WOULDN'T HAVE DIED.

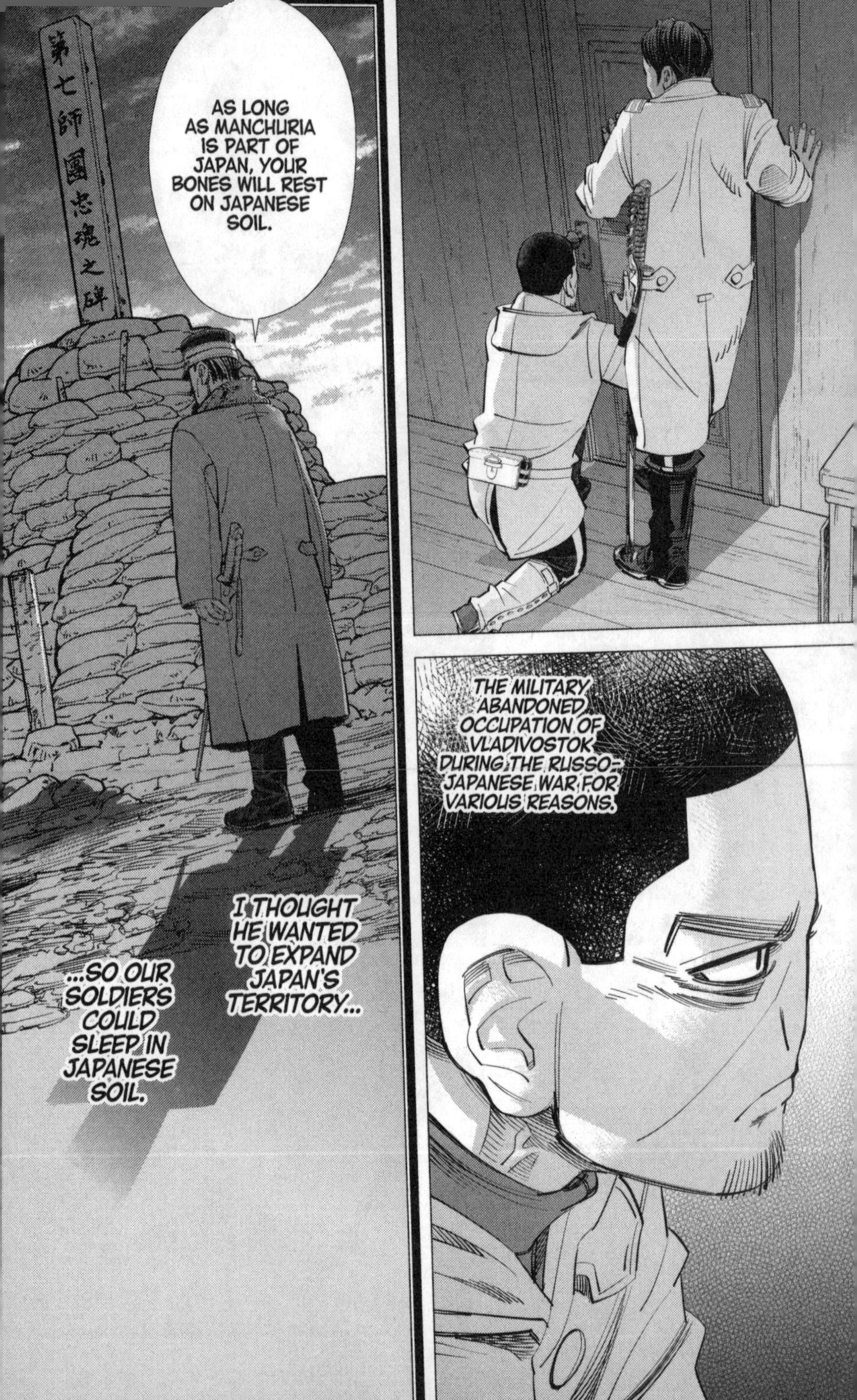
THE MILITARY ABANDONED OCCUPATION OF VLADIVOSTOK DURING THE RUSSO-JAPANESE WAR FOR VARIOUS REASONS.
AS LONG AS MANCHURIA IS PART OF JAPAN, YOUR BONES WILL REST ON JAPANESE SOIL.
第七師團忠魂之碑
I THOUGHT HE WANTED TO EXPAND JAPAN'S TERRITORY...
...SO OUR SOLDIERS COULD SLEEP IN JAPANESE SOIL.

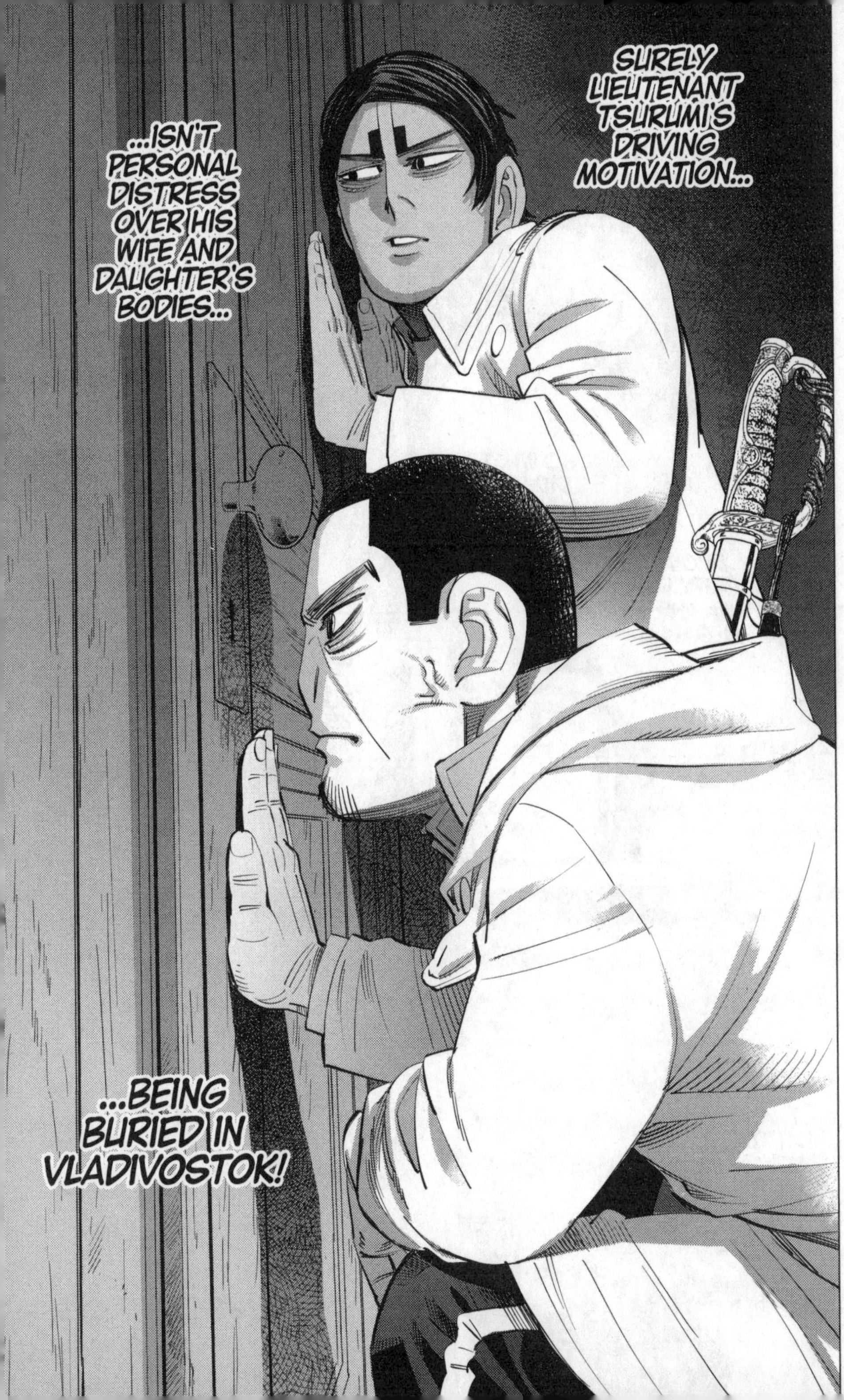
SURELY LIEUTENANT TSURUMI'S DRIVING MOTIVATION...
...ISN'T PERSONAL DISTRESS OVER HIS WIFE AND DAUGHTER'S BODIES...
...BEING BURIED IN VLADIVOSTOK!

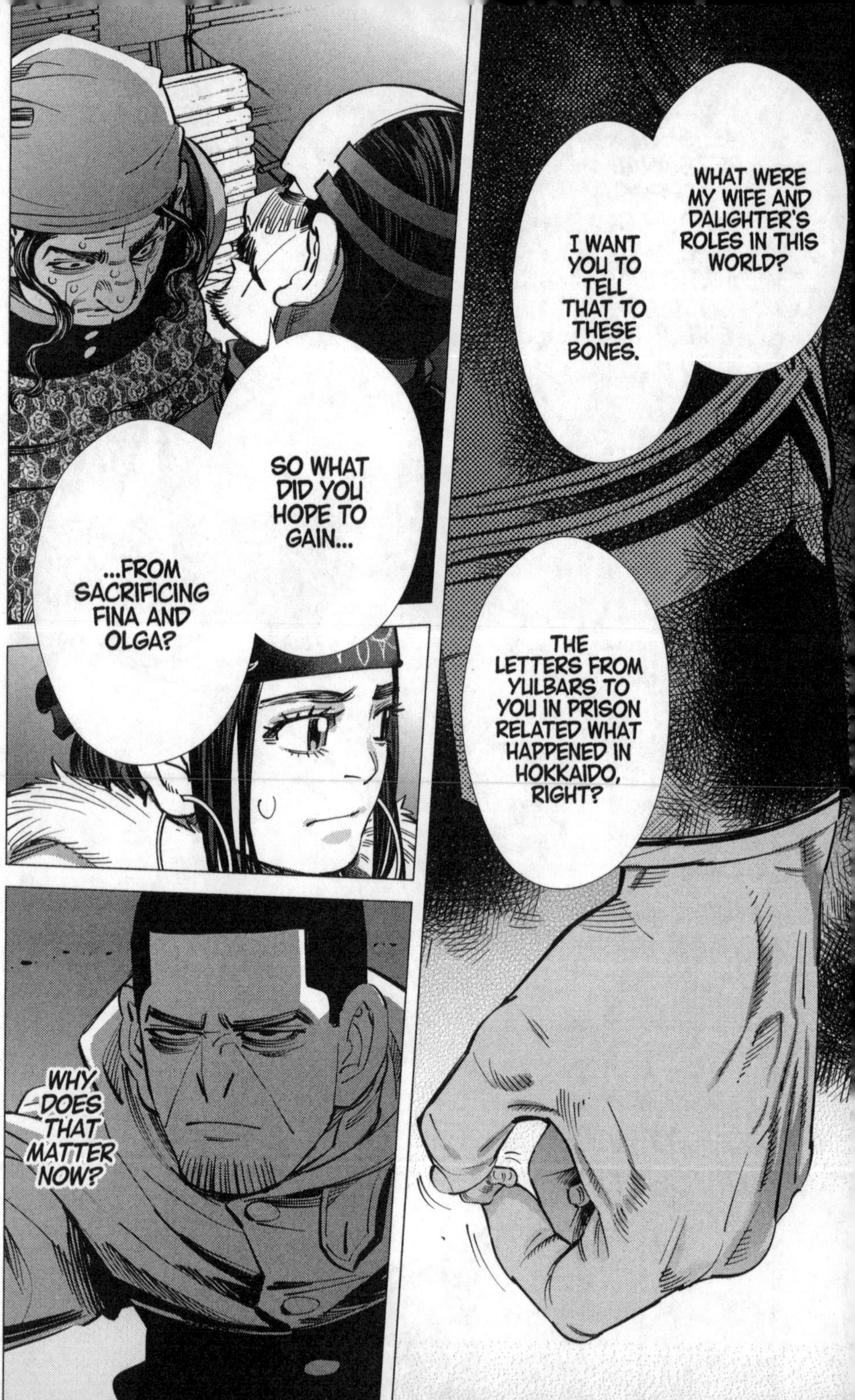
WHAT WERE MY WIFE AND DAUGHTER'S ROLES IN THIS WORLD?
I WANT YOU TO TELL THAT TO THESE BONES.
THE LETTERS FROM YULBARS TO YOU IN PRISON RELATED WHAT HAPPENED IN HOKKAIDO, RIGHT?
SO WHAT DID YOU HOPE TO GAIN...
...FROM SACRIFICING FINA AND OLGA?
WHY DOES THAT MATTER NOW?

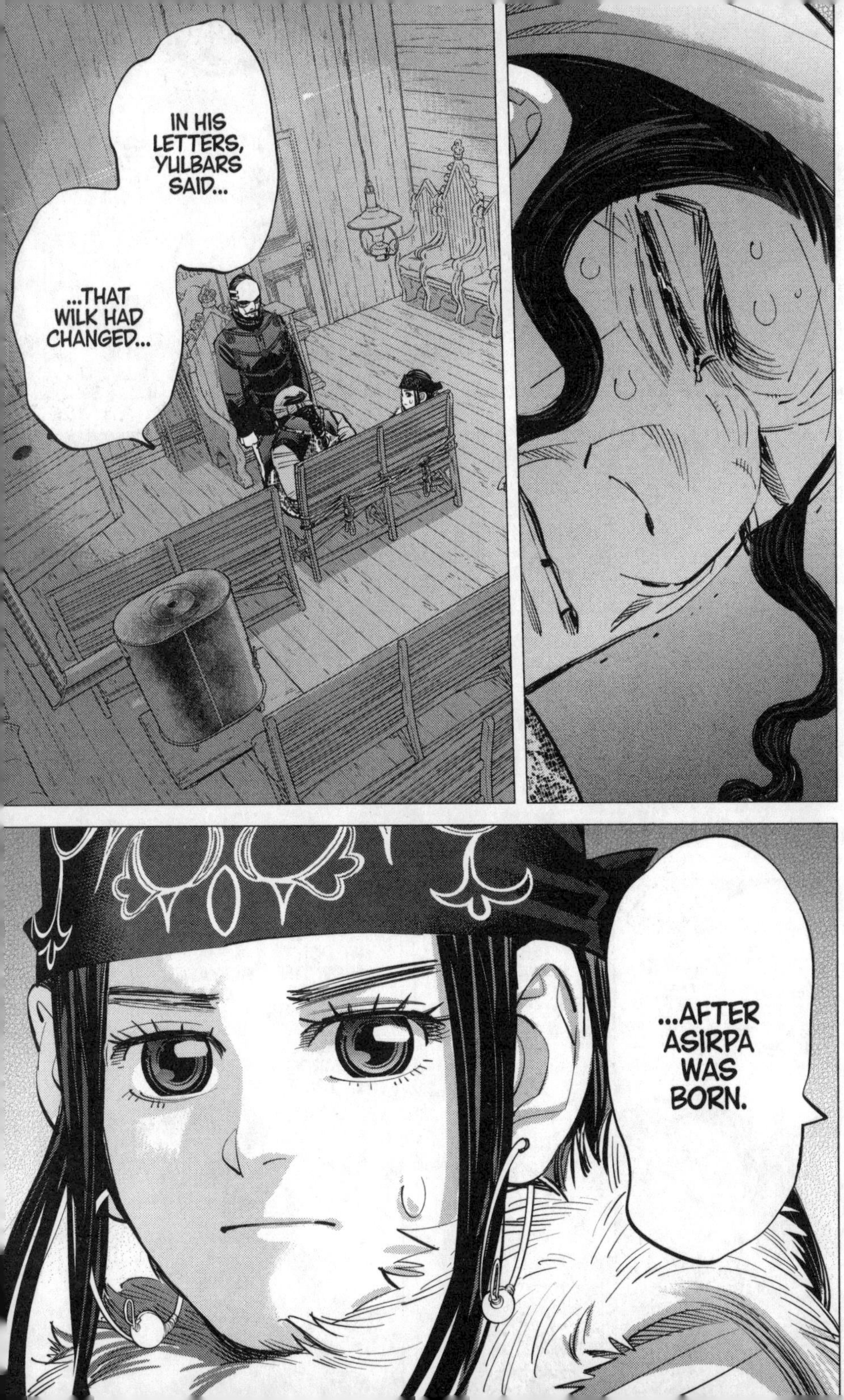
IN HIS LETTERS, YULBARS SAID...
...THAT WILK HAD CHANGED...
...AFTER ASIRPA WAS BORN.

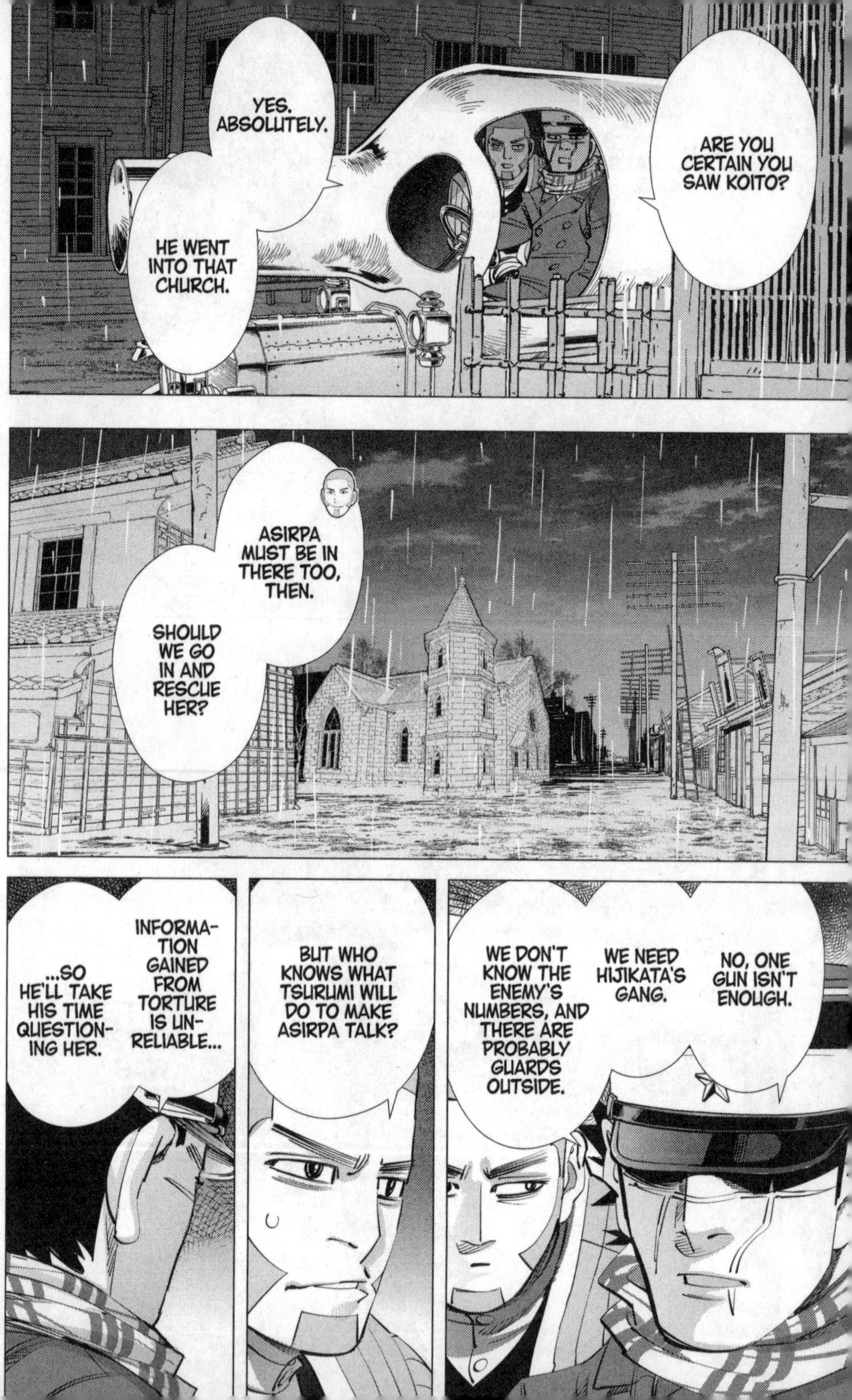
ARE YOU CERTAIN YOU SAW KOITO?
YES. ABSOLUTELY.
HE WENT INTO THAT CHURCH.
ASIRPA MUST BE IN THERE TOO, THEN.
SHOULD WE GO IN AND RESCUE HER?
NO, ONE GUN ISN'T ENOUGH.
WE NEED HIJIKATA'S GANG.
WE DON'T KNOW THE ENEMY'S NUMBERS, AND THERE ARE PROBABLY GUARDS OUTSIDE.
BUT WHO KNOWS WHAT TSURUMI WILL DO TO MAKE ASIRPA TALK?
INFORMATION GAINED FROM TORTURE IS UNRELIABLE...
...SO HE'LL TAKE HIS TIME QUESTIONING HER.

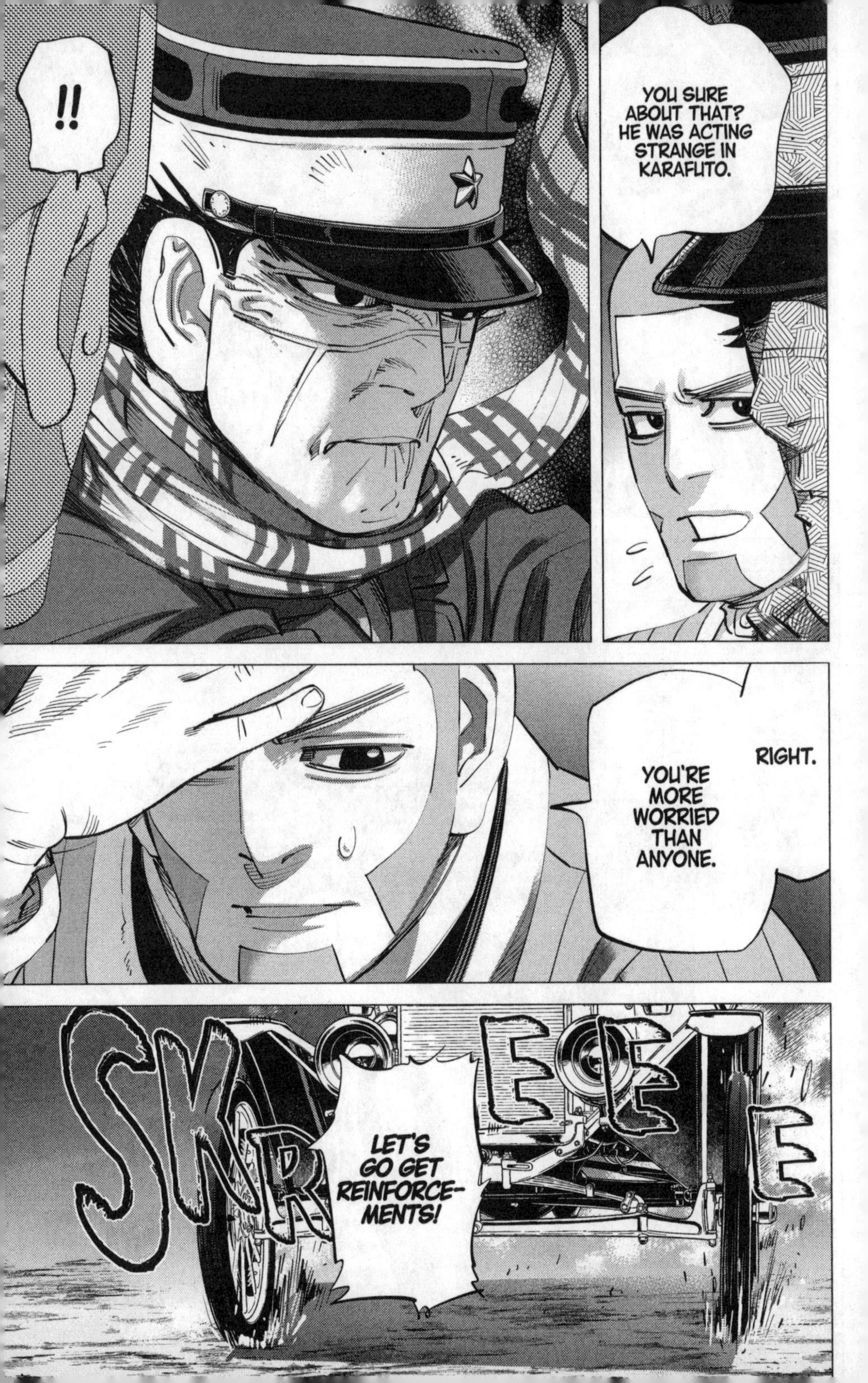
YOU SURE ABOUT THAT? HE WAS ACTING STRANGE IN KARAFUTO.
!!
RIGHT.
YOU'RE MORE WORRIED THAN ANYONE.
SKREEEEE
LET'S GO GET REINFORCE-MENTS!

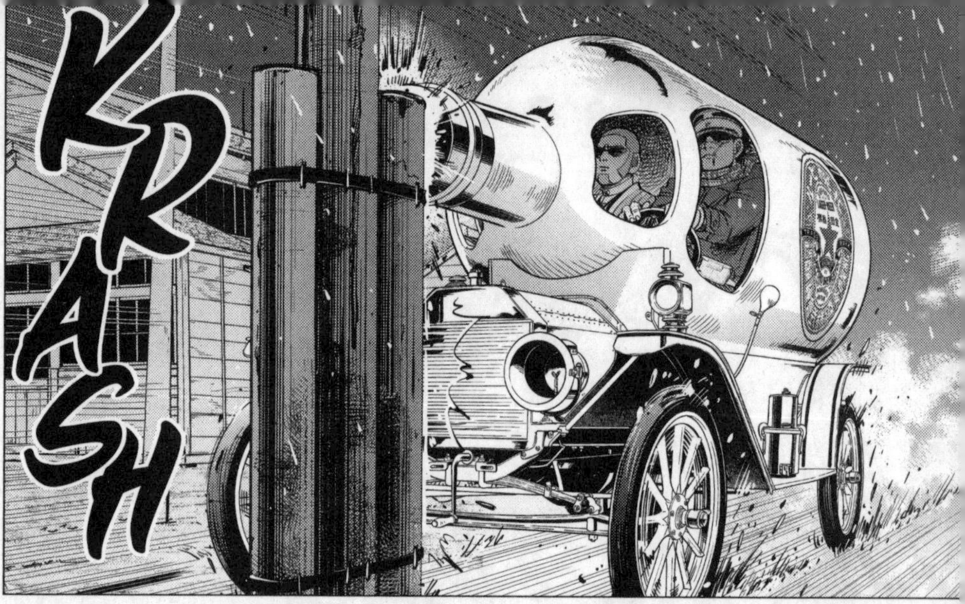
KRASH
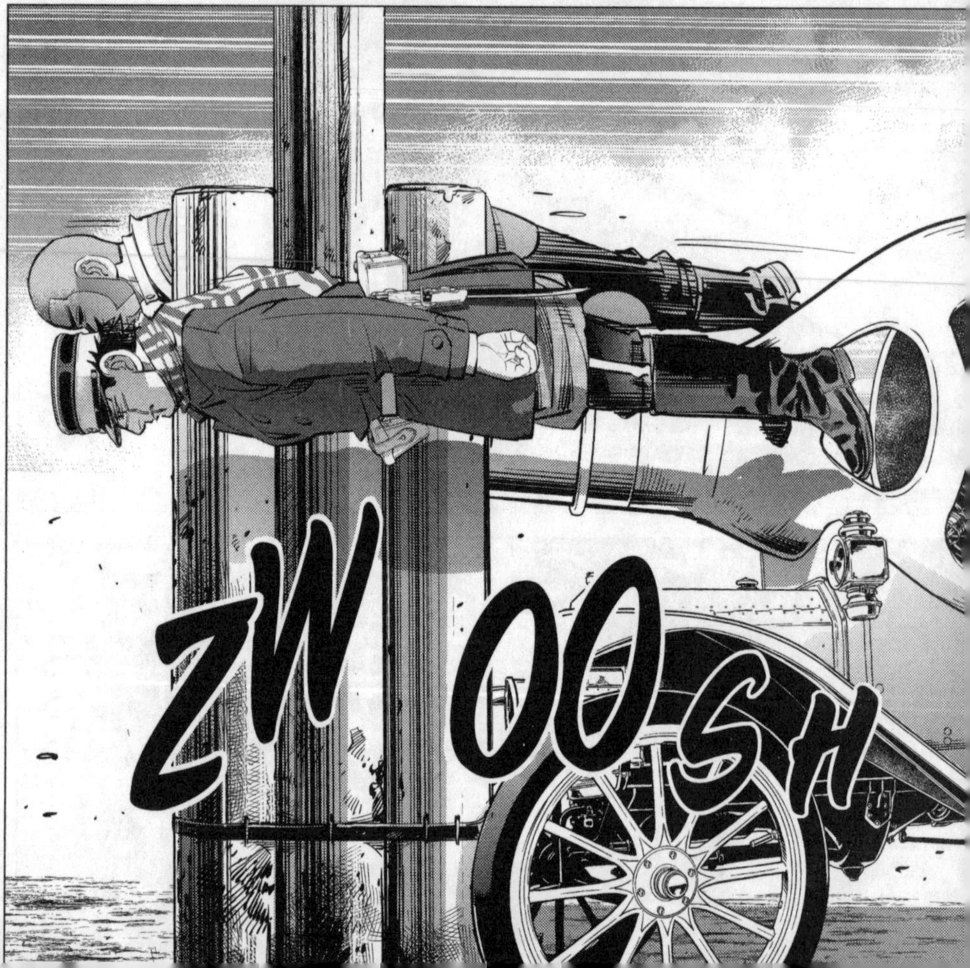
ZWOOSH

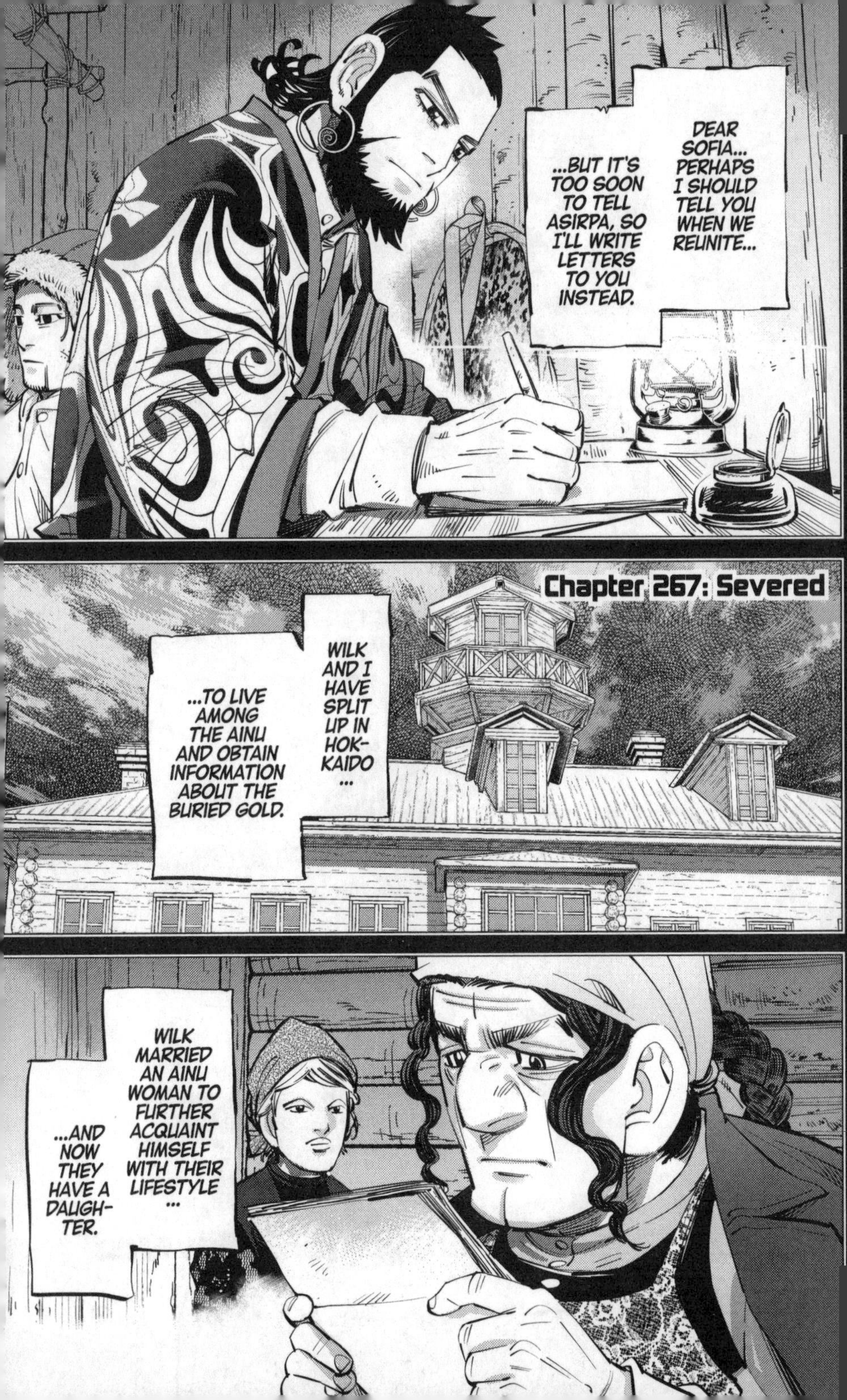
DEAR SOFIA... PERHAPS I SHOULD TELL YOU WHEN WE REUNITE...
...BUT IT'S TOO SOON TO TELL ASIRPA, SO I'LL WRITE LETTERS TO YOU INSTEAD.
Chapter 267: Severed
WILK AND I HAVE SPLIT UP IN HOKKAIDO...
...TO LIVE AMONG THE AINU AND OBTAIN INFORMATION ABOUT THE BURIED GOLD.
WILK MARRIED AN AINU WOMAN TO FURTHER ACQUAINT HIMSELF WITH THEIR LIFESTYLE...
...AND NOW THEY HAVE A DAUGHTER.

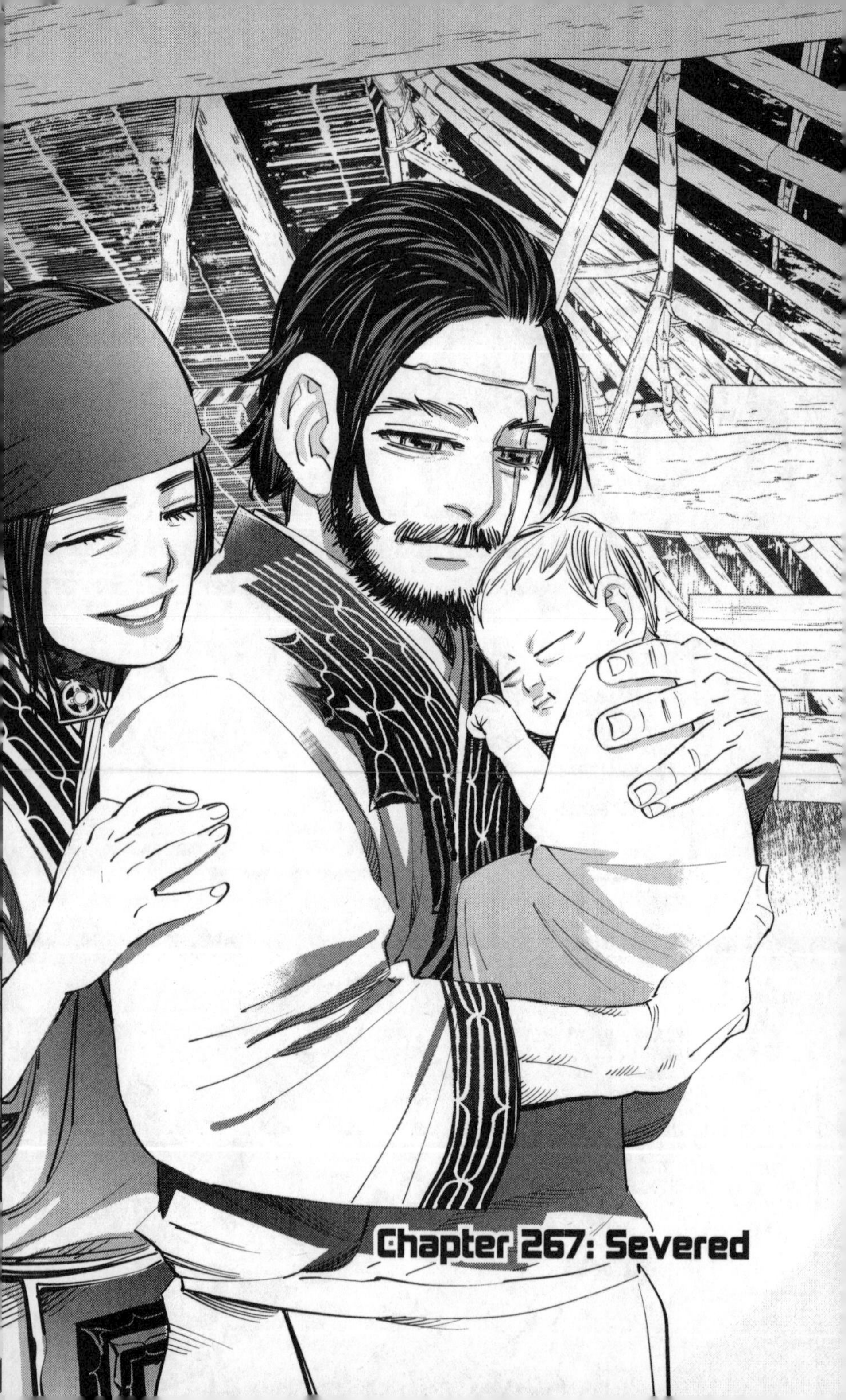
Chapter 267: Severed

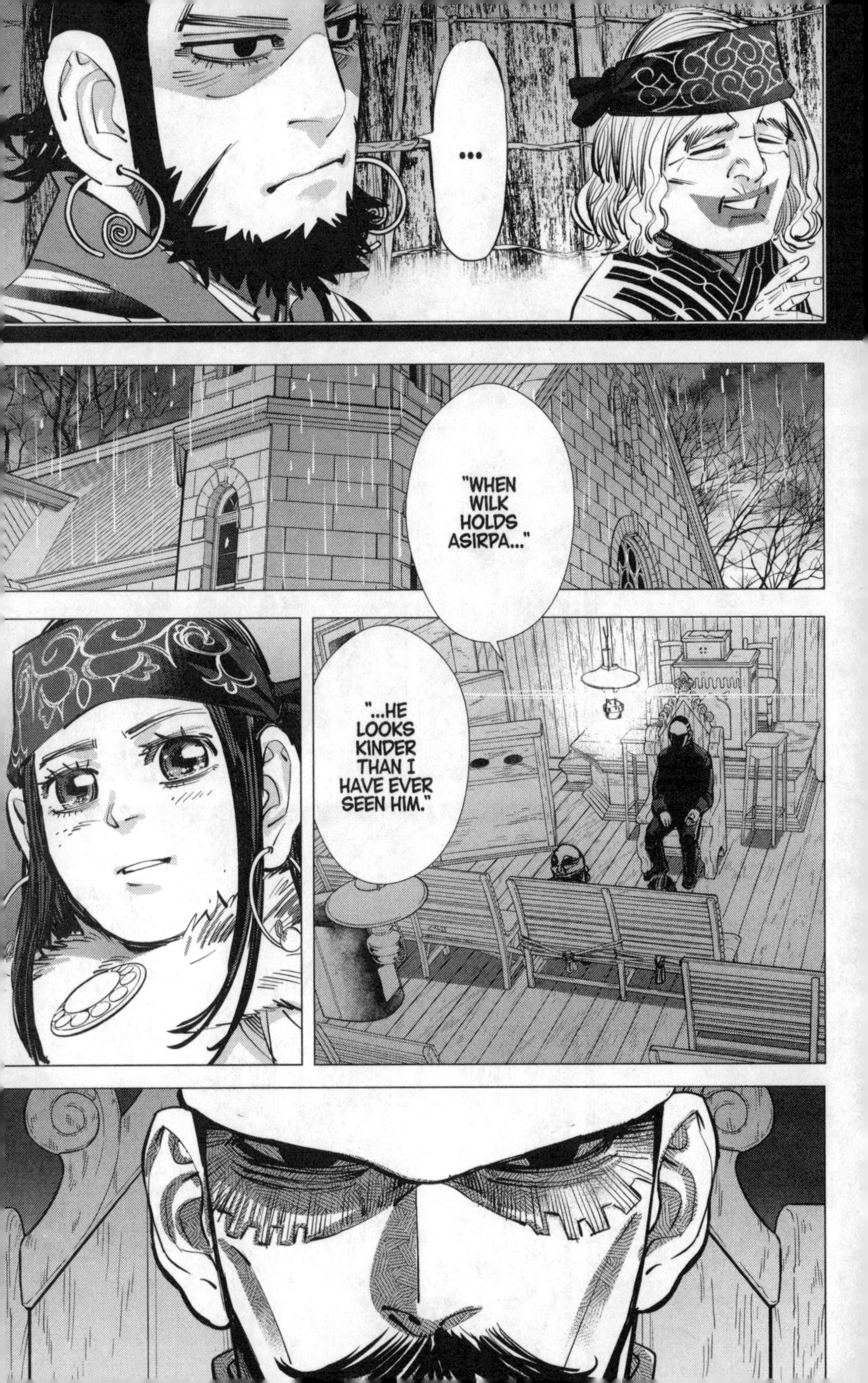
...
"WHEN WILK HOLDS ASIRPA..."
"...HE LOOKS KINDER THAN I HAVE EVER SEEN HIM."

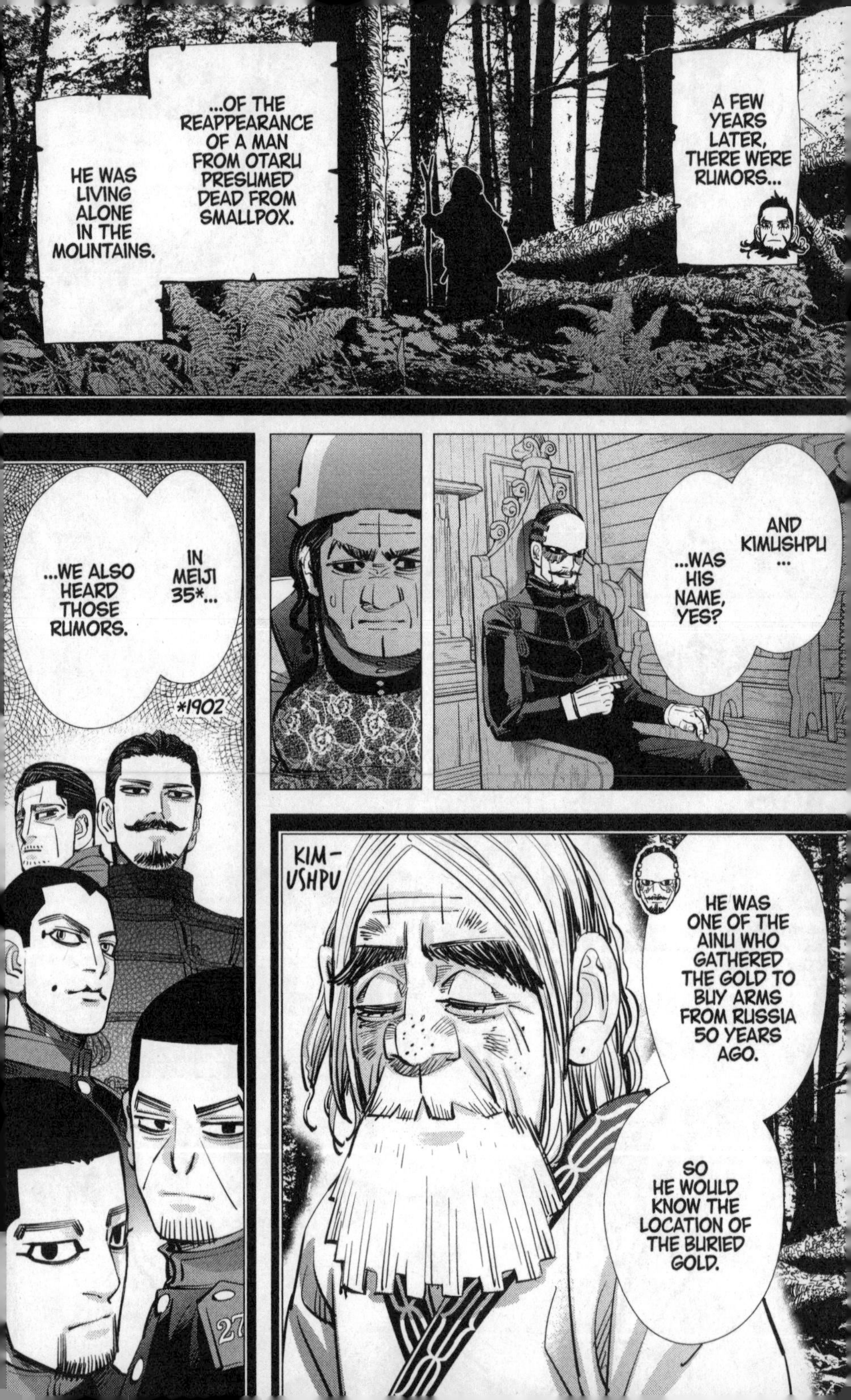
A FEW YEARS LATER, THERE WERE RUMORS...
...OF THE REAPPEARANCE OF A MAN FROM OTARU PRESUMED DEAD FROM SMALLPOX.
HE WAS LIVING ALONE IN THE MOUNTAINS.
AND KIMUSHPU...
...WAS HIS NAME, YES?
KIM-USHPU
HE WAS ONE OF THE AINU WHO GATHERED THE GOLD TO BUY ARMS FROM RUSSIA 50 YEARS AGO.
SO HE WOULD KNOW THE LOCATION OF THE BURIED GOLD.
IN MEIJI 35*...
...WE ALSO HEARD THOSE RUMORS.
*1902
27

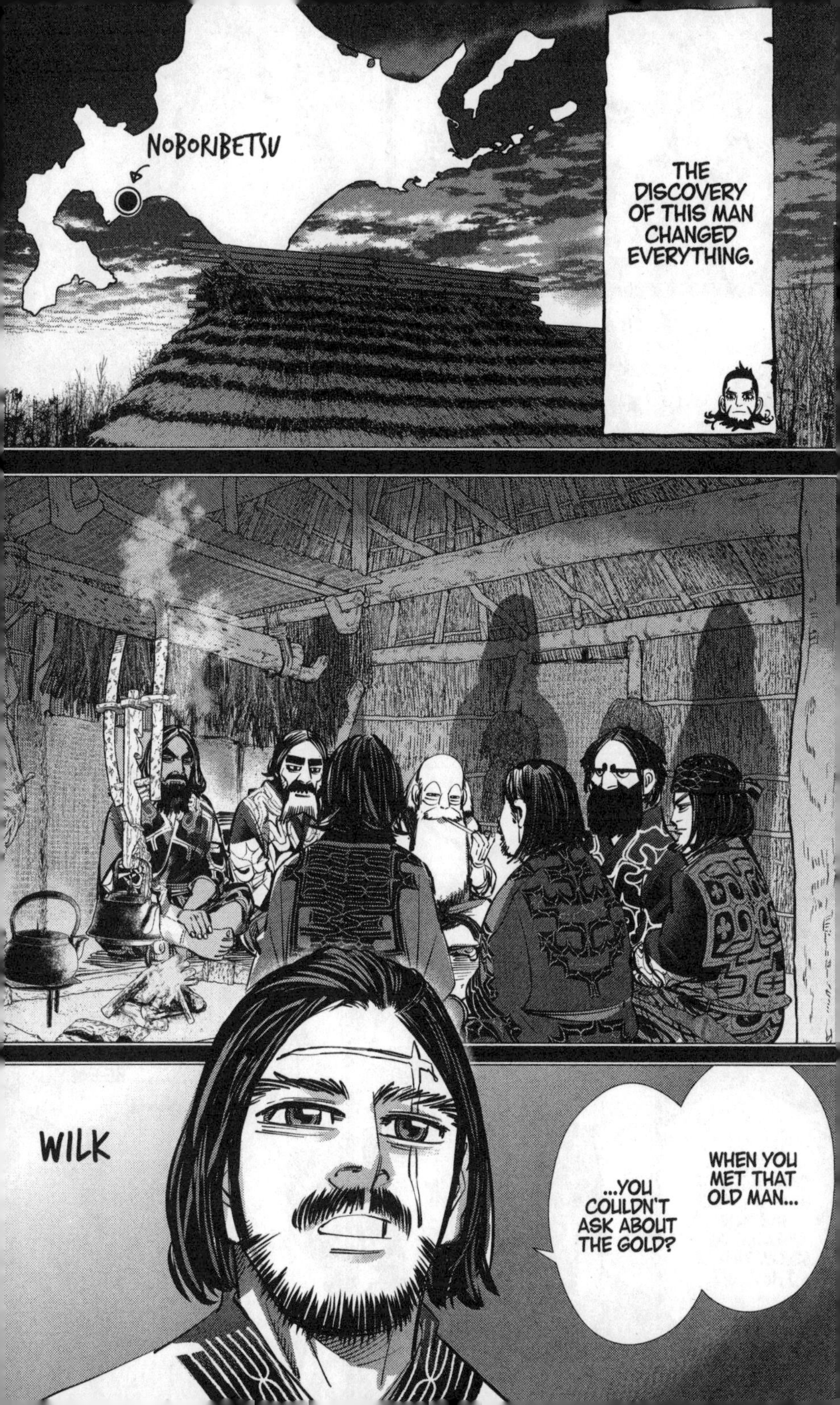
THE DISCOVERY OF THIS MAN CHANGED EVERYTHING.
NOBORIBETSU
WHEN YOU MET THAT OLD MAN...
...YOU COULDN'T ASK ABOUT THE GOLD?
WILK

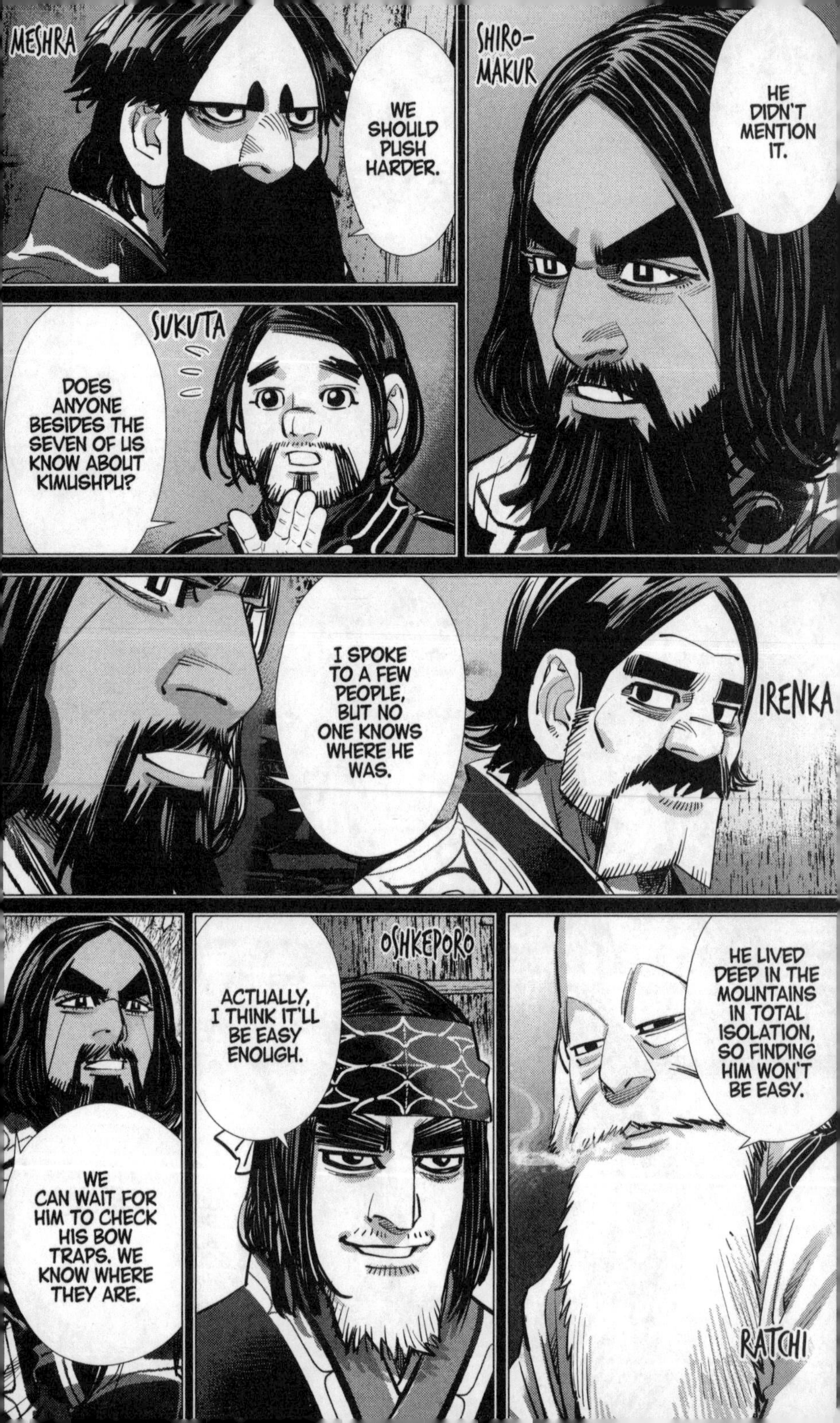
SHIRO-MAKUR
HE DIDN'T MENTION IT.
MESHRA
WE SHOULD PUSH HARDER.
SUKUTA
DOES ANYONE BESIDES THE SEVEN OF US KNOW ABOUT KIMUSHPU?
IRENKA
I SPOKE TO A FEW PEOPLE, BUT NO ONE KNOWS WHERE HE WAS.
HE LIVED DEEP IN THE MOUNTAINS IN TOTAL ISOLATION, SO FINDING HIM WON'T BE EASY.
RATCHI
OSHKEPORO
ACTUALLY, I THINK IT'LL BE EASY ENOUGH.
WE CAN WAIT FOR HIM TO CHECK HIS BOW TRAPS. WE KNOW WHERE THEY ARE.

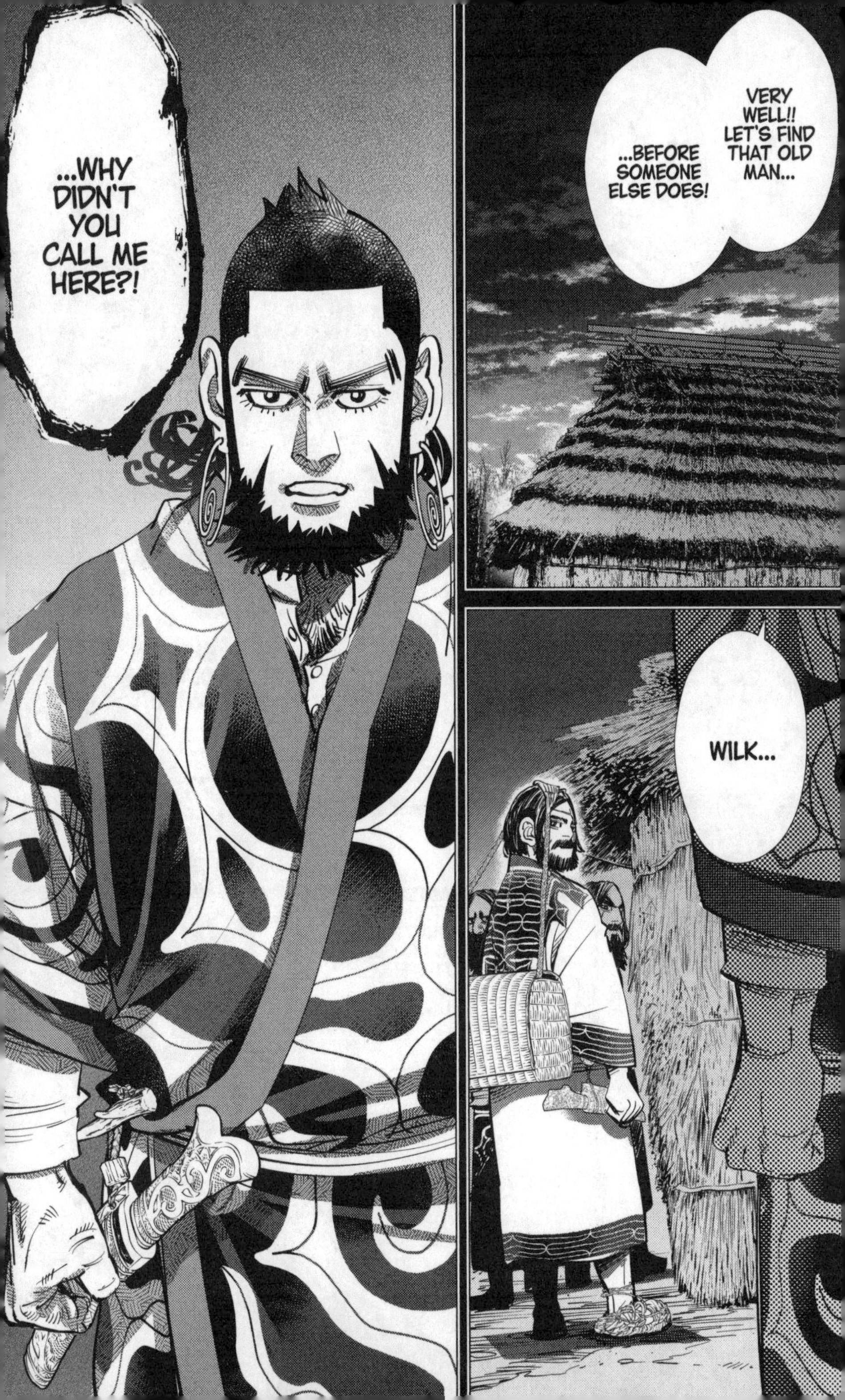
VERY WELL!! LET'S FIND THAT OLD MAN...
...BEFORE SOMEONE ELSE DOES!
WILK...
...WHY DIDN'T YOU CALL ME HERE?!

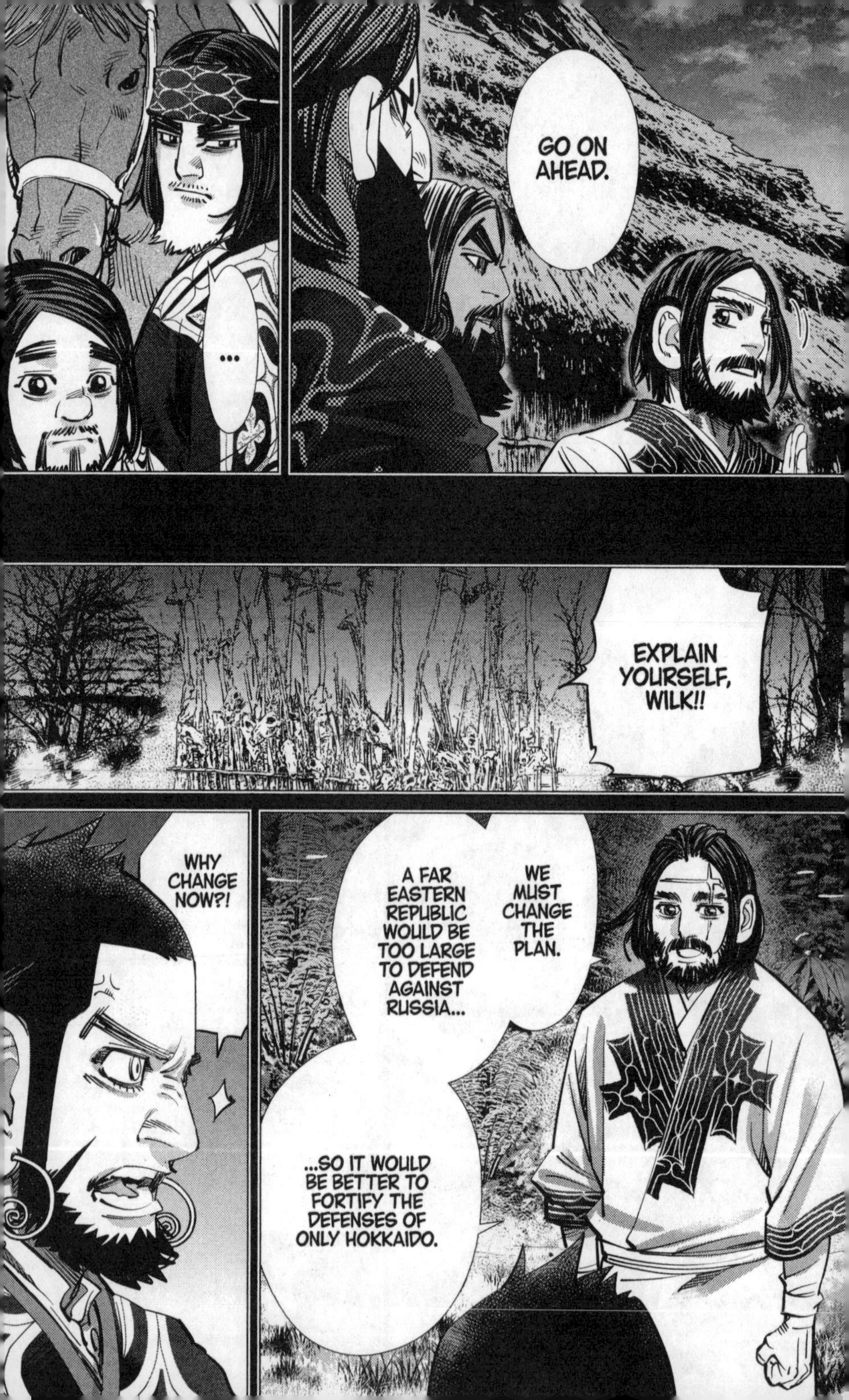
GO ON AHEAD.
...
EXPLAIN YOURSELF, WILK!!
WE MUST CHANGE THE PLAN.
A FAR EASTERN REPUBLIC WOULD BE TOO LARGE TO DEFEND AGAINST RUSSIA...
...SO IT WOULD BE BETTER TO FORTIFY THE DEFENSES OF ONLY HOKKAIDO.
WHY CHANGE NOW?!

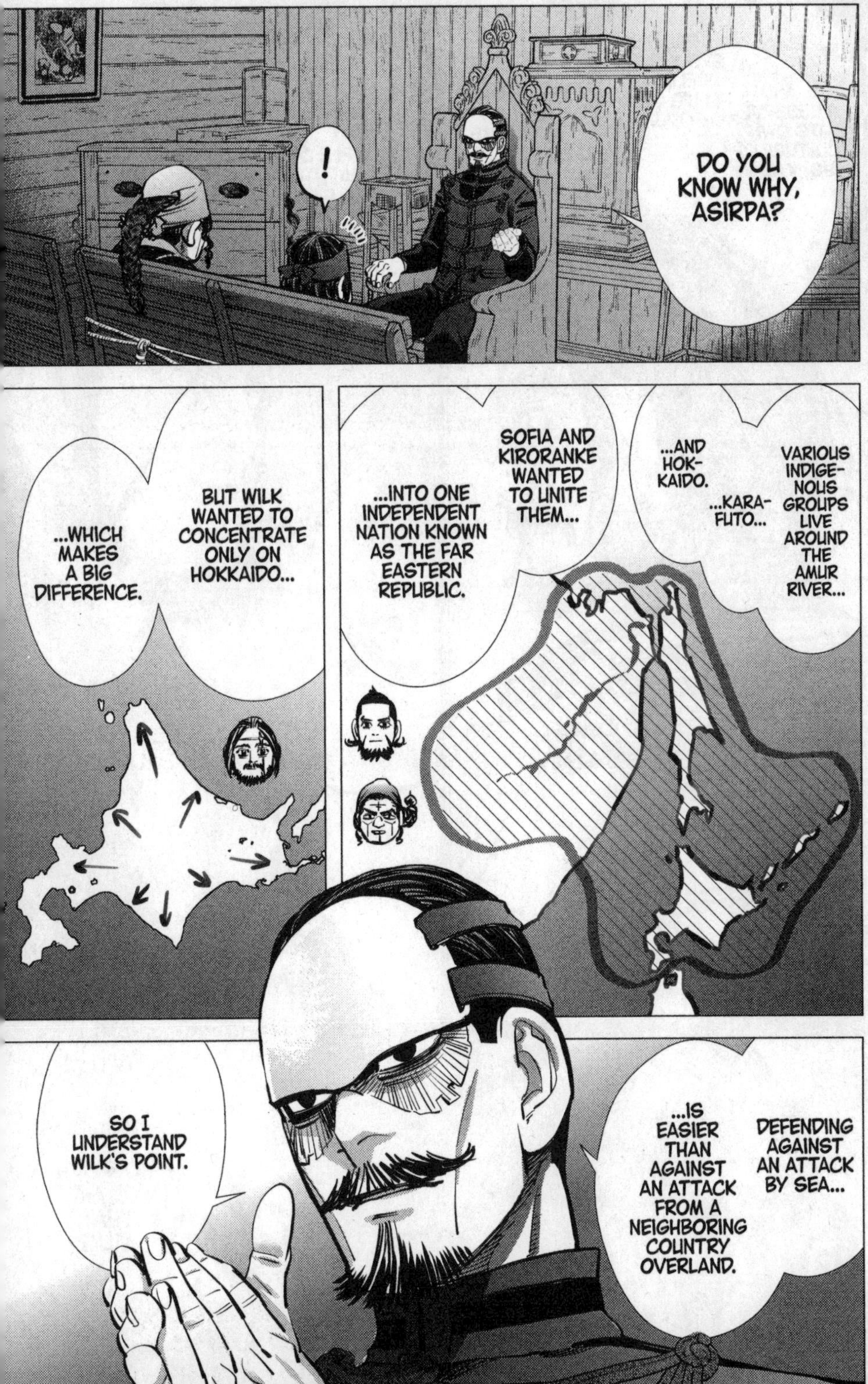
DO YOU KNOW WHY, ASIRPA?
!
VARIOUS INDIGENOUS GROUPS LIVE AROUND THE AMUR RIVER...
...KARAFUTO...
...AND HOKKAIDO.
SOFIA AND KIRORANKE WANTED TO UNITE THEM...
...INTO ONE INDEPENDENT NATION KNOWN AS THE FAR EASTERN REPUBLIC.
BUT WILK WANTED TO CONCENTRATE ONLY ON HOKKAIDO...
...WHICH MAKES A BIG DIFFERENCE.
DEFENDING AGAINST AN ATTACK BY SEA...
...IS EASIER THAN AGAINST AN ATTACK FROM A NEIGHBORING COUNTRY OVERLAND.
SO I UNDERSTAND WILK'S POINT.

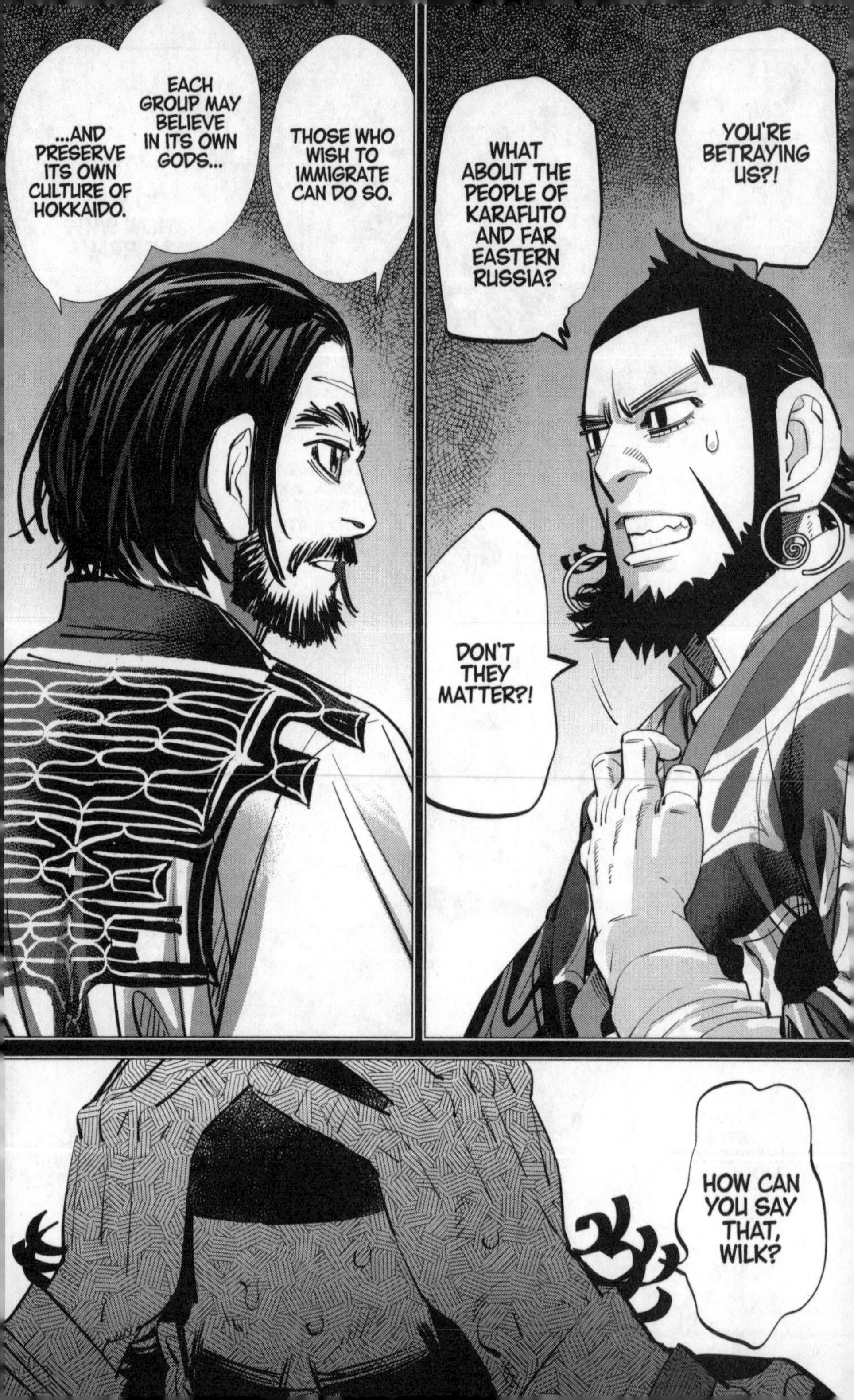
YOU'RE BETRAYING US?!
WHAT ABOUT THE PEOPLE OF KARAFUTO AND FAR EASTERN RUSSIA?
DON'T THEY MATTER?!
THOSE WHO WISH TO IMMIGRATE CAN DO SO.
EACH GROUP MAY BELIEVE IN ITS OWN GODS...
...AND PRESERVE ITS OWN CULTURE OF HOKKAIDO.
HOW CAN YOU SAY THAT, WILK?

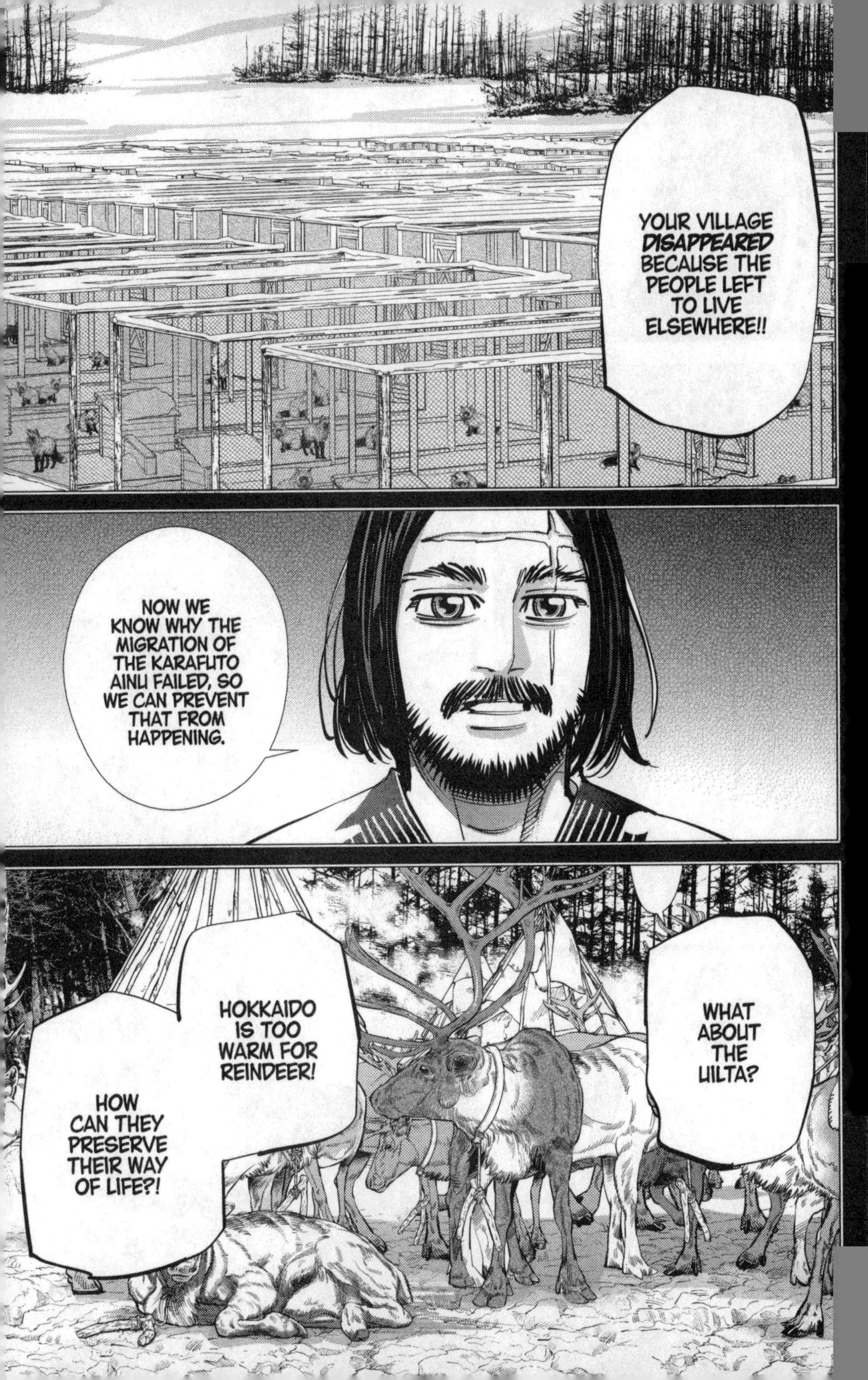
YOUR VILLAGE DISAPPEARED BECAUSE THE PEOPLE LEFT TO LIVE ELSEWHERE!!
NOW WE KNOW WHY THE MIGRATION OF THE KARAFUTO AINU FAILED, SO WE CAN PREVENT THAT FROM HAPPENING.
WHAT ABOUT THE UILTA?
HOKKAIDO IS TOO WARM FOR REINDEER!
HOW CAN THEY PRESERVE THEIR WAY OF LIFE?!

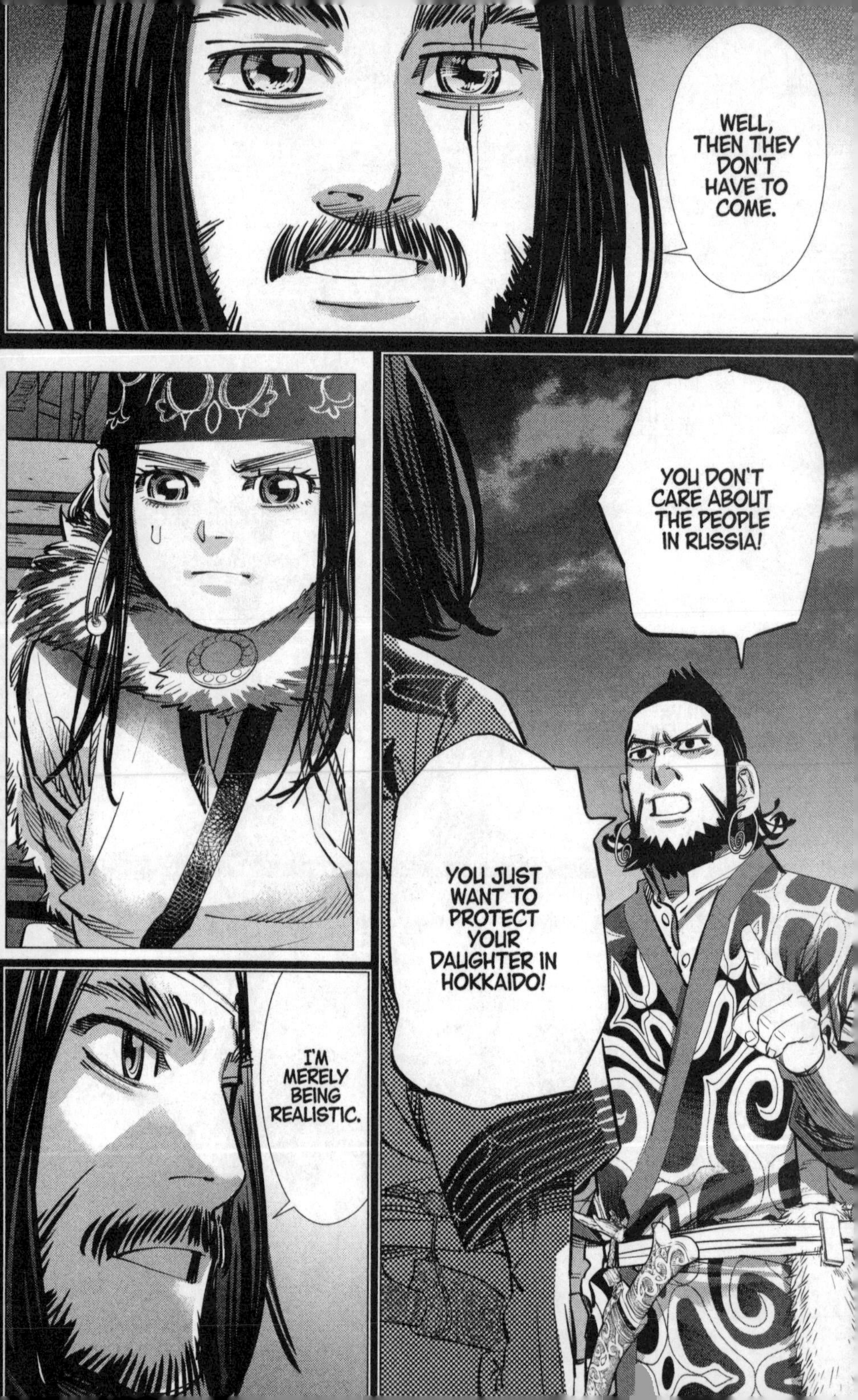
WELL, THEN THEY DON'T HAVE TO COME.
YOU DON'T CARE ABOUT THE PEOPLE IN RUSSIA!
YOU JUST WANT TO PROTECT YOUR DAUGHTER IN HOKKAIDO!
I'M MERELY BEING REALISTIC.

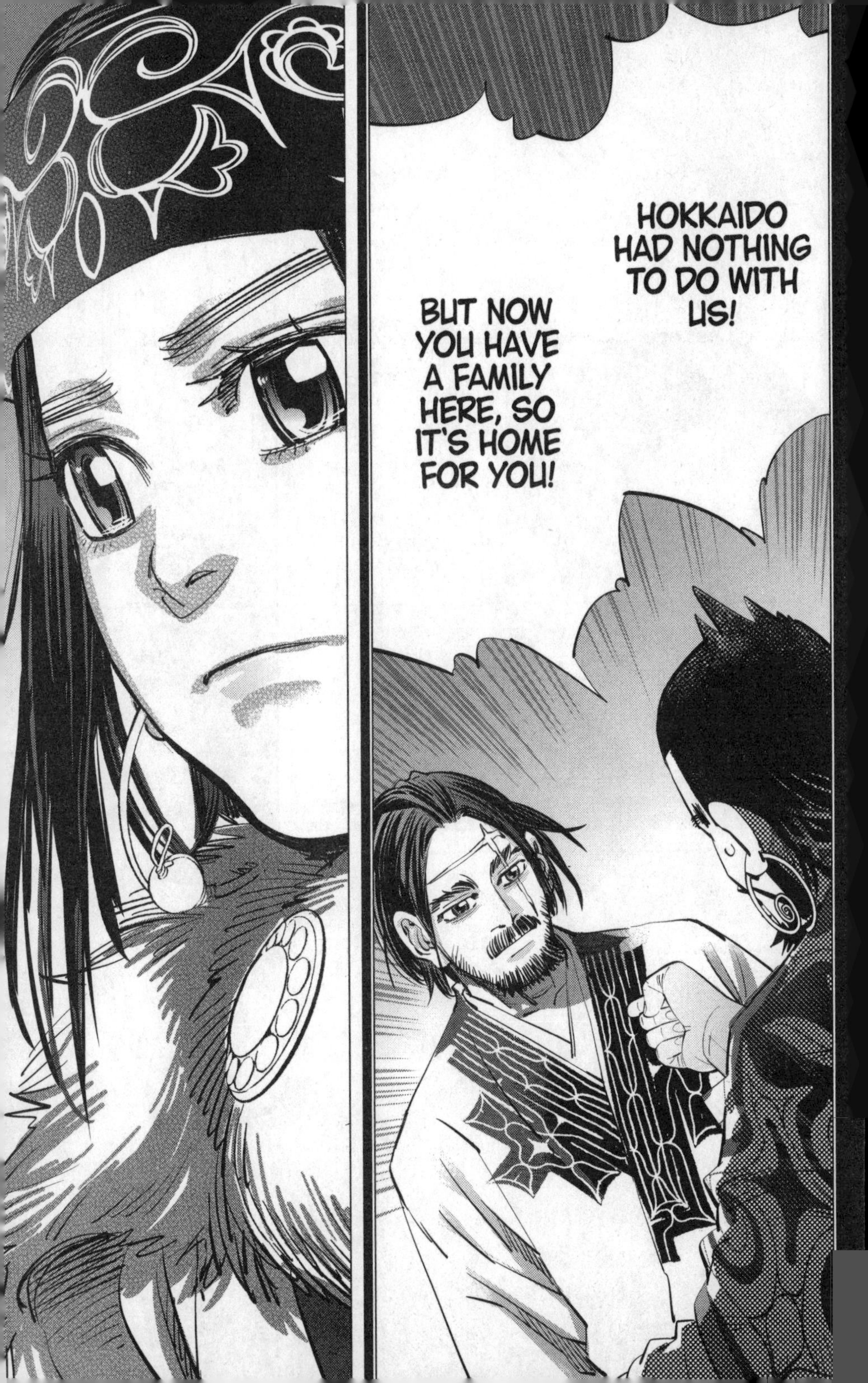
HOKKAIDO HAD NOTHING TO DO WITH US!
BUT NOW YOU HAVE A FAMILY HERE, SO IT'S HOME FOR YOU!

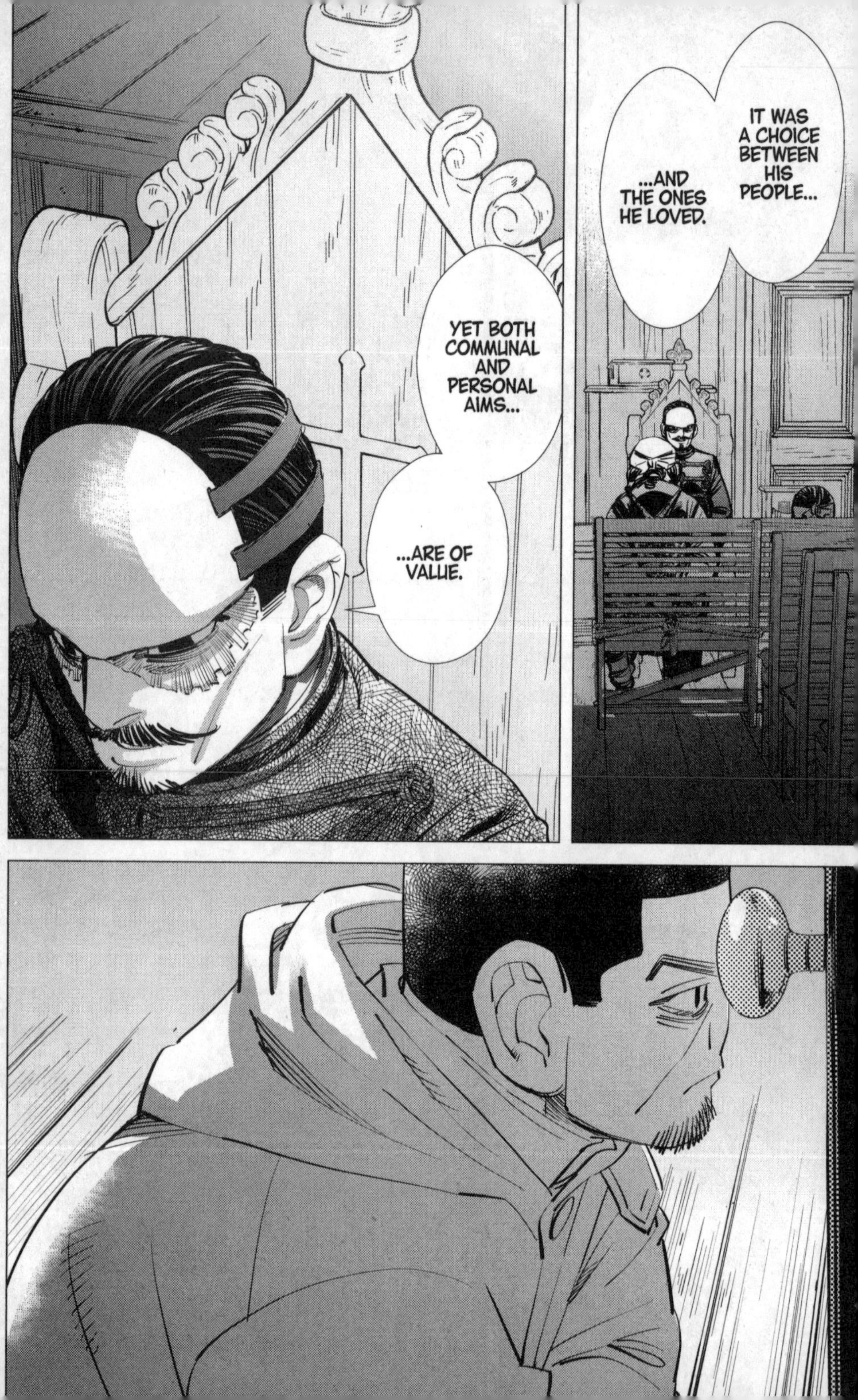
IT WAS A CHOICE BETWEEN HIS PEOPLE...
...AND THE ONES HE LOVED.
YET BOTH COMMUNAL AND PERSONAL AIMS...
...ARE OF VALUE.

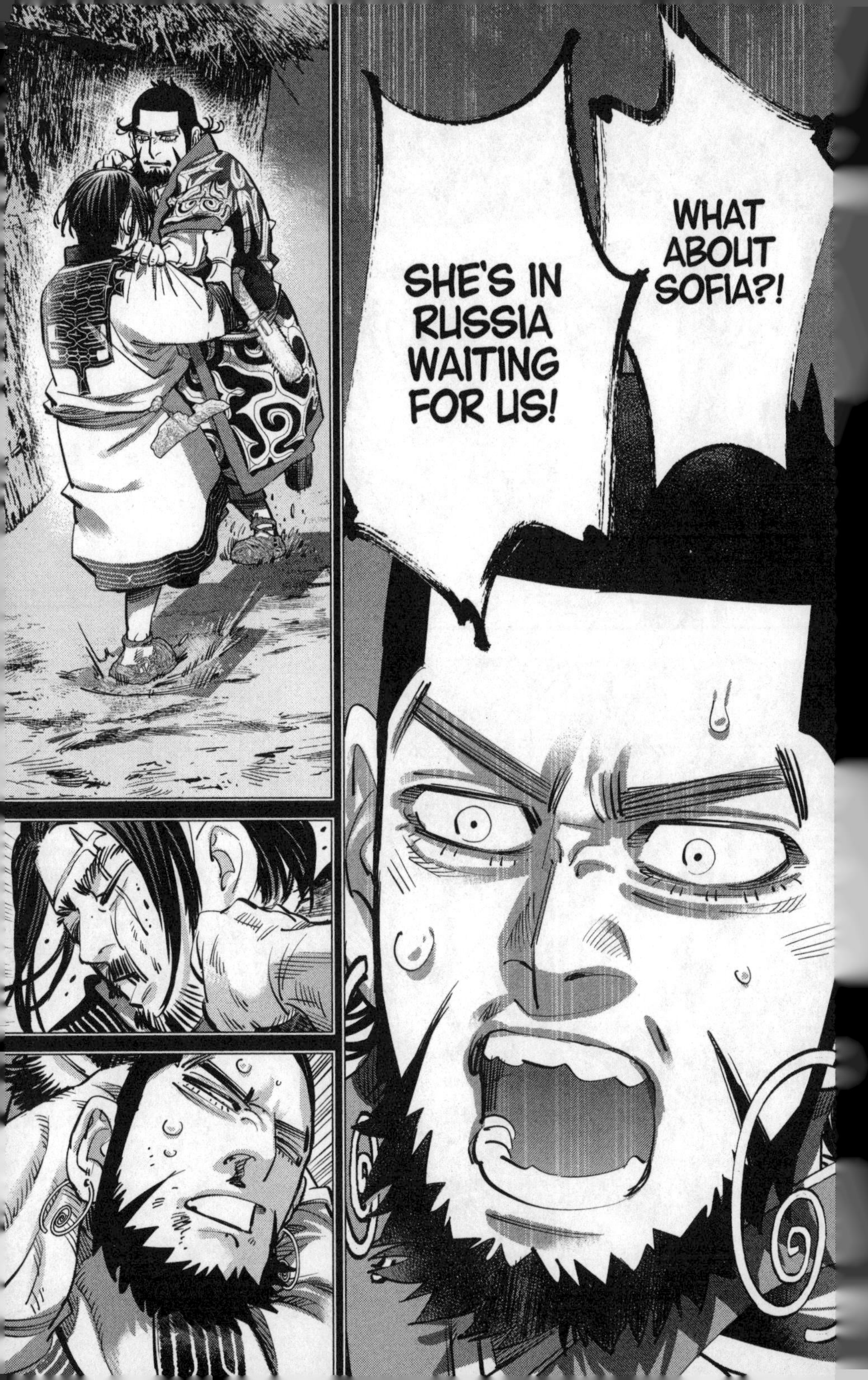
WHAT ABOUT SOFIA?!
SHE'S IN RUSSIA WAITING FOR US!

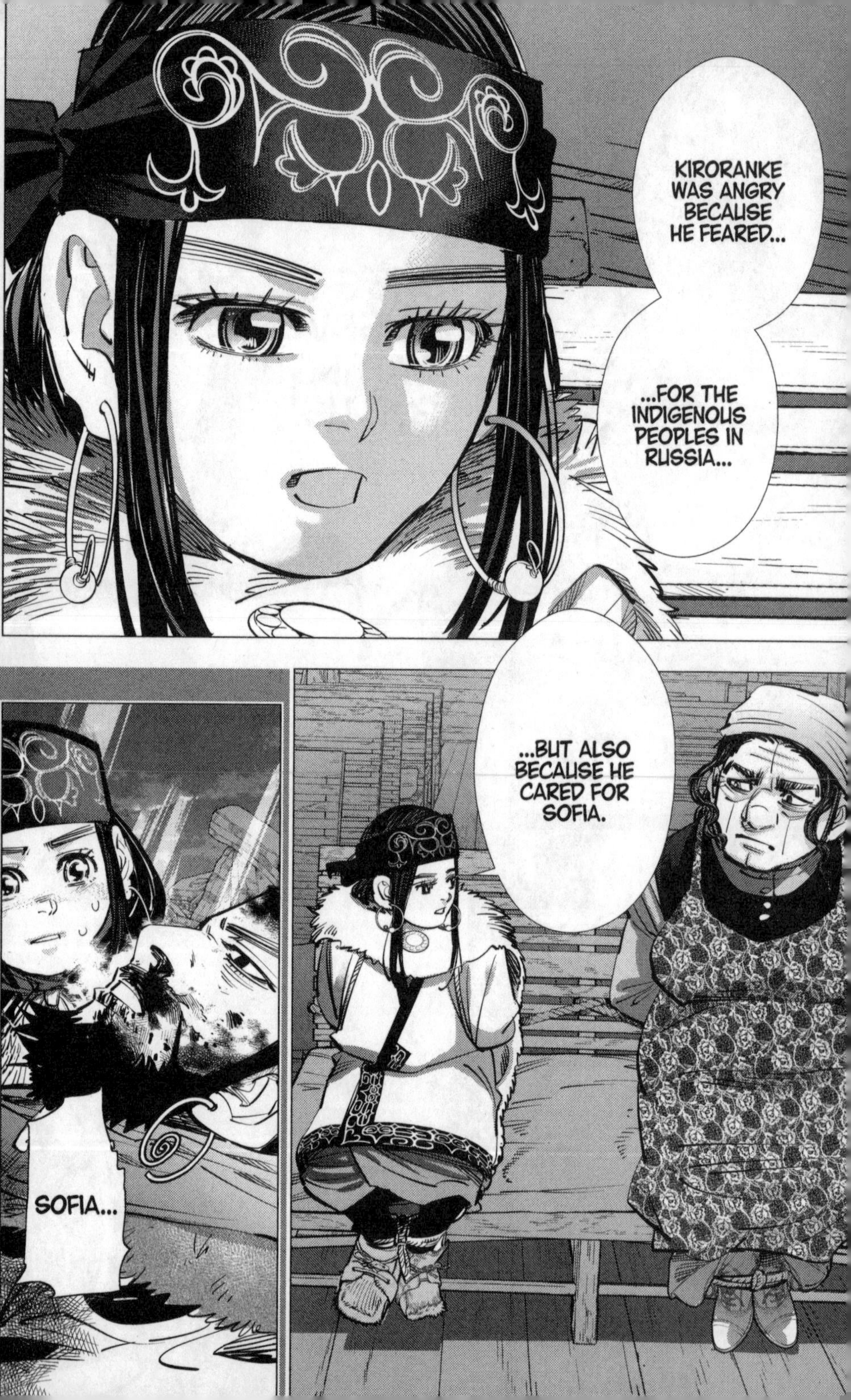
KIRORANKE WAS ANGRY BECAUSE HE FEARED...
...FOR THE INDIGENOUS PEOPLES IN RUSSIA...
...BUT ALSO BECAUSE HE CARED FOR SOFIA.
SOFIA...

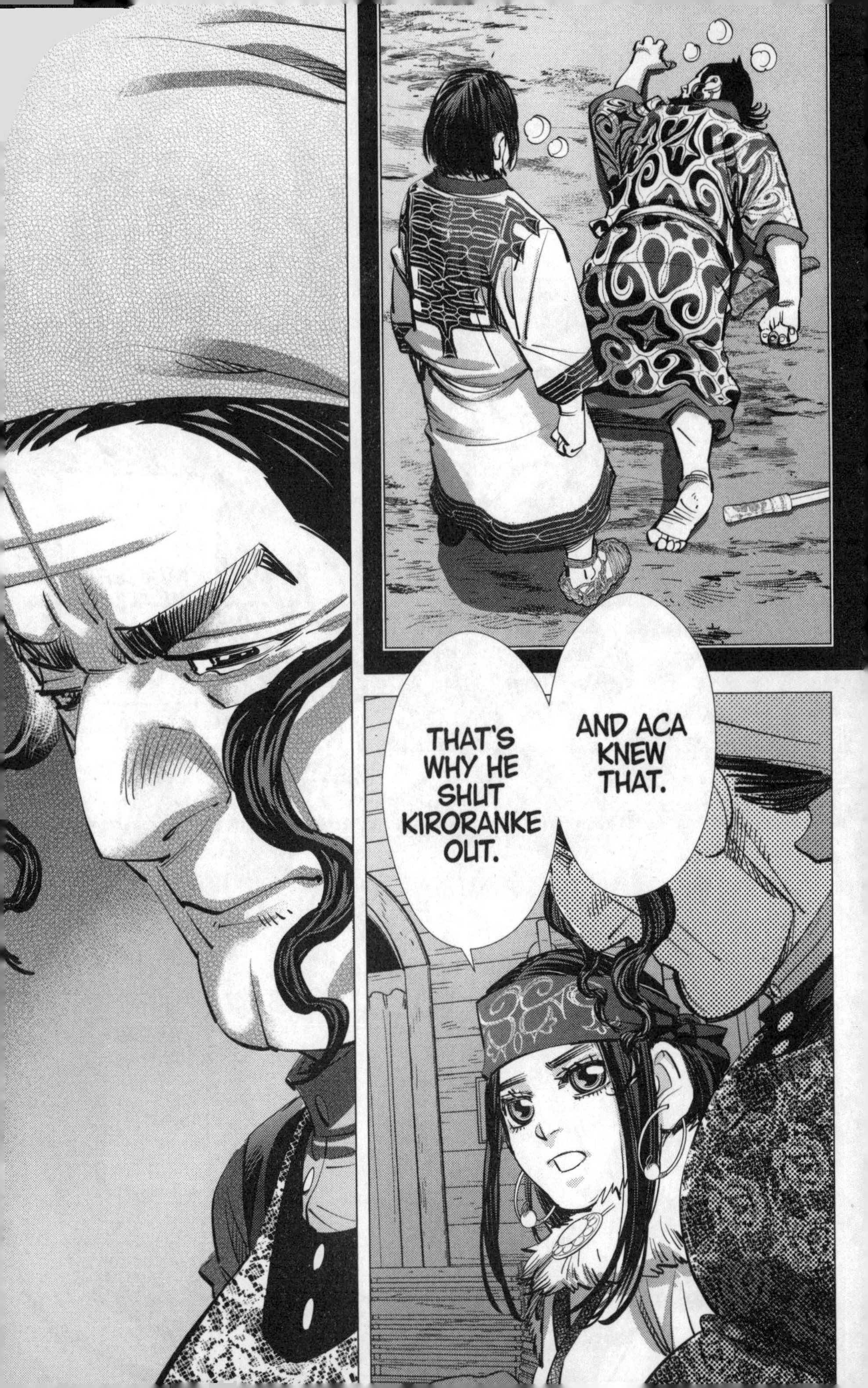
AND ACA KNEW THAT.
THAT'S WHY HE SHUT KIRORANKE OUT.

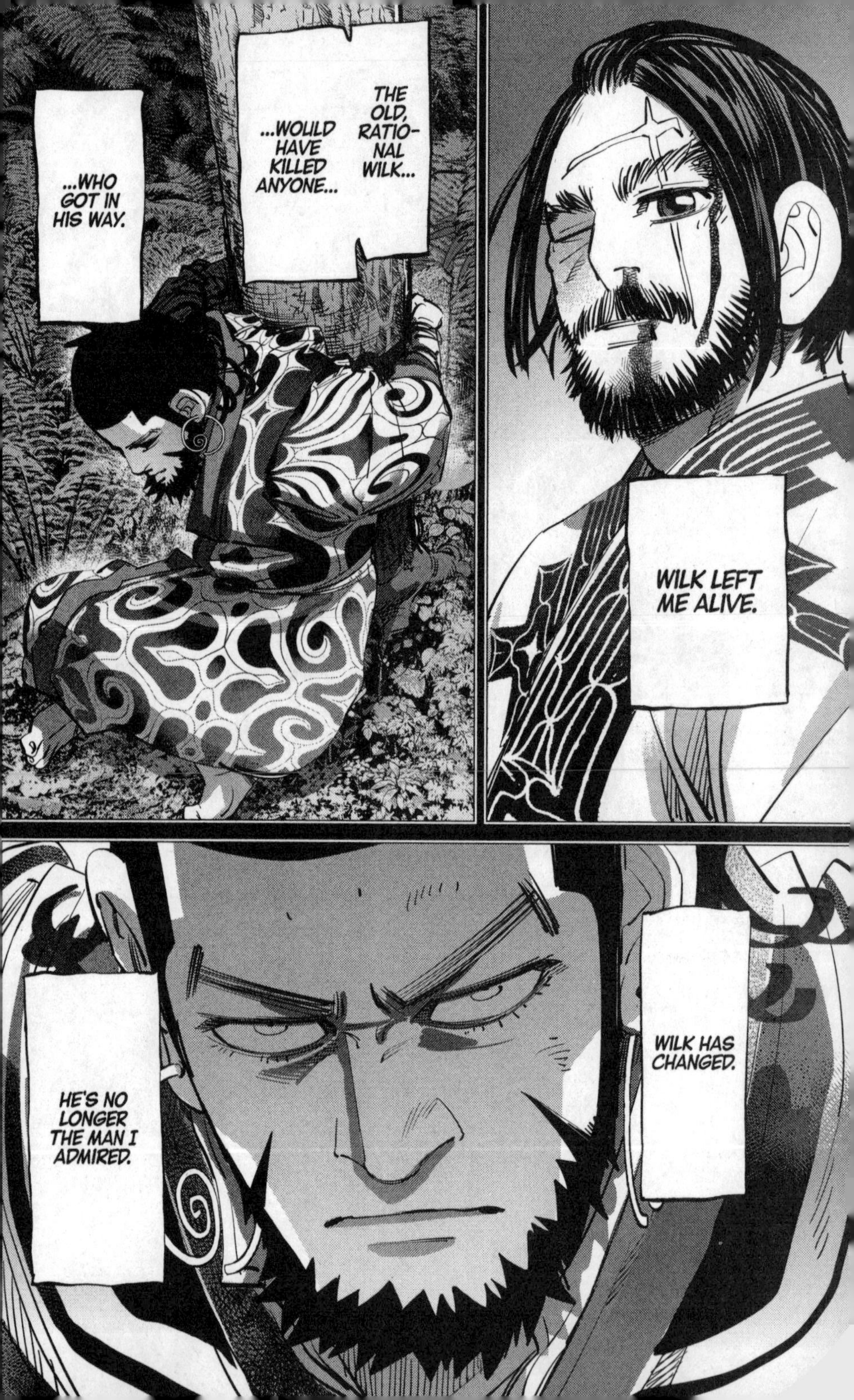
WILK LEFT ME ALIVE.
THE OLD, RATIO-NAL WILK...
...WOULD HAVE KILLED ANYONE...
...WHO GOT IN HIS WAY.
WILK HAS CHANGED.
HE'S NO LONGER THE MAN I ADMIRED.

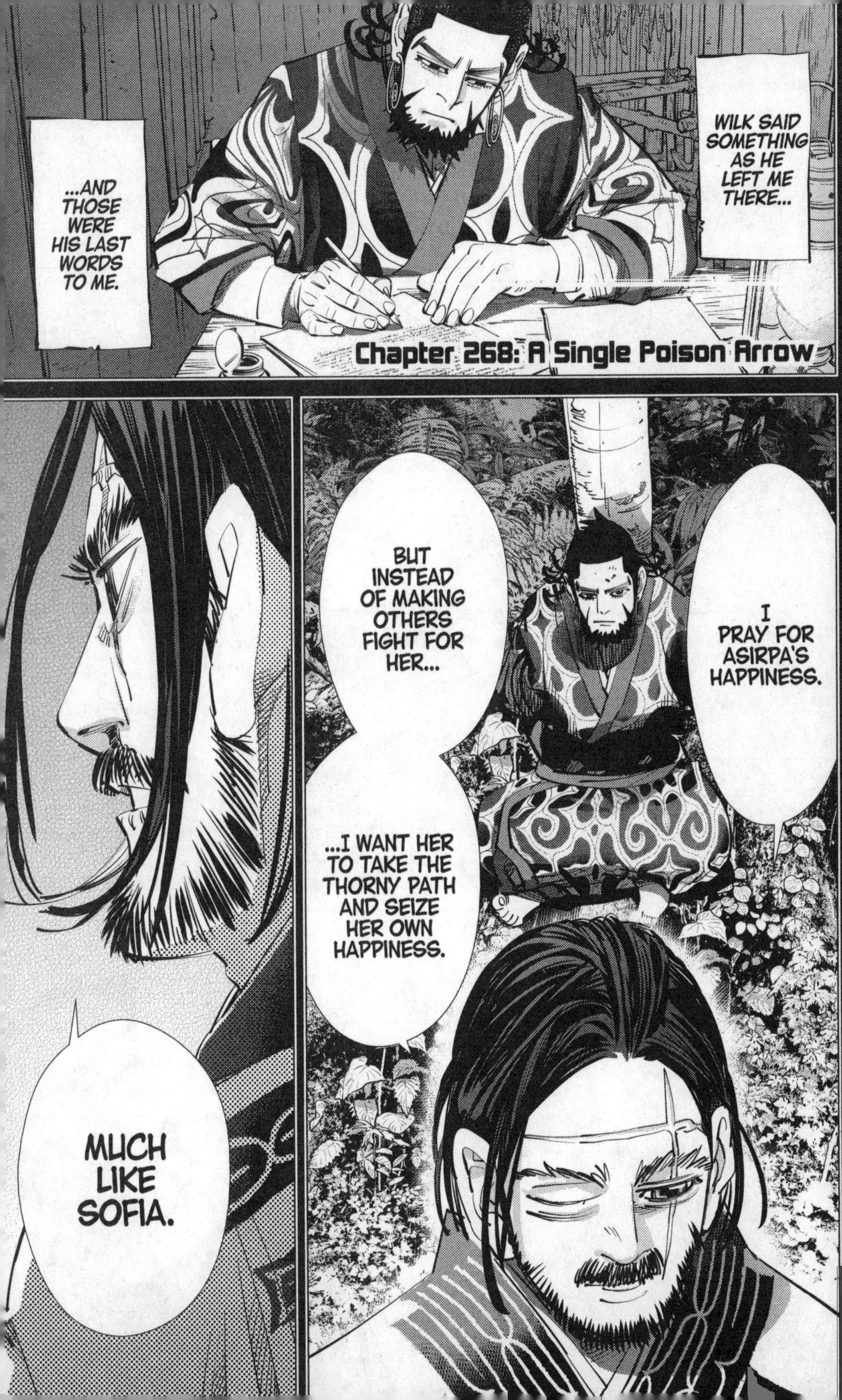
WILK SAID SOMETHING AS HE LEFT ME THERE...
...AND THOSE WERE HIS LAST WORDS TO ME.
Chapter 268: A Single Poison Arrow
I PRAY FOR ASIRPA'S HAPPINESS.
BUT INSTEAD OF MAKING OTHERS FIGHT FOR HER...
...I WANT HER TO TAKE THE THORNY PATH AND SEIZE HER OWN HAPPINESS.
MUCH LIKE SOFIA.

Chapter 268: A Single Poison Arrow

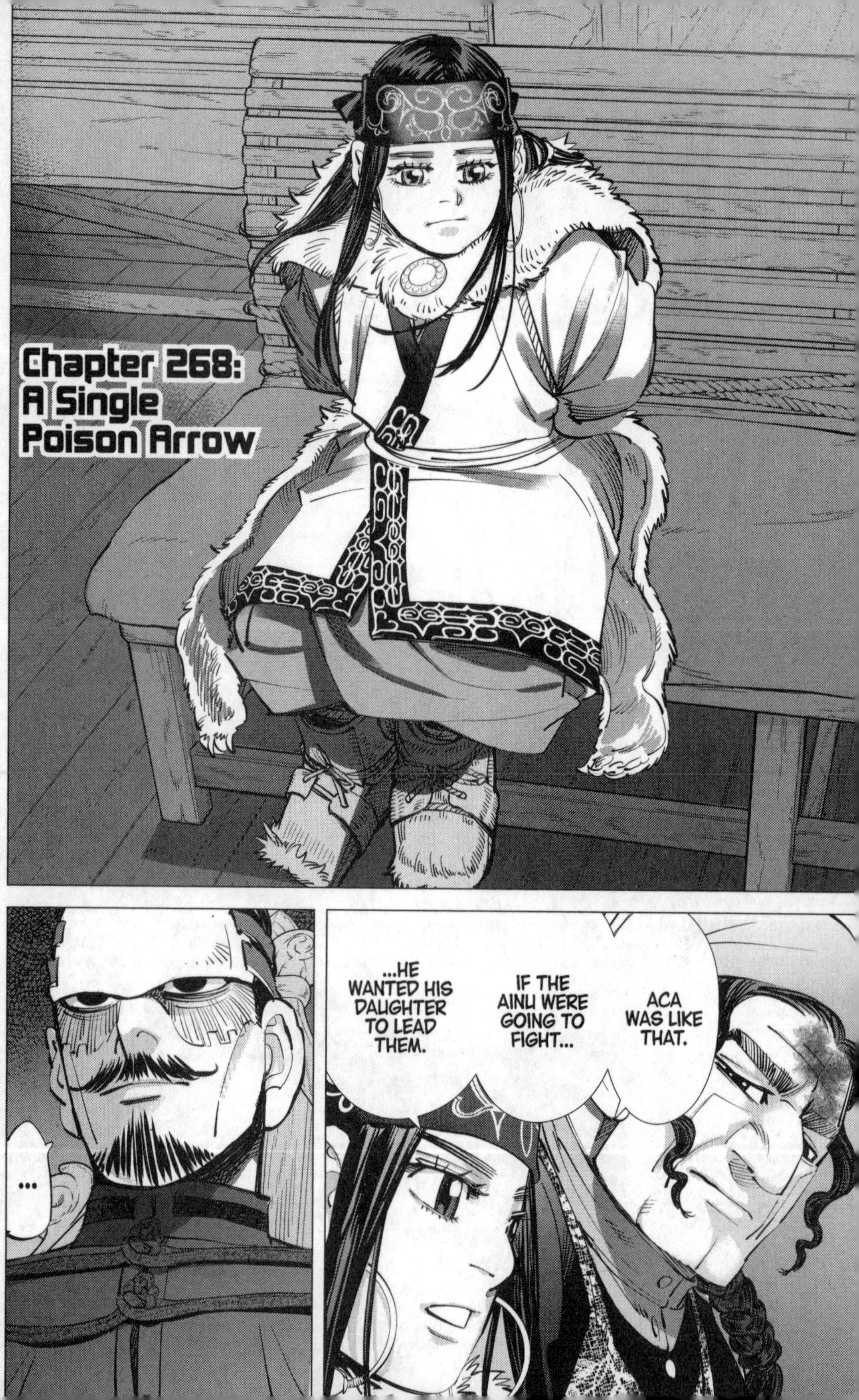

ACA WAS LIKE THAT.
IF THE AINU WERE GOING TO FIGHT...
...HE WANTED HIS DAUGHTER TO LEAD THEM.
...

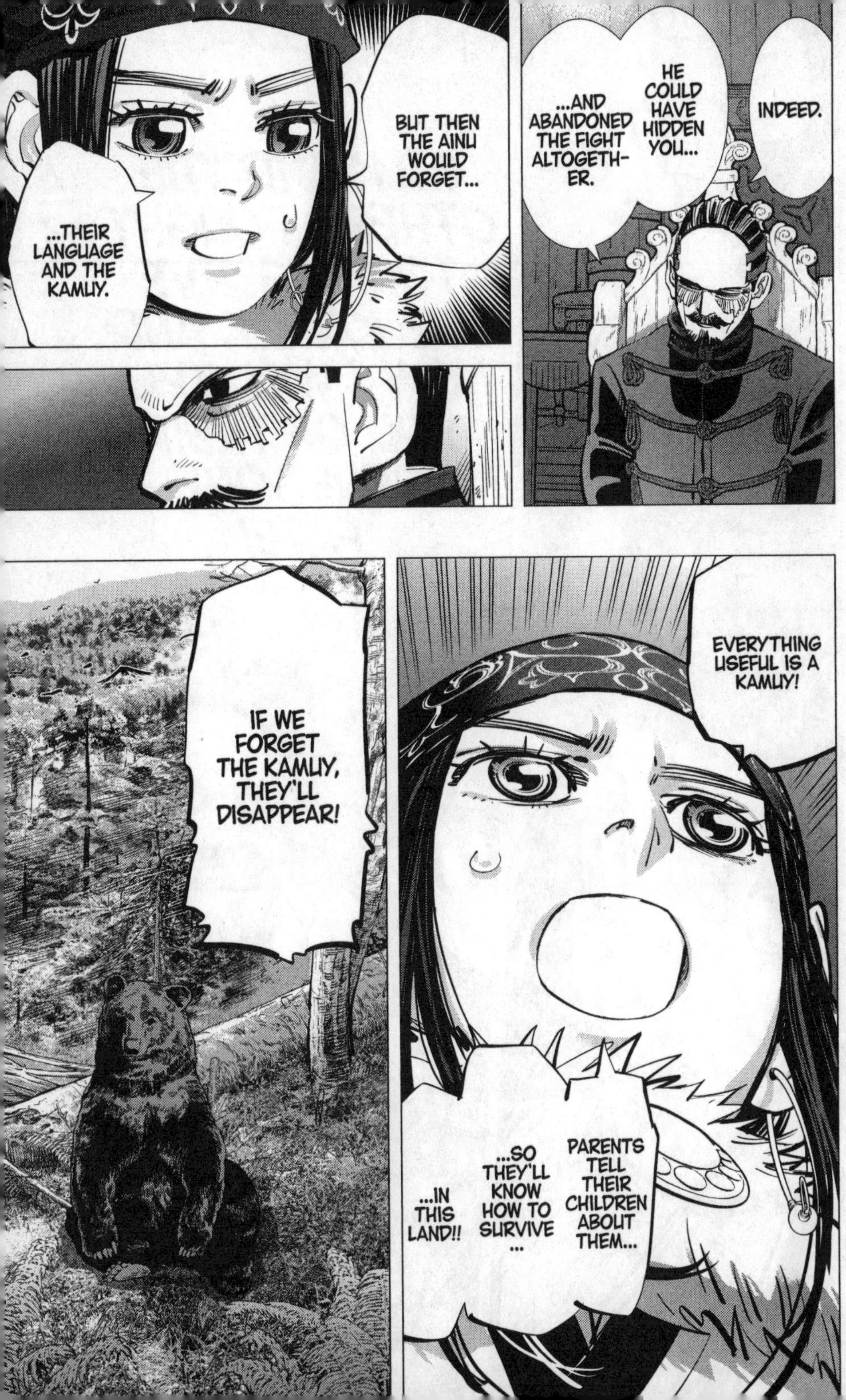
INDEED.
HE COULD HAVE HIDDEN YOU...
...AND ABANDONED THE FIGHT ALTOGETH-ER.
BUT THEN THE AINU WOULD FORGET...
...THEIR LANGUAGE AND THE KAMUY.
EVERYTHING USEFUL IS A KAMUY!
PARENTS TELL THEIR CHILDREN ABOUT THEM...
...SO THEY'LL KNOW HOW TO SURVIVE ...
...IN THIS LAND!!
IF WE FORGET THE KAMUY, THEY'LL DISAPPEAR!

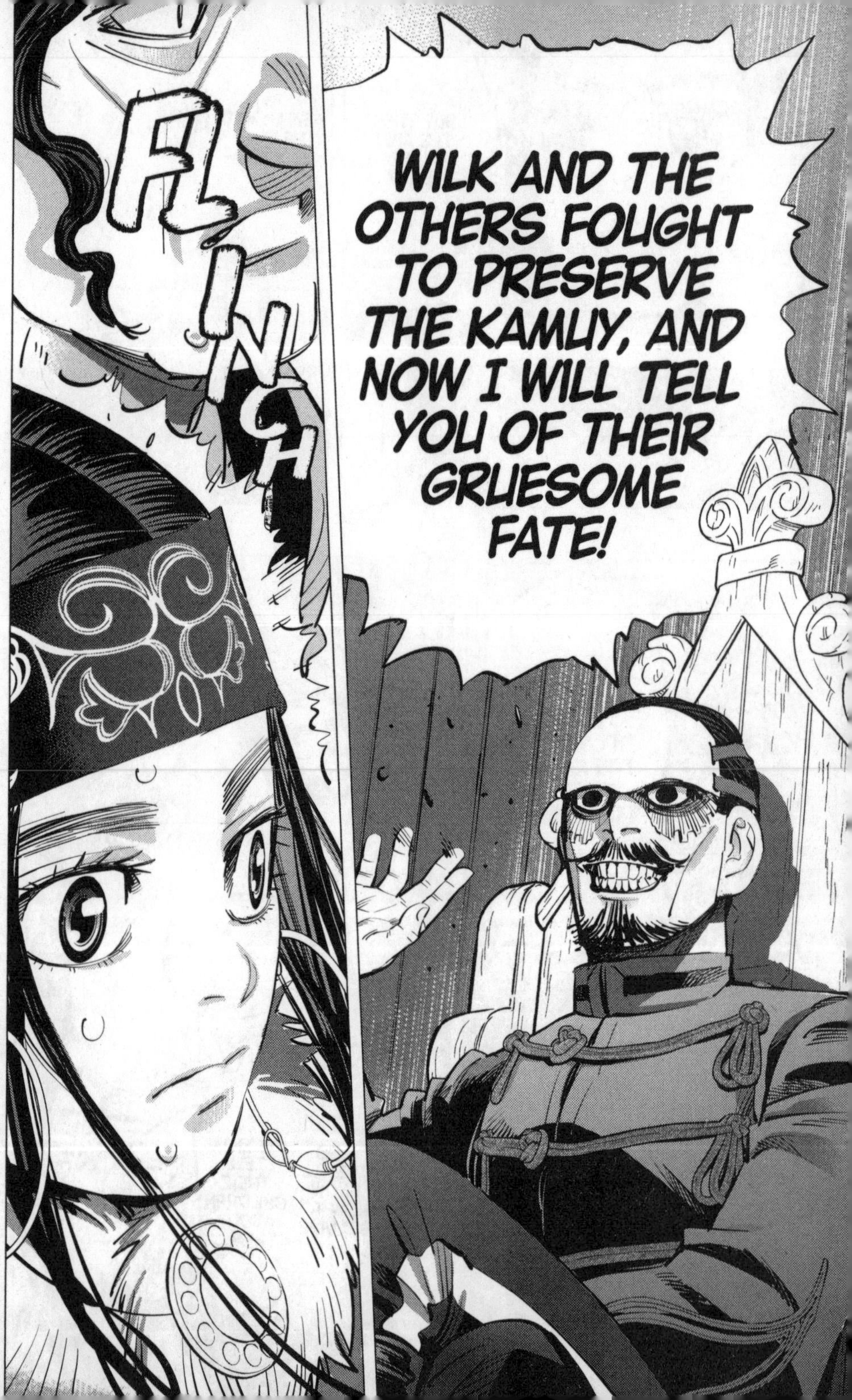
WILK AND THE OTHERS FOUGHT TO PRESERVE THE KAMUY, AND NOW I WILL TELL YOU OF THEIR GRUESOME FATE!
FLINCH

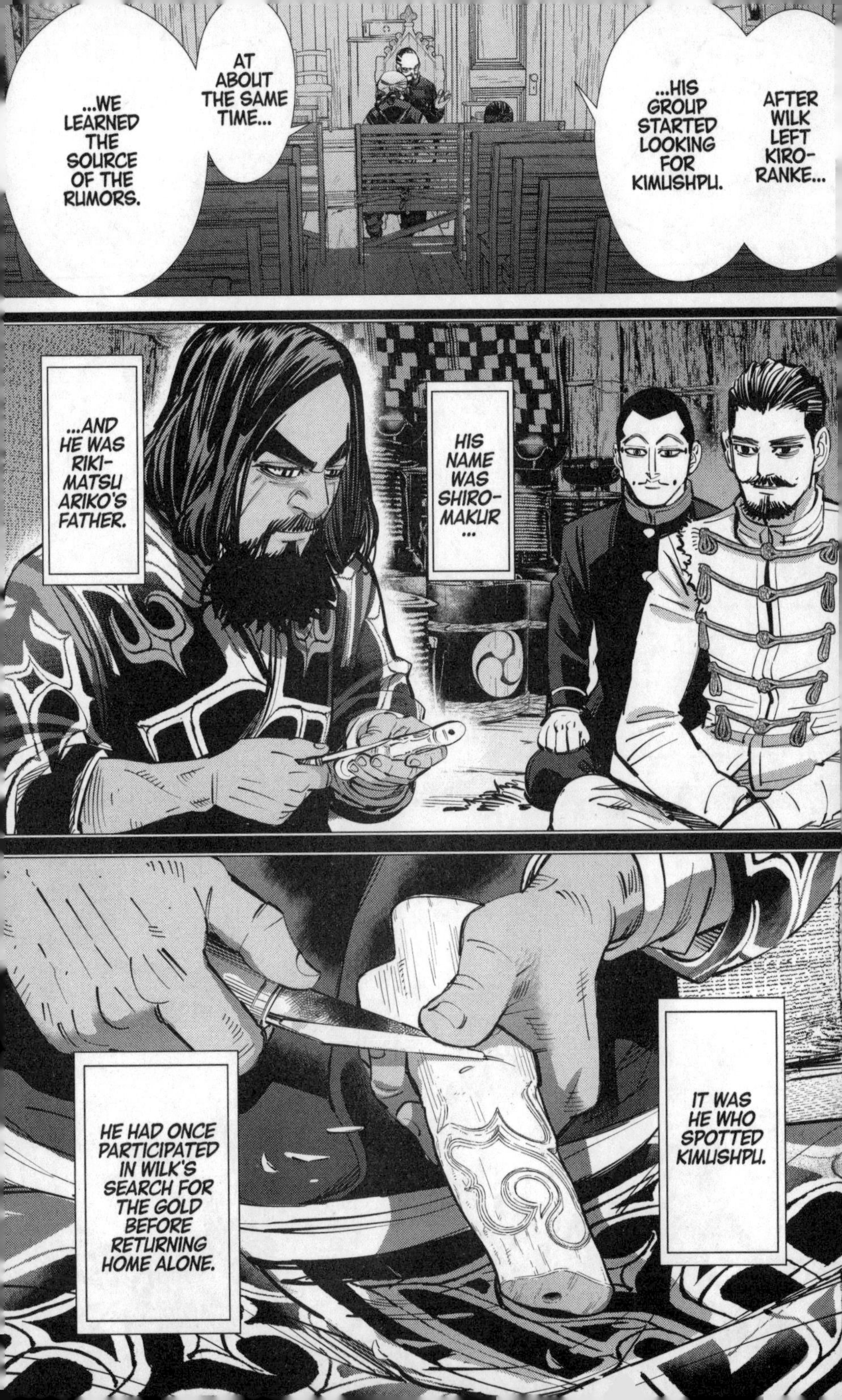
AFTER WILK LEFT KIRO-RANKE...
...HIS GROUP STARTED LOOKING FOR KIMUSHPU.
AT ABOUT THE SAME TIME...
...WE LEARNED THE SOURCE OF THE RUMORS.
HIS NAME WAS SHIRO-MAKUR...
...AND HE WAS RIKI-MATSU ARIKO'S FATHER.
IT WAS HE WHO SPOTTED KIMUSHPU.
HE HAD ONCE PARTICIPATED IN WILK'S SEARCH FOR THE GOLD BEFORE RETURNING HOME ALONE.

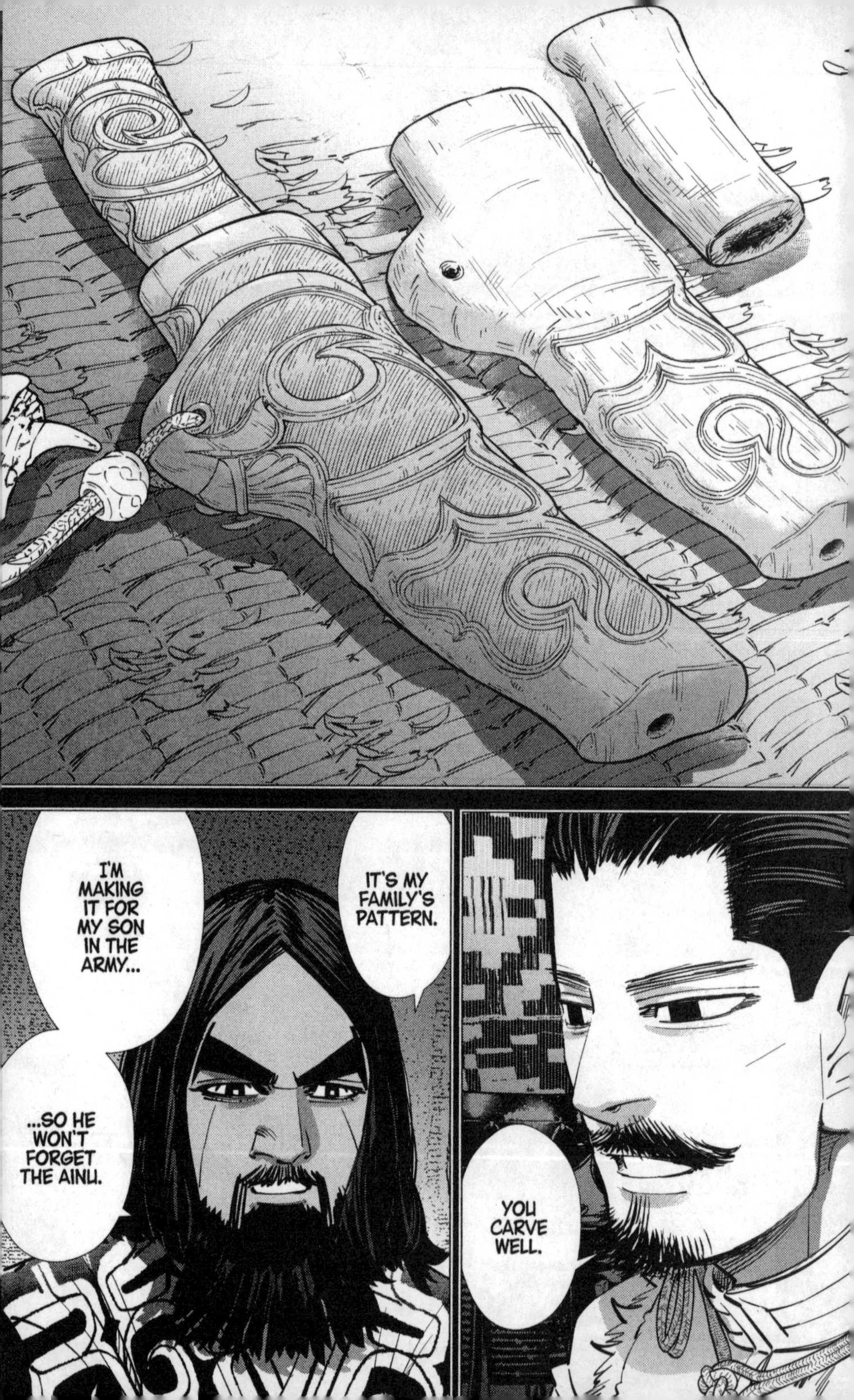
YOU CARVE WELL.
IT'S MY FAMILY'S PATTERN.
I'M MAKING IT FOR MY SON IN THE ARMY...
...SO HE WON'T FORGET THE AINU.

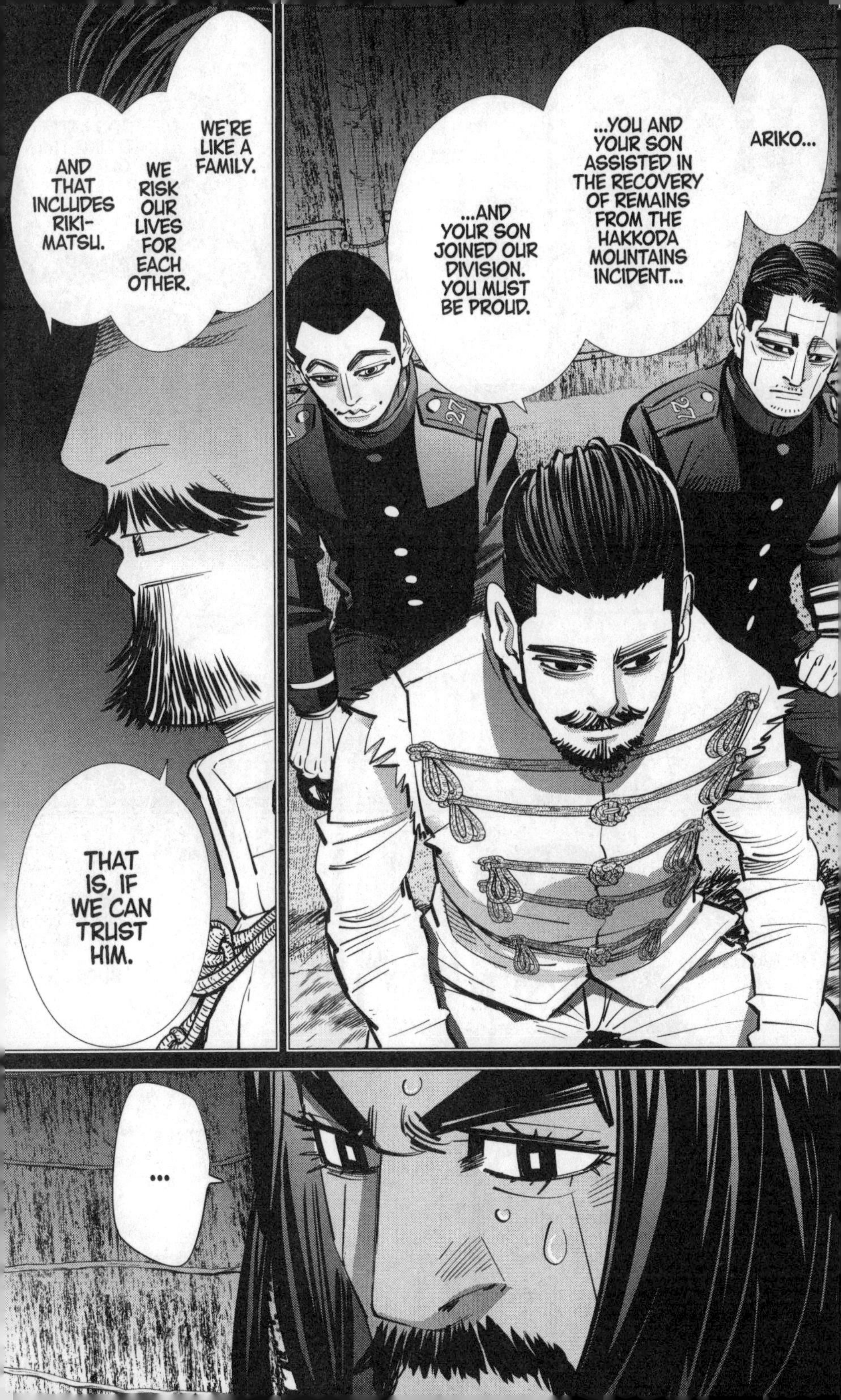
ARIKO...
...YOU AND YOUR SON ASSISTED IN THE RECOVERY OF REMAINS FROM THE HAKKODA MOUNTAINS INCIDENT...
...AND YOUR SON JOINED OUR DIVISION. YOU MUST BE PROUD.
WE'RE LIKE A FAMILY.
WE RISK OUR LIVES FOR EACH OTHER.
AND THAT INCLUDES RIKI-MATSU.
THAT IS, IF WE CAN TRUST HIM.
...

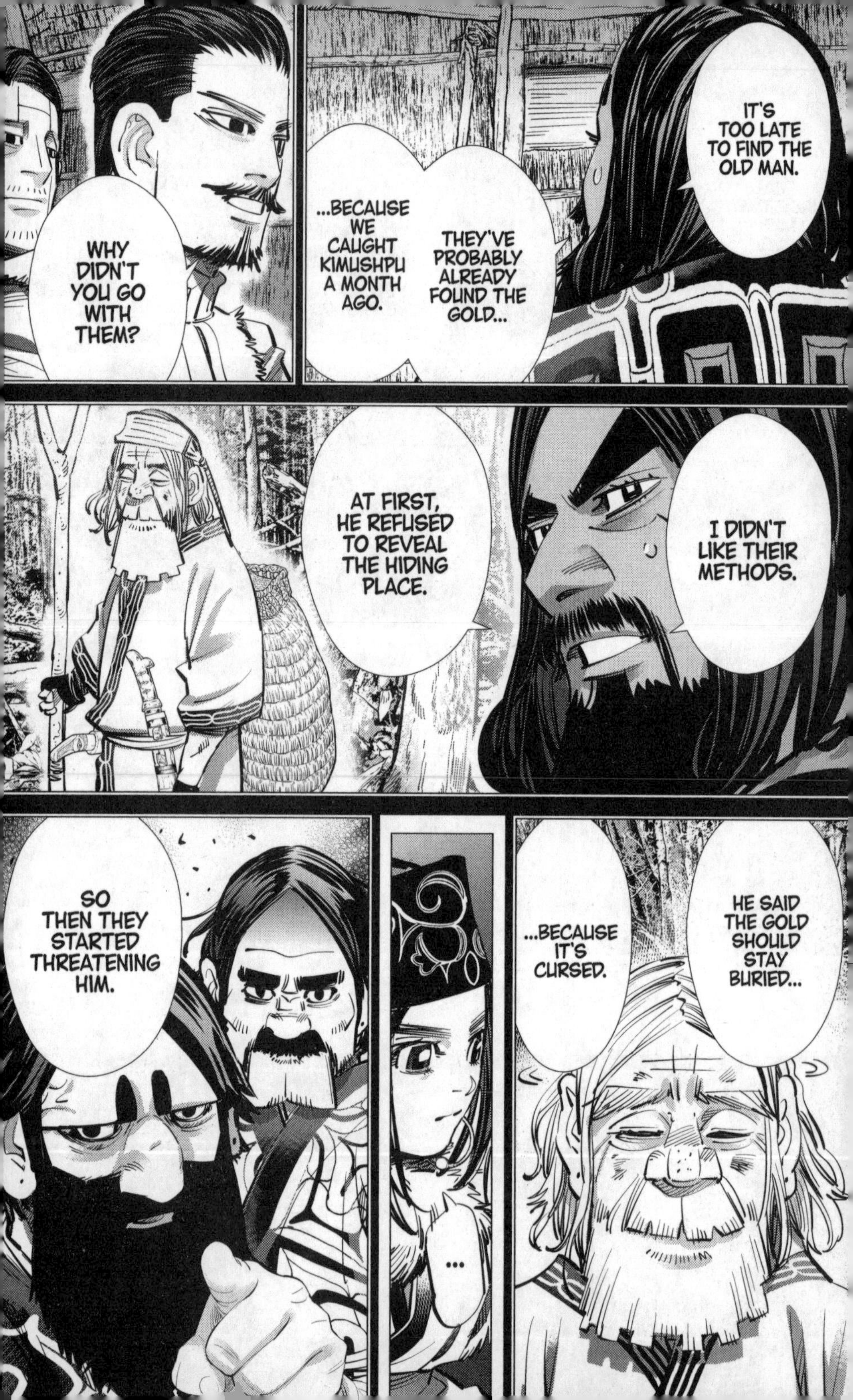
IT'S TOO LATE TO FIND THE OLD MAN.
THEY'VE PROBABLY ALREADY FOUND THE GOLD...
...BECAUSE WE CAUGHT KIMUSHPU A MONTH AGO.
WHY DIDN'T YOU GO WITH THEM?
I DIDN'T LIKE THEIR METHODS.
AT FIRST, HE REFUSED TO REVEAL THE HIDING PLACE.
HE SAID THE GOLD SHOULD STAY BURIED...
...BECAUSE IT'S CURSED.
...
SO THEN THEY STARTED THREATENING HIM.

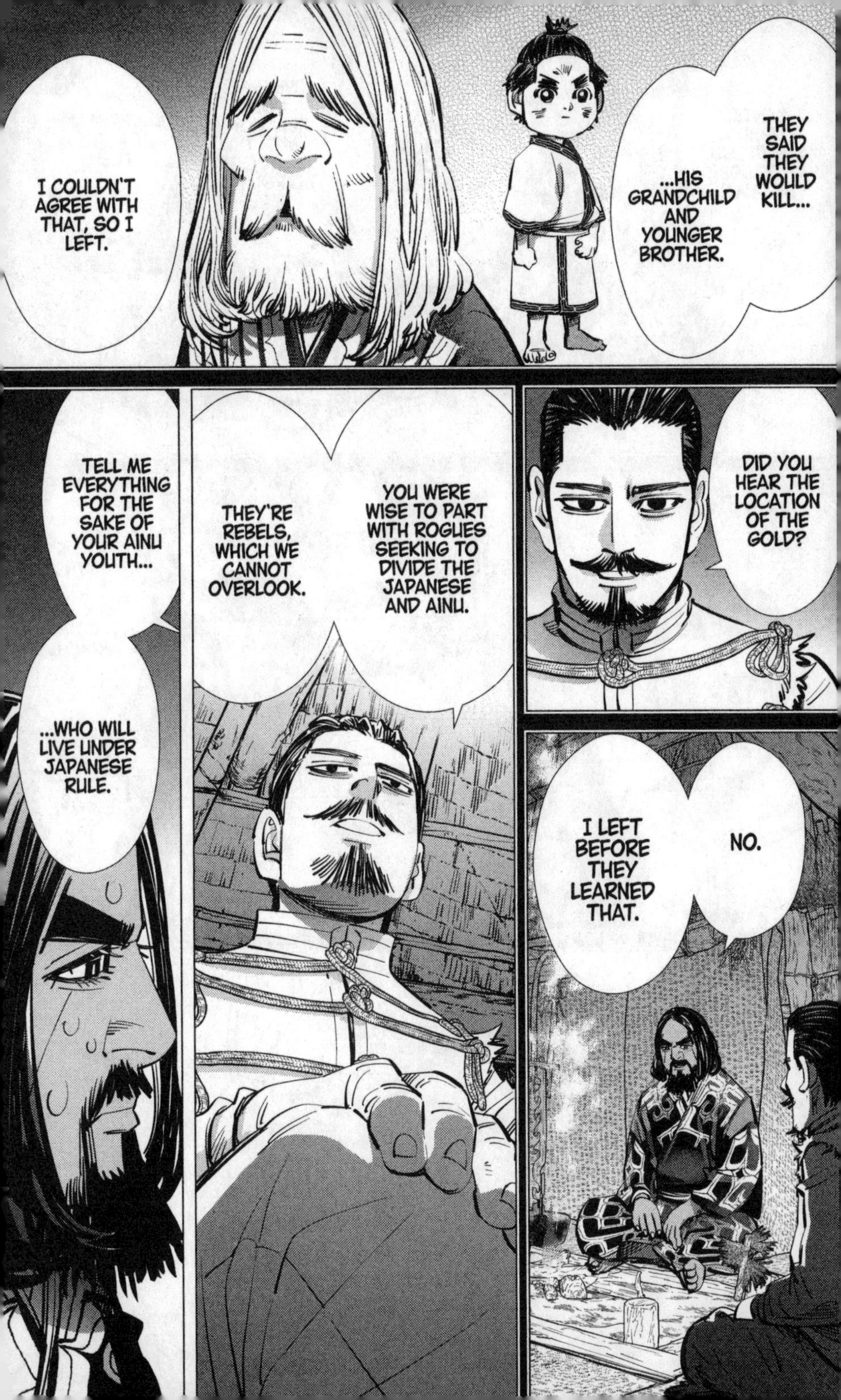
THEY SAID THEY WOULD KILL...
...HIS GRANDCHILD AND YOUNGER BROTHER.
I COULDN'T AGREE WITH THAT, SO I LEFT.
DID YOU HEAR THE LOCATION OF THE GOLD?
NO.
I LEFT BEFORE THEY LEARNED THAT.
YOU WERE WISE TO PART WITH ROGUES SEEKING TO DIVIDE THE JAPANESE AND AINU.
THEY'RE REBELS, WHICH WE CANNOT OVERLOOK.
TELL ME EVERYTHING FOR THE SAKE OF YOUR AINU YOUTH...
...WHO WILL LIVE UNDER JAPANESE RULE.

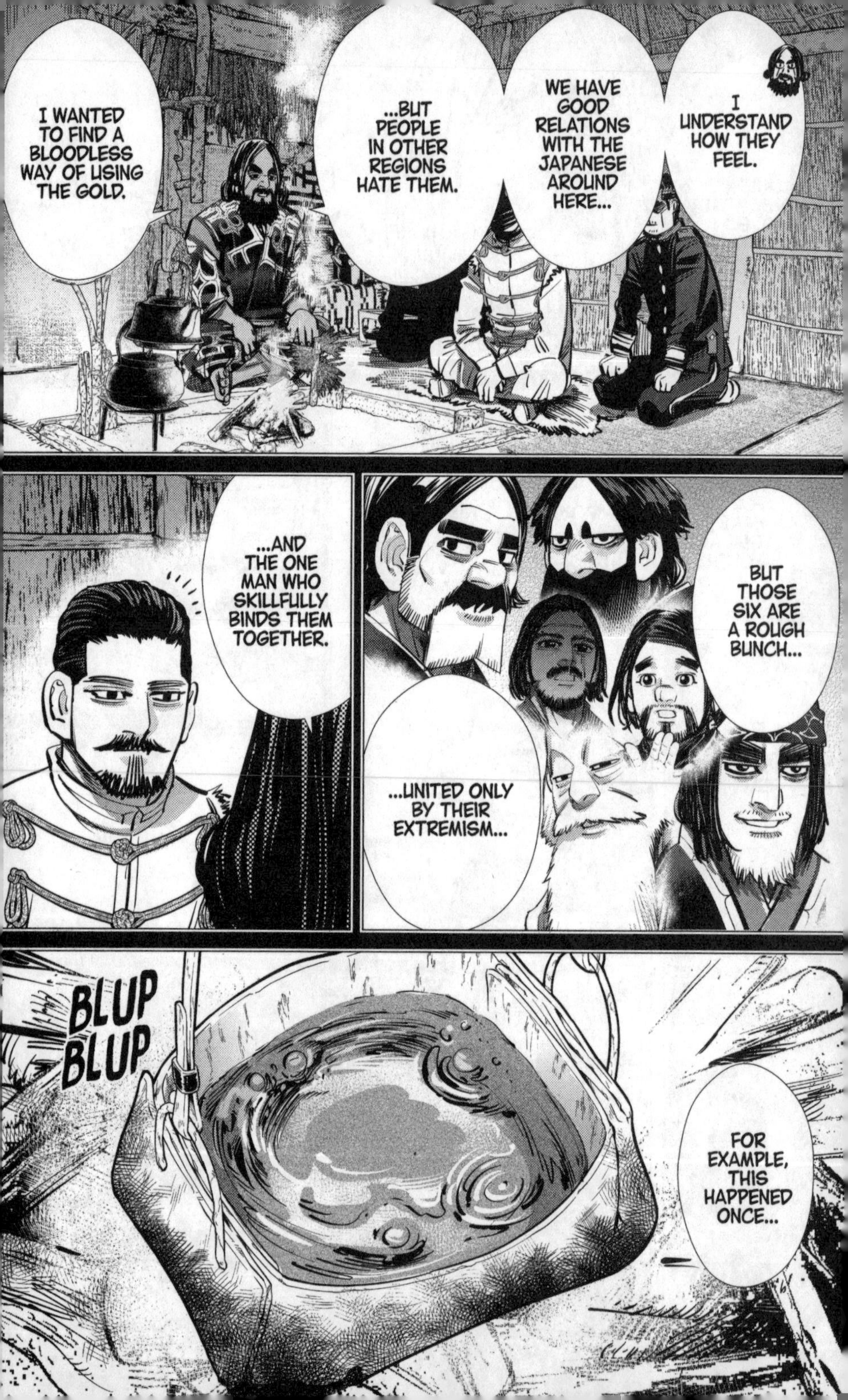
I UNDERSTAND HOW THEY FEEL.
WE HAVE GOOD RELATIONS WITH THE JAPANESE AROUND HERE...
...BUT PEOPLE IN OTHER REGIONS HATE THEM.
I WANTED TO FIND A BLOODLESS WAY OF USING THE GOLD.
BUT THOSE SIX ARE A ROUGH BUNCH...
...UNITED ONLY BY THEIR EXTREMISM...
...AND THE ONE MAN WHO SKILLFULLY BINDS THEM TOGETHER.
BLUP BLUP
FOR EXAMPLE, THIS HAPPENED ONCE...

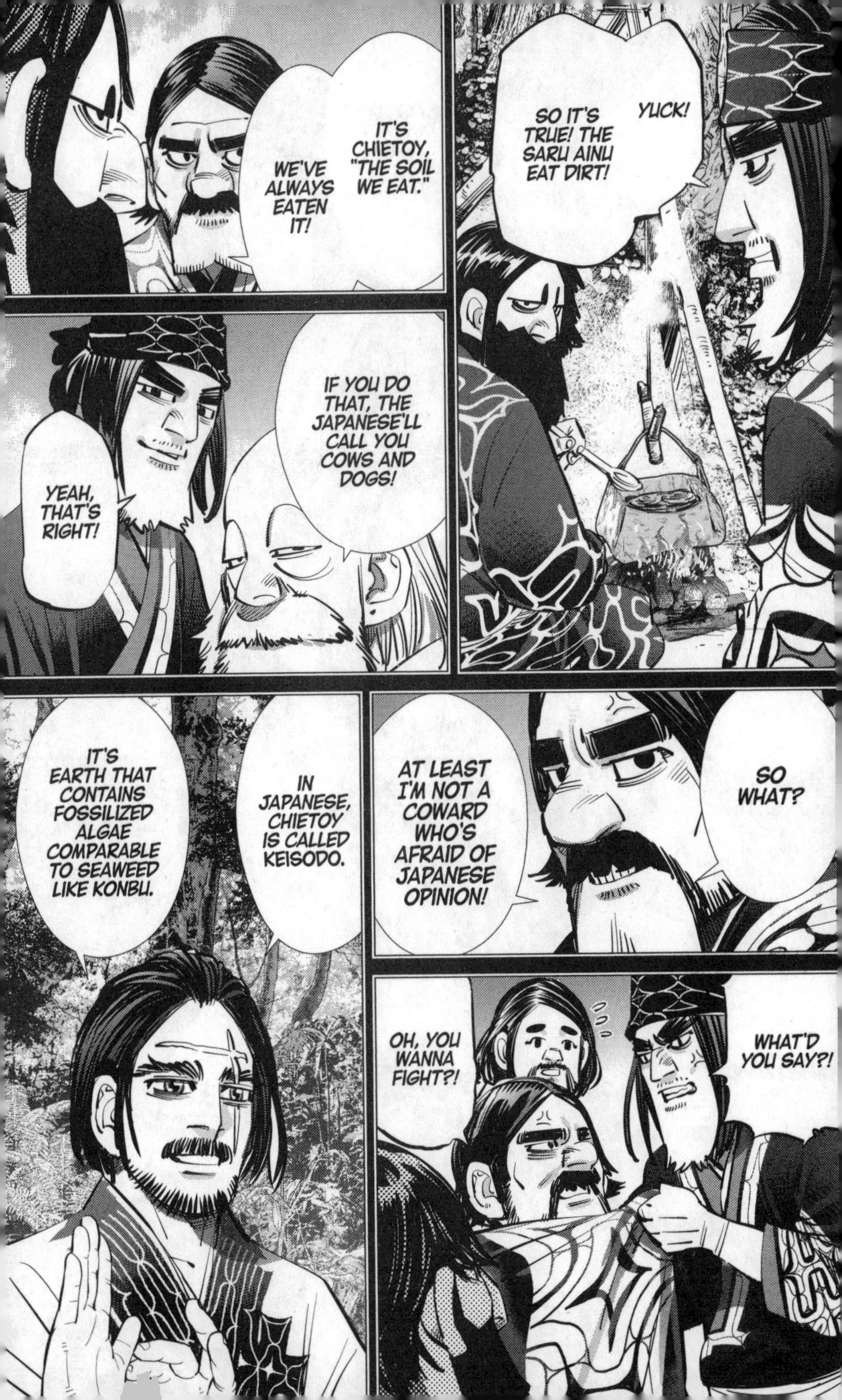
YUCK!
SO IT'S TRUE! THE SARU AINU EAT DIRT!
IT'S CHIETOY, "THE SOIL WE EAT."
WE'VE ALWAYS EATEN IT!
IF YOU DO THAT, THE JAPANESE'LL CALL YOU COWS AND DOGS!
YEAH, THAT'S RIGHT!
SO WHAT?
AT LEAST I'M NOT A COWARD WHO'S AFRAID OF JAPANESE OPINION!
WHAT'D YOU SAY?!
OH, YOU WANNA FIGHT?!
IN JAPANESE, CHIETOY IS CALLED KEISODO.
IT'S EARTH THAT CONTAINS FOSSILIZED ALGAE COMPARABLE TO SEAWEED LIKE KONBU.

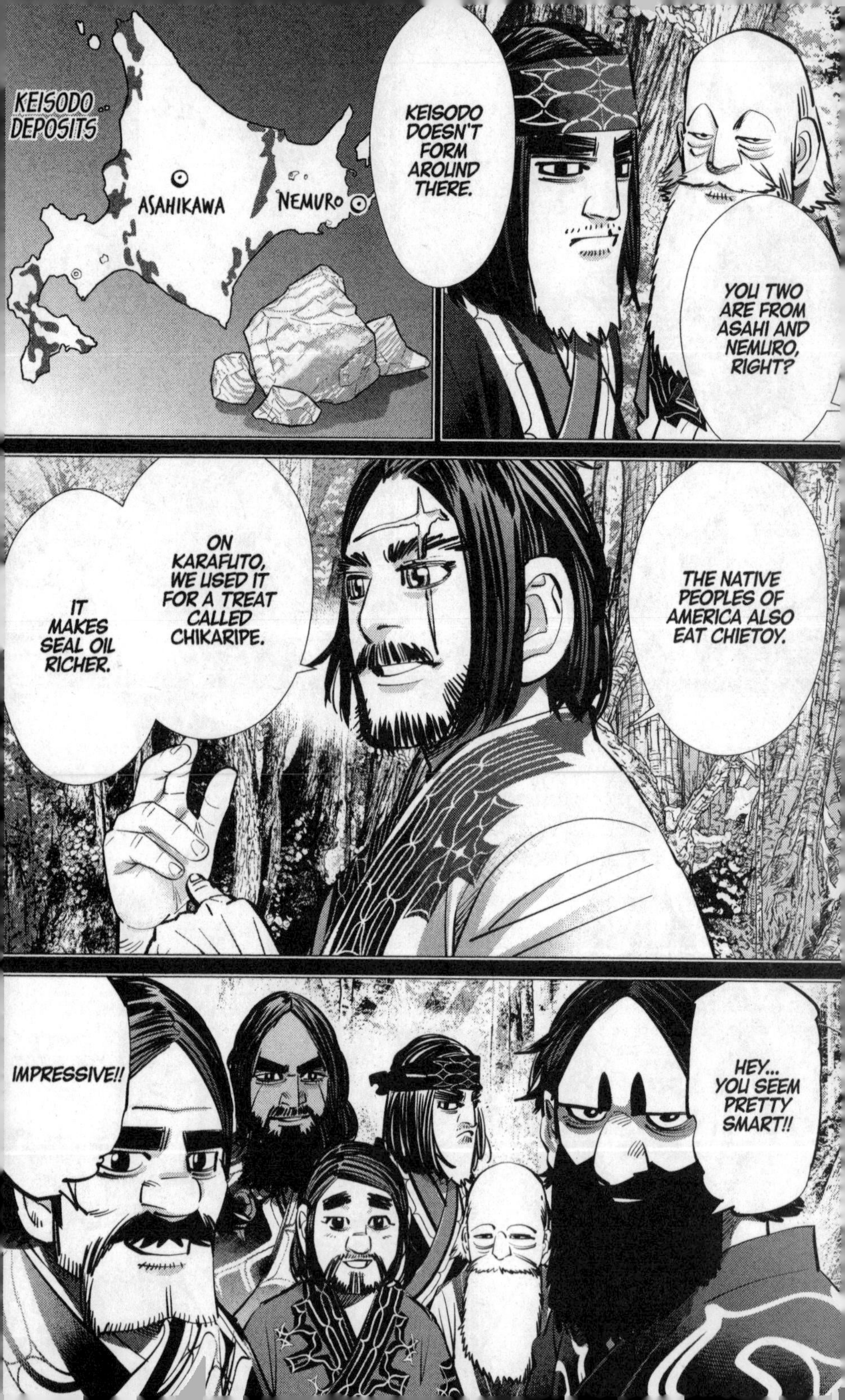
YOU TWO ARE FROM ASAHI AND NEMURO, RIGHT?
KEISODO DOESN'T FORM AROUND THERE.
KEISODO DEPOSITS
ASAHIKAWA
NEMURO
THE NATIVE PEOPLES OF AMERICA ALSO EAT CHIETOY.
ON KARAFUTO, WE USED IT FOR A TREAT CALLED CHIKARIPE.
IT MAKES SEAL OIL RICHER.
HEY... YOU SEEM PRETTY SMART!!
IMPRESSIVE!!

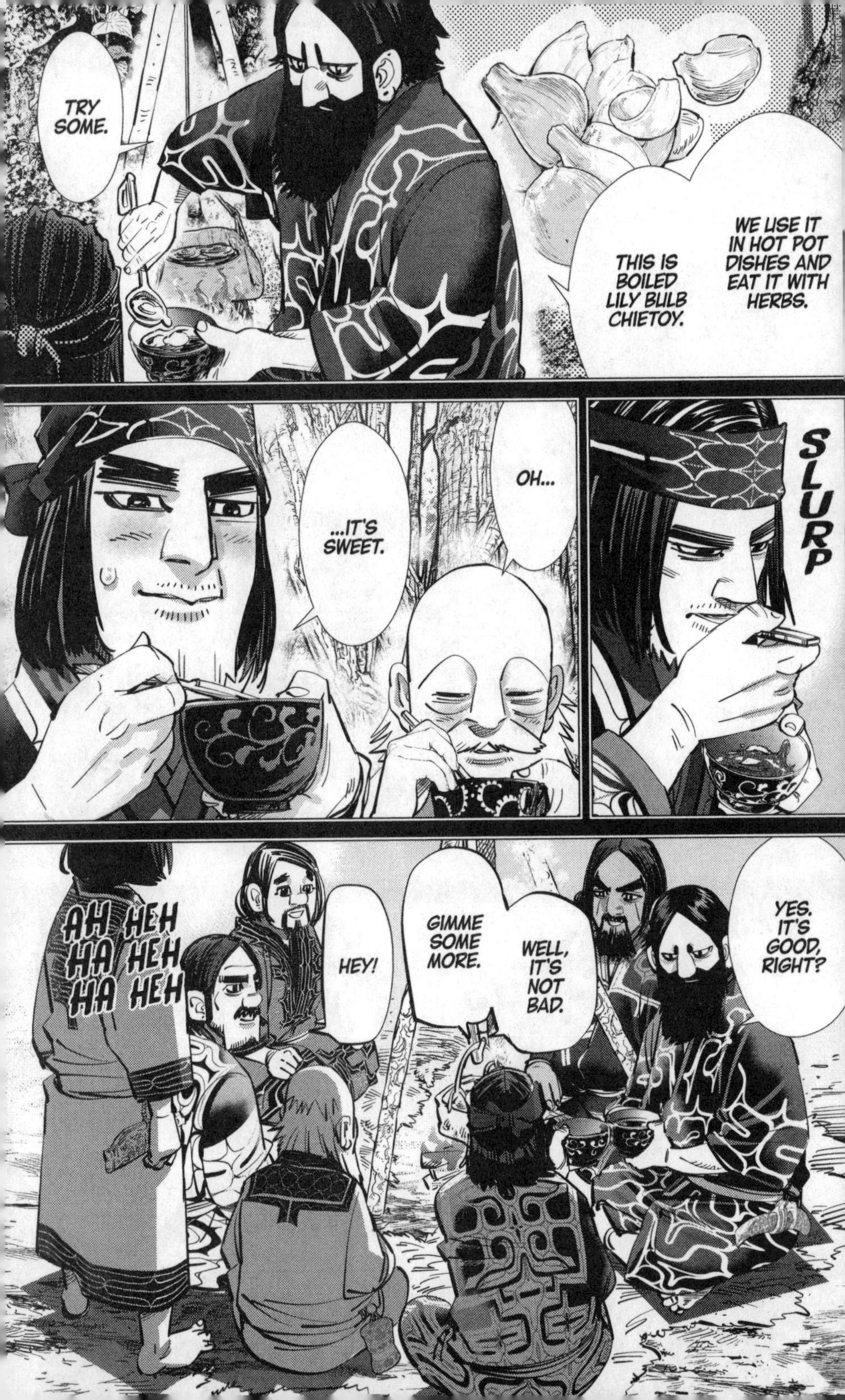
THIS IS BOILED LILY BULB CHIETOY.
WE USE IT IN HOT POT DISHES AND EAT IT WITH HERBS.
TRY SOME.
SLURP
OH...
...IT'S SWEET.
YES. IT'S GOOD, RIGHT?
WELL, IT'S NOT BAD.
GIMME SOME MORE.
HEY!
HEH HEH HEH
AH HA HA HA

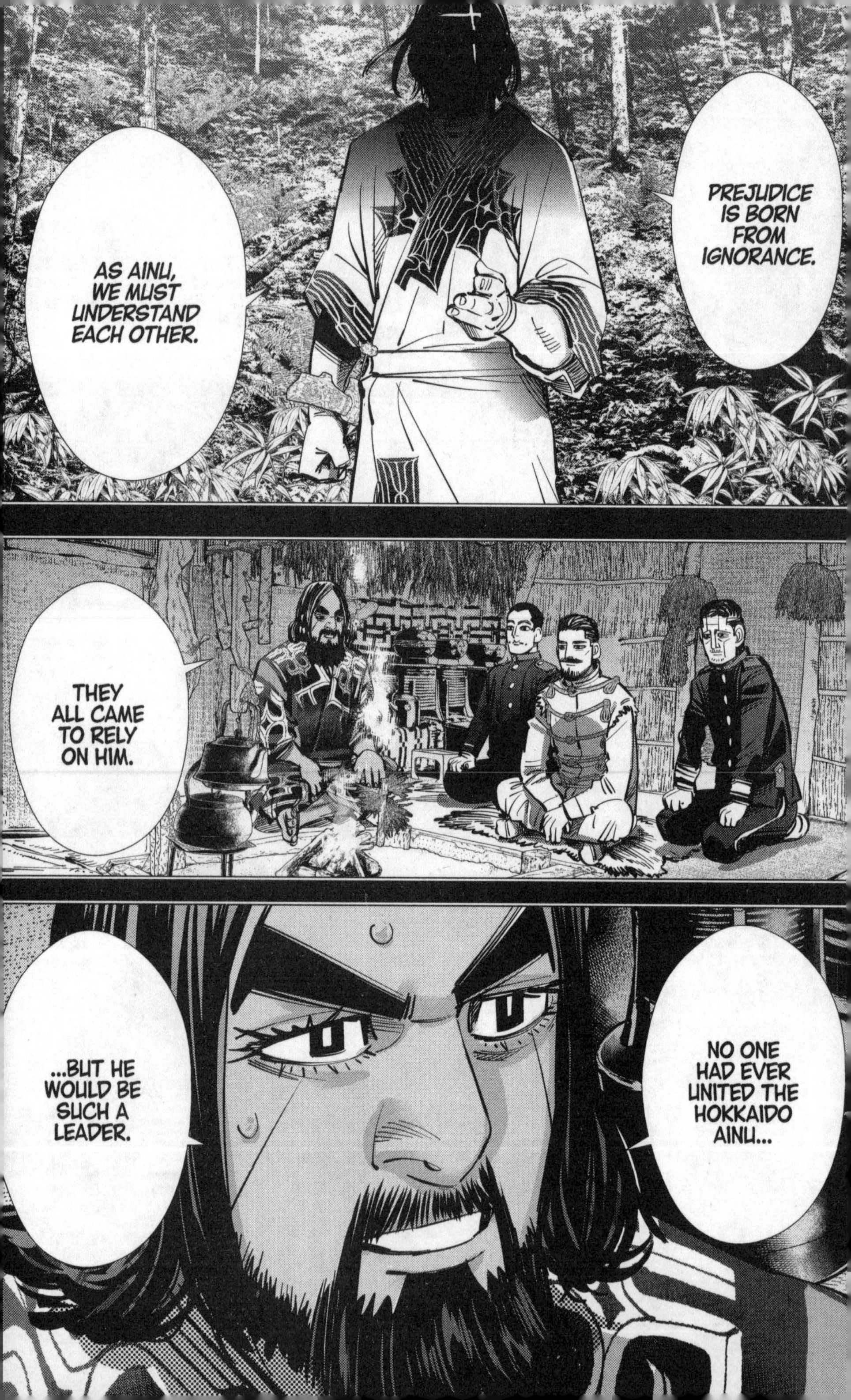
PREJUDICE IS BORN FROM IGNORANCE.
AS AINU, WE MUST UNDERSTAND EACH OTHER.
THEY ALL CAME TO RELY ON HIM.
NO ONE HAD EVER UNITED THE HOKKAIDO AINU...
...BUT HE WOULD BE SUCH A LEADER.

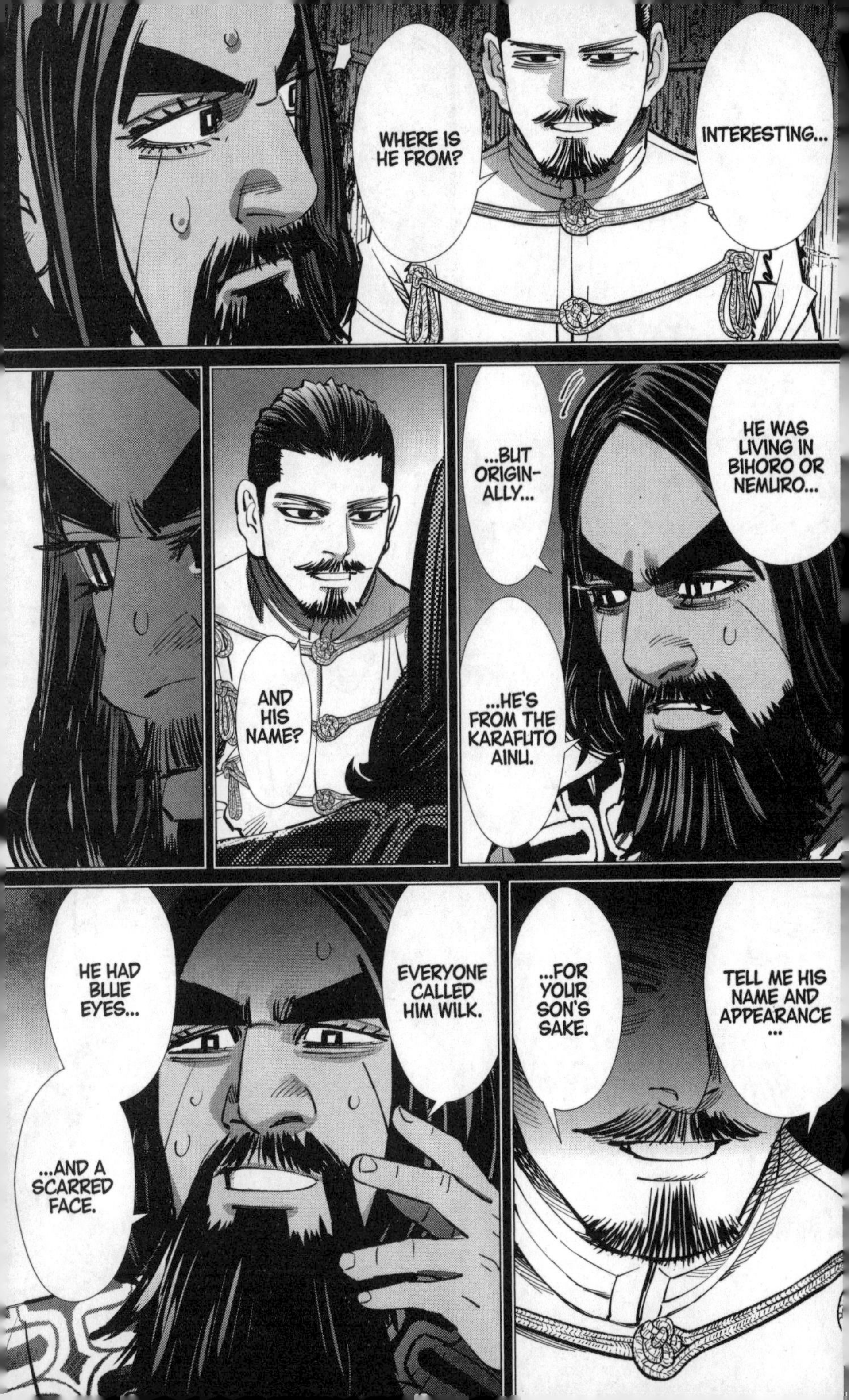
INTERESTING...
WHERE IS HE FROM?
HE WAS LIVING IN BIHORO OR NEMURO...
...BUT ORIGIN-ALLY...
...HE'S FROM THE KARAFUTO AINU.
AND HIS NAME?
TELL ME HIS NAME AND APPEARANCE ...
...FOR YOUR SON'S SAKE.
EVERYONE CALLED HIM WILK.
HE HAD BLUE EYES...
...AND A SCARRED FACE.

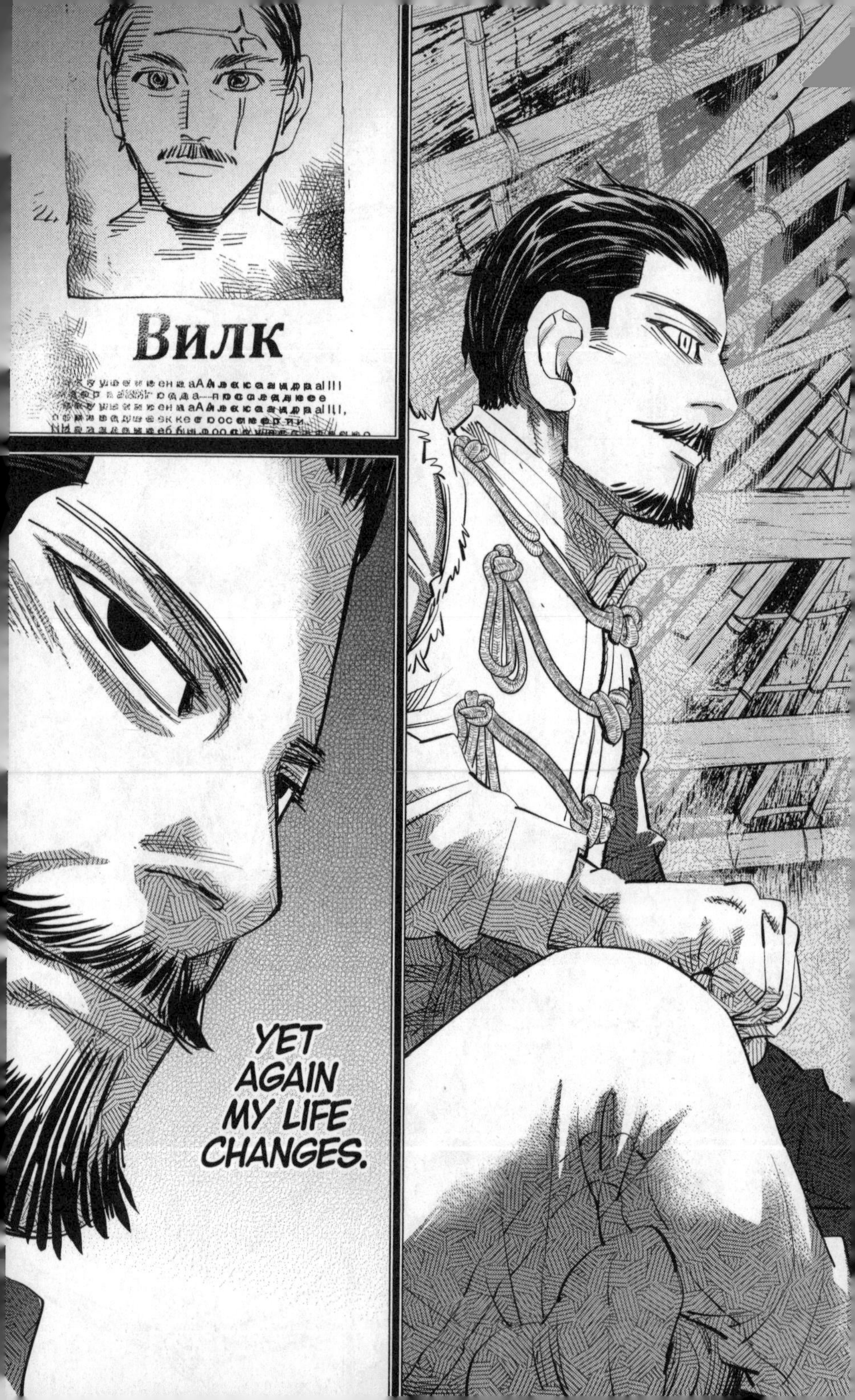
Вилк
YET AGAIN MY LIFE CHANGES.

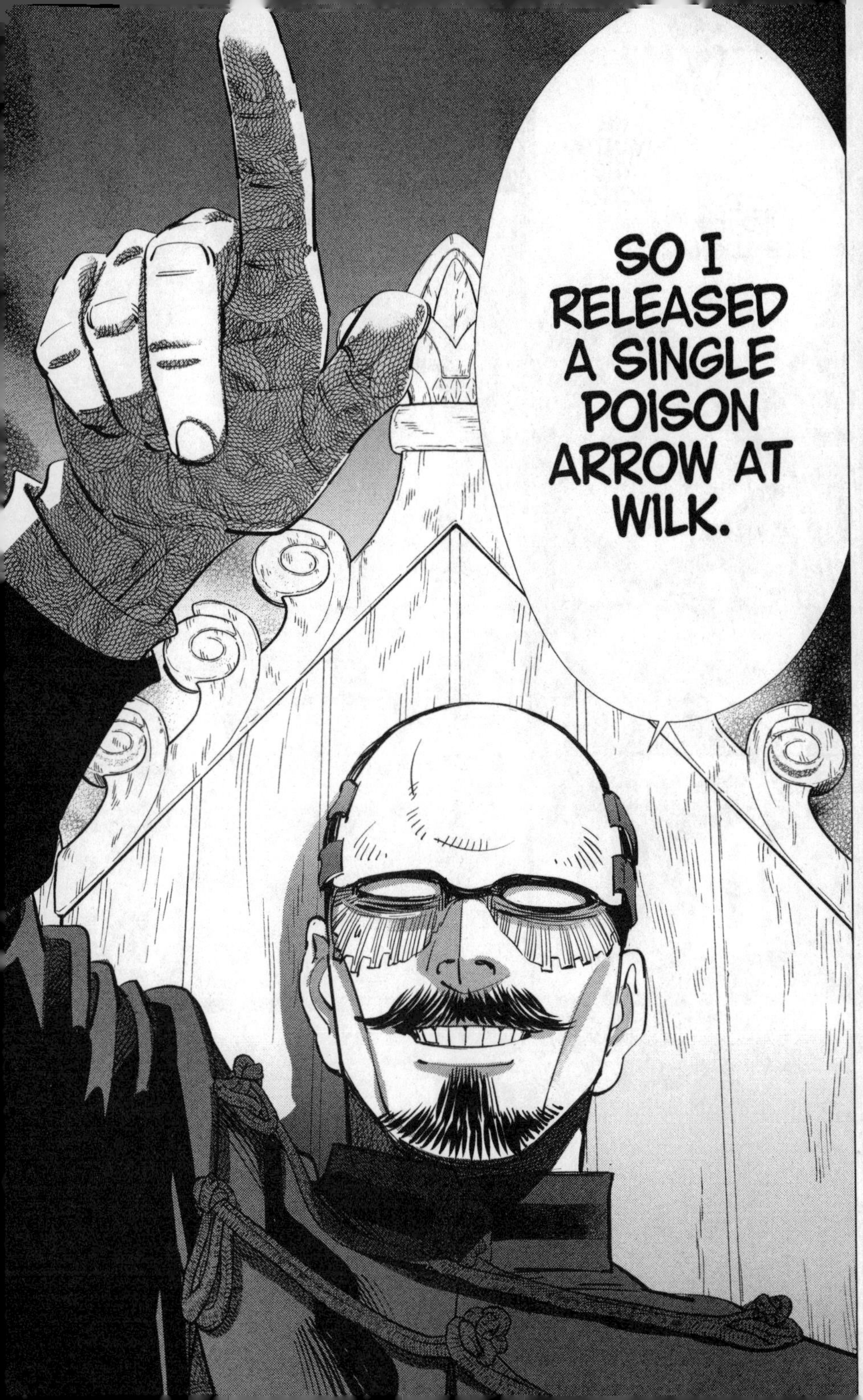
SO I RELEASED A SINGLE POISON ARROW AT WILK.

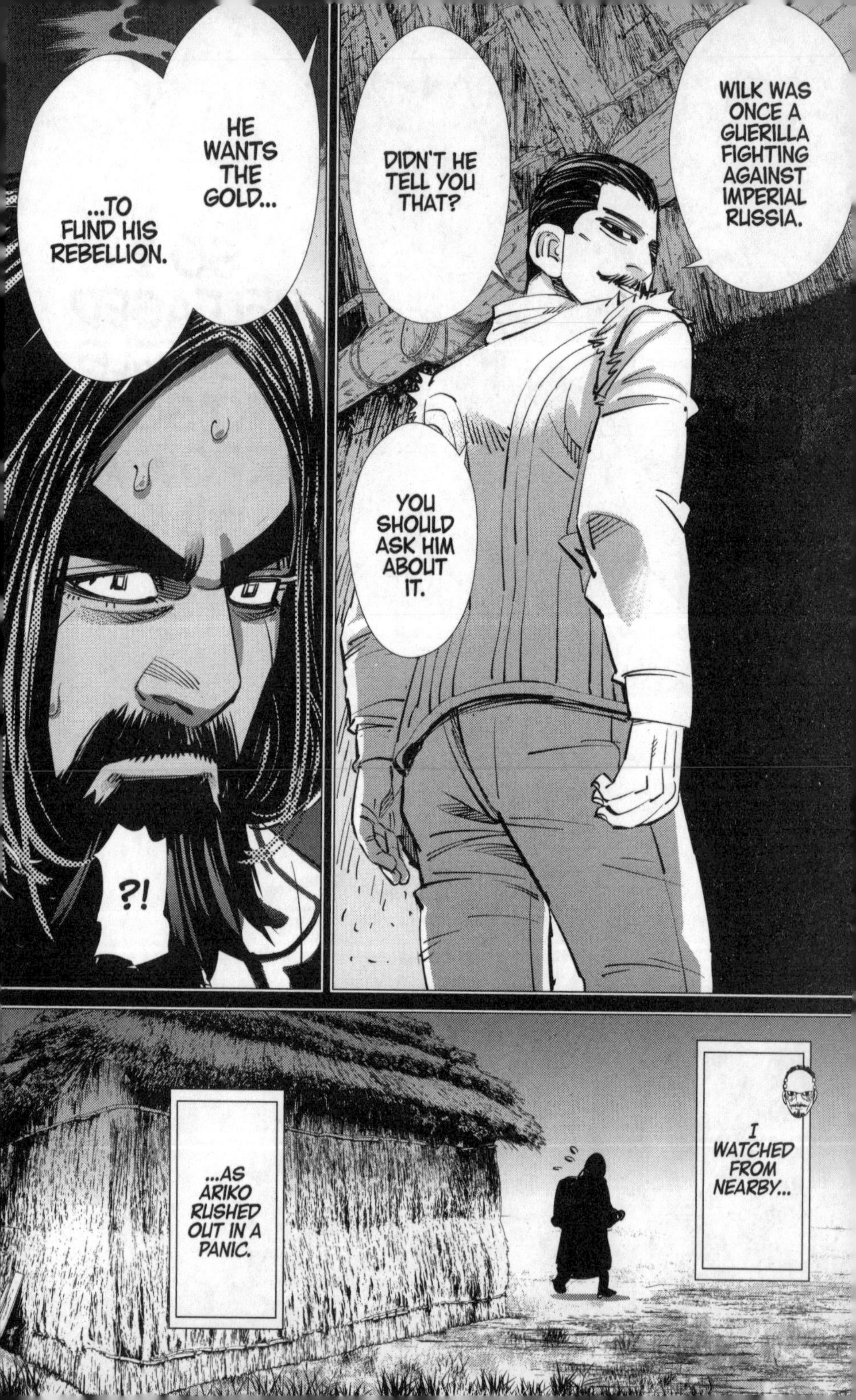
WILK WAS ONCE A GUERILLA FIGHTING AGAINST IMPERIAL RUSSIA.
DIDN'T HE TELL YOU THAT?
YOU SHOULD ASK HIM ABOUT IT.
HE WANTS THE GOLD...
...TO FUND HIS REBELLION.
?!
I WATCHED FROM NEARBY...
...AS ARIKO RUSHED OUT IN A PANIC.

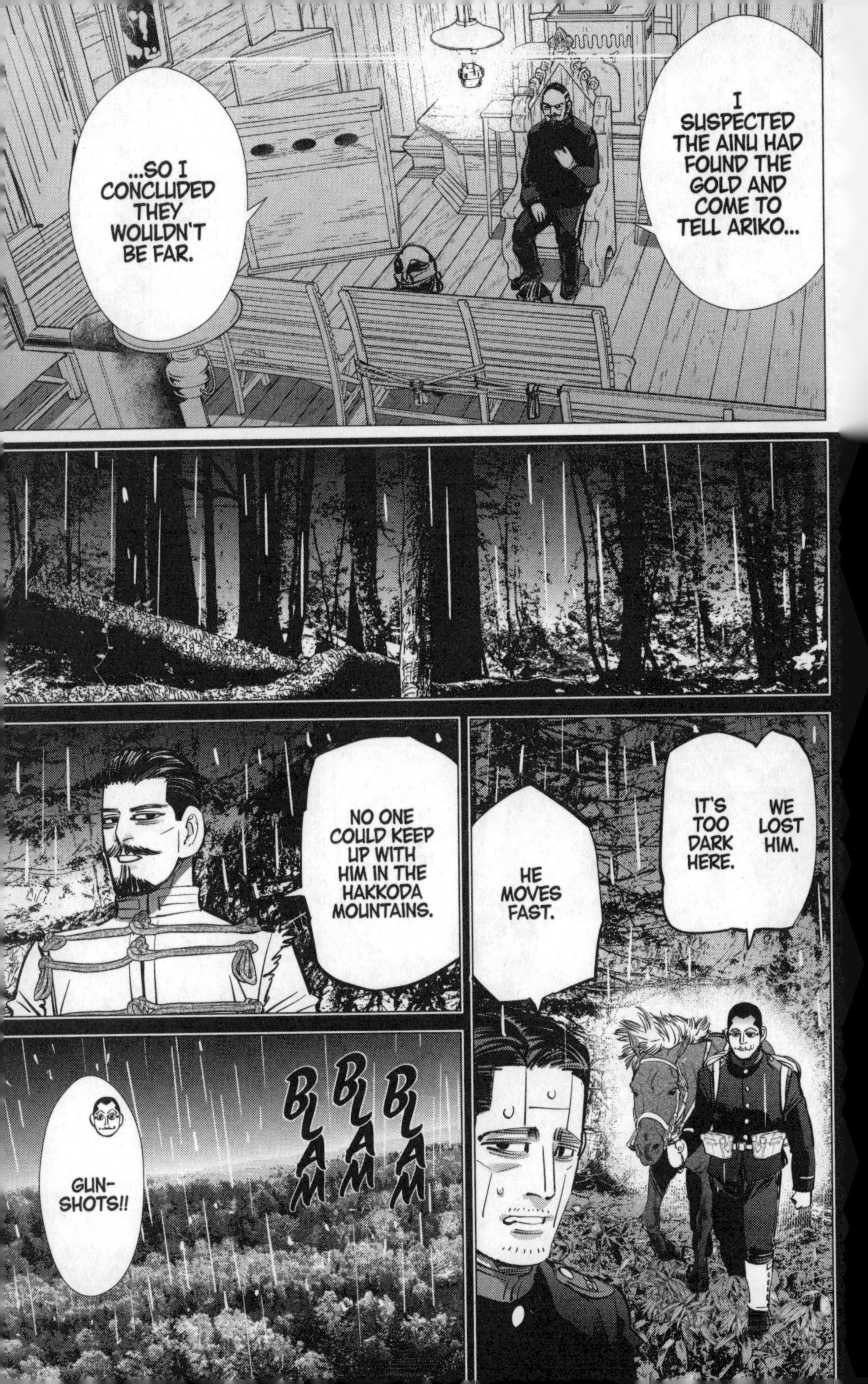
I SUSPECTED THE AINU HAD FOUND THE GOLD AND COME TO TELL ARIKO...
...SO I CONCLUDED THEY WOULDN'T BE FAR.
WE LOST HIM.
IT'S TOO DARK HERE.
HE MOVES FAST.
NO ONE COULD KEEP UP WITH HIM IN THE HAKKODA MOUNTAINS.
BLAM BLAM BLAM
GUN-SHOTS!!

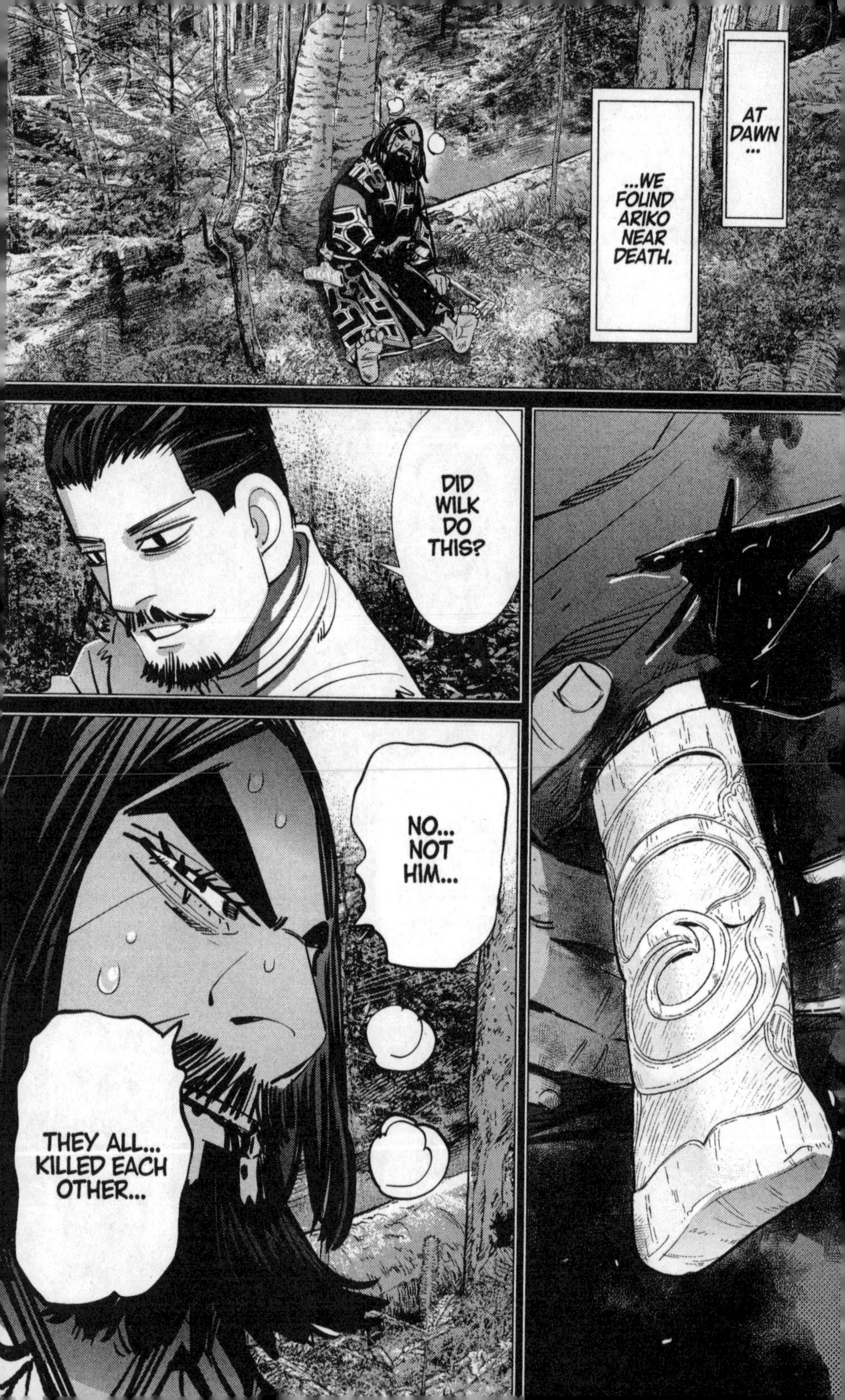
AT DAWN...
...WE FOUND ARIKO NEAR DEATH.
DID WILK DO THIS?
NO... NOT HIM...
THEY ALL... KILLED EACH OTHER...

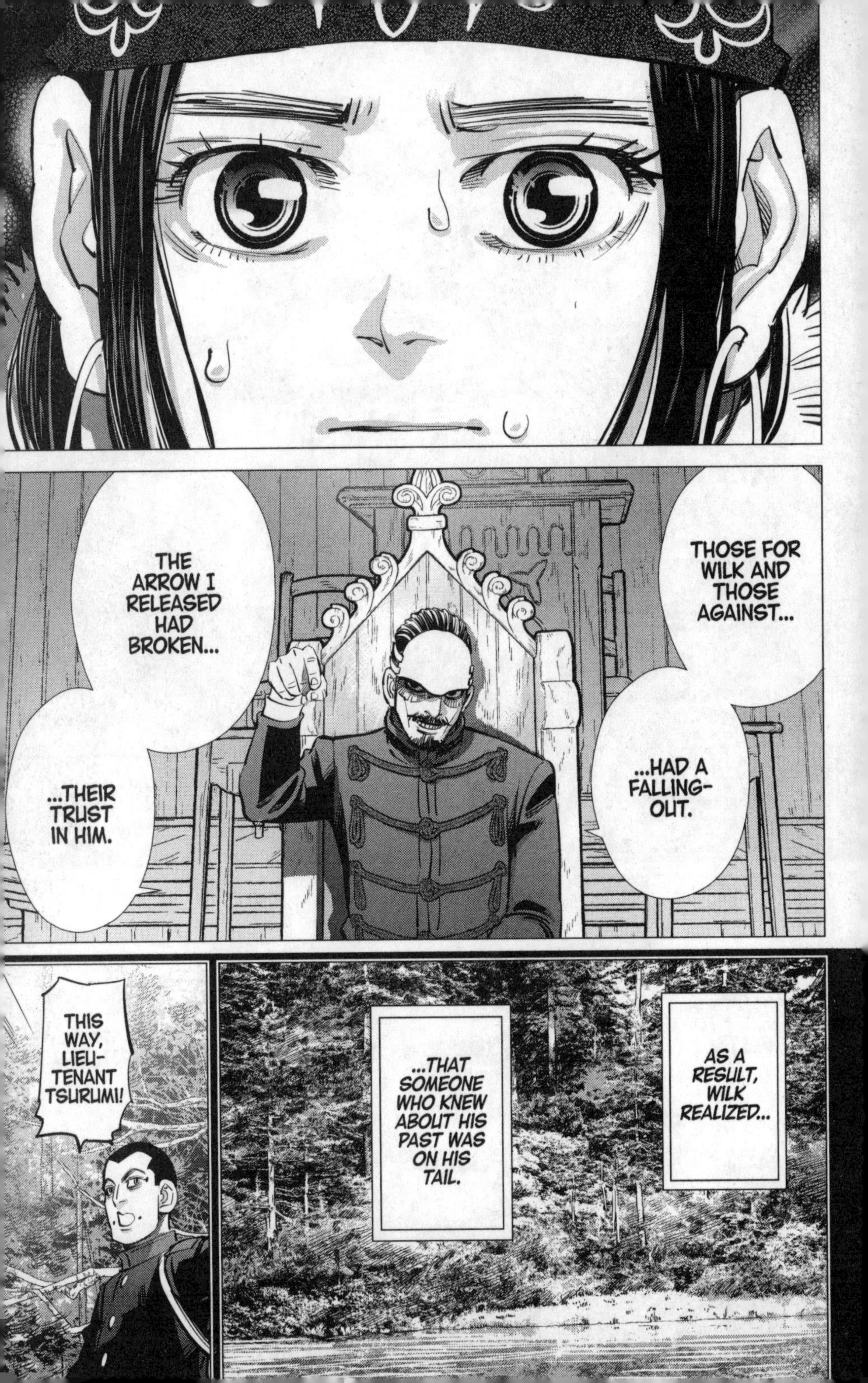
THOSE FOR WILK AND THOSE AGAINST...
...HAD A FALLING-OUT.
THE ARROW I RELEASED HAD BROKEN...
...THEIR TRUST IN HIM.
AS A RESULT, WILK REALIZED...
...THAT SOMEONE WHO KNEW ABOUT HIS PAST WAS ON HIS TAIL.
THIS WAY, LIEUTENANT TSURUMI!

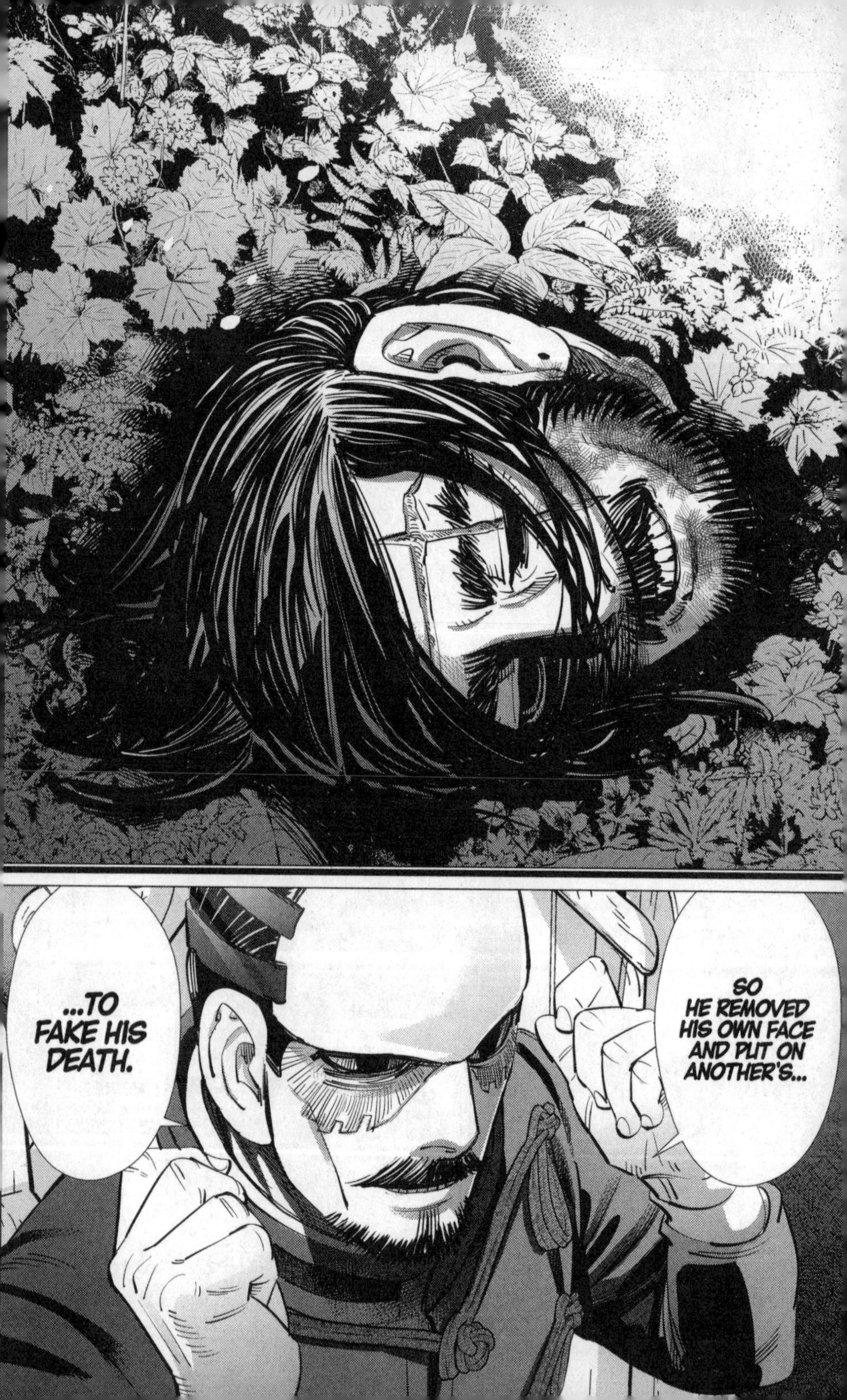
SO HE REMOVED HIS OWN FACE AND PUT ON ANOTHER'S...
...TO FAKE HIS DEATH.

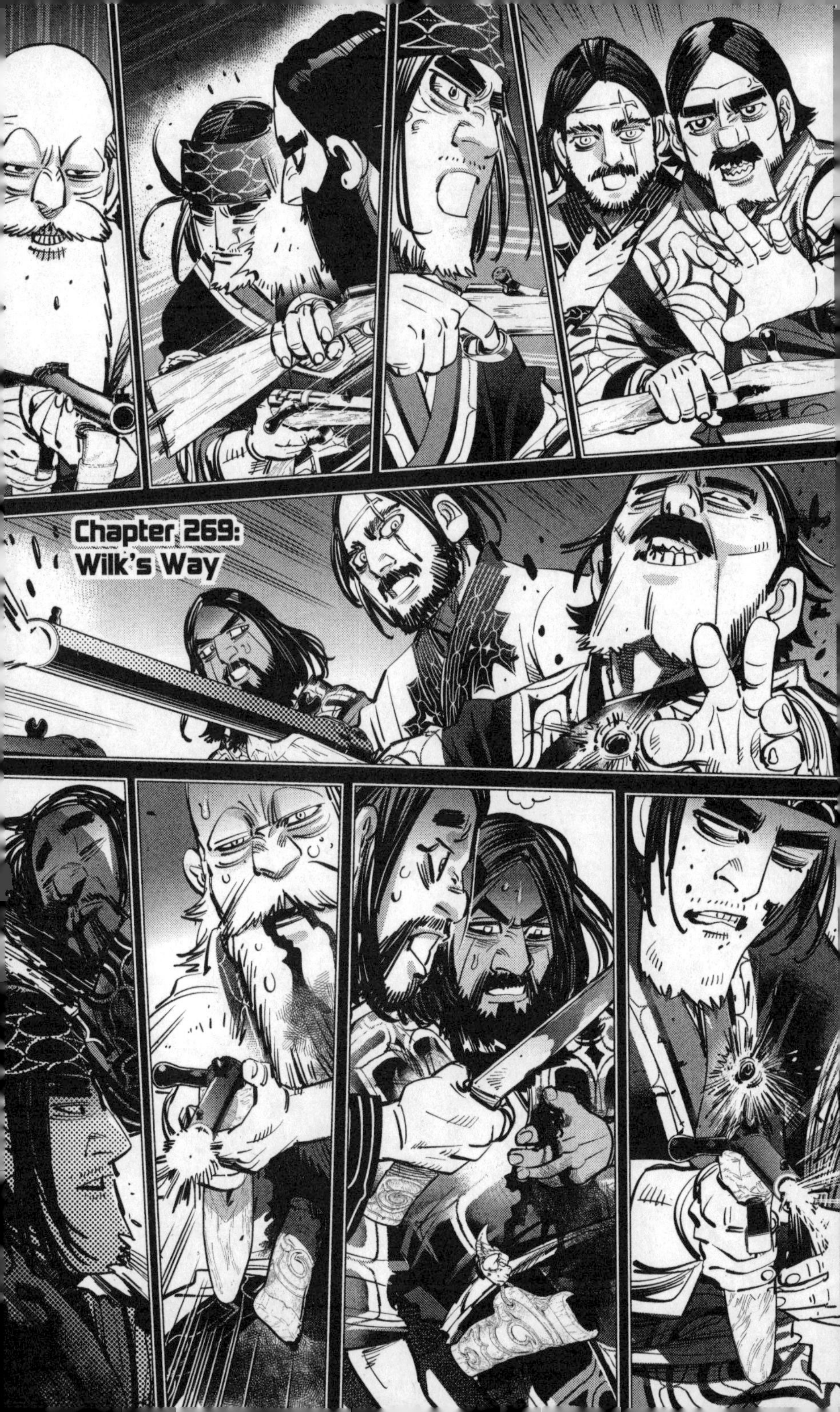
Chapter 269:
Wilk's Way

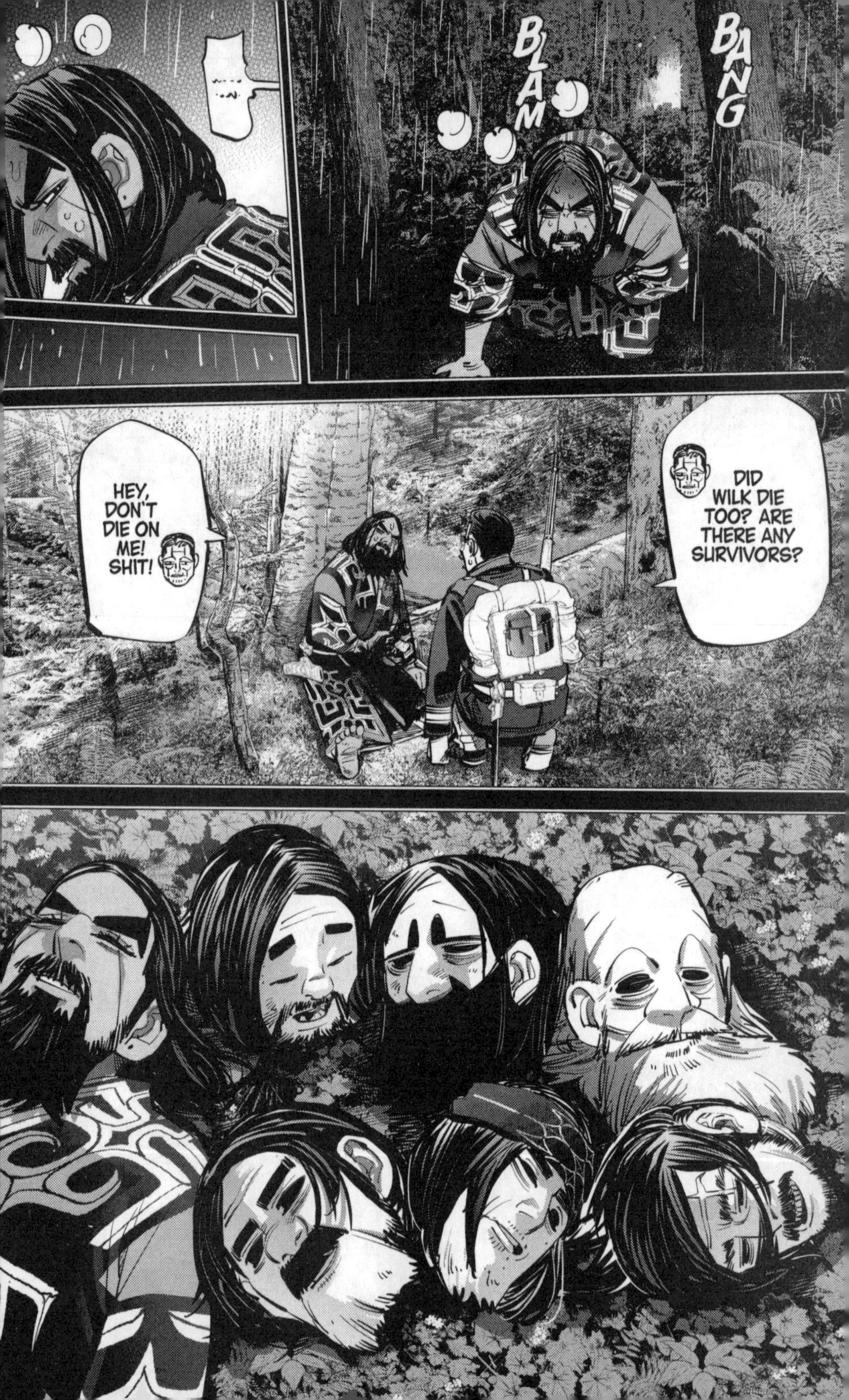
BANG
BLAM
DID WILK DIE TOO? ARE THERE ANY SURVIVORS?
HEY, DON'T DIE ON ME! SHIT!

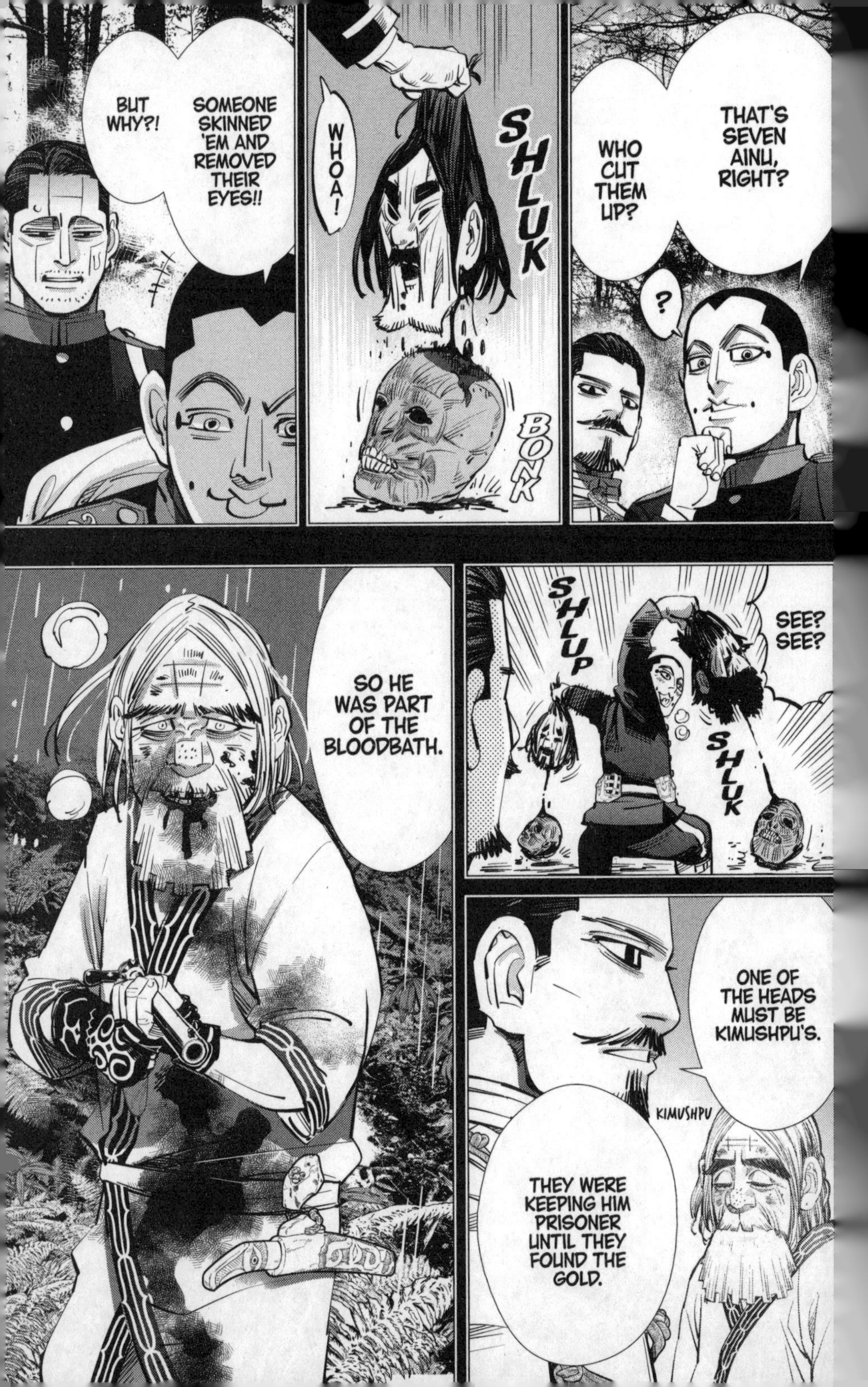
THAT'S SEVEN AINU, RIGHT?
WHO CUT THEM UP?
?
SHLUK
WHOA!
BONK
SOMEONE SKINNED 'EM AND REMOVED THEIR EYES!!
BUT WHY?!
SEE? SEE?
SHLUK
SHLUP
ONE OF THE HEADS MUST BE KIMUSHPU'S.
KIMUSHPU
THEY WERE KEEPING HIM PRISONER UNTIL THEY FOUND THE GOLD.
SO HE WAS PART OF THE BLOODBATH.

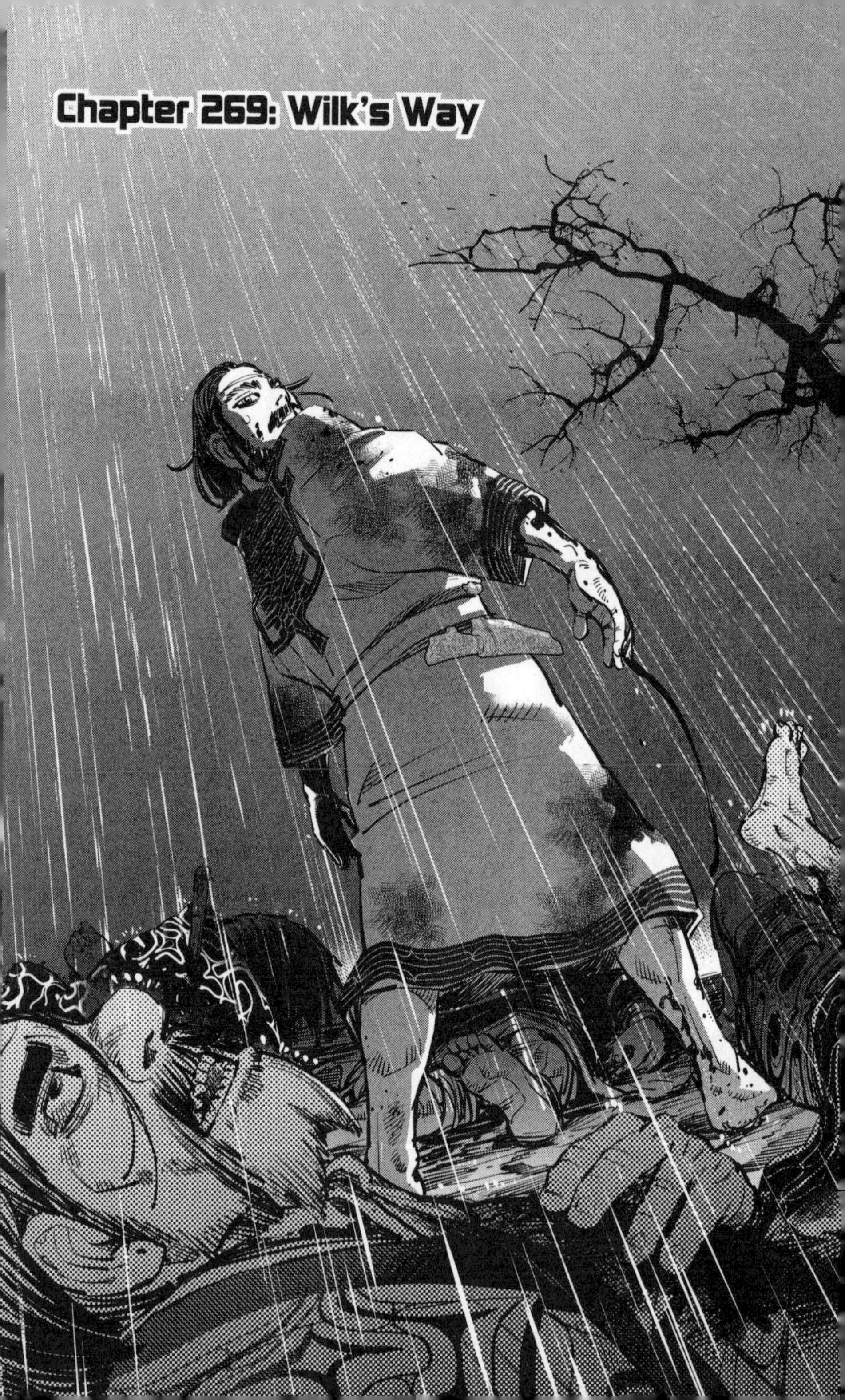
Chapter 269: Wilk's Way

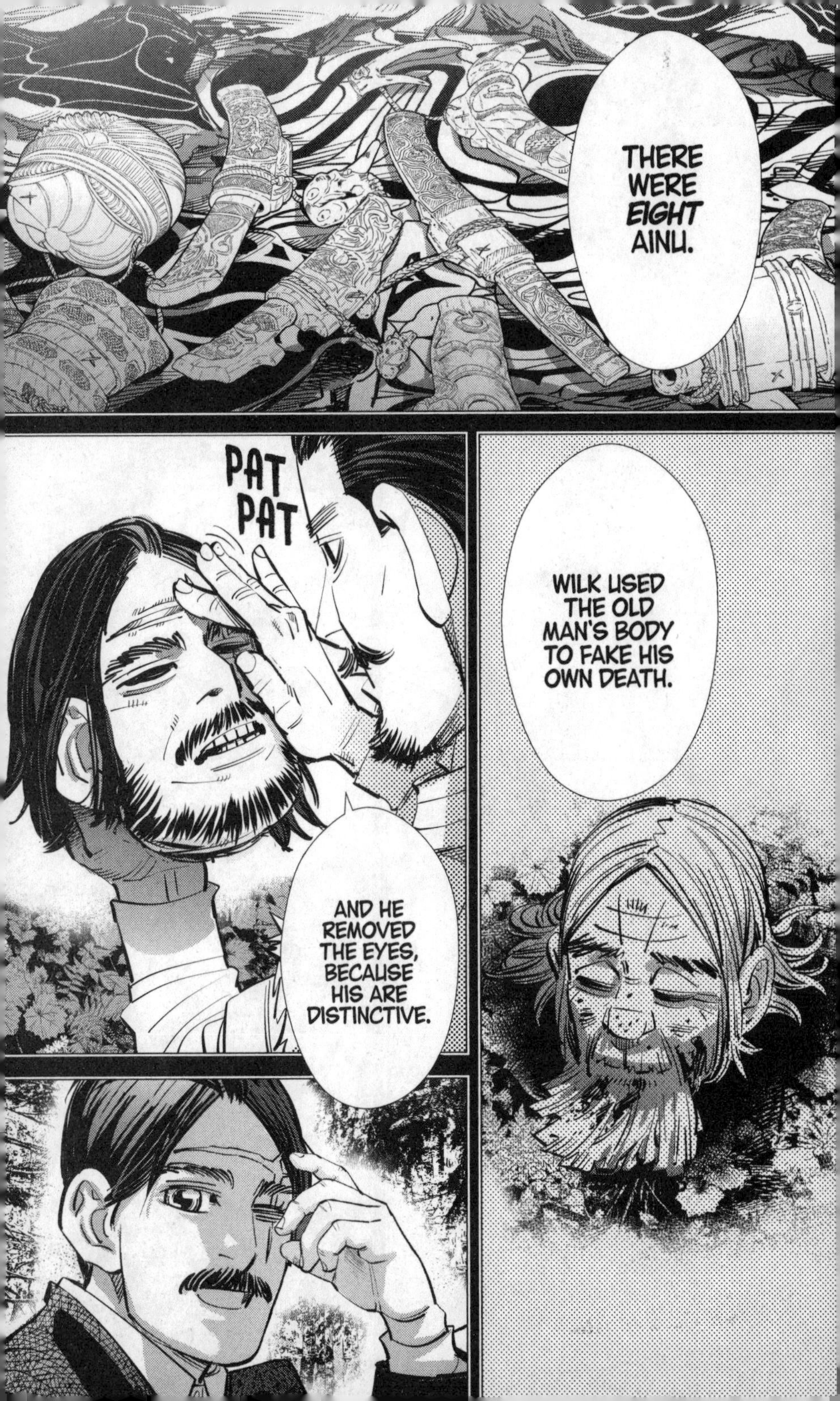
THERE WERE EIGHT AINU.
WILK USED THE OLD MAN'S BODY TO FAKE HIS OWN DEATH.
PAT PAT
AND HE REMOVED THE EYES, BECAUSE HIS ARE DISTINCTIVE.

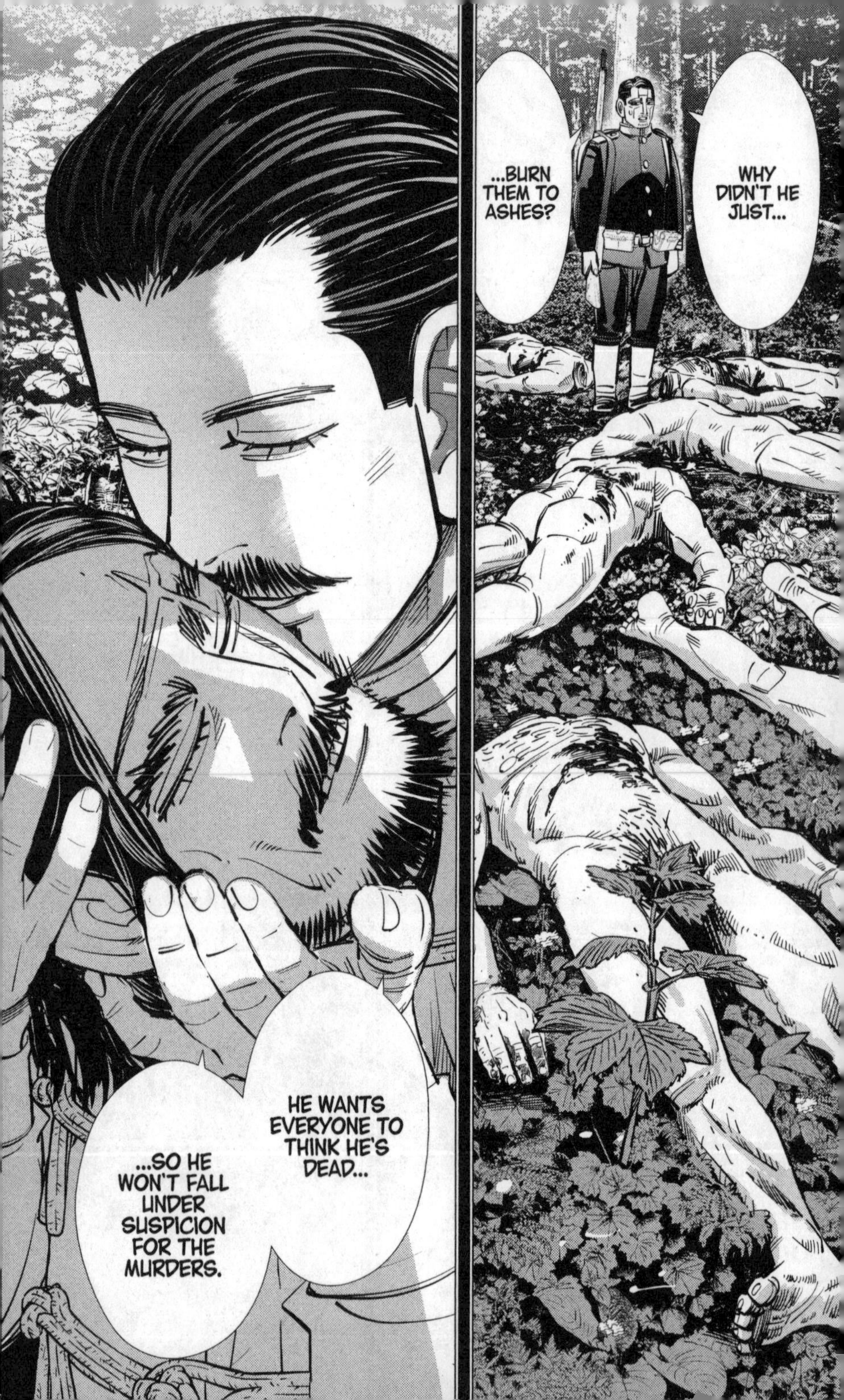
WHY DIDN'T HE JUST...
...BURN THEM TO ASHES?
HE WANTS EVERYONE TO THINK HE'S DEAD...
...SO HE WON'T FALL UNDER SUSPICION FOR THE MURDERS.

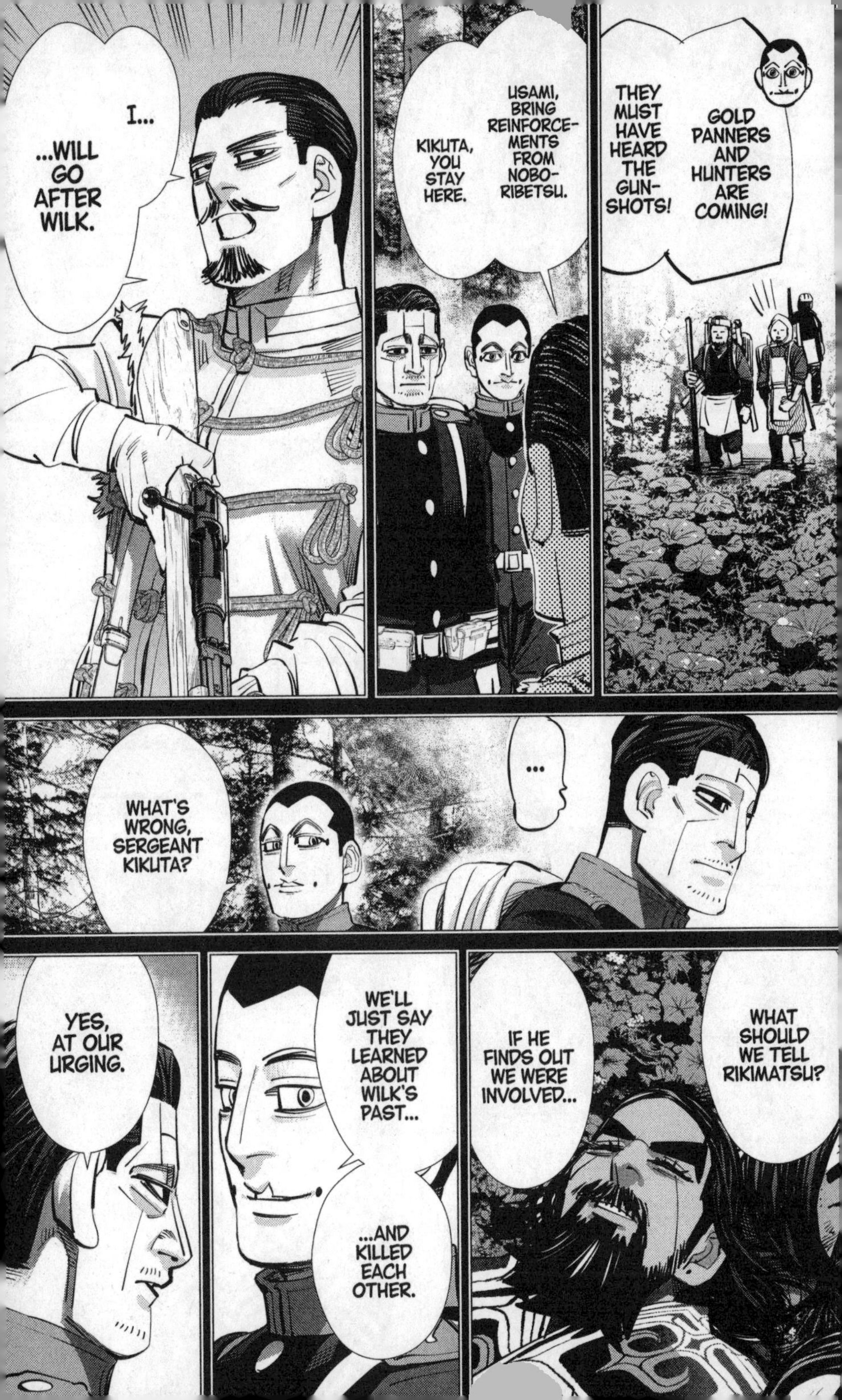
GOLD PANNERS AND HUNTERS ARE COMING!
THEY MUST HAVE HEARD THE GUNSHOTS!
USAMI, BRING REINFORCEMENTS FROM NOBORIBETSU.
KIKUTA, YOU STAY HERE.
I...
...WILL GO AFTER WILK.
...
WHAT'S WRONG, SERGEANT KIKUTA?
WHAT SHOULD WE TELL RIKIMATSU?
IF HE FINDS OUT WE WERE INVOLVED...
WE'LL JUST SAY THEY LEARNED ABOUT WILK'S PAST...
...AND KILLED EACH OTHER.
YES, AT OUR URGING.

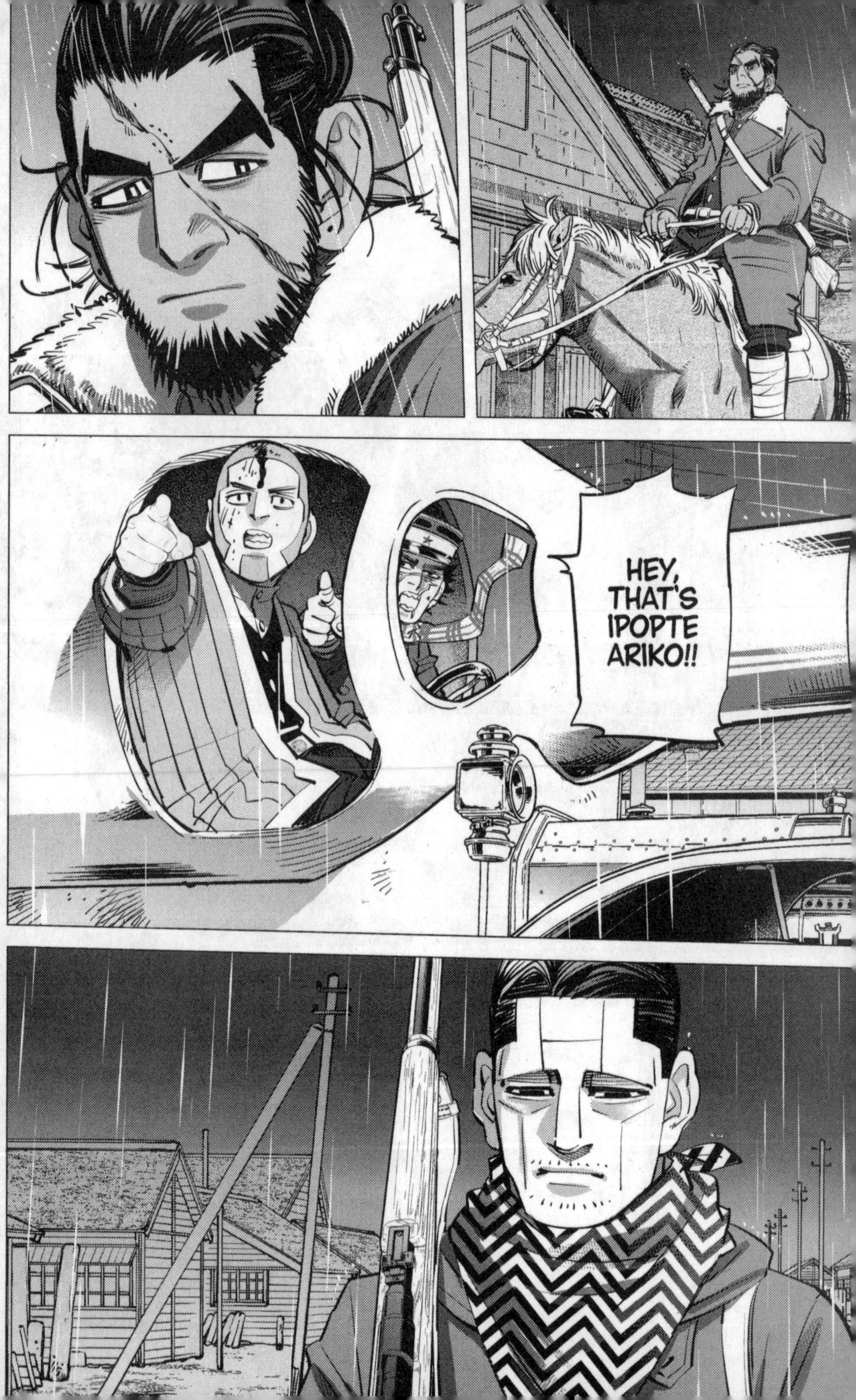
HEY, THAT'S IPOPTE ARIKO!!

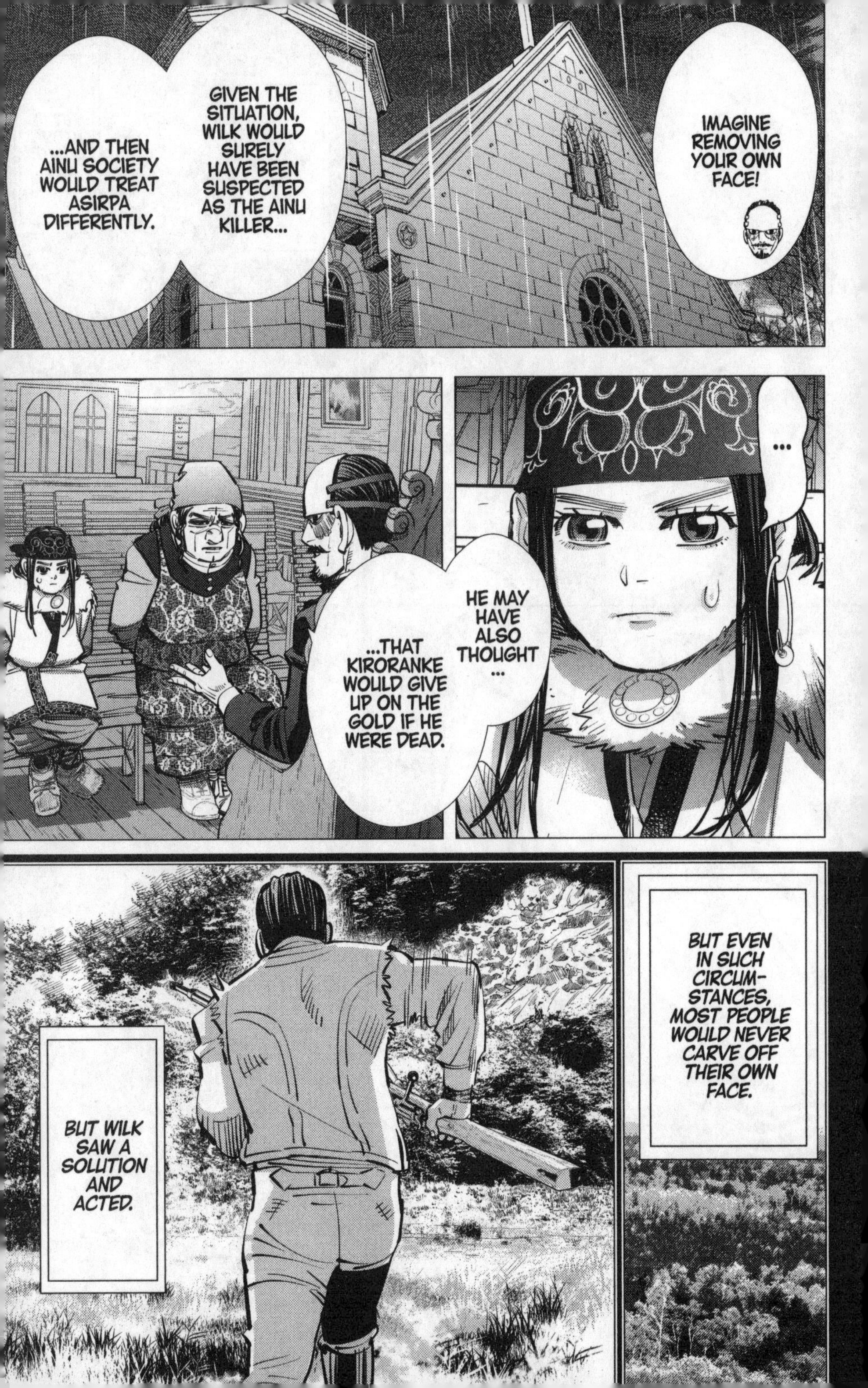
IMAGINE REMOVING YOUR OWN FACE!
GIVEN THE SITUATION, WILK WOULD SURELY HAVE BEEN SUSPECTED AS THE AINU KILLER...
...AND THEN AINU SOCIETY WOULD TREAT ASIRPA DIFFERENTLY.
...
HE MAY HAVE ALSO THOUGHT ...
...THAT KIRORANKE WOULD GIVE UP ON THE GOLD IF HE WERE DEAD.
BUT EVEN IN SUCH CIRCUM-STANCES, MOST PEOPLE WOULD NEVER CARVE OFF THEIR OWN FACE.
BUT WILK SAW A SOLUTION AND ACTED.

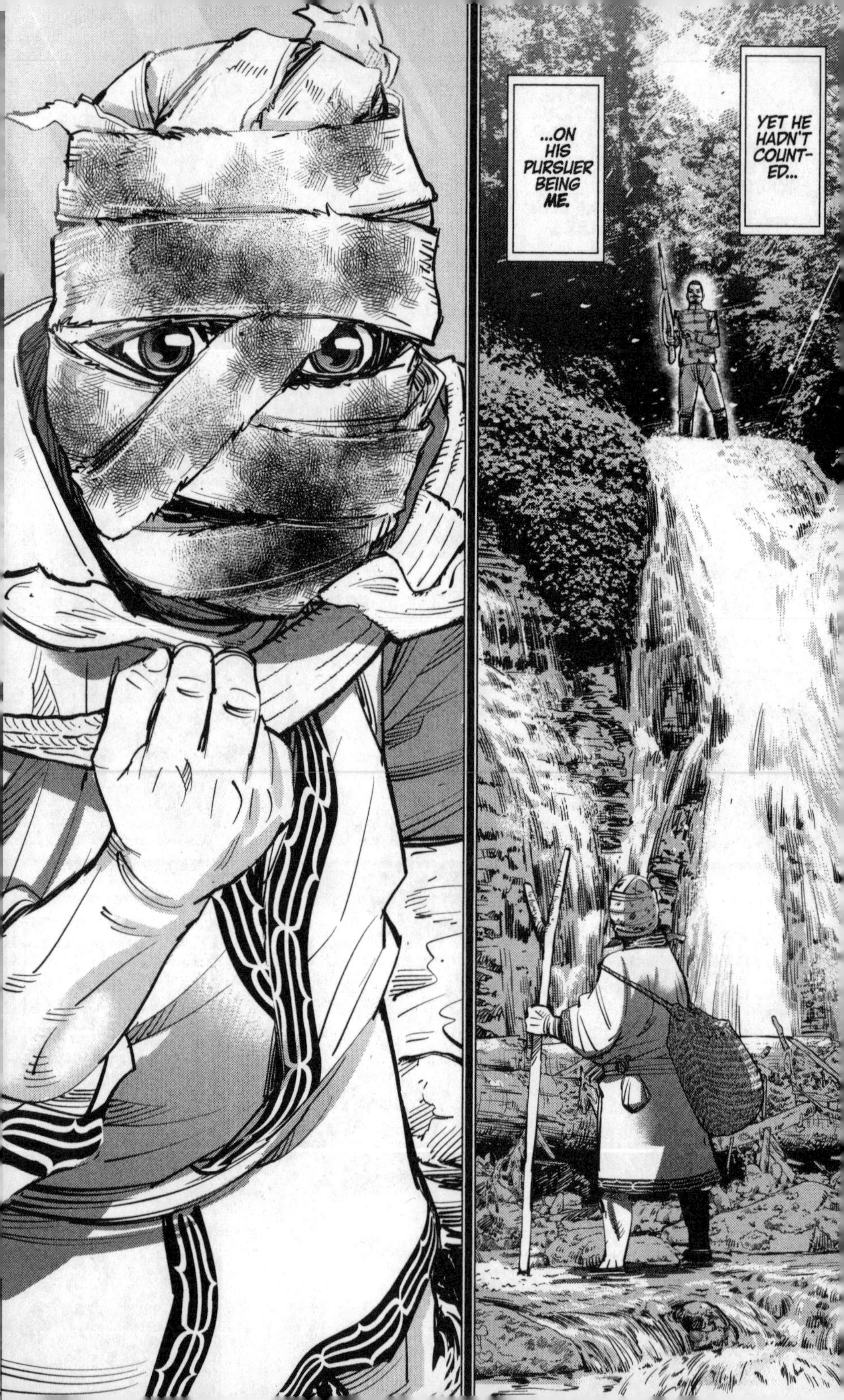
YET HE HADN'T COUNTED...
...ON HIS PURSUER BEING ME.

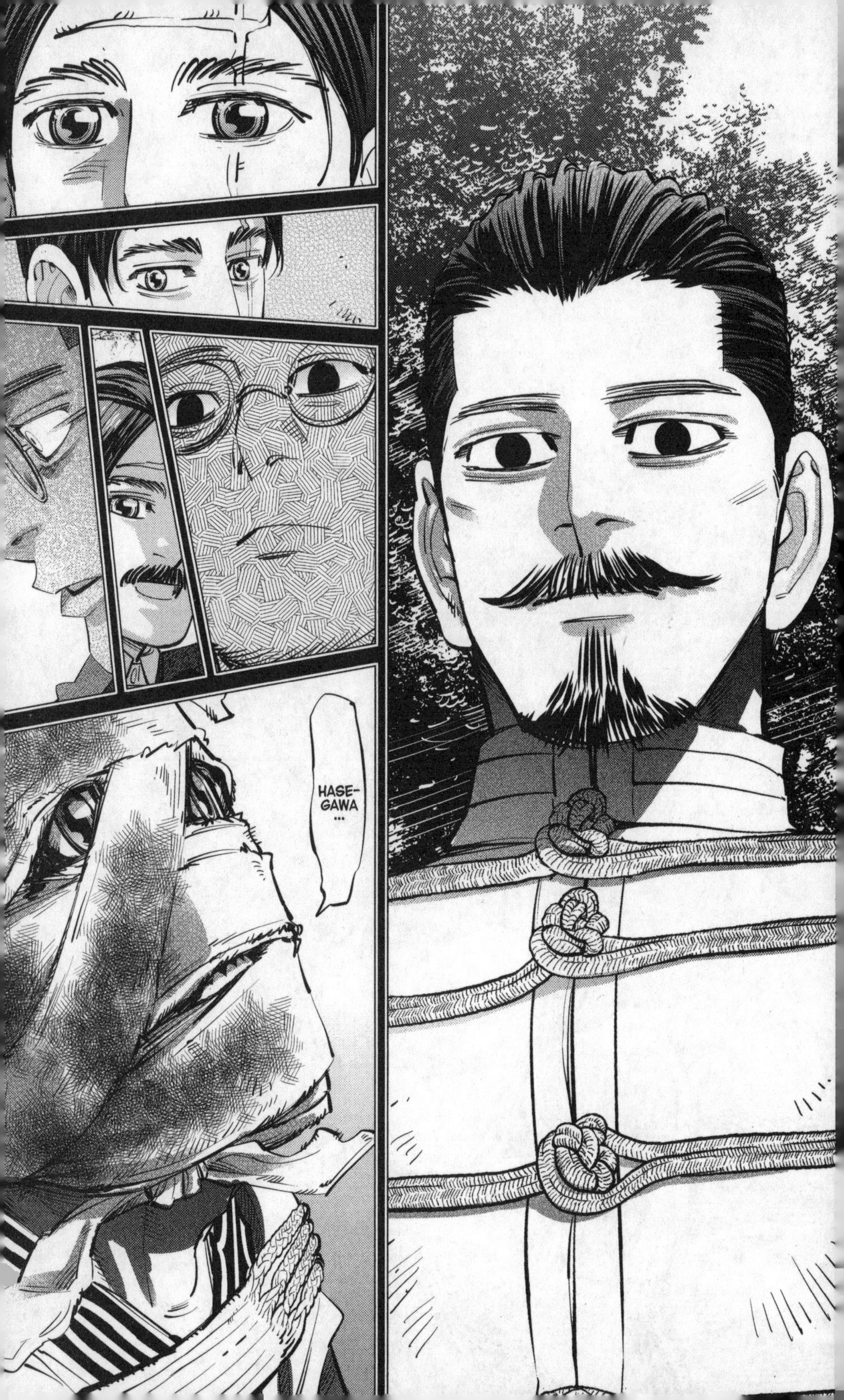
HASE-GAWA...

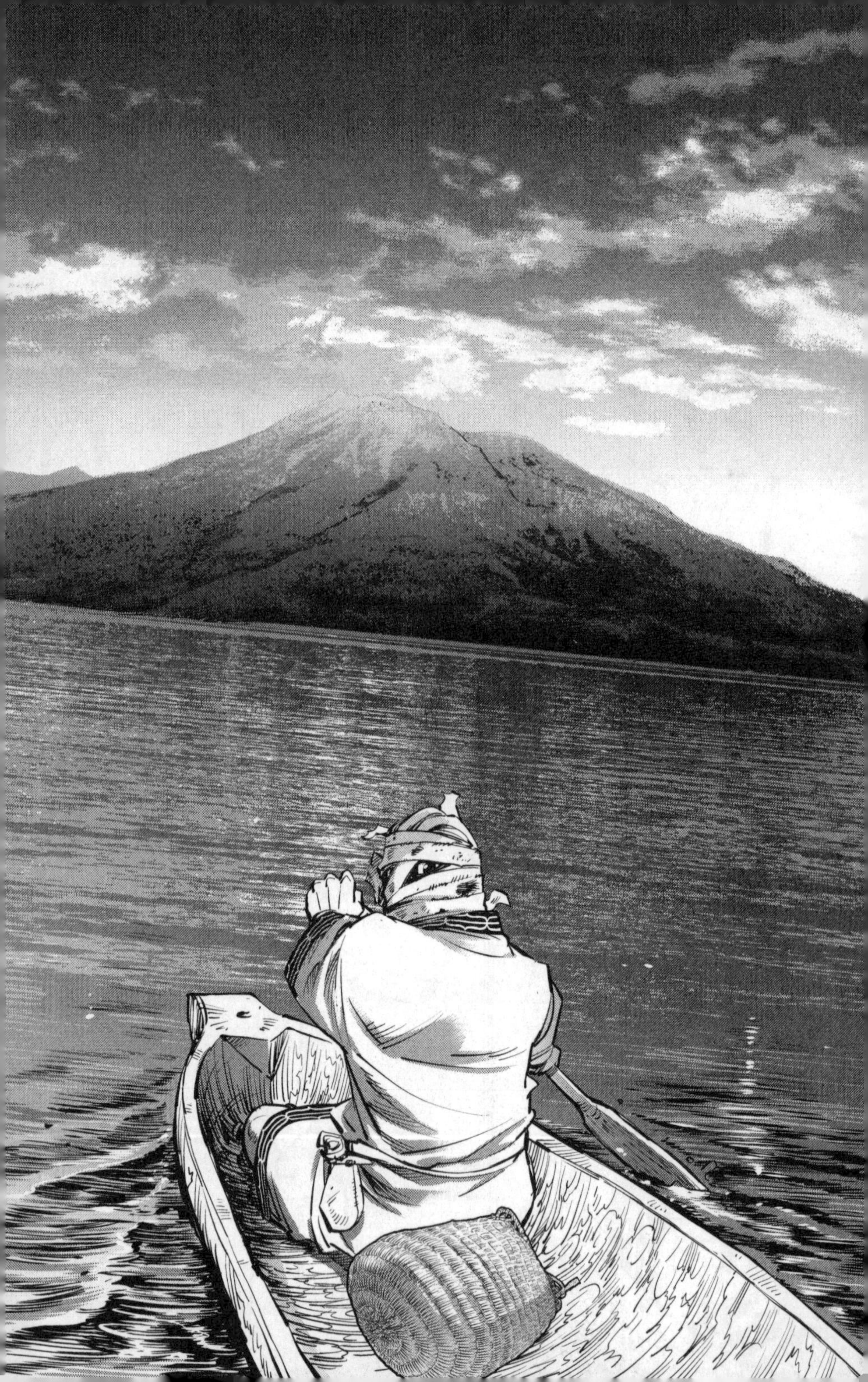

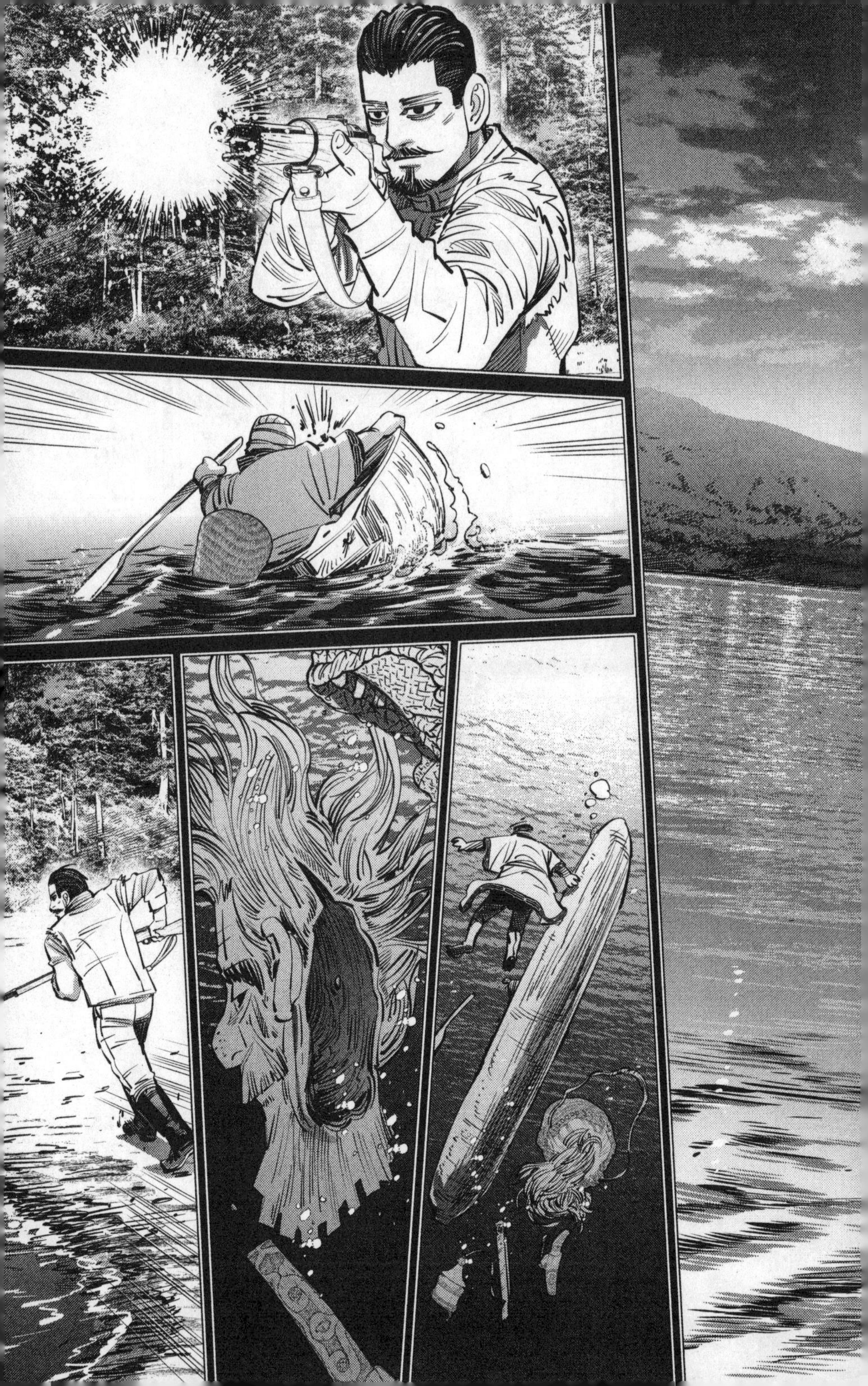

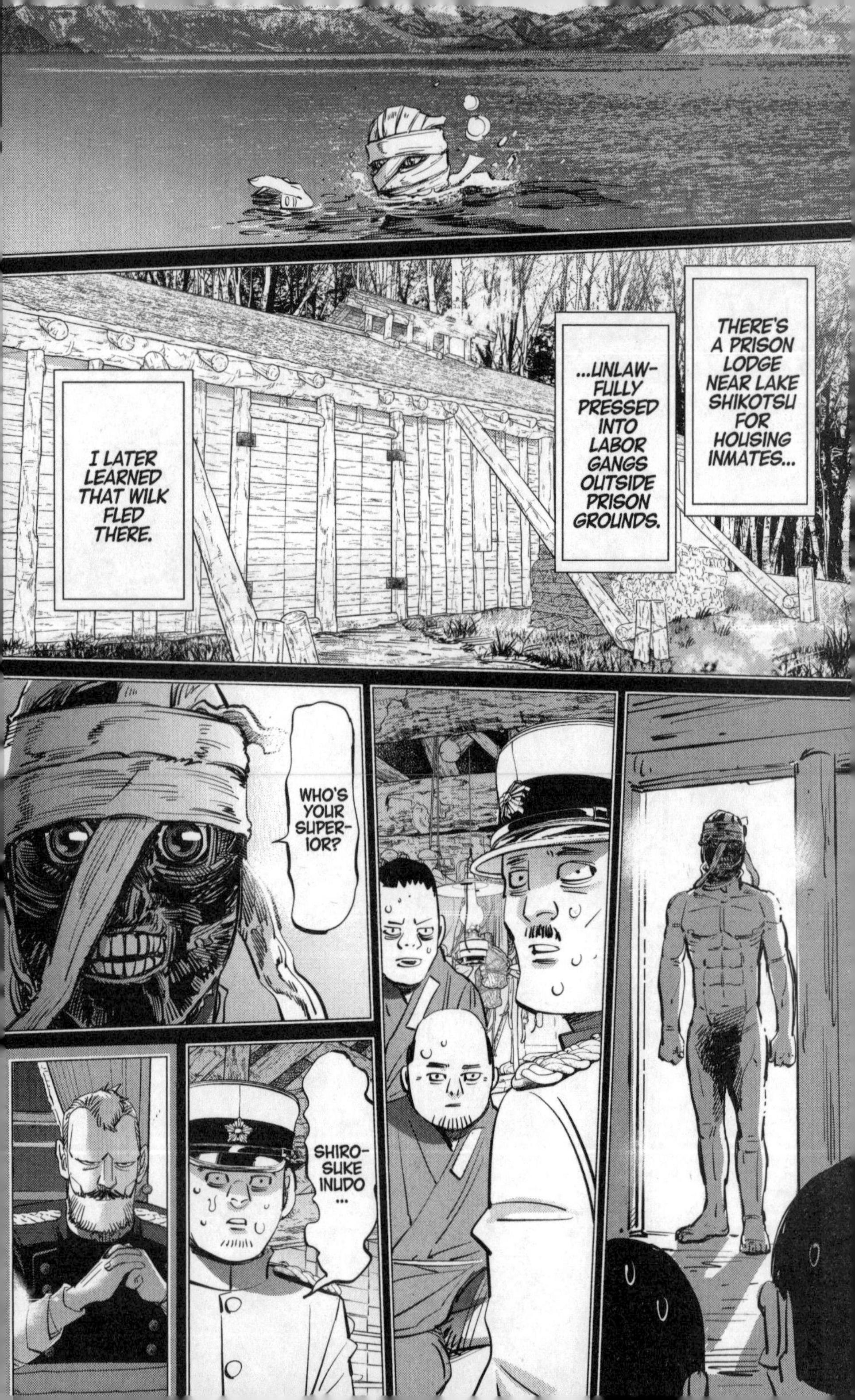
THERE'S A PRISON LODGE NEAR LAKE SHIKOTSU FOR HOUSING INMATES...
...UNLAWFULLY PRESSED INTO LABOR GANGS OUTSIDE PRISON GROUNDS.
I LATER LEARNED THAT WILK FLED THERE.
WHO'S YOUR SUPERIOR?
SHIROSUKE INUDO...

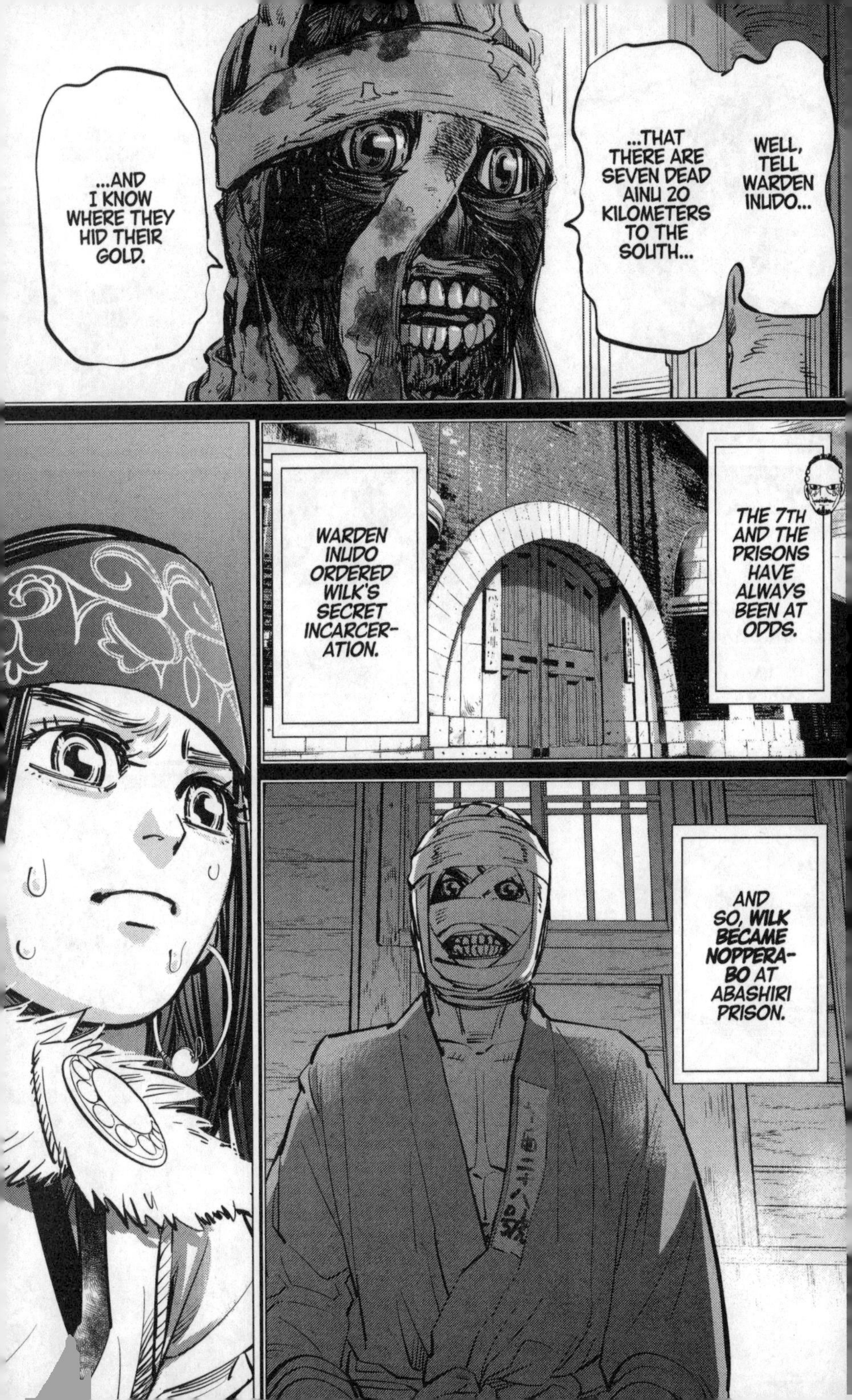
WELL, TELL WARDEN INUDO...
...THAT THERE ARE SEVEN DEAD AINU 20 KILOMETERS TO THE SOUTH...
...AND I KNOW WHERE THEY HID THEIR GOLD.
THE 7TH AND THE PRISONS HAVE ALWAYS BEEN AT ODDS.
WARDEN INUDO ORDERED WILK'S SECRET INCARCERATION.
AND SO, WILK BECAME NOPPERABO AT ABASHIRI PRISON.

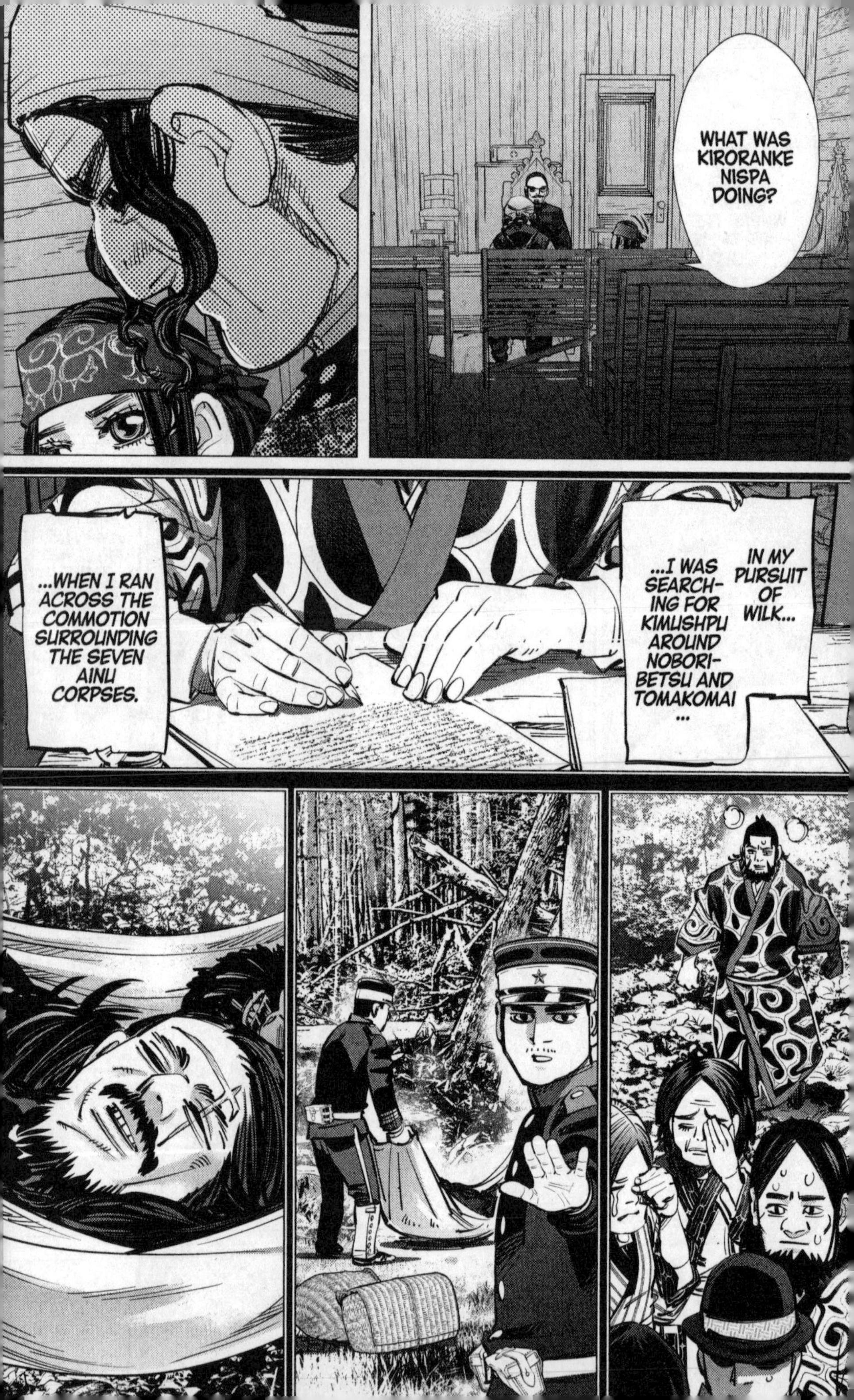
WHAT WAS KIRORANKE NISPA DOING?
IN MY PURSUIT OF WILK...
...I WAS SEARCHING FOR KIMUSHPU AROUND NOBORIBETSU AND TOMAKOMAI ...
...WHEN I RAN ACROSS THE COMMOTION SURROUNDING THE SEVEN AINU CORPSES.

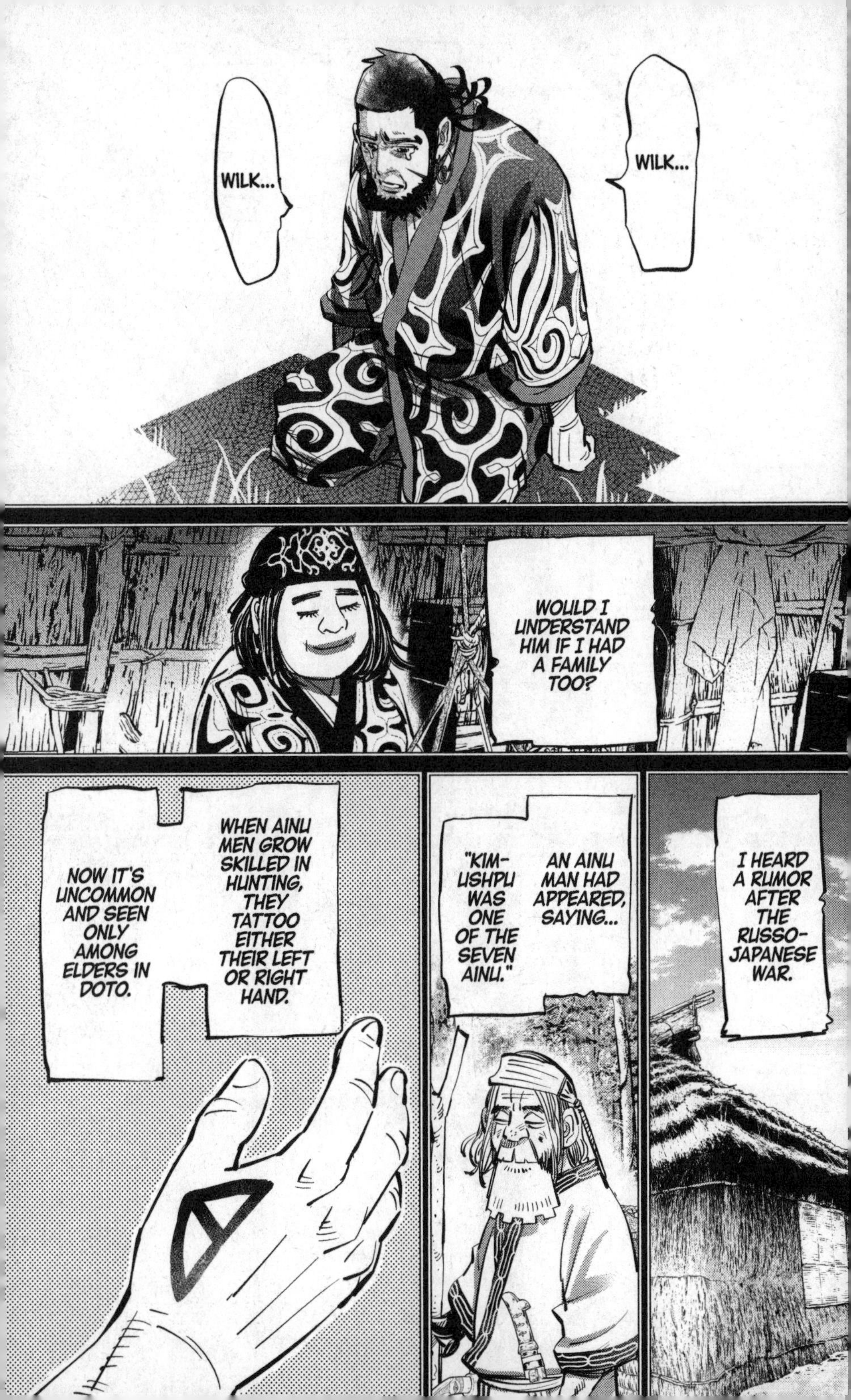
WILK...
WILK...
WOULD I UNDERSTAND HIM IF I HAD A FAMILY TOO?
I HEARD A RUMOR AFTER THE RUSSO-JAPANESE WAR.
AN AINU MAN HAD APPEARED, SAYING...
"KIM-USHPU WAS ONE OF THE SEVEN AINU."
WHEN AINU MEN GROW SKILLED IN HUNTING, THEY TATTOO EITHER THEIR LEFT OR RIGHT HAND.
NOW IT'S UNCOMMON AND SEEN ONLY AMONG ELDERS IN DOTO.

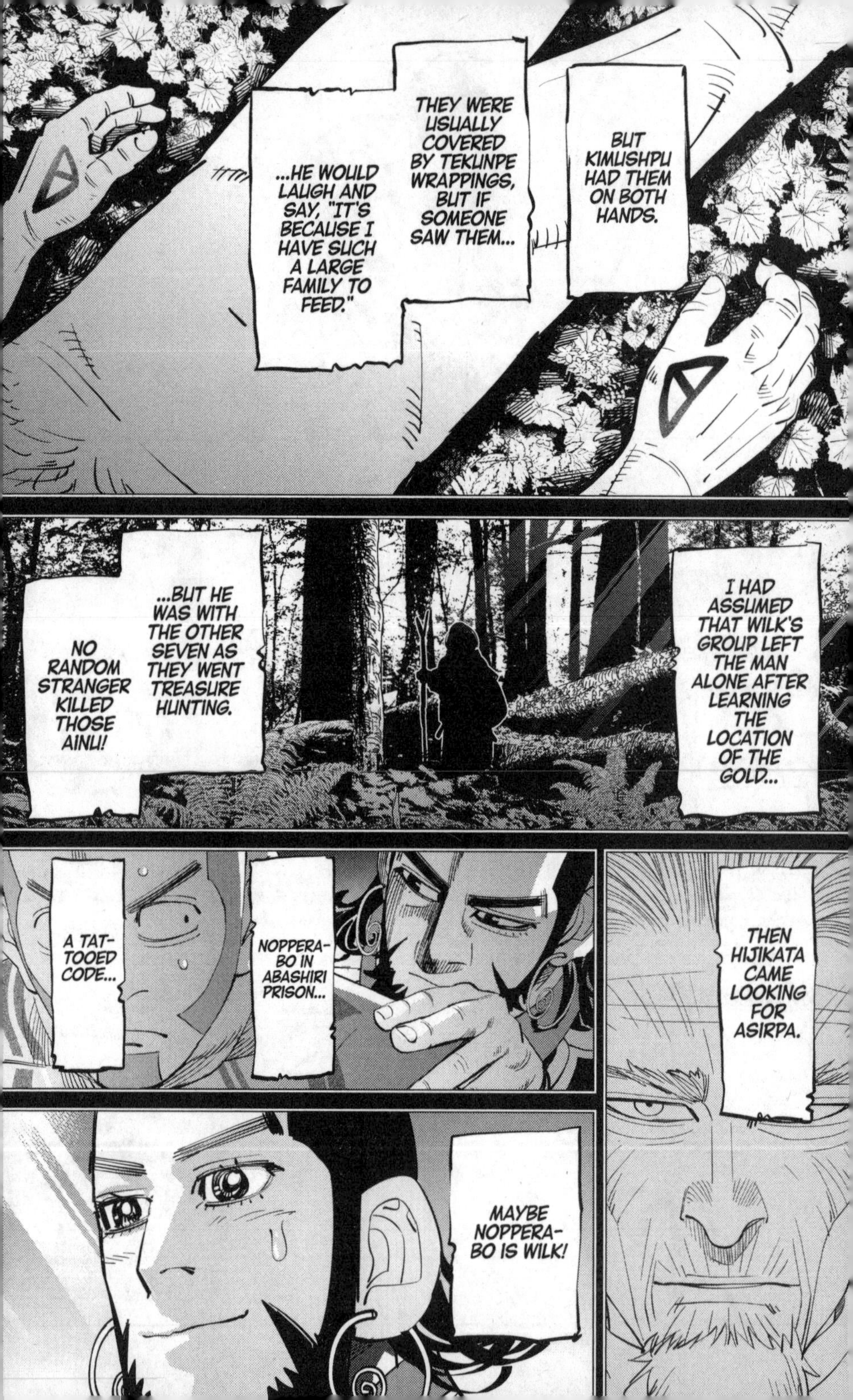
BUT KIMUSHPU HAD THEM ON BOTH HANDS.
THEY WERE USUALLY COVERED BY TEKUNPE WRAPPINGS, BUT IF SOMEONE SAW THEM...
...HE WOULD LAUGH AND SAY, "IT'S BECAUSE I HAVE SUCH A LARGE FAMILY TO FEED."
I HAD ASSUMED THAT WILK'S GROUP LEFT THE MAN ALONE AFTER LEARNING THE LOCATION OF THE GOLD...
...BUT HE WAS WITH THE OTHER SEVEN AS THEY WENT TREASURE HUNTING.
NO RANDOM STRANGER KILLED THOSE AINU!
THEN HIJIKATA CAME LOOKING FOR ASIRPA.
NOPPERA-BO IN ABASHIRI PRISON...
A TAT-TOOED CODE...
MAYBE NOPPERA-BO IS WILK!

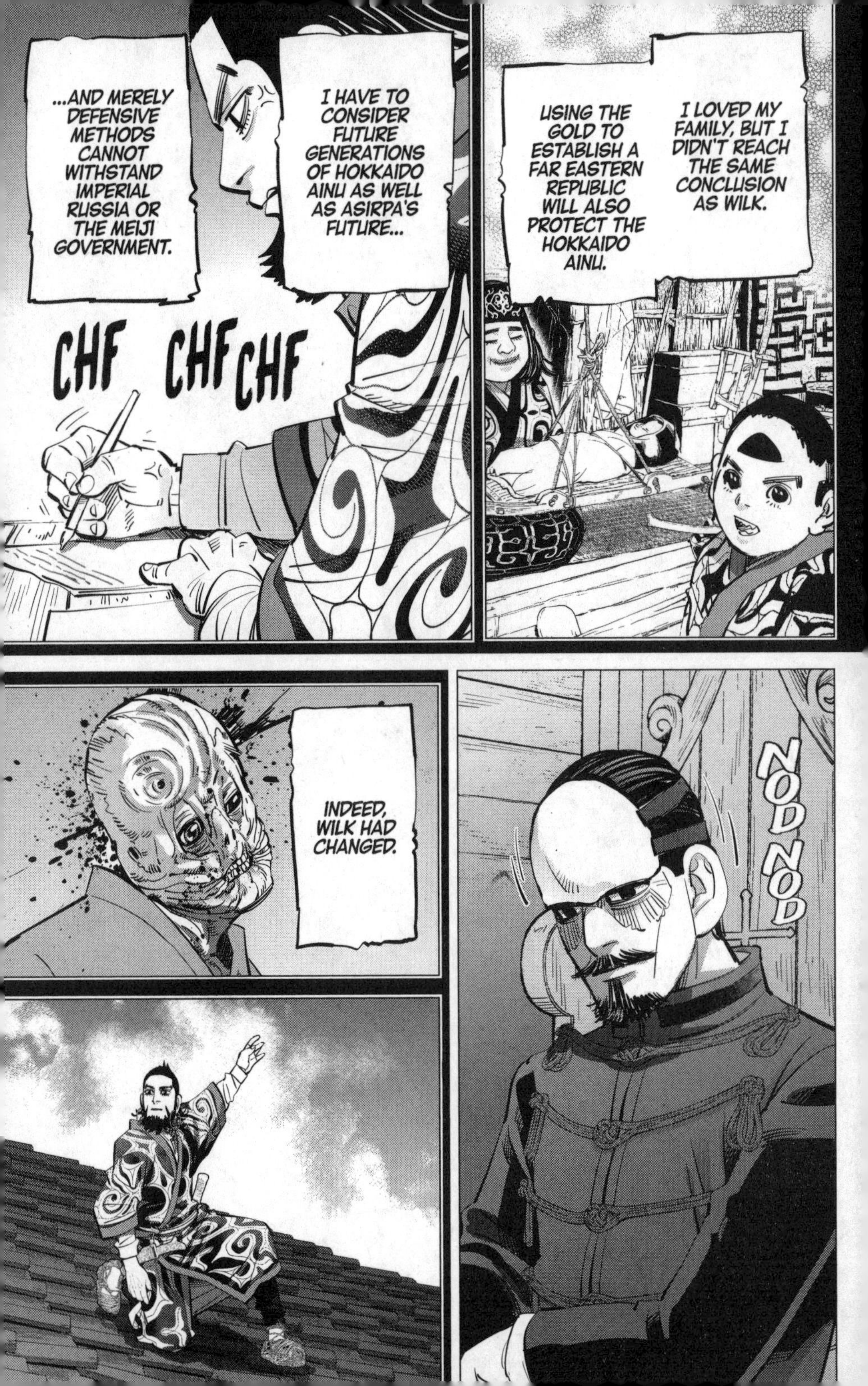
I LOVED MY FAMILY, BUT I DIDN'T REACH THE SAME CONCLUSION AS WILK.
USING THE GOLD TO ESTABLISH A FAR EASTERN REPUBLIC WILL ALSO PROTECT THE HOKKAIDO AINU.
I HAVE TO CONSIDER FUTURE GENERATIONS OF HOKKAIDO AINU AS WELL AS ASIRPA'S FUTURE...
...AND MERELY DEFENSIVE METHODS CANNOT WITHSTAND IMPERIAL RUSSIA OR THE MEIJI GOVERNMENT.
CHF CHF CHF
NOD NOD
INDEED, WILK HAD CHANGED.

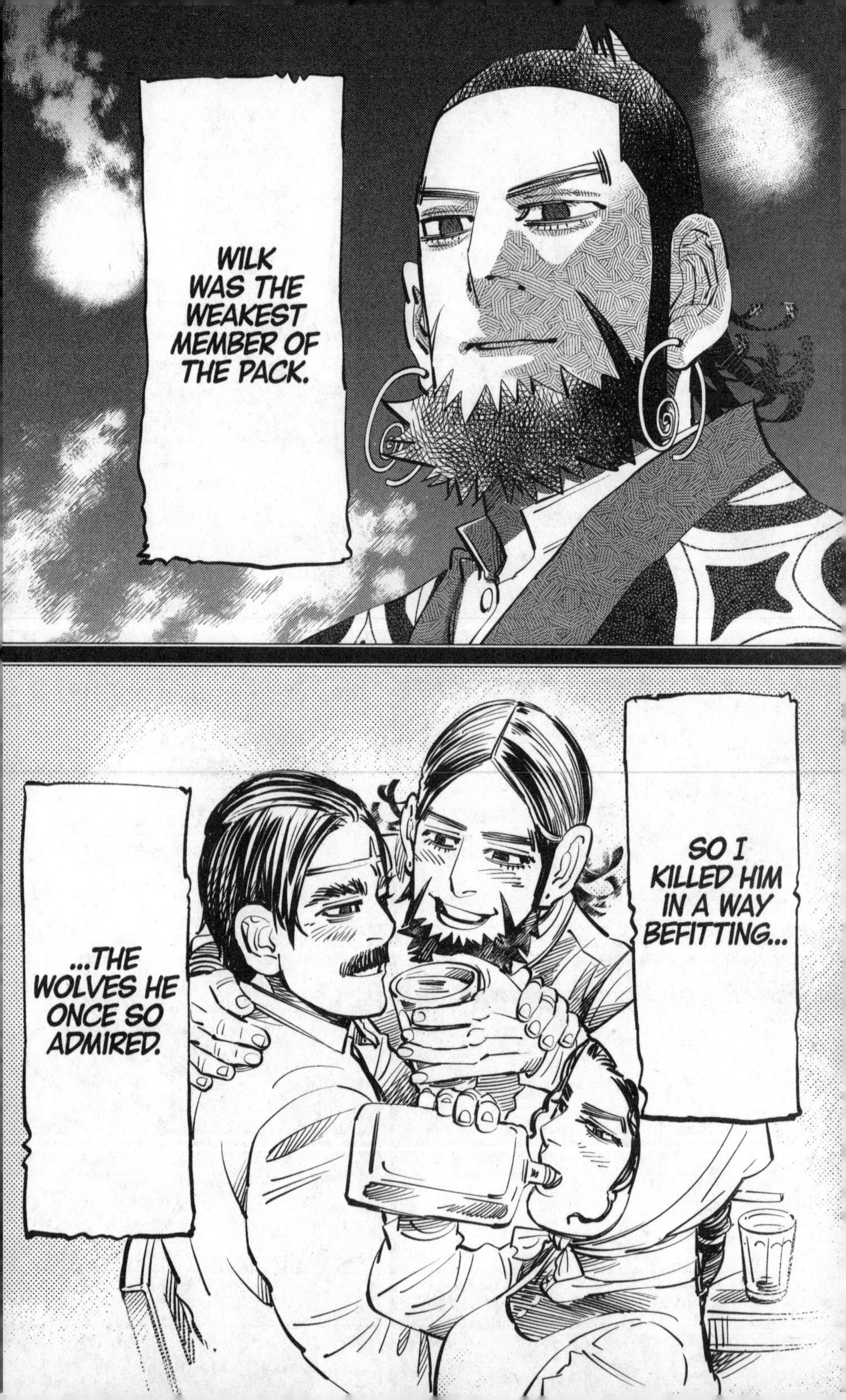
WILK WAS THE WEAKEST MEMBER OF THE PACK.
SO I KILLED HIM IN A WAY BEFITTING...
...THE WOLVES HE ONCE SO ADMIRED.

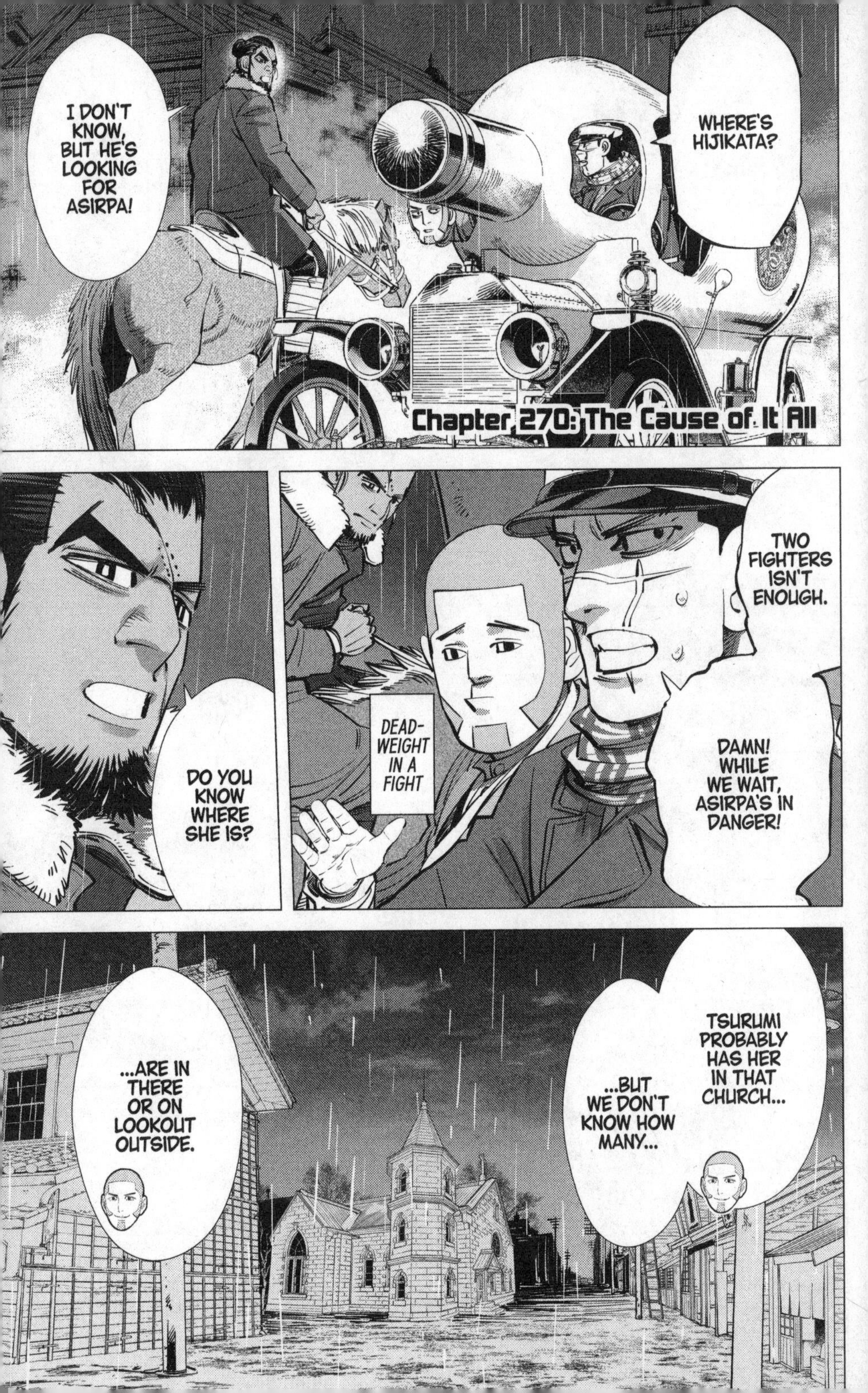
WHERE'S HIJIKATA?
I DON'T KNOW, BUT HE'S LOOKING FOR ASIRPA!
Chapter 270: The Cause of It All
TWO FIGHTERS ISN'T ENOUGH.
DAMN! WHILE WE WAIT, ASIRPA'S IN DANGER!
DEAD-WEIGHT IN A FIGHT
DO YOU KNOW WHERE SHE IS?
TSURUMI PROBABLY HAS HER IN THAT CHURCH...
...BUT WE DON'T KNOW HOW MANY...
...ARE IN THERE OR ON LOOKOUT OUTSIDE.

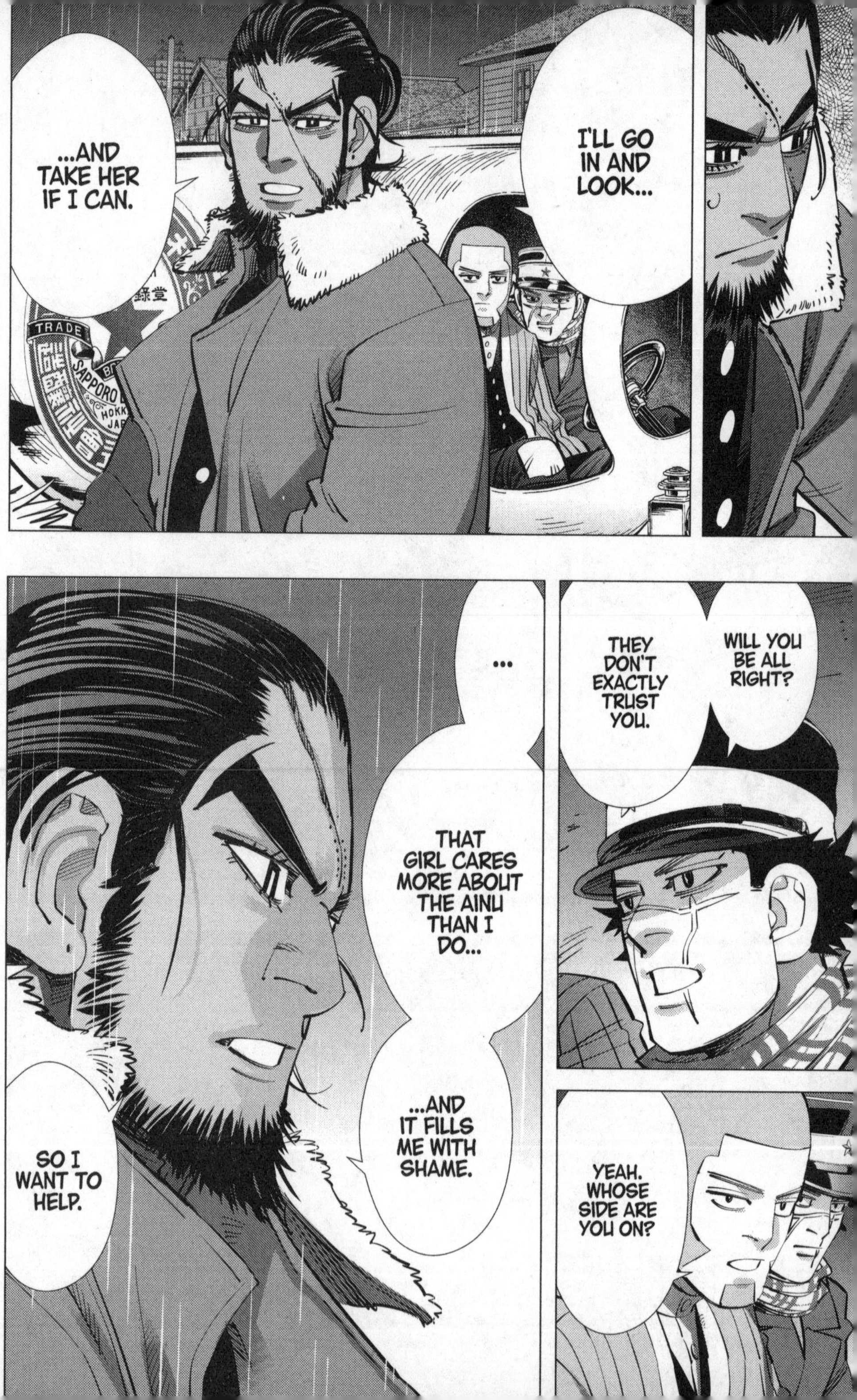
I'LL GO IN AND LOOK...
...AND TAKE HER IF I CAN.
WILL YOU BE ALL RIGHT?
THEY DON'T EXACTLY TRUST YOU.
YEAH. WHOSE SIDE ARE YOU ON?
...
THAT GIRL CARES MORE ABOUT THE AINU THAN I DO...
...AND IT FILLS ME WITH SHAME.
SO I WANT TO HELP.

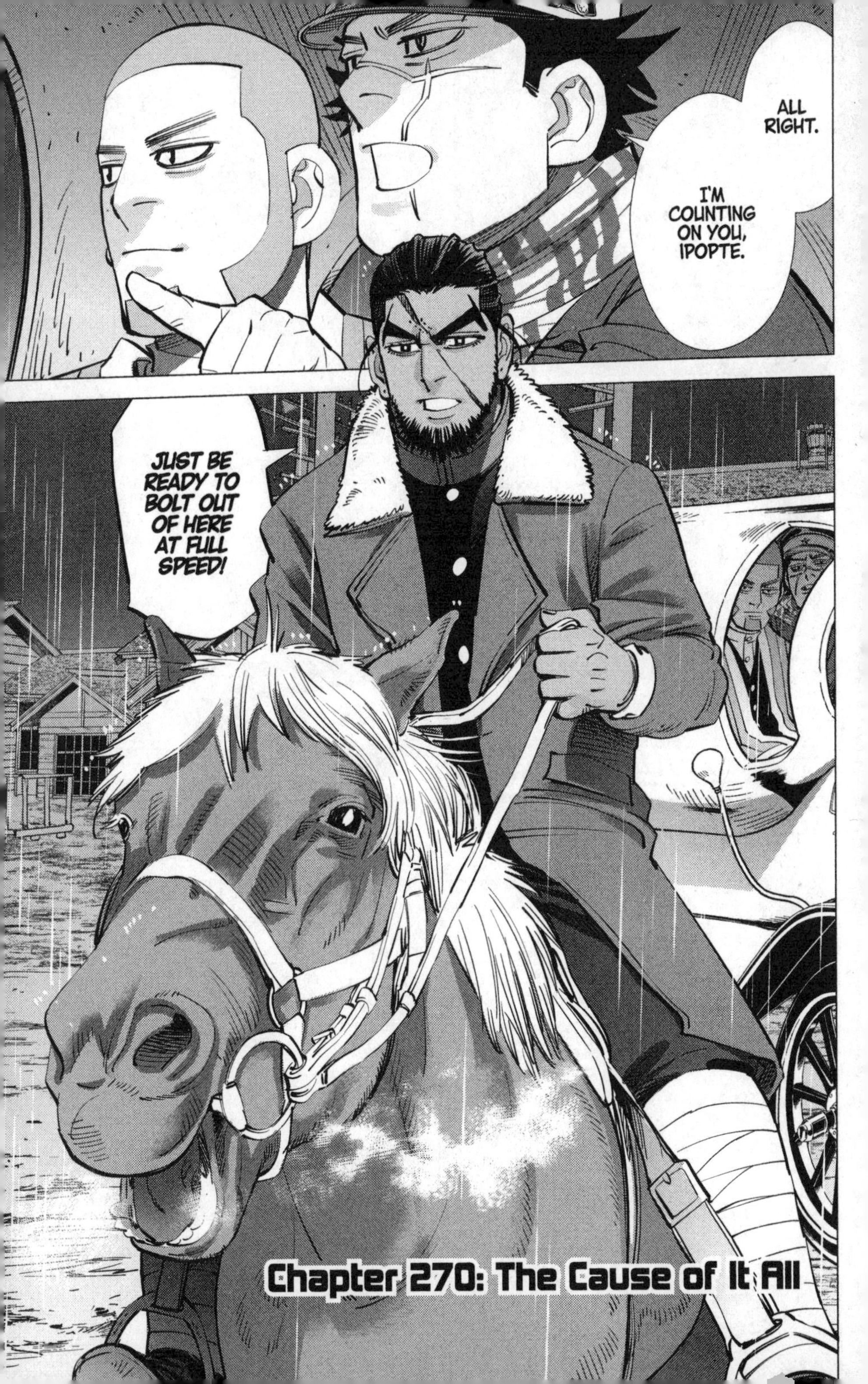
ALL RIGHT.
I'M COUNTING ON YOU, IPOPTE.
JUST BE READY TO BOLT OUT OF HERE AT FULL SPEED!
Chapter 270: The Cause of It All

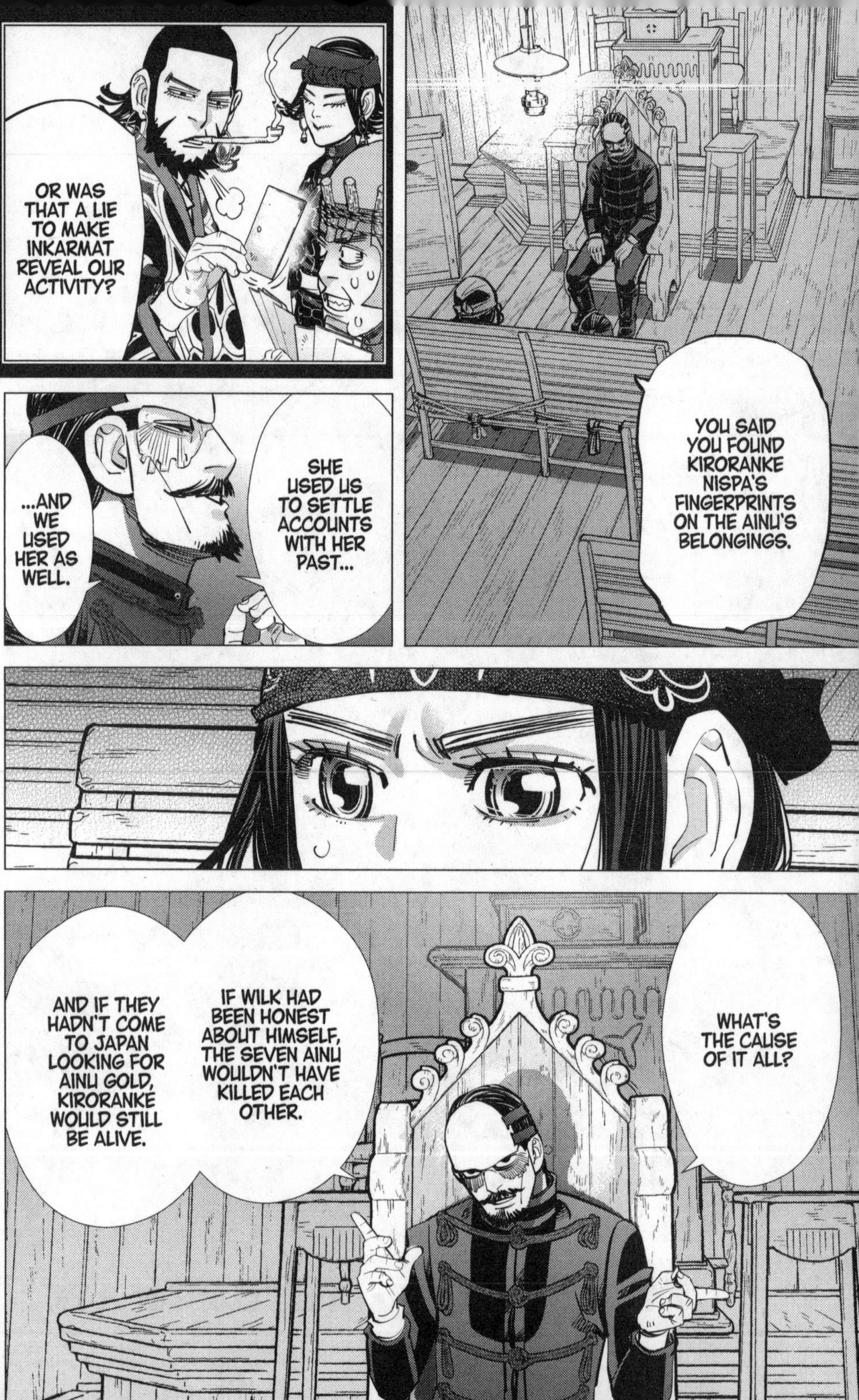
YOU SAID YOU FOUND KIRORANKE NISPA'S FINGERPRINTS ON THE AINU'S BELONGINGS.
OR WAS THAT A LIE TO MAKE INKARMAT REVEAL OUR ACTIVITY?
SHE USED US TO SETTLE ACCOUNTS WITH HER PAST...
...AND WE USED HER AS WELL.
WHAT'S THE CAUSE OF IT ALL?
IF WILK HAD BEEN HONEST ABOUT HIMSELF, THE SEVEN AINU WOULDN'T HAVE KILLED EACH OTHER.
AND IF THEY HADN'T COME TO JAPAN LOOKING FOR AINU GOLD, KIRORANKE WOULD STILL BE ALIVE.

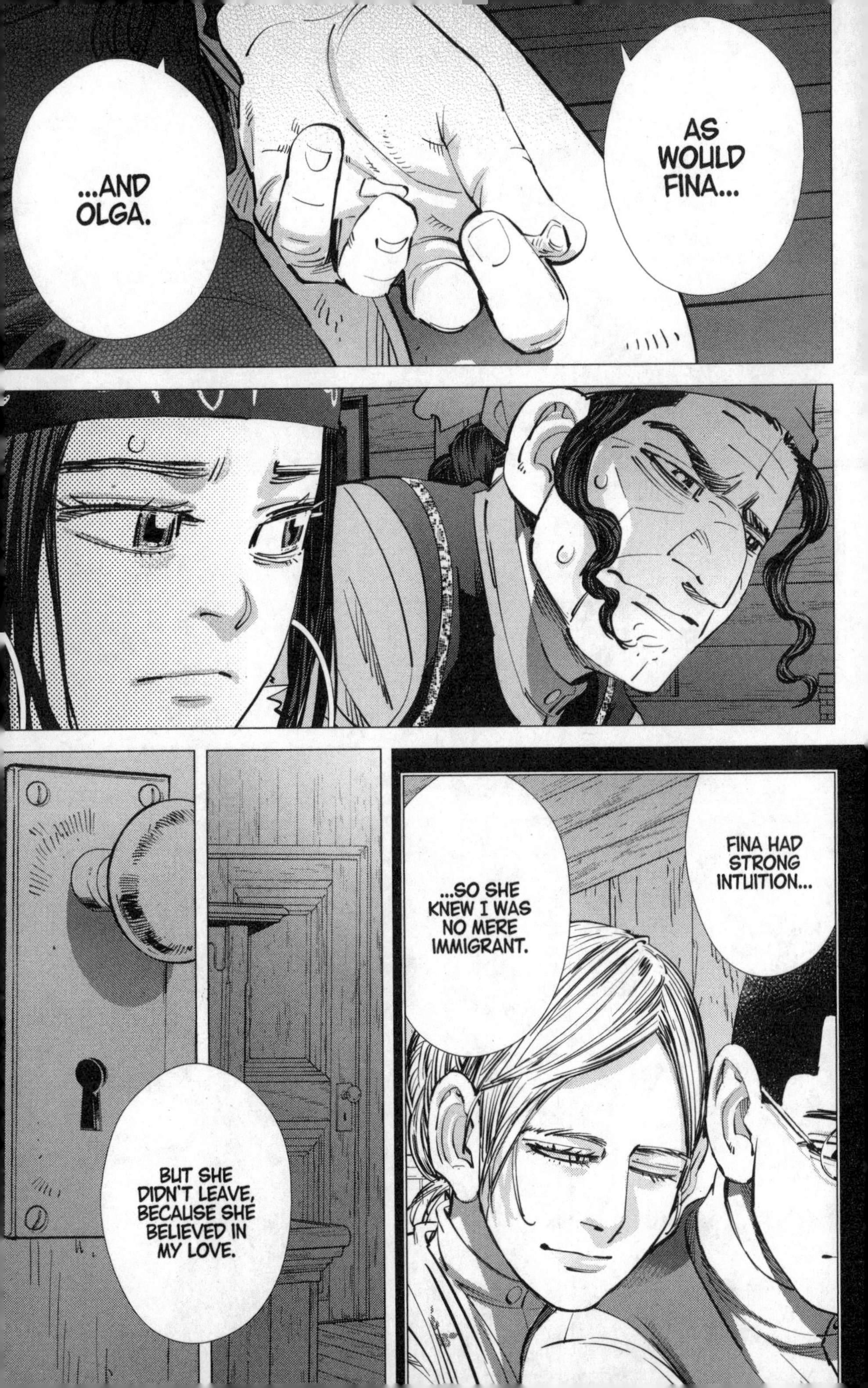
AS WOULD FINA...
...AND OLGA.
FINA HAD STRONG INTUITION...
...SO SHE KNEW I WAS NO MERE IMMIGRANT.
BUT SHE DIDN'T LEAVE, BECAUSE SHE BELIEVED IN MY LOVE.

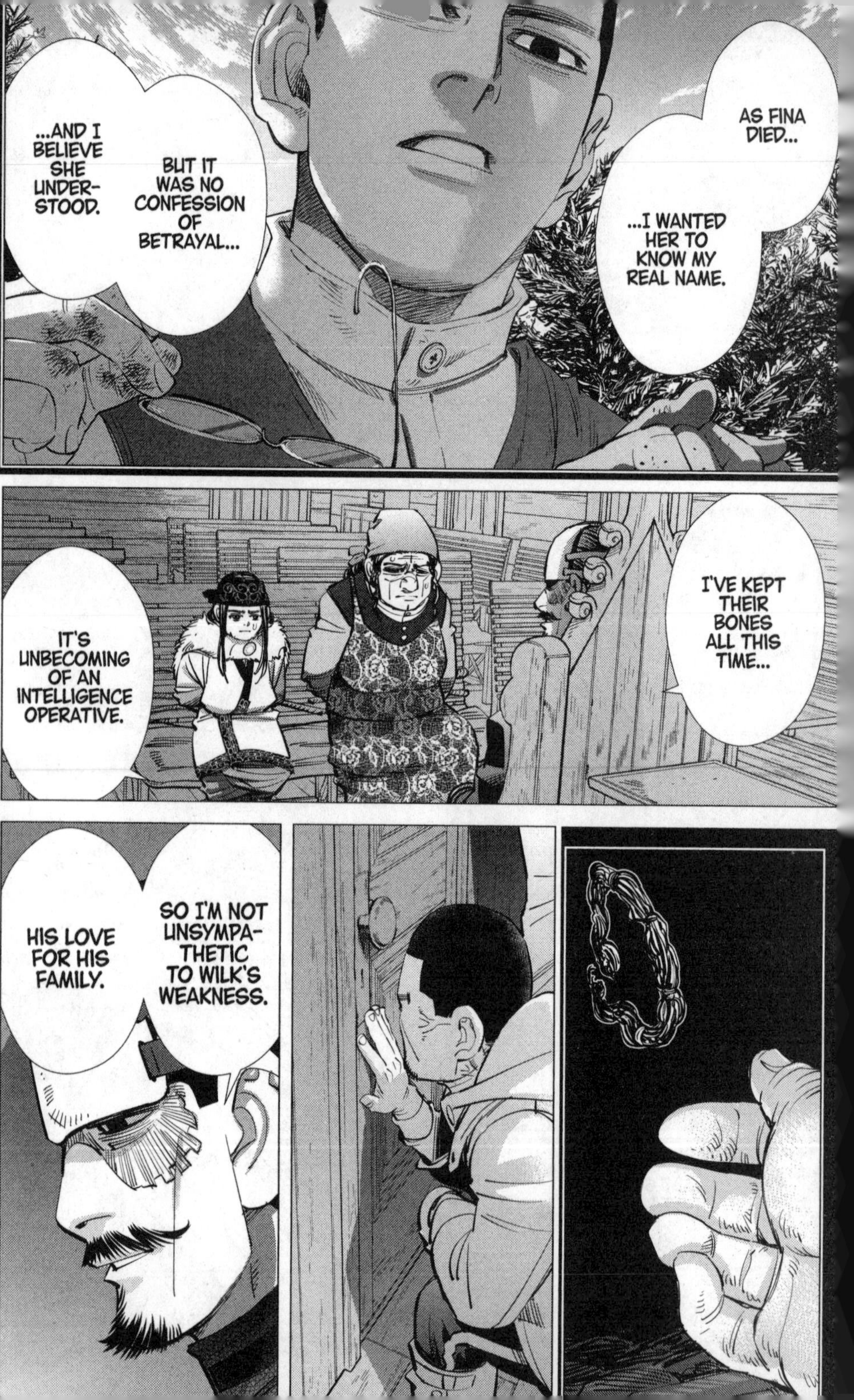
AS FINA DIED...
...I WANTED HER TO KNOW MY REAL NAME.
BUT IT WAS NO CONFESSION OF BETRAYAL...
...AND I BELIEVE SHE UNDER-STOOD.
I'VE KEPT THEIR BONES ALL THIS TIME...
IT'S UNBECOMING OF AN INTELLIGENCE OPERATIVE.
SO I'M NOT UNSYMPA-THETIC TO WILK'S WEAKNESS.
HIS LOVE FOR HIS FAMILY.

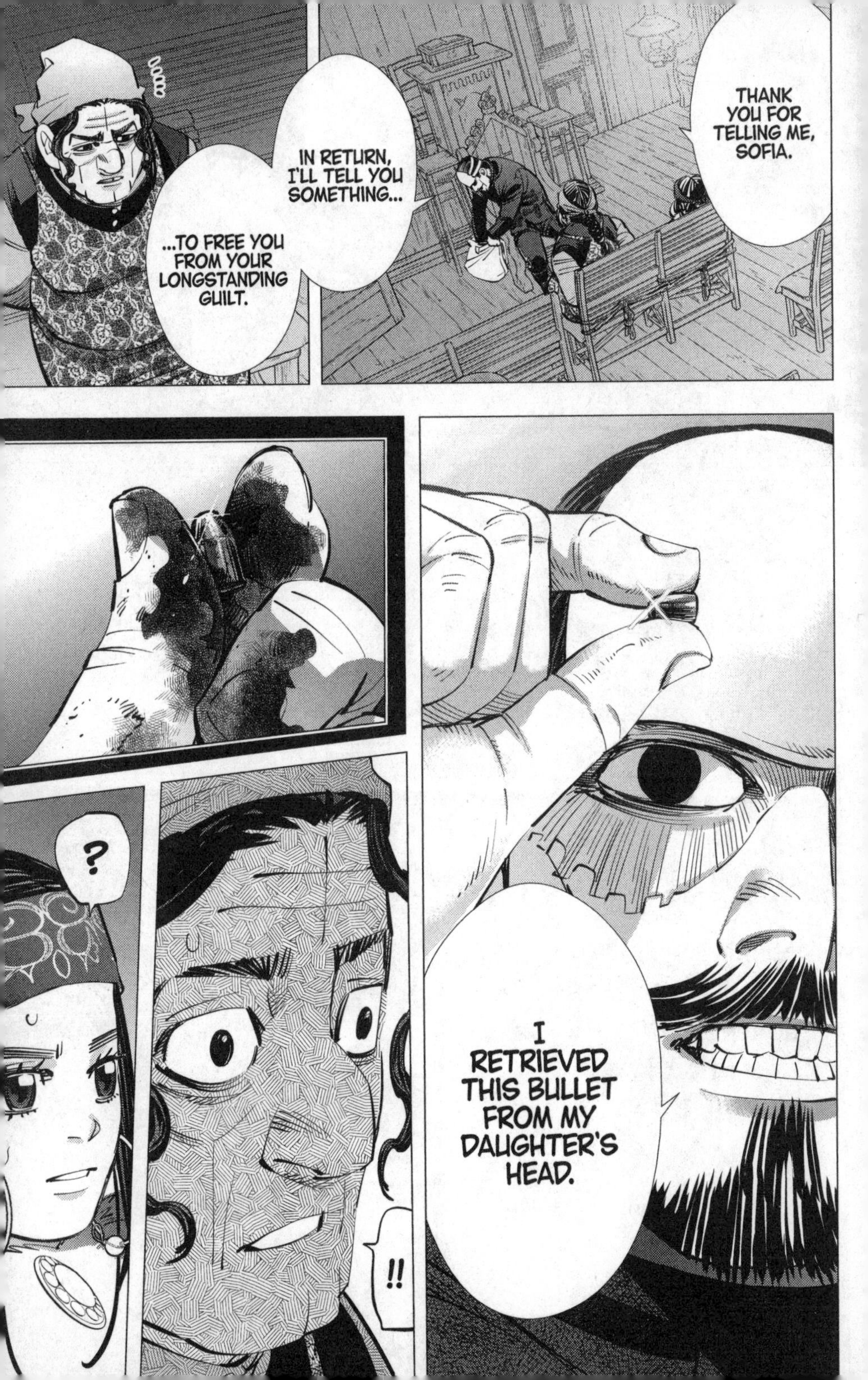
THANK YOU FOR TELLING ME, SOFIA.
IN RETURN, I'LL TELL YOU SOMETHING...
...TO FREE YOU FROM YOUR LONGSTANDING GUILT.
I RETRIEVED THIS BULLET FROM MY DAUGHTER'S HEAD.
!!
?

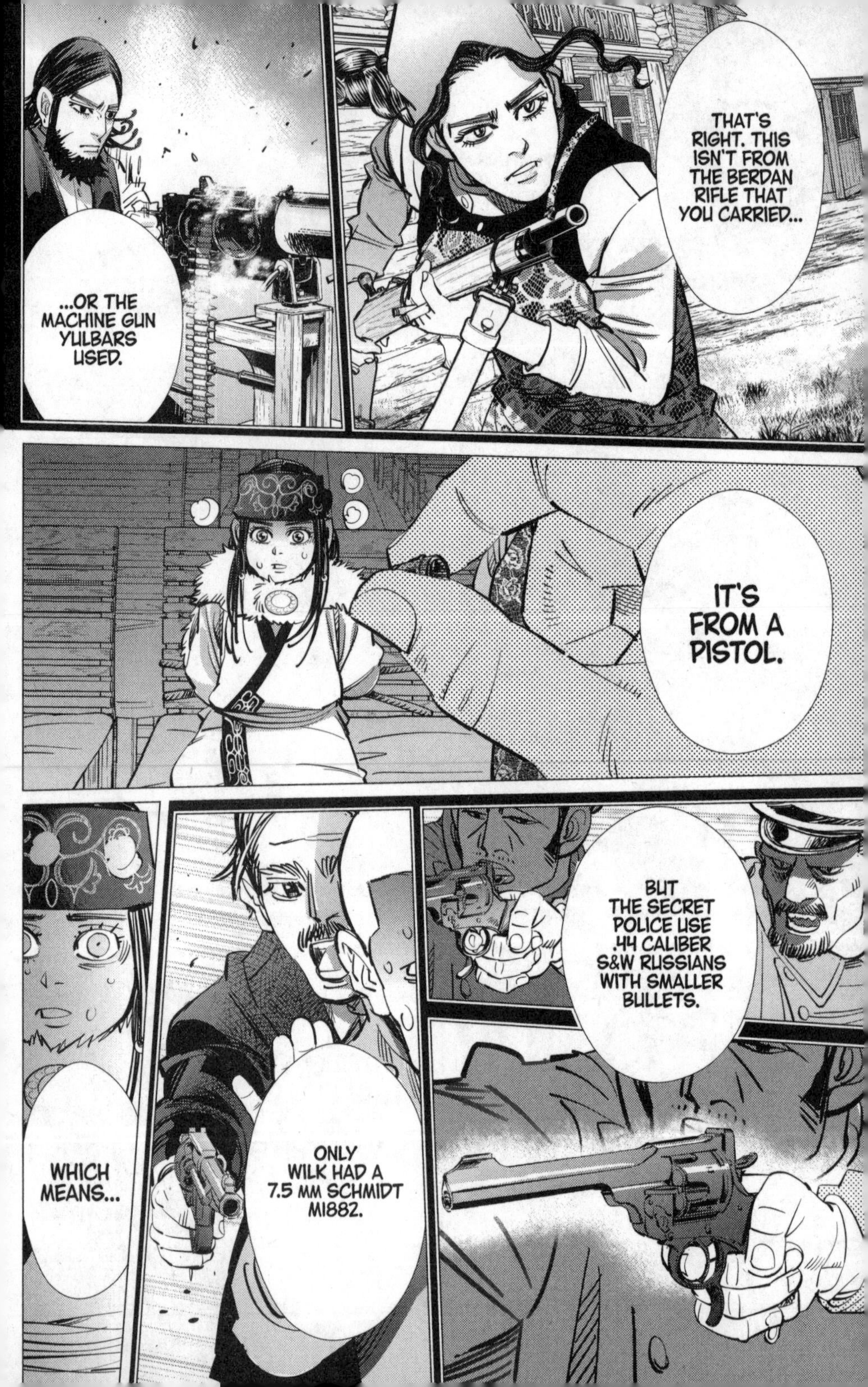
THAT'S RIGHT. THIS ISN'T FROM THE BERDAN RIFLE THAT YOU CARRIED...
...OR THE MACHINE GUN YULBARS USED.
IT'S FROM A PISTOL.
BUT THE SECRET POLICE USE .44 CALIBER S&W RUSSIANS WITH SMALLER BULLETS.
ONLY WILK HAD A 7.5 MM SCHMIDT M1882.
WHICH MEANS...

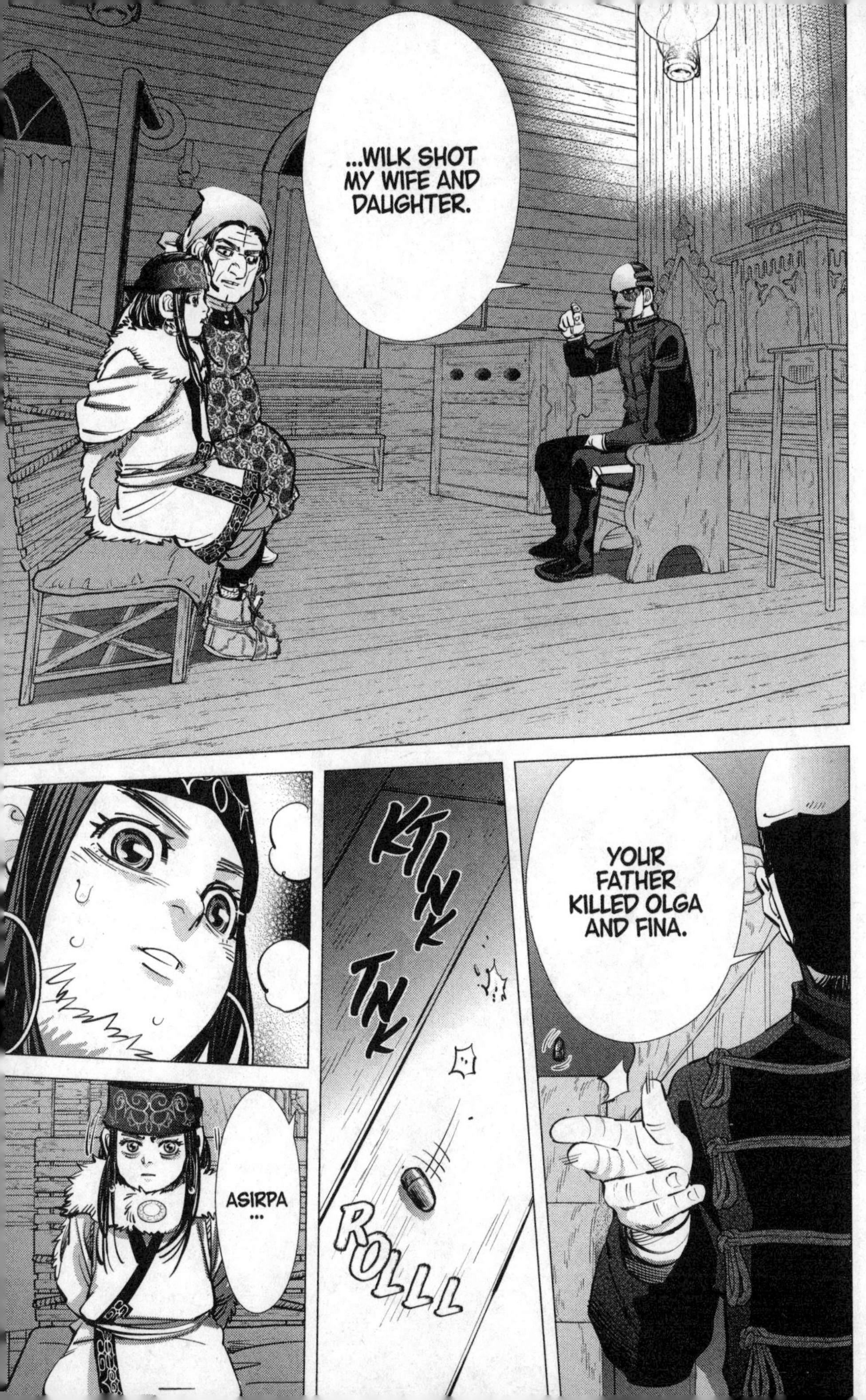
...WILK SHOT MY WIFE AND DAUGHTER.
YOUR FATHER KILLED OLGA AND FINA.
KTINK
TNK
ROLLL
ASIRPA ...

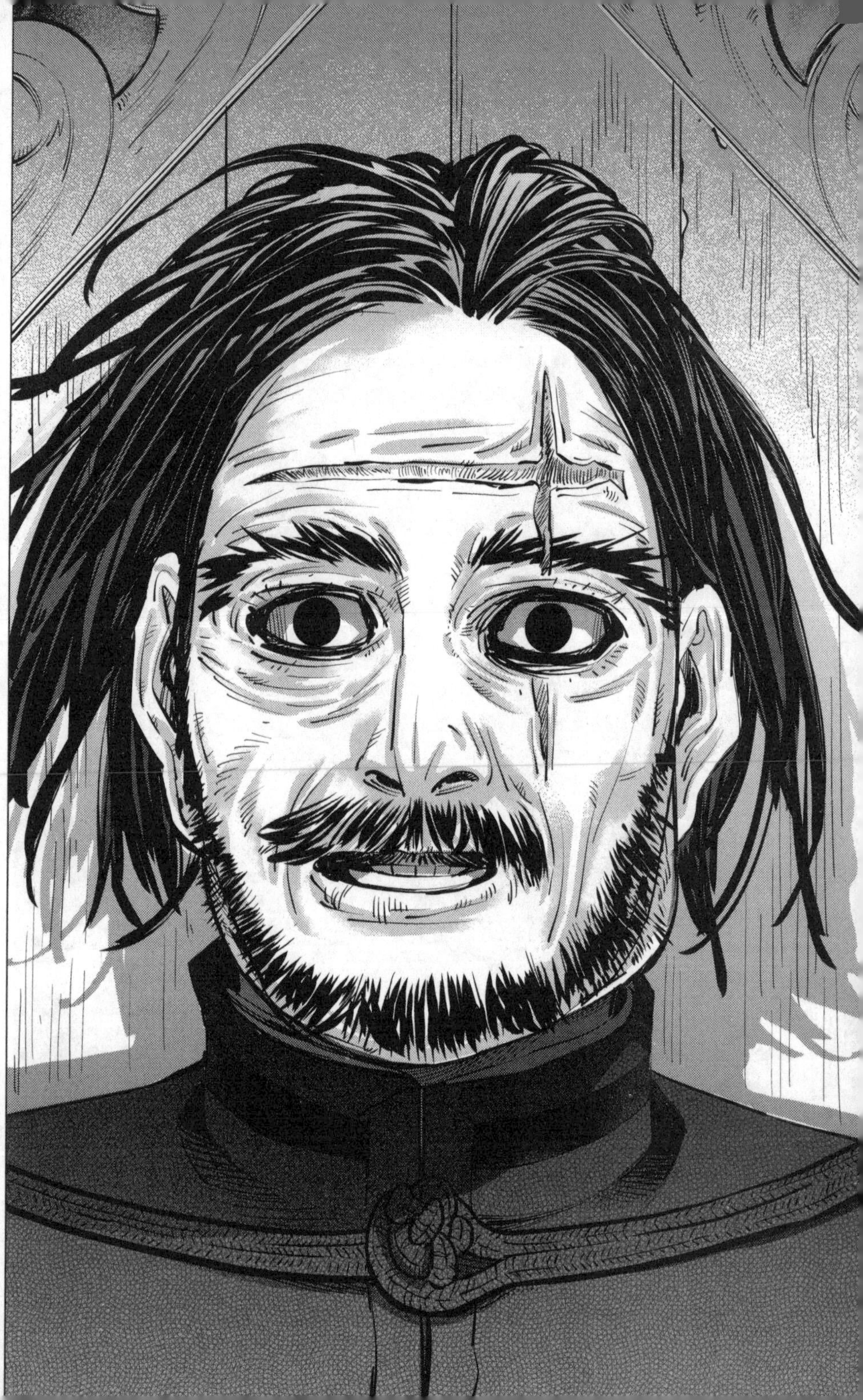

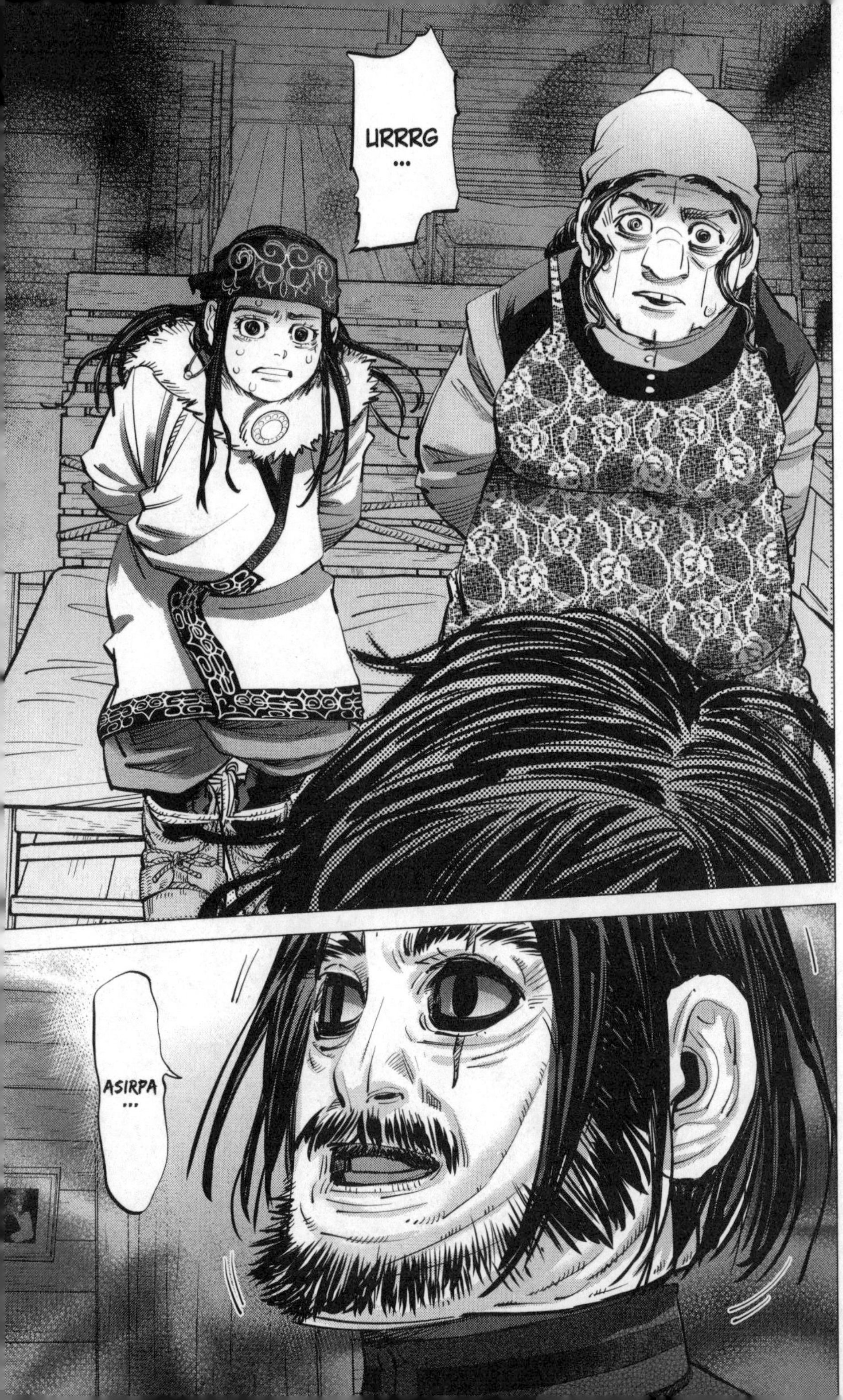
URRRG
...
ASIRPA
...

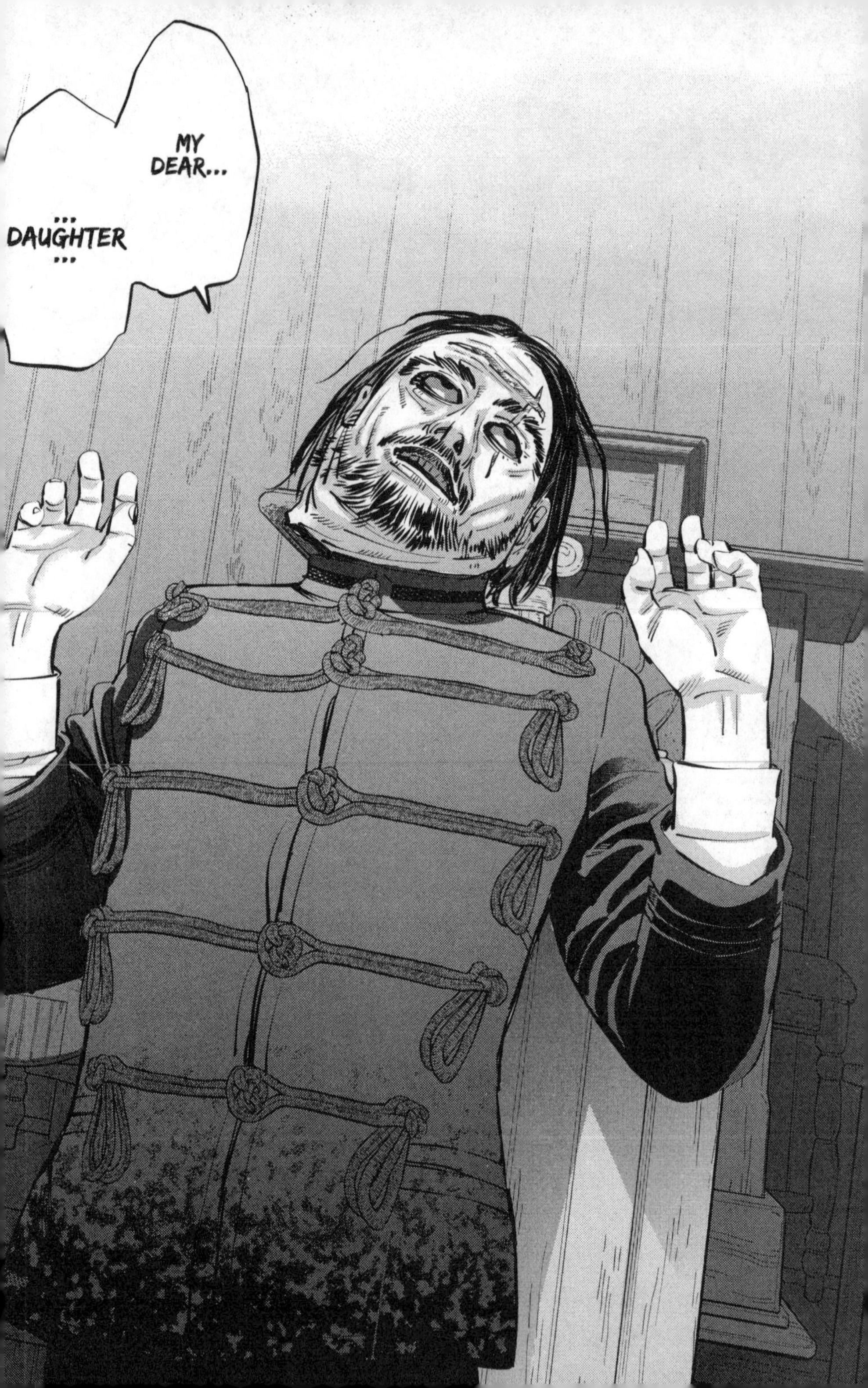
MY DEAR...
...DAUGHTER...

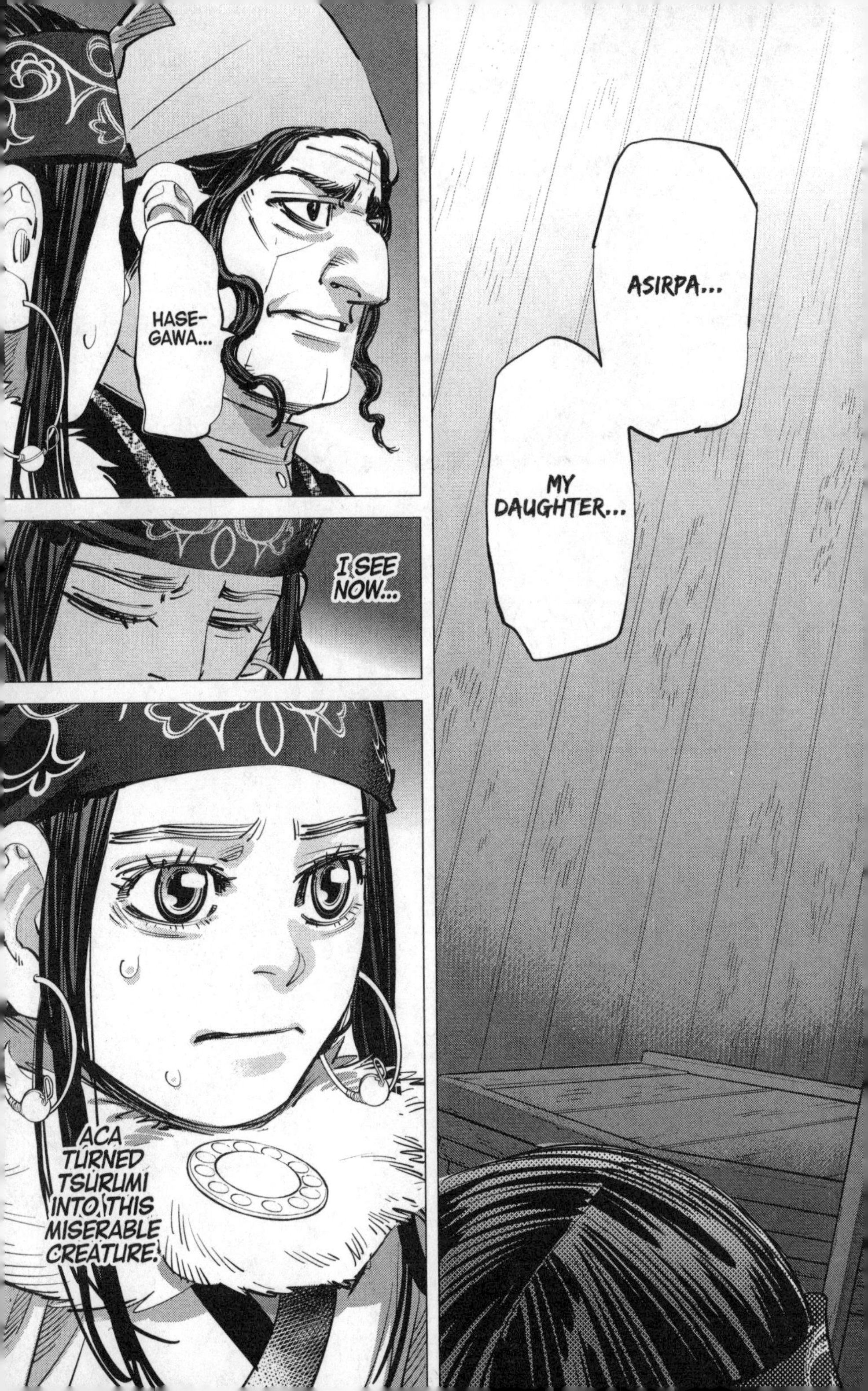
ASIRPA...
MY DAUGHTER...
HASE-GAWA...
I SEE NOW...
ACA TURNED TSURUMI INTO THIS MISERABLE CREATURE.

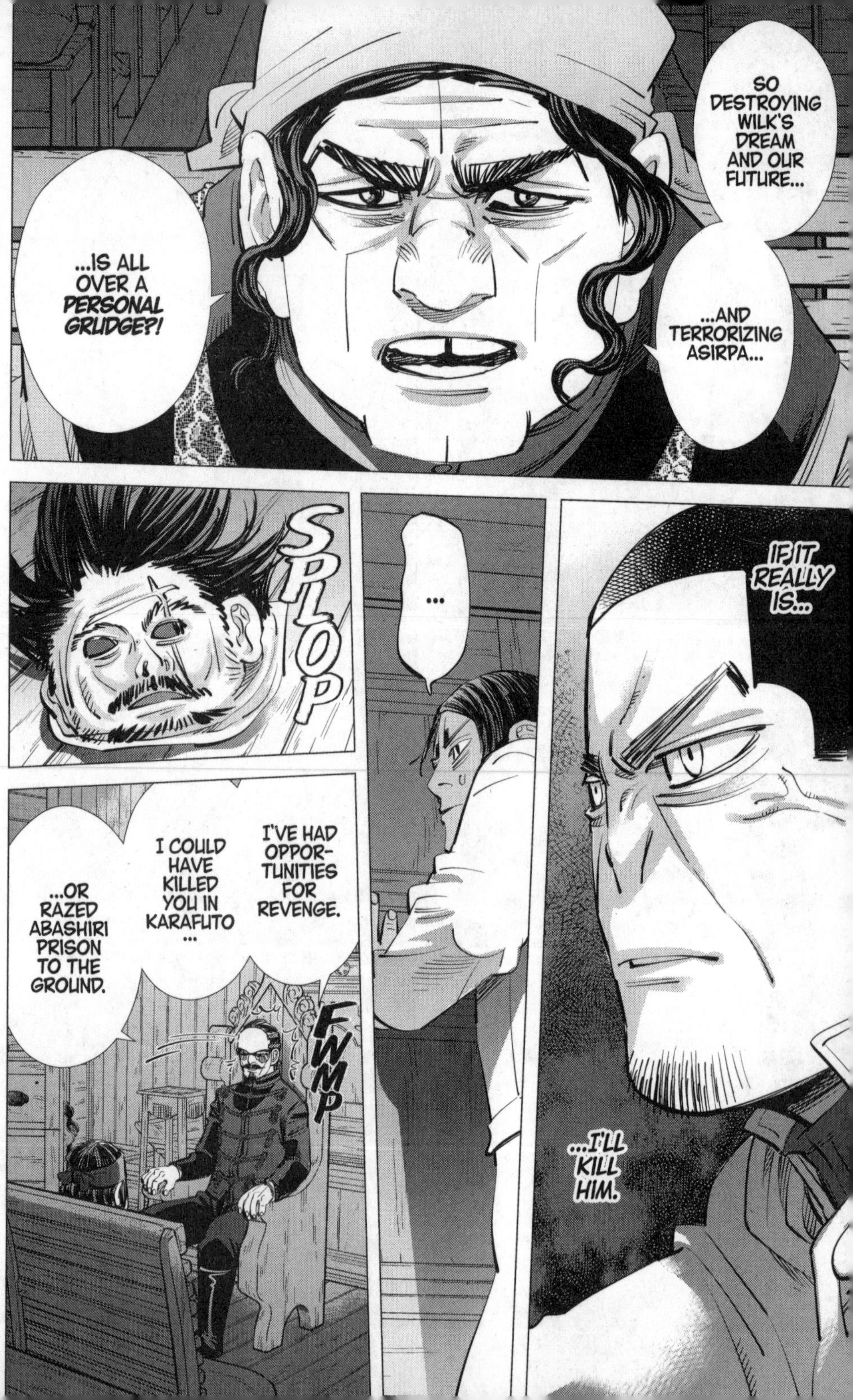
SO DESTROYING WILK'S DREAM AND OUR FUTURE...
...AND TERRORIZING ASIRPA...
...IS ALL OVER A PERSONAL GRUDGE?!
IF IT REALLY IS...
...I'LL KILL HIM.
...
SPLOP
I'VE HAD OPPOR-TUNITIES FOR REVENGE.
I COULD HAVE KILLED YOU IN KARAFUTO...
...OR RAZED ABASHIRI PRISON TO THE GROUND.
FWMP

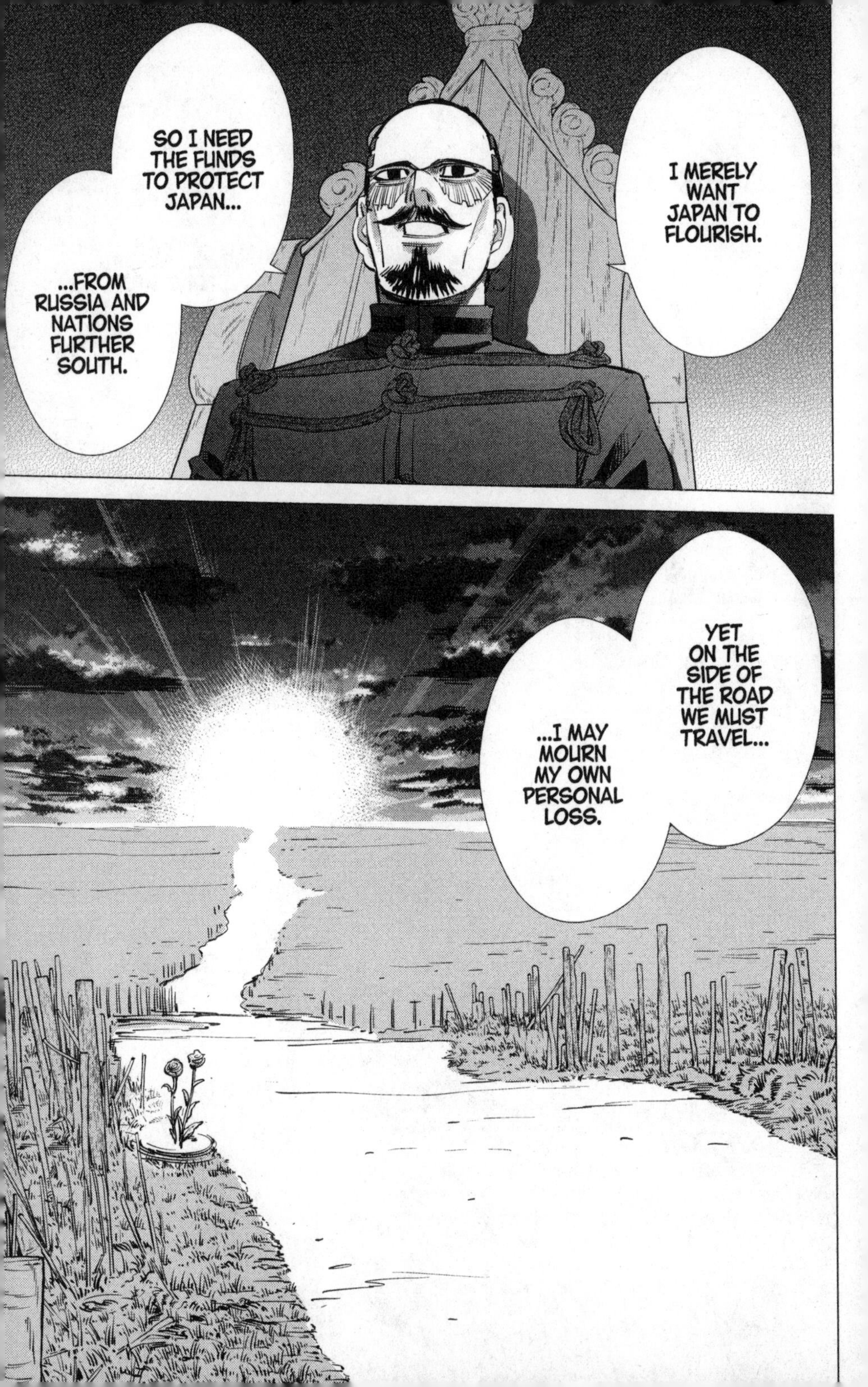
I MERELY WANT JAPAN TO FLOURISH.
SO I NEED THE FUNDS TO PROTECT JAPAN...
...FROM RUSSIA AND NATIONS FURTHER SOUTH.
YET ON THE SIDE OF THE ROAD WE MUST TRAVEL...
...I MAY MOURN MY OWN PERSONAL LOSS.

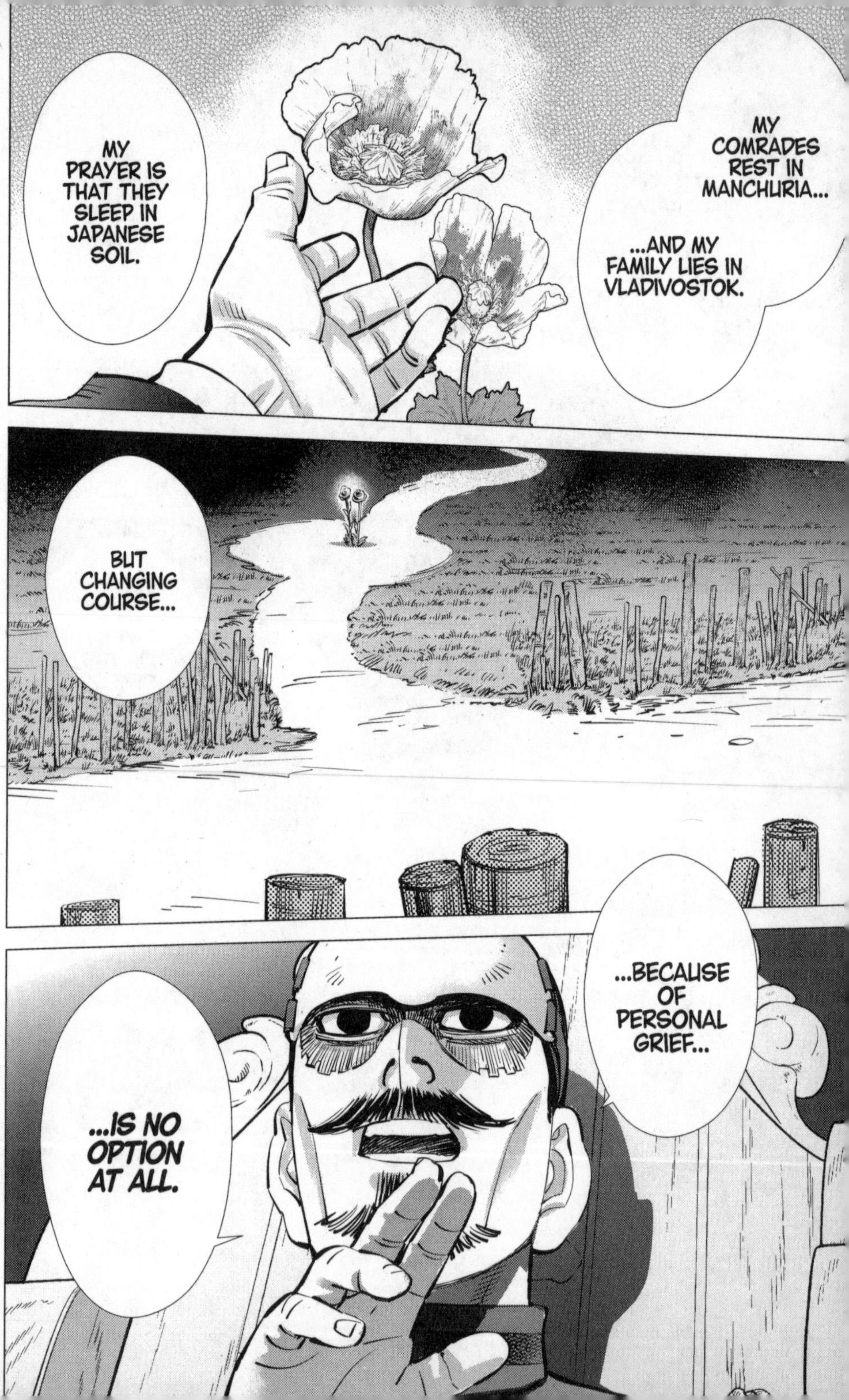
MY COMRADES REST IN MANCHURIA...
...AND MY FAMILY LIES IN VLADIVOSTOK.
MY PRAYER IS THAT THEY SLEEP IN JAPANESE SOIL.
BUT CHANGING COURSE...
...BECAUSE OF PERSONAL GRIEF...
...IS NO OPTION AT ALL.

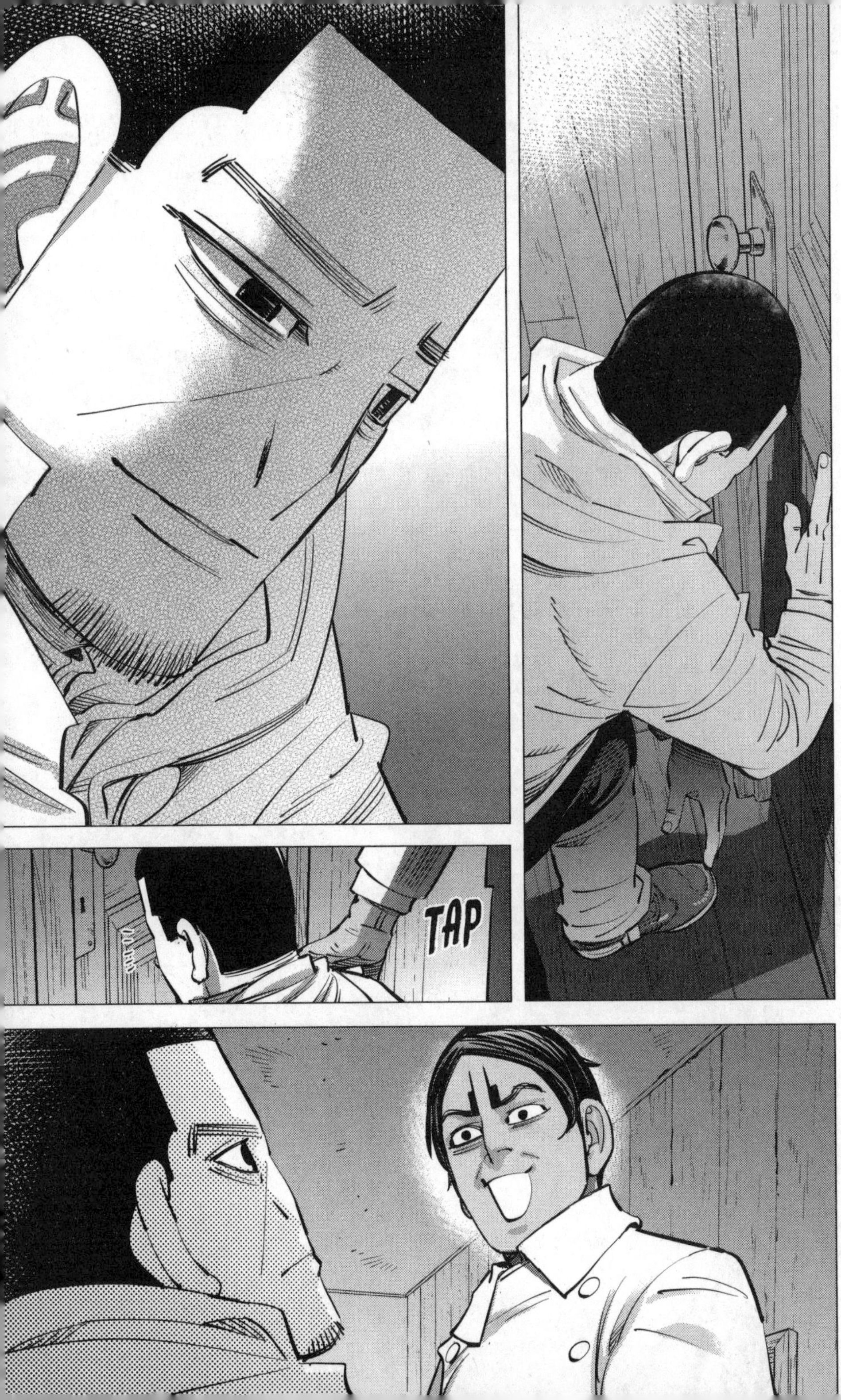
TAP

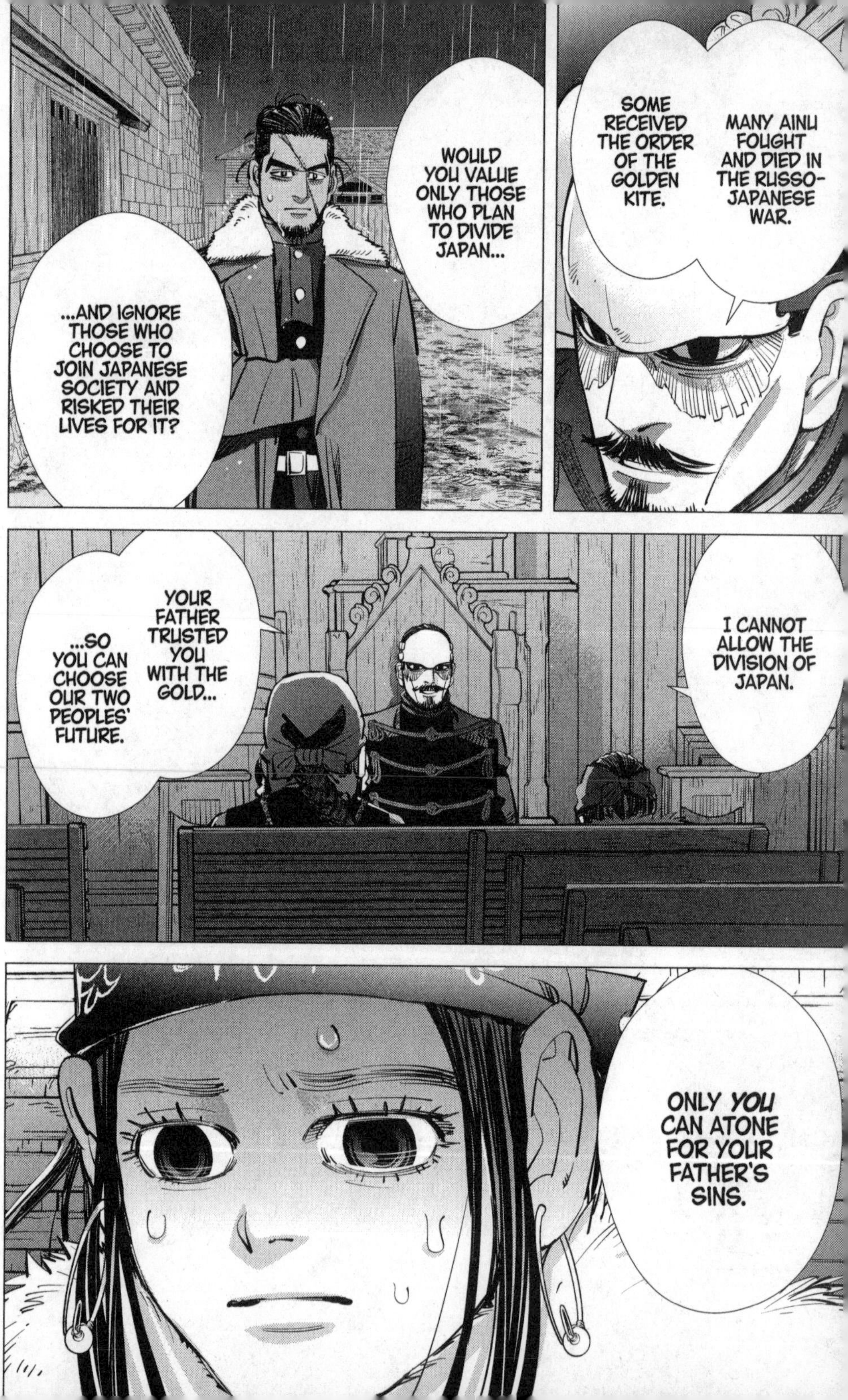
MANY AINU FOUGHT AND DIED IN THE RUSSO-JAPANESE WAR.
SOME RECEIVED THE ORDER OF THE GOLDEN KITE.
WOULD YOU VALUE ONLY THOSE WHO PLAN TO DIVIDE JAPAN...
...AND IGNORE THOSE WHO CHOOSE TO JOIN JAPANESE SOCIETY AND RISKED THEIR LIVES FOR IT?
I CANNOT ALLOW THE DIVISION OF JAPAN.
YOUR FATHER TRUSTED YOU WITH THE GOLD...
...SO YOU CAN CHOOSE OUR TWO PEOPLES' FUTURE.
ONLY *YOU* CAN ATONE FOR YOUR FATHER'S SINS.

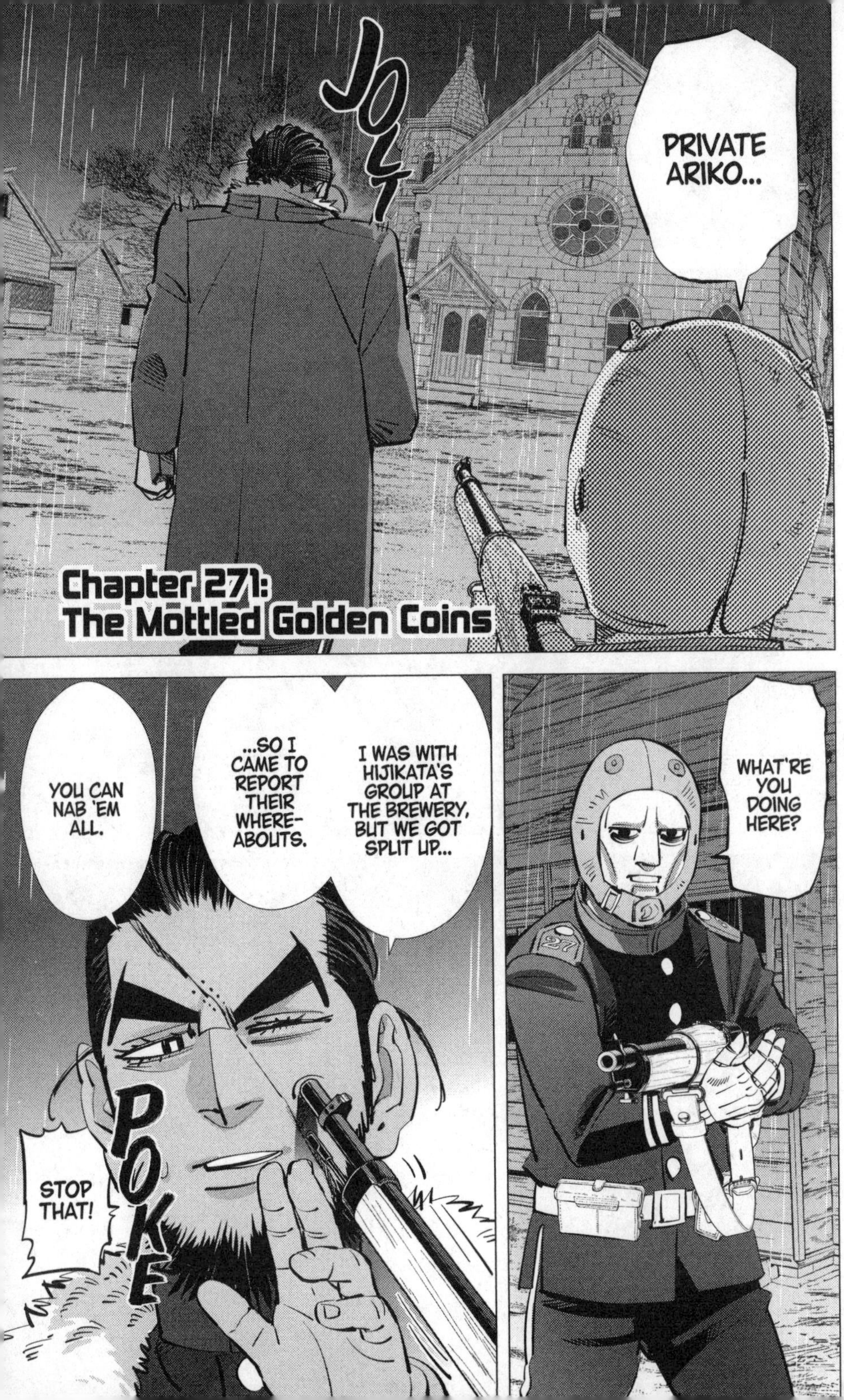
JOLT
PRIVATE ARIKO...
Chapter 271: The Mottled Golden Coins
WHAT'RE YOU DOING HERE?
I WAS WITH HIJIKATA'S GROUP AT THE BREWERY, BUT WE GOT SPLIT UP...
...SO I CAME TO REPORT THEIR WHERE-ABOUTS.
YOU CAN NAB 'EM ALL.
POKE
STOP THAT!

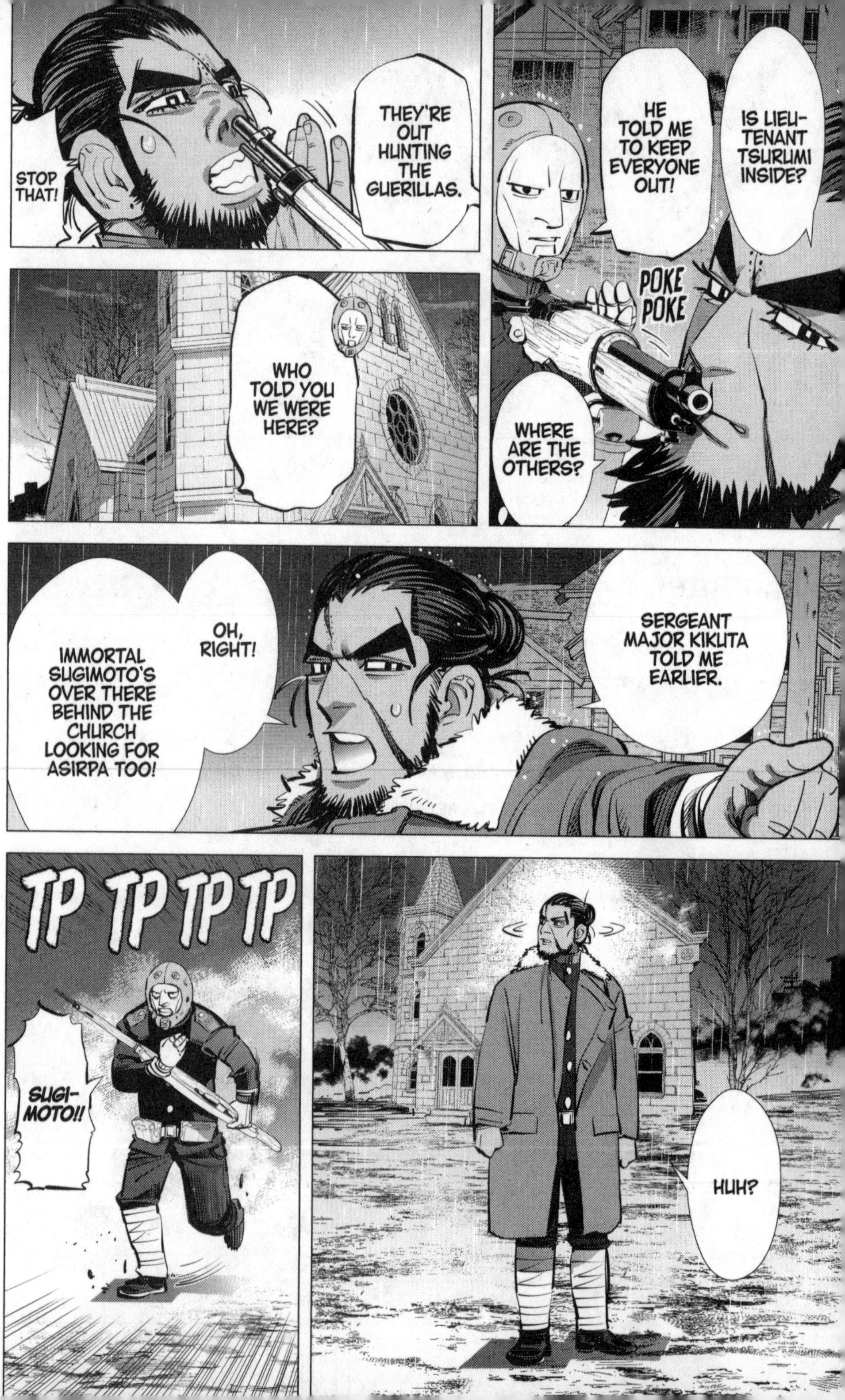
IS LIEUTENANT TSURUMI INSIDE?
HE TOLD ME TO KEEP EVERYONE OUT!
POKE POKE
WHERE ARE THE OTHERS?
THEY'RE OUT HUNTING THE GUERILLAS.
STOP THAT!
WHO TOLD YOU WE WERE HERE?
SERGEANT MAJOR KIKUTA TOLD ME EARLIER.
OH, RIGHT!
IMMORTAL SUGIMOTO'S OVER THERE BEHIND THE CHURCH LOOKING FOR ASIRPA TOO!
HUH?
TP TP TP TP
SUGIMOTO!!

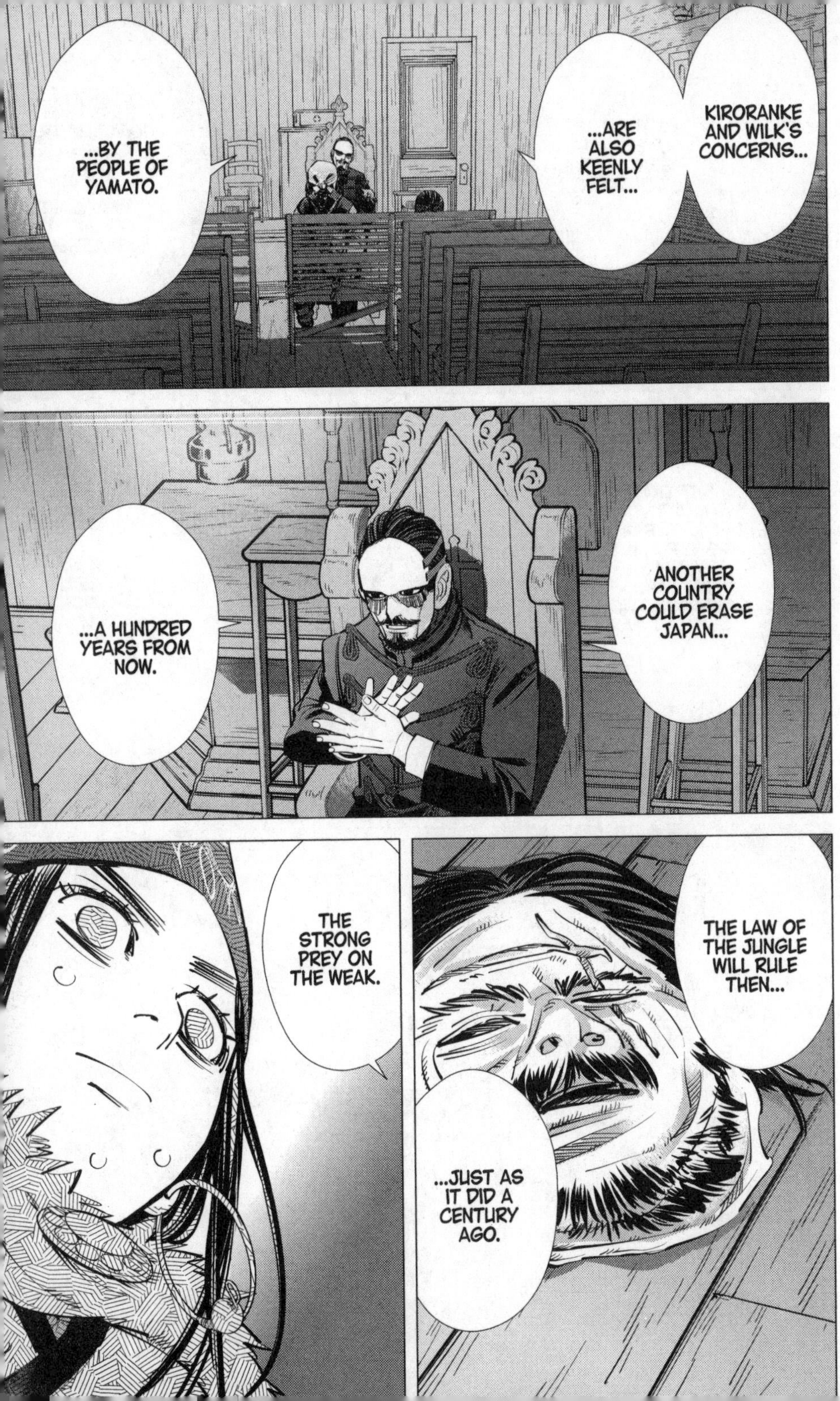
KIRORANKE AND WILK'S CONCERNS...
...ARE ALSO KEENLY FELT...
...BY THE PEOPLE OF YAMATO.
ANOTHER COUNTRY COULD ERASE JAPAN...
...A HUNDRED YEARS FROM NOW.
THE LAW OF THE JUNGLE WILL RULE THEN...
...JUST AS IT DID A CENTURY AGO.
THE STRONG PREY ON THE WEAK.

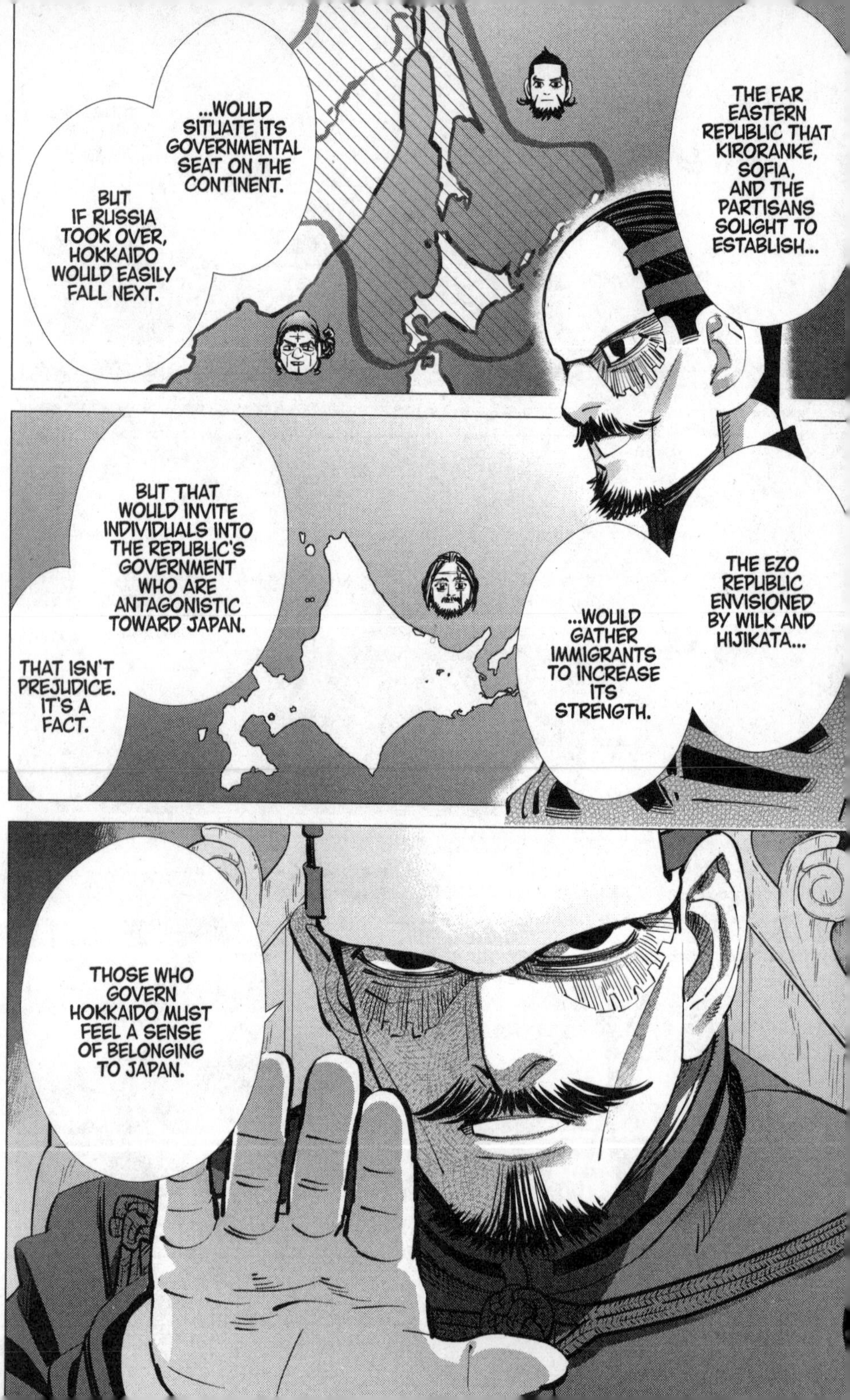
THE FAR EASTERN REPUBLIC THAT KIRORANKE, SOFIA, AND THE PARTISANS SOUGHT TO ESTABLISH...
...WOULD SITUATE ITS GOVERNMENTAL SEAT ON THE CONTINENT.
BUT IF RUSSIA TOOK OVER, HOKKAIDO WOULD EASILY FALL NEXT.
THE EZO REPUBLIC ENVISIONED BY WILK AND HIJIKATA...
...WOULD GATHER IMMIGRANTS TO INCREASE ITS STRENGTH.
BUT THAT WOULD INVITE INDIVIDUALS INTO THE REPUBLIC'S GOVERNMENT WHO ARE ANTAGONISTIC TOWARD JAPAN.
THAT ISN'T PREJUDICE. IT'S A FACT.
THOSE WHO GOVERN HOKKAIDO MUST FEEL A SENSE OF BELONGING TO JAPAN.

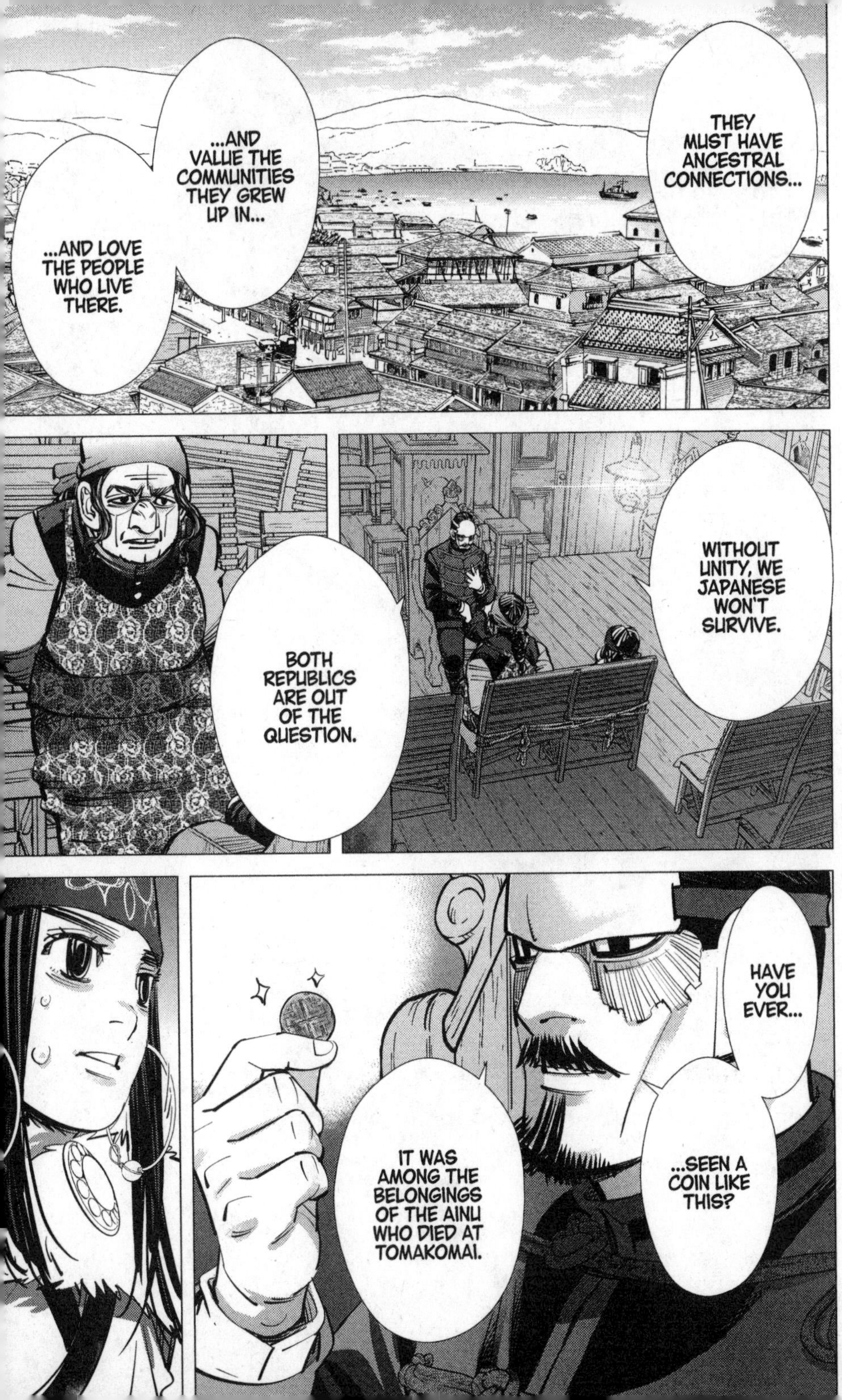
THEY MUST HAVE ANCESTRAL CONNECTIONS...
...AND VALUE THE COMMUNITIES THEY GREW UP IN...
...AND LOVE THE PEOPLE WHO LIVE THERE.
WITHOUT UNITY, WE JAPANESE WON'T SURVIVE.
BOTH REPUBLICS ARE OUT OF THE QUESTION.
HAVE YOU EVER...
...SEEN A COIN LIKE THIS?
IT WAS AMONG THE BELONGINGS OF THE AINU WHO DIED AT TOMAKOMAI.

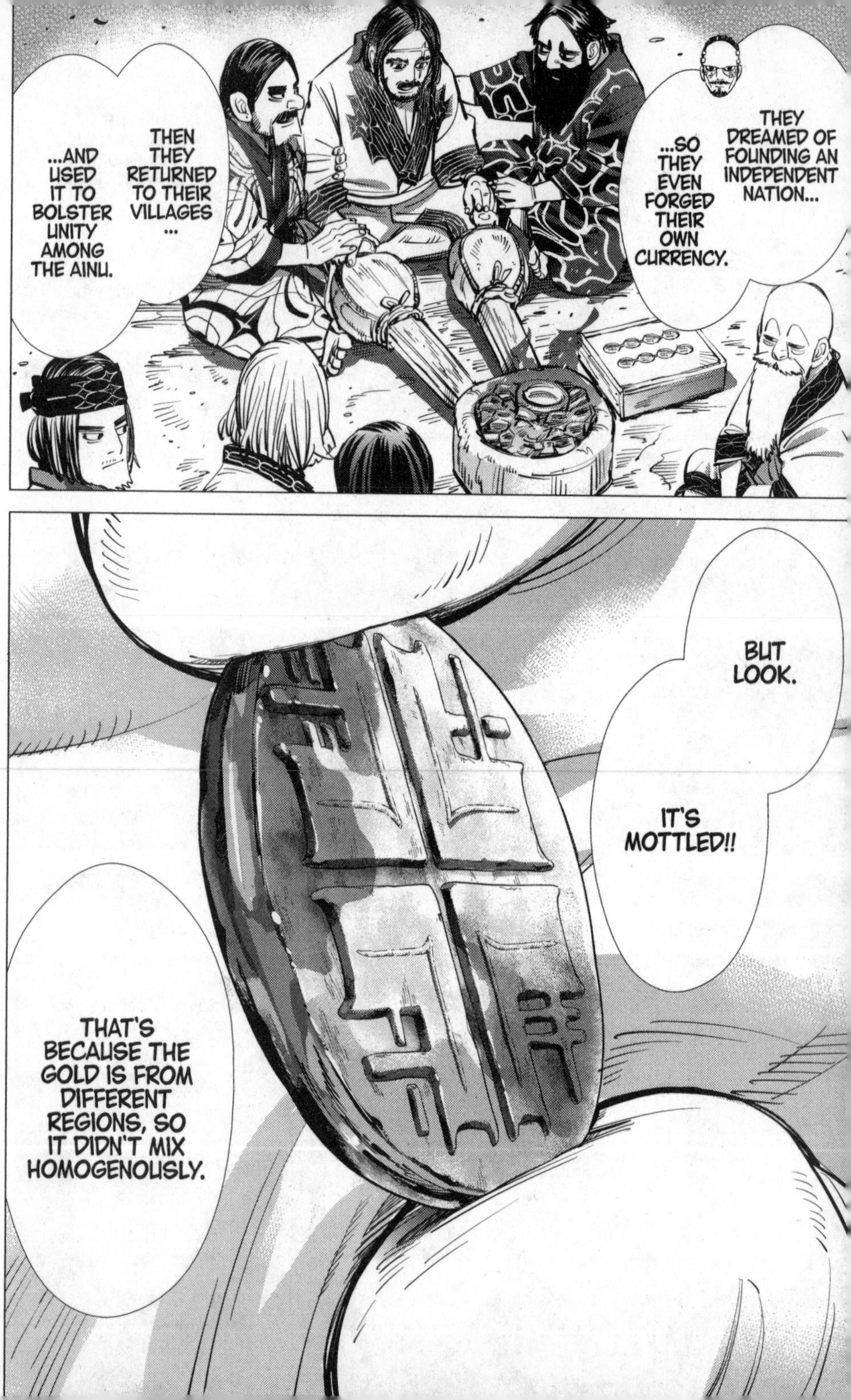
THEY DREAMED OF FOUNDING AN INDEPENDENT NATION...
...SO THEY EVEN FORGED THEIR OWN CURRENCY.
THEN THEY RETURNED TO THEIR VILLAGES...
...AND USED IT TO BOLSTER UNITY AMONG THE AINU.
BUT LOOK.
IT'S MOTTLED!!
THAT'S BECAUSE THE GOLD IS FROM DIFFERENT REGIONS, SO IT DIDN'T MIX HOMOGENOUSLY.

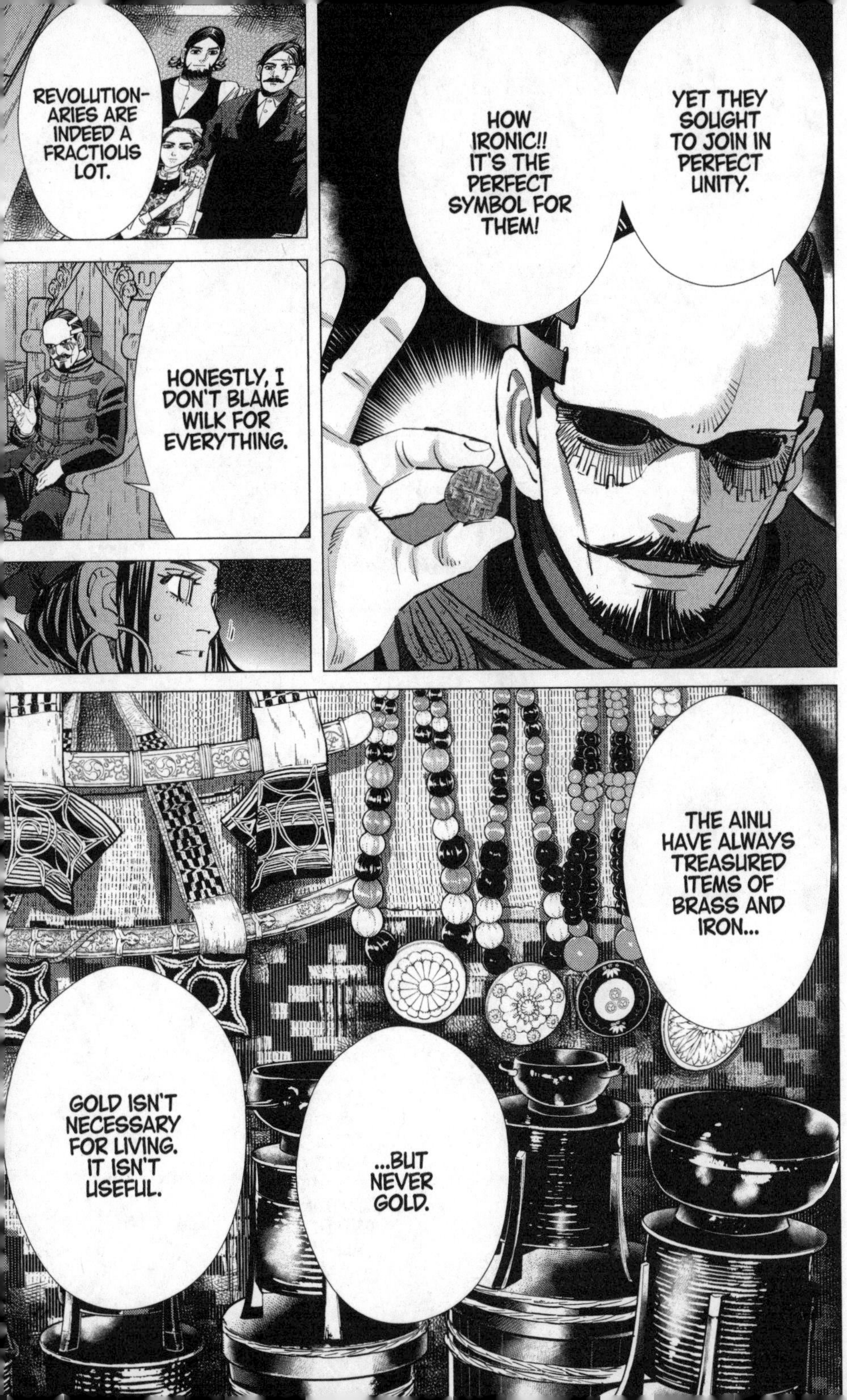
YET THEY SOUGHT TO JOIN IN PERFECT UNITY.
HOW IRONIC!! IT'S THE PERFECT SYMBOL FOR THEM!
REVOLUTION-ARIES ARE INDEED A FRACTIOUS LOT.
HONESTLY, I DON'T BLAME WILK FOR EVERYTHING.
THE AINU HAVE ALWAYS TREASURED ITEMS OF BRASS AND IRON...
...BUT NEVER GOLD.
GOLD ISN'T NECESSARY FOR LIVING. IT ISN'T USEFUL.

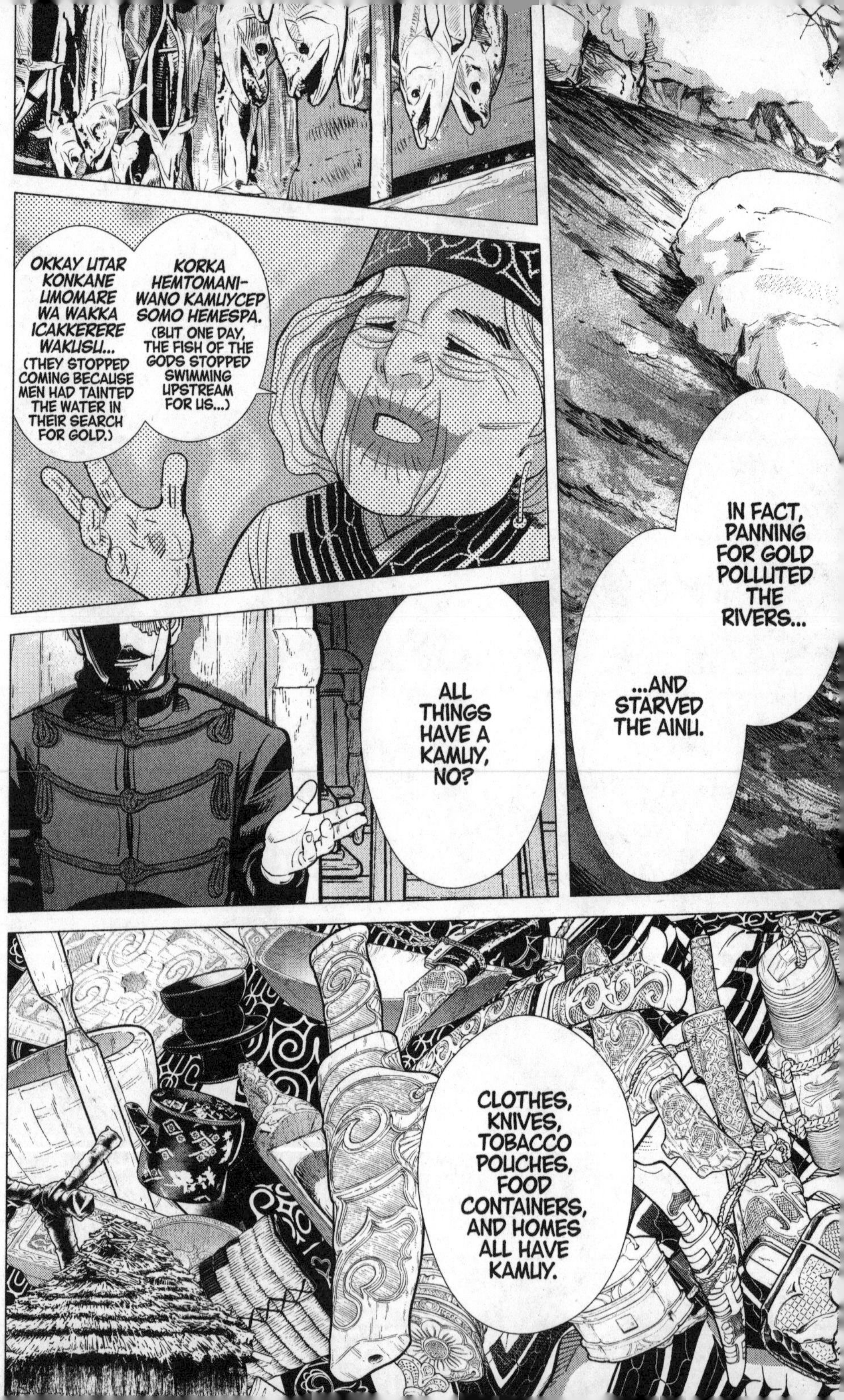
IN FACT, PANNING FOR GOLD POLLUTED THE RIVERS...
...AND STARVED THE AINU.
KORKA HEMTOMANI-WANO KAMUYCEP SOMO HEMESPA. (BUT ONE DAY, THE FISH OF THE GODS STOPPED SWIMMING UPSTREAM FOR US...)
OKKAY UTAR KONKANE UMOMARE WA WAKKA ICAKKERERE WAKUSU... (THEY STOPPED COMING BECAUSE MEN HAD TAINTED THE WATER IN THEIR SEARCH FOR GOLD.)
ALL THINGS HAVE A KAMUY, NO?
CLOTHES, KNIVES, TOBACCO POUCHES, FOOD CONTAINERS, AND HOMES ALL HAVE KAMUY.

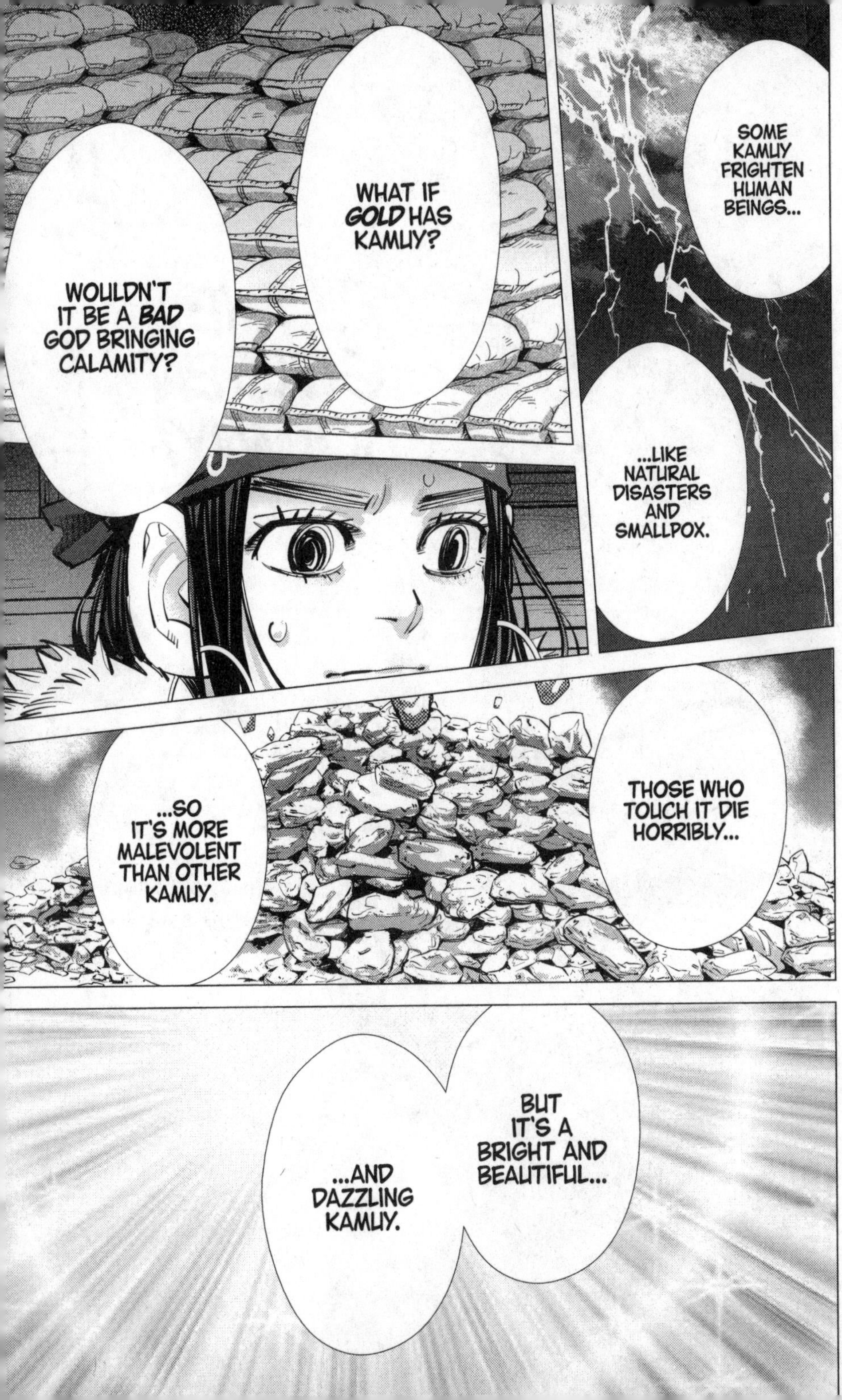
SOME KAMUY FRIGHTEN HUMAN BEINGS...
...LIKE NATURAL DISASTERS AND SMALLPOX.
WHAT IF GOLD HAS KAMUY?
WOULDN'T IT BE A BAD GOD BRINGING CALAMITY?
THOSE WHO TOUCH IT DIE HORRIBLY...
...SO IT'S MORE MALEVOLENT THAN OTHER KAMUY.
BUT IT'S A BRIGHT AND BEAUTIFUL...
...AND DAZZLING KAMUY.

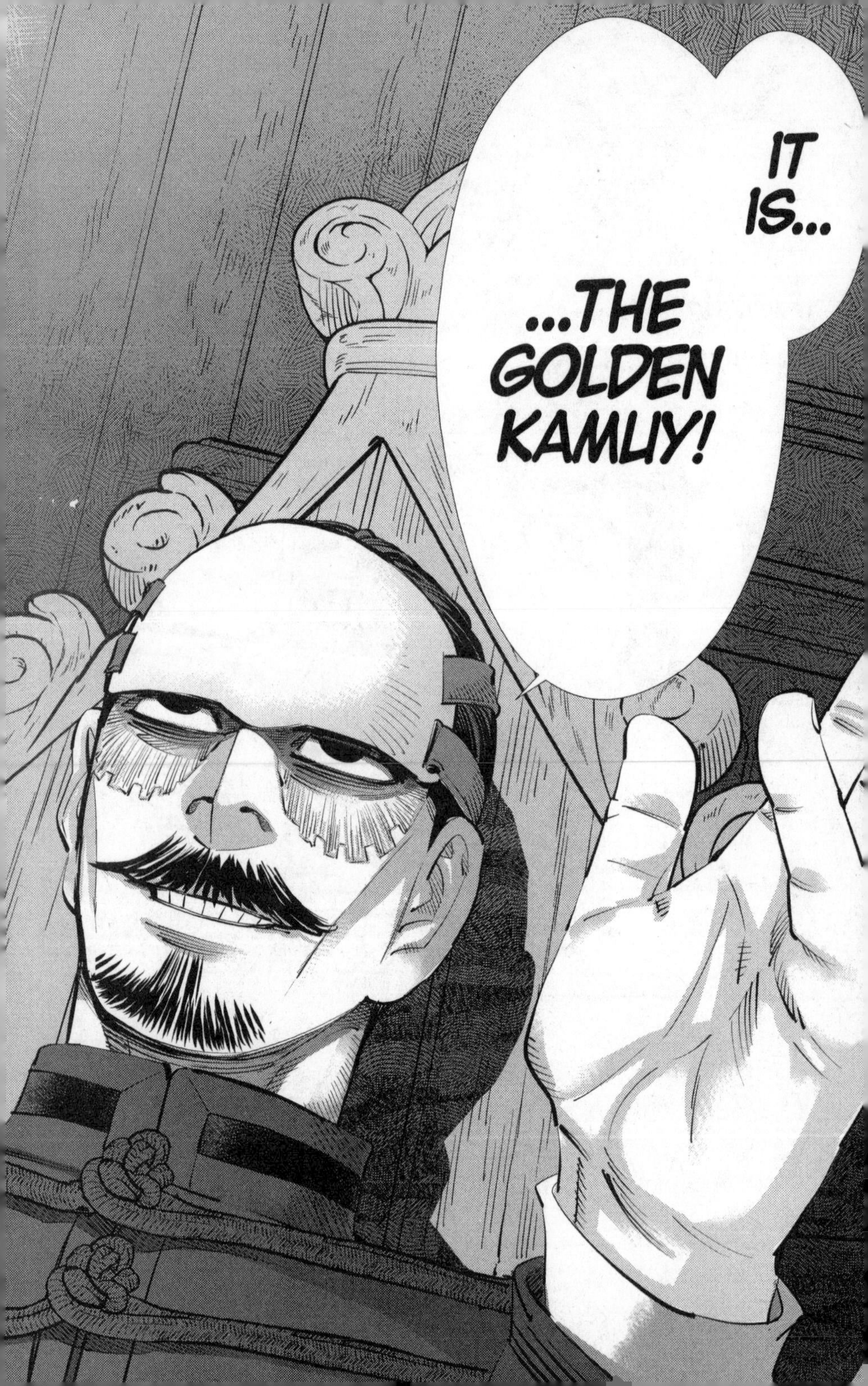
IT IS... ...THE GOLDEN KAMUY!

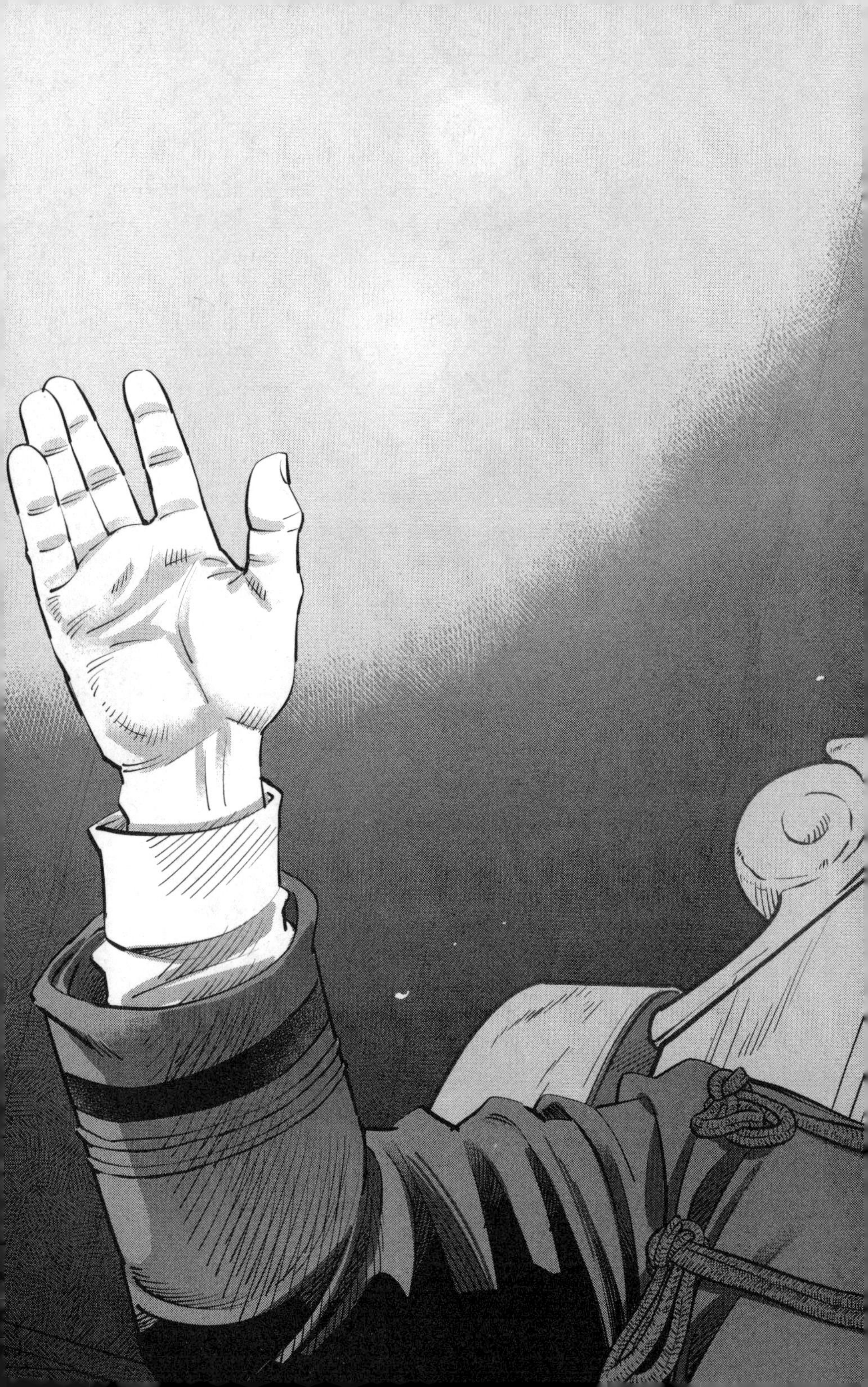

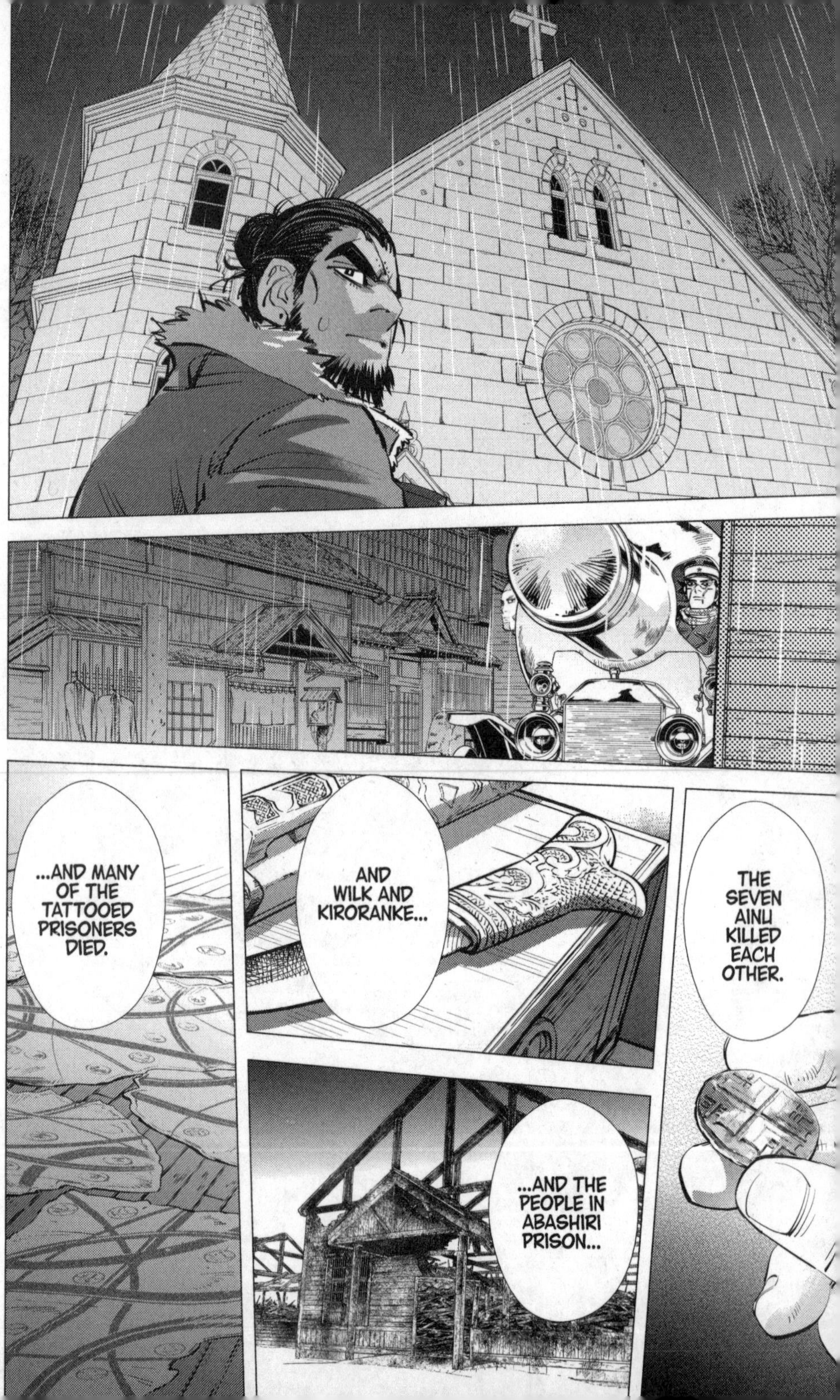
THE SEVEN AINU KILLED EACH OTHER.
AND WILK AND KIRORANKE...
...AND THE PEOPLE IN ABASHIRI PRISON...
...AND MANY OF THE TATTOOED PRISONERS DIED.

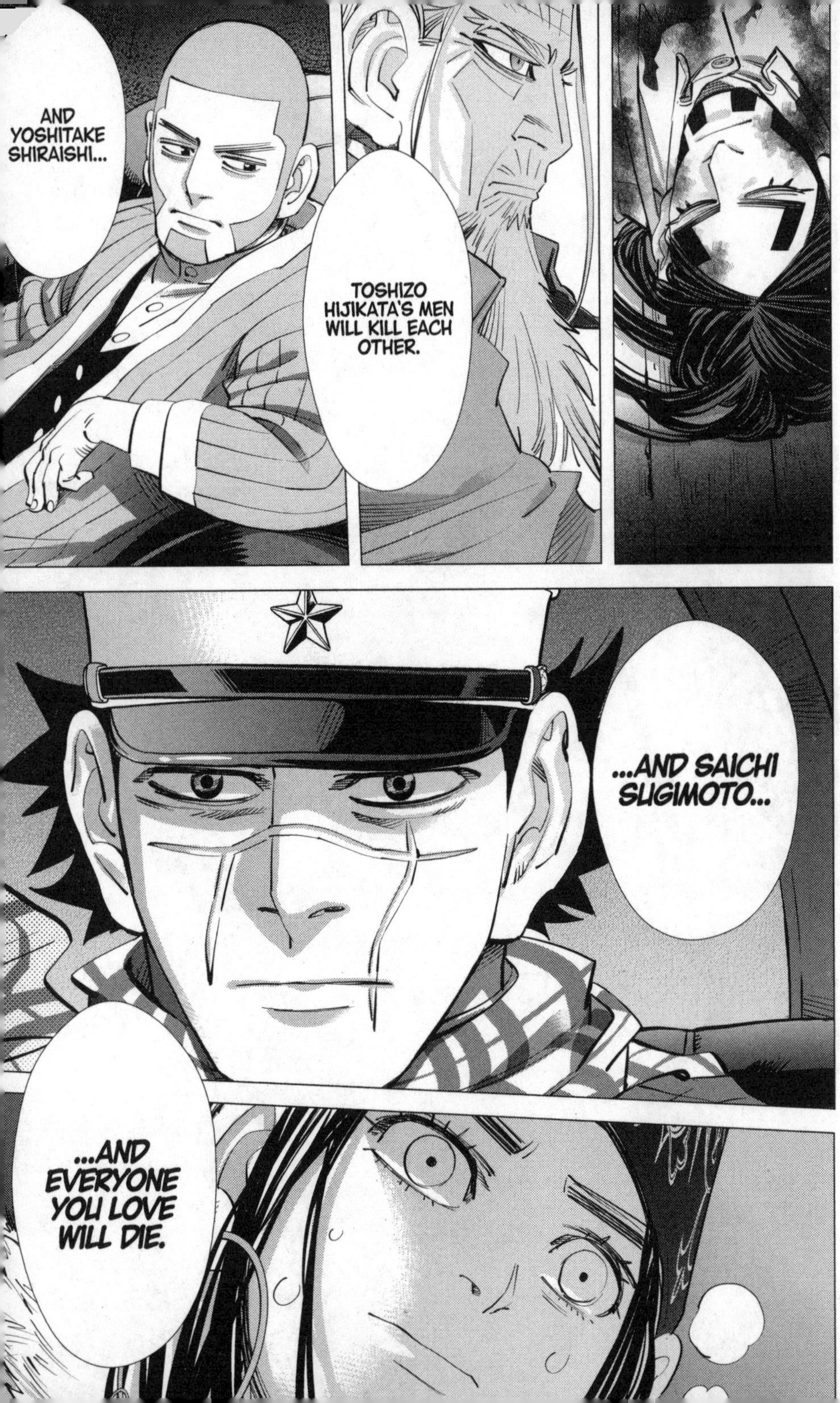
TOSHIZO HIJIKATA'S MEN WILL KILL EACH OTHER.
AND YOSHITAKE SHIRAISHI...
...AND SAICHI SUGIMOTO...
...AND EVERYONE YOU LOVE WILL DIE.

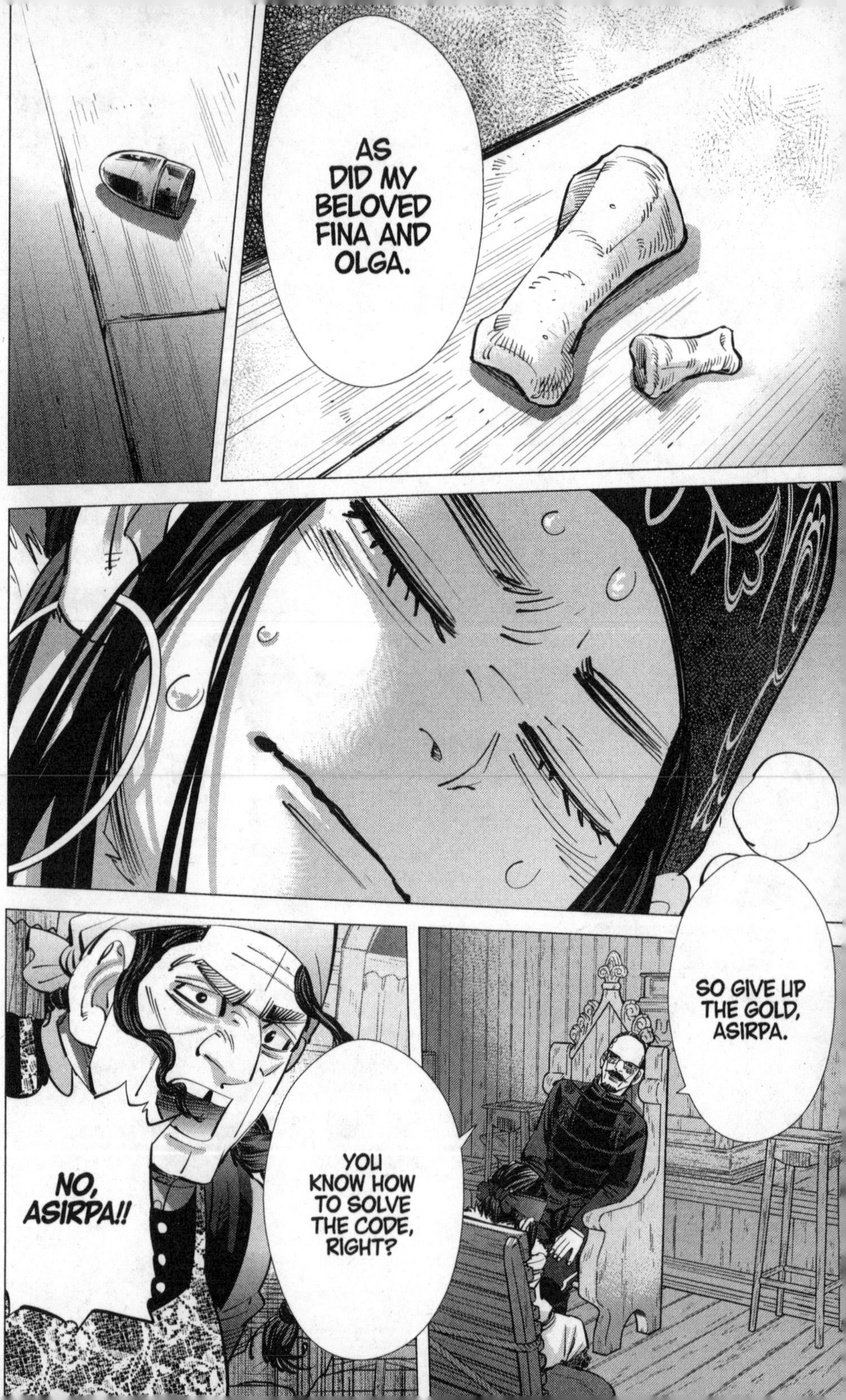
AS DID MY BELOVED FINA AND OLGA.
SO GIVE UP THE GOLD, ASIRPA.
YOU KNOW HOW TO SOLVE THE CODE, RIGHT?
NO, ASIRPA!!

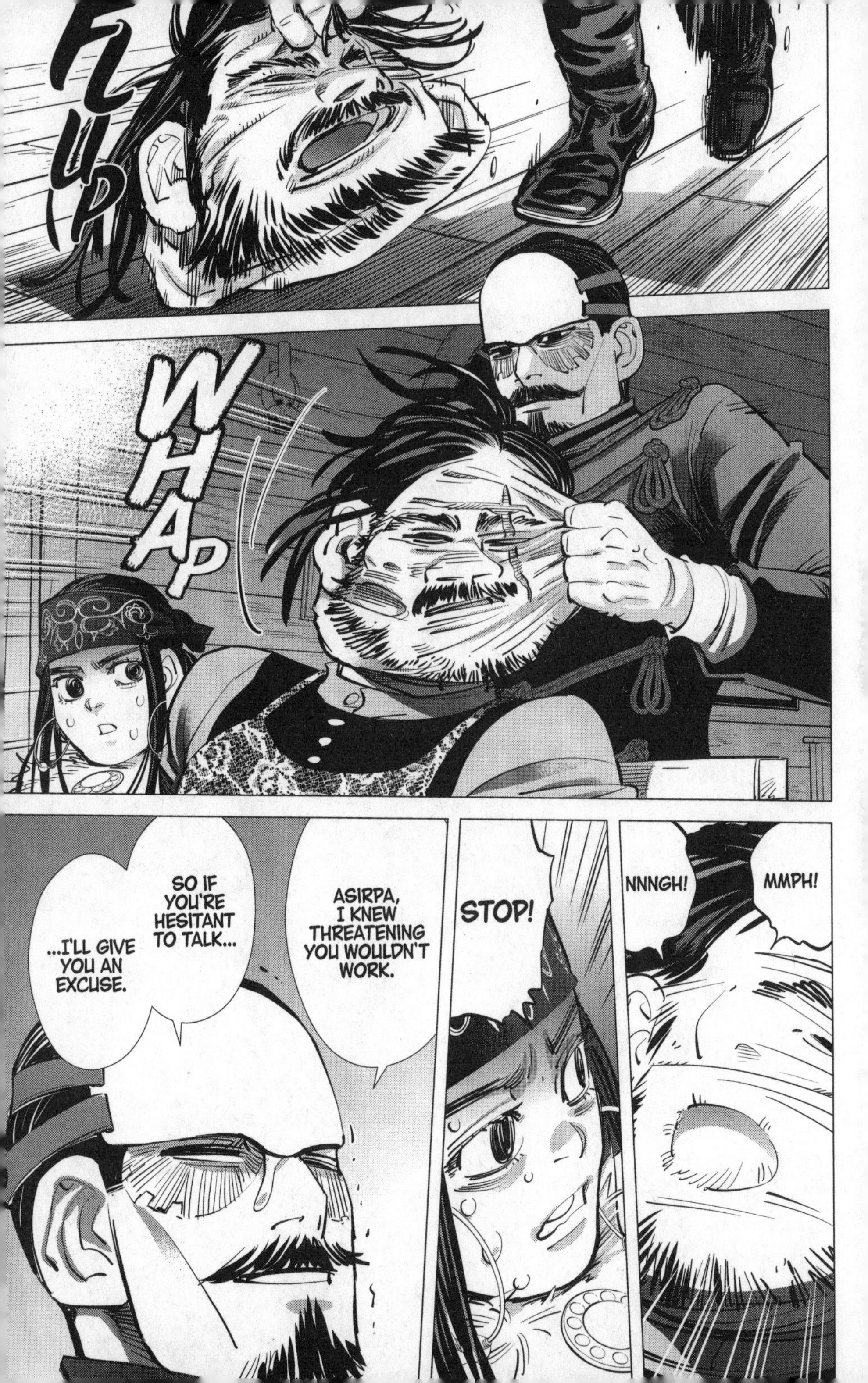
FLUP
WHAP
MMPH!
NNNGH!
STOP!
ASIRPA, I KNEW THREATENING YOU WOULDN'T WORK.
SO IF YOU'RE HESITANT TO TALK...
...I'LL GIVE YOU AN EXCUSE.

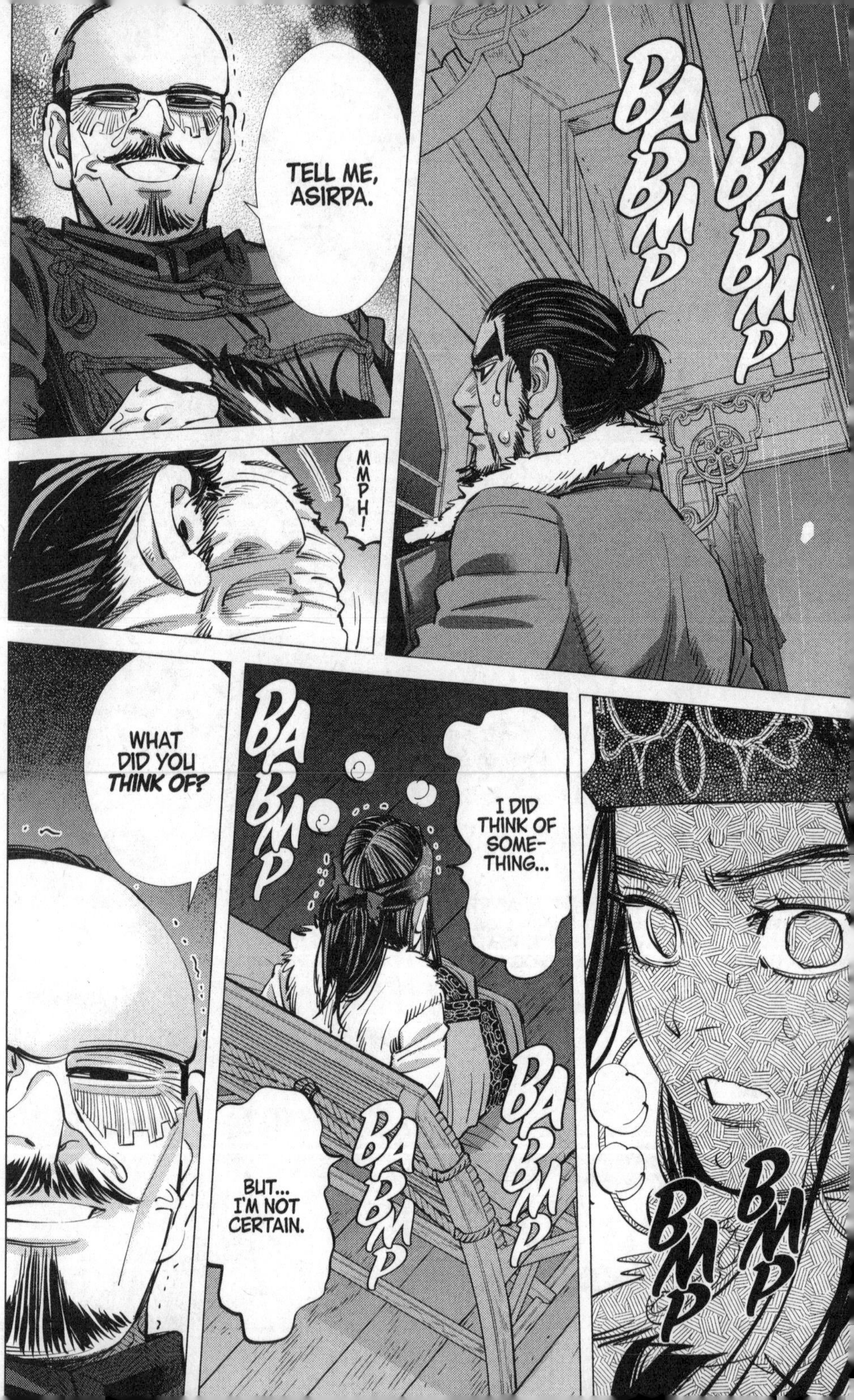

BABMP
BABMP
TELL ME, ASIRPA.
MMPH!
BMP
BMP
BABMP
I DID THINK OF SOME-THING...
BABMP
BABMP
BUT... I'M NOT CERTAIN.
WHAT DID YOU *THINK OF?*

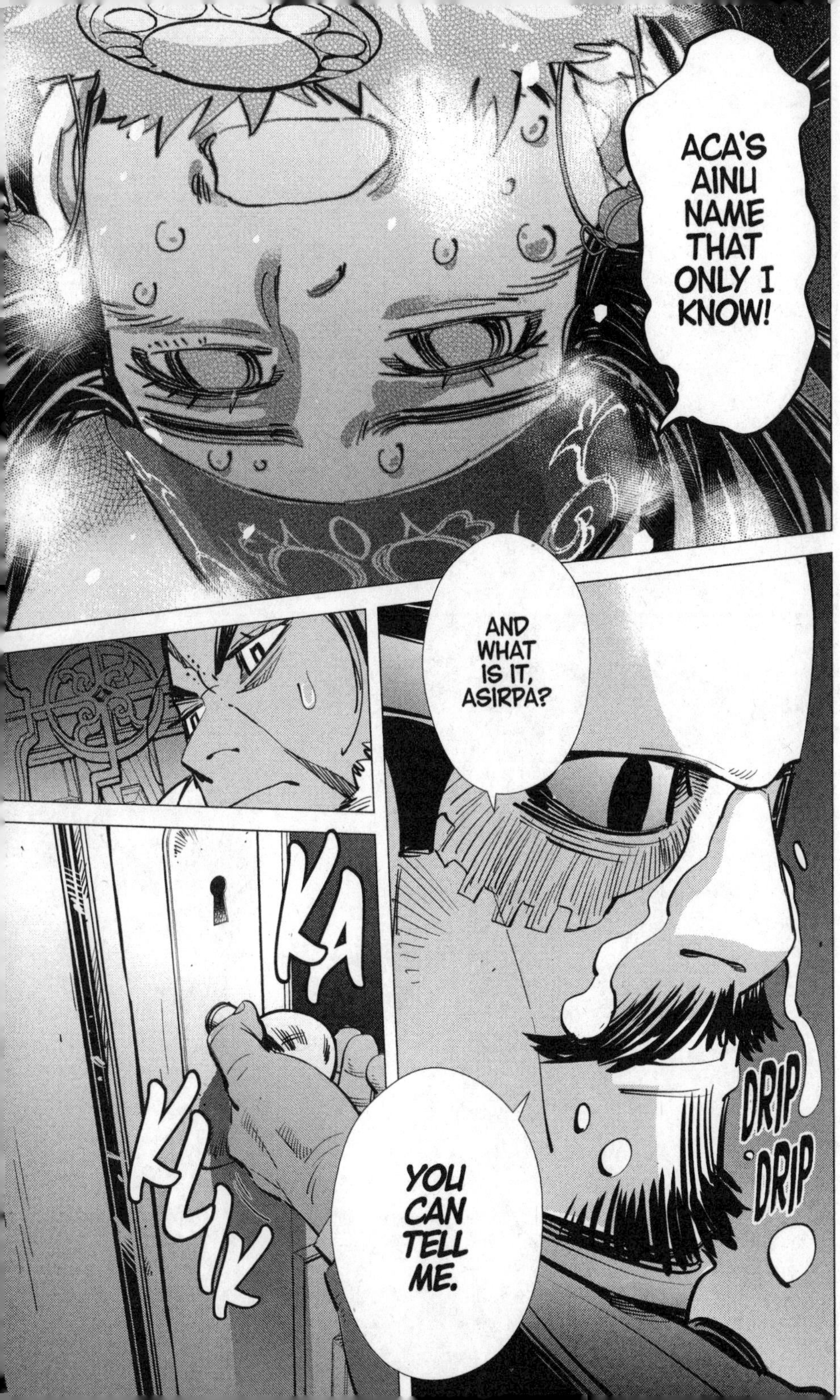
ACA'S AINU NAME THAT ONLY I KNOW!
AND WHAT IS IT, ASIRPA?
DRIP DRIP
YOU CAN TELL ME.
KA
KLIK

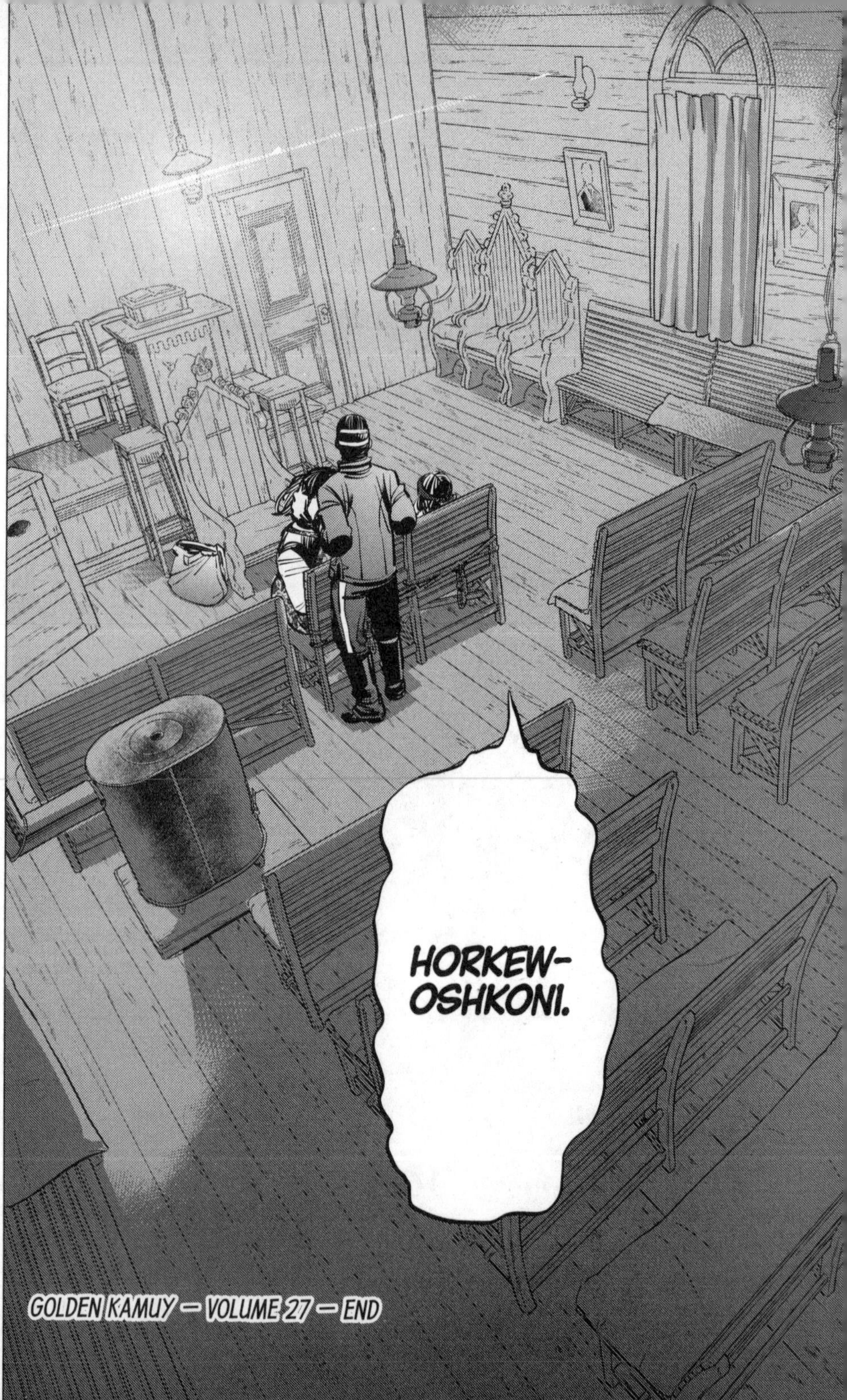
HORKEW-
OSHKONI.
GOLDEN KAMUY — VOLUME 27 — END

Ainu Language Supervision • Hiroshi Nakagawa •
Russian Language Supervision • Eugenio Uzhinin •
Uilta Language Supervision • Yoshiko Yamada • Satsuma Dialect Supervision •
Shogo Nakamura • Niigata Dialect Supervision • Fumiya Ito

Cooperation from • Hokkaido Ainu Association and the Abashiri Prison Museum • Otaru City General Museum • Waseda University Aizu Museum • Kazunobu Goto, • Botanic Garden and Museum, Hokkaido University • National Museum of Ethnology • Nibutani Ainu Culture Museum • The Ainu Museum • Moon Kabato Museum • Kushiro City Museum • Atsuyo Hisai • Tatsuhiro Tokuda • Shigeharu Terui • All Japan Federation of Karafuto • Tokyo National Museum • Sakhalin Regional Museum • Shiraishi Hidetoshi • Masato Tamura • Historical Village of Hokkaido • Asahikawa City Museum • Hokuchin Museum • Tomakomai City Museum • Museum Meijimura • Sapporo Breweries Ltd.

Photo Credits • Takayuki Monma, Takanori Matsuda, Kozo Ishikawa, Shigekazu Kizu, Minoru Noda

Ainu Culture References

Chiri, Takanaka and Yokoyama, Takao. *Ainugo Eiri Jiten* (Ainu Language Illustrated Dictionary). Tokyo: Kagyusha, 1994

Kayano, Shigeru. *Ainu no Mingu* (Ainu Folkcrafts). Kawagoe: Suzusawa Book Store, 1978

Kayano, Shigeru. *Kayano Shigeru no Ainugo Jiten* (KayanoShigeru's Ainu Language Dictionary). Tokyo: Sanseido, 1996

Musashino Art University – The Research Institute for Culture and Cultural History. *Ainu no Mingu Jissoku Zushu* (Ainu Folkcrafts – Collection of Drawing and Figures). Biratori: Biratori-cho Council for Promoting Ainu Culture, 2014

Satouchi, Ai. *Ainu-shiki ekoroji-seikatsu: Haruzo Ekashi ni manabu shizen no chie* (Ainu Style Ecological Living: Haruzo Ekashi Teaches the Wisdom of Nature). Tokyo: Kabushiki gaisha Shogakukan, 2008

Chiri, Yukie. *Ainu Shin'yoshu* (Chiri Yukie's Ainu Epic Tales). Tokyo: Iwanami Shoten, 1978

Namikawa, Kenji. *Ainu Minzoku no Kiseki* (The Path of the Ainu People). Tokyo: Yamakawa Publishing, 2004

Mook. *Senjuumin Ainu Minzoku* (Bessatsu Taiyo) (The Ainu People (Extra Issue Taiyo). Tokyo: Heibonsha, 2004

Kinoshita, Seizo. *Shiraoikotan Kinoshita Seizo Isaku Shashin Shu* (Shiraoikotan: Kinoshita Seizo's Posthumous Photography Collection). Hokkaido Shiraoi-gun Shiraoi-cho: Shiraoi Heritage Conservation Foundation, 1988

The Ainu Museum. *Ainu no Ifuku Bunka* (The Culture of Ainu Clothing). Hokkaido Shiraoi-gun Shiraoi-cho: Shiraoi Ainu Museum, 1991

Keira, Tomoko and Kaji, Sayaka. *Ainu no Shiki* (Ainu's Four Seasons). Tokyo: Akashi Shoten, 1995

Fukuoka, Itoko and Sato, Kazuko. *Ainu Shokubutsushi* (Ainu Botanical Journal). Chiba Urayasu-Shi: Sofukan, 1995

Hayakawa, Noboru. *Ainu no Minzoku* (Ainu Folklore). Iwasaki Bijutsusha, 1983

Sunazawa, Kura. *Ku Sukuppu Orushibe* (The Memories of My Generation). Hokkaido, Sapporo-shi: Miyama Shobo, 1983

Haginaka, Miki et al. *Kikigaki Ainu no Shokuji* (Oral History of Ainu Diet). Tokyo: Rural Culture Association Japan, 1992

Nakagawa, Hiroshi. *New Express Ainu Go*. Tokyo: Hakusuisha, 2013

Nakagawa, Hiroshi. *Ainugo Chitose Hogen Jiten* (The Ainu-Japanese dictionary). Chiba Urayasu-Shi: Sofukan, 1995

Nakagawa, Hiroshi and Nakamoto, Mutsuko. *Kamuy Yukara de Ainu Go wo Manabu* (Learning Ainu with Kamuy Yukar). Tokyo: Hakusuisha, 2007

Nakagawa, Hiroshi. *Katari au Kotoba no Chikara – Kamuy tachi to Ikiru Sekai* (The Power of Spoken Words – Living in a World with Kamuy). Tokyo: Iwanami Shoten, 2010

Sarashina, Genzo and Sarashina, Hikari. *Kotan Seibutsu Ki <1 Juki / Zassou hen>* (Kotan Wildlife Vol. 1 – Trees and Weeds). Hosei University Publishing, 1992/2007

Sarashina, Genzo and Sarashina, Hikari. *Kotan Seibutsu Ki <2 Yacho / Kaijuu / Gyozoku hen>* (Kotan Wildlife Vol. 2 – Birds, Sea Creatures, and Fish). Hosei University Publishing, 1992/2007

Sarashina, Genzo and Sarashina, Hikari. *Kotan Seibutsu Ki <3 Yachou / Mizudori / Konchu hen>* (Kotan Wildlife Vol. 3 – Shorebirds, Seabirds, and Insects). Hosei University Publishing, 1992/2007

Sarashina, Genzo. *Ainu Minwashu* (Collection of Ainu Folktales). Kita Shobou, 1963

Sarashina, Genzo. *Ainu Rekishi to Minzoku* (Ainu History and Folklore). Shakai Shisousha, 1968

Kawakami Yuji. *Sarunkur Ainu Monogatari* (The Tale of Sarunkur Ainu). Kawagoe: Suzusawa Book Store, 2003/2005

Kawakami, Yuji. *Ekashi to Fuchi wo Tazunete* (Visiting Ekashi and Fuchi). Kawagoe: Suzusawa Book Store, 1991

Council for the Conservation of Ainu Culture. *Ainu Minzokushi* (Ainu People Magazine). Dai-ichi Hoki, 1970

Okamura, Kichiemon and Clancy, Judith A. *Ainu no Ishou* (The Clothes of the Ainu People). Kyoto Shoin, 1993

Hokkaido Cultural Property Protection Association. *Ainu Ifuku Chousa Houkokusho <1 Ainu Josei ga Denshou Suru Ibunka>* (The Ainu Clothing Research Report Vol. 1 – Traditional Clothing Passed Down Through Generations of Ainu Women). 1986

Yotsuji, Ichiro. Photos by Mizutani, Morio. *Ainu no Monyo* (Decorative Arts of the Ainu). Kasakura Publishing, 1981

Yoshida, Iwao. *Ainushi Shiryoshu* (Collection of Ainu Historical Documents). Hokkaido Publication Project Center, 1983

Kubodera, Itsuhiko. *Ainu no Mukashibanashi* (Old Stories of the Ainu). Miyaishoten, 1972

Kubodera, Itsuhiko (trans.). *Ainu Minzokushi* (Ainu People Magazine). Dai-ichi Hoki

Inoue, Koichi and Latyshev, Vladislav M. (coed.). *Karafuto Ainu no Mingu* (Karafuto Ainu Folkcraft). Hokkaido Publication Project Center, 2002

Russia ga Mita Ainu Bunka (Ainu Culture as Seen by Russia). The Foundation for Research and Promotion of Ainu Culture, 2013

Russia Minzokugaku Hakubutsukan Ainu Shiryoten—Russia ga Mita Shimaguni no Hitobito (Russia Museum of Ethnology Ainu Materials Exhibition—Island Peoples as Seen by Russia). The Foundation for Research and Promotion of Ainu Culture, 2005

The Foundation for Research and Promotion of Ainu Culture (ed.). *Senjima, Karafuto, Hokkaido—Ainu no Kurashi* (Ainu Life on the Kuril Islands, Karafuto and Hokkaido). The Senri Foundation, 2011

SPb-Ainu Project Group (ed.). *Russia Kagaku Academy Jinruigaku Minzokugaku Hakubutsukan Shozo Ainu Shiryo Mokuroku* (Ainu Collections of Peter the Great Museum of Anthropology and Ethnography Russian Academy of Sciences Catalogue). Sofukan, 1998

Yamamoto, Yuko. *Karafuto Ainu—Jukyo to Mingu* (Residences and Folkcraft of the Karafuto Ainu). Sagami Shobo, 1970

Yamamoto, Yuko (author and ed.). Chiri, Mashiho and Onuki, Emiko co-authors). *Karafuto Shizen Minzoku no Seikatsu* (Lifestyles of Karafuto Natural Peoples). Sagami Shobo, 1979

Chiri, Mashiho. *Chiri Mashiho Chosakushu 3 Seikatsu-shi / Minzokugaku-hen* (Mashiho Chiri Collected Works, Vol. 3: Lifestyles and Ethnology). Heibonsha, 1973

Yamamoto, Yuko. *Hoppo Shizen Minzoku Minwa Shusei* (Northern Natural Peoples Folk Tales Compilation). Sagami Shobo, 1968

Yamamoto, Yuko. *Karafuto Genshi Minzoku no Seikatsu* (Lifestyles of Karafuto Primitive Peoples). ARS, 1943

Nishitsuru, Sadaka. *Karafuto Ainu*. Miyama Shobo, 1974

Kasai, Takechiyo. *Karafuto Ainu no Minzoku* (Folklore of the Karafuto Ainu). Miyama Shobo, 1975

Tanigawa, Kenichi. Kita no Minzokushi-Sakhalin / Chishima no Minzoku (Northern Ethnography—Sakhalin / People of the Kuril Islands). San-Ichi Shobo Publishing Inc., 1997

Takabeya, Fukuhei. *Hoppoken no Ie* (Houses of the Northern Regions). Shokokusha Publishing Co., Ltd., 1943

Abashiri City Northern Folkore Cultural Preservation Society. *Uiruta no Kurashi to Mingu* (Uilta Lifestyles and Folkcraft). 1982

The Foundation for Research and Promotion of Ainu Culture (ed.). *Zaidan Hojin Ainu Bunka Fukko / Kenkyu Suishin Kiko Shuzo Mokuroku 7 (Ishida Shuzo Kyuzo Shashin)* (The Foundation for Research and Promotion of Ainu Culture Collection Catalog 7 (Ishida Collection Old Collection Photograph). The Foundation for Research and Promotion of Ainu Culture, 2012

Uilta Society Museum Steering Committee (ed.). *Shiryokan Jakka Duxuni Tenji Sakuhinshu* (Museum Jakka Duxuni Exhibition Works Collection), 2002

Bird, Isabella L. (author), Kobari, Kosai (trans.) *Meiji Shoki no Emishi Tanboki* (Report on Emishi in the Early Meiji Era). Sarorun Shobo, 1977

Munro, N.G. (author), Seligman, B.Z. (ed.), Tetsuro, Komatsu (trans.). *Ainu no Shinko to Sono Gishiki* (Ainu Creed and Cult). Kokushokankokai, 2002

Batchelor, John (author), Tetsuro, Komatsu (trans.). *Ainu no Kurashi to Densho* (Ainu Life and Lore). Hokkaido Publication Project Center, 1999

Shinmyo, Hidehito. *Ainu Fuzokuga no Kenkyu: Kinsei Hokkaido ni Okeru Ainu to Bijutsu* (Study of Ainu Genre Painting: Ainu and Art in Modern Hokkaido). Nakanishi Publishing, 2011

Aoki, Aiko (teller). Nagai, Hiroshi (recorder). Ainu O-san Baa-chan no Upashikuma Densho no Chie no Kiroku (Ainu Midwife Upaskuma: A Record of Traditional Wisdom). Jushinsha, 1998

Segawa, Kiyoko. *Ainu no Konin* (Married Ainu). Miraisha, 1998

Hitchcock, R. (author) Kitakamae, Yasuo (trans.). *Ainujin to Sono Bunka—Meiji Chuki no Ainu no Mura Kara—* (The Ainu People and Their Culture: From the Ainu Villages of the Mid-Meiji Era). Rokko Shuppan, 1990

Landor, A.S. (author). Toda, Sachiko (trans.). *Ezo-chi Isshu Hitori Tabi: Omoide no Ainu Country* (Traveling Alone Around Ezo: Ainu Country as I Remember It). Miraisha, 1985

Kono, Motomichi (ed.). Hoppo no Mingu <1>—Nikubun, Uita, Orochon no Kogei to Shishu— (Northern Folk Art <1>... Arts and Embroidery of the Nivkh, Uilta, Oroqen). Hokkaido Publication Project Center, 1976

Kono, Motomichi (ed.). Hoppo no Mingu <2>—Enchu (Karafuto Ainu) no Busshitsu Bunka— (Northern Folk Art <2>... Material Culture of the Enchiw (Karafuto Ainu)). Hokkaido Publication Project Center, 1979

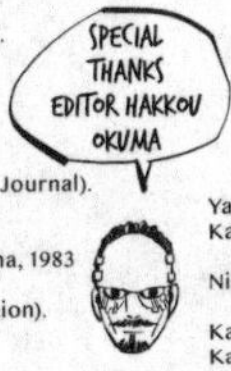
SPECIAL THANKS EDITOR HAKKOU OKUMA

Kanto or wa yaku sak no arankep sinep ka isam.

Nothing comes from heaven without purpose. —Ainu proverb

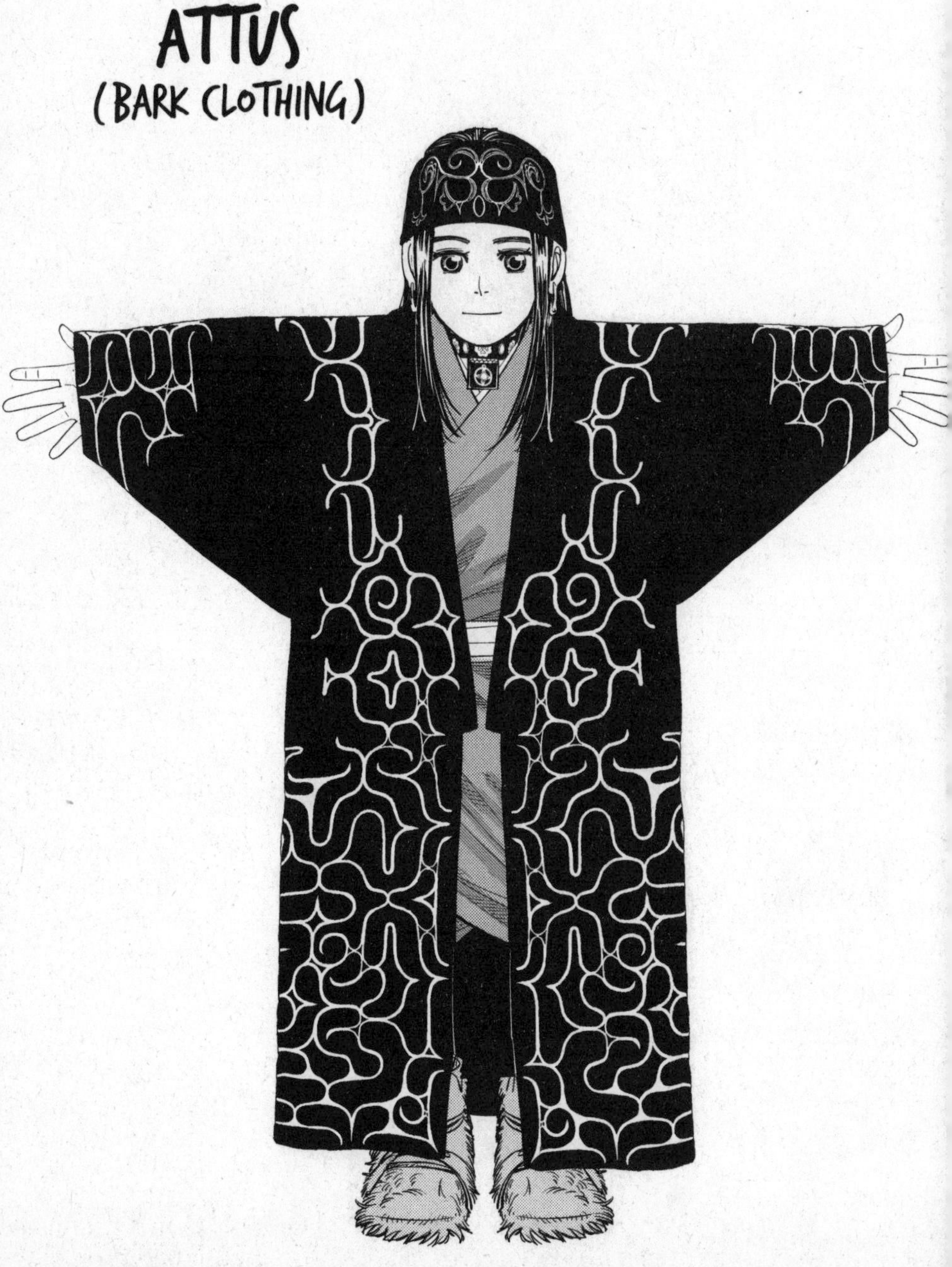
ATTUS
(BARK CLOTHING)

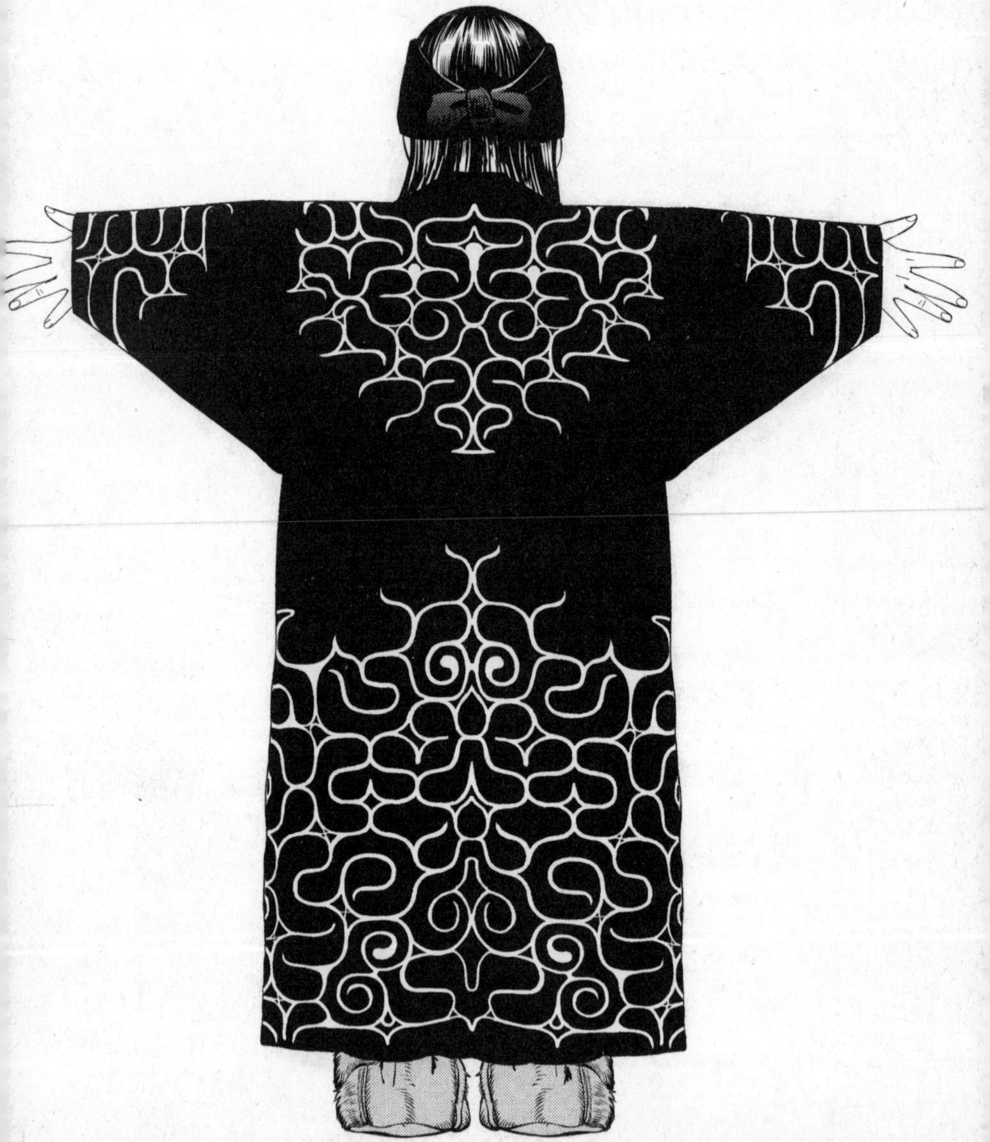

GOLDEN KAMUY

Volume 27
VIZ Signature Edition

Story/Art by **Satoru Noda**

GOLDEN KAMUY © 2014 by Satoru Noda
All rights reserved.
First published in Japan in 2014 by SHUEISHA Inc., Tokyo.
English translation rights arranged by SHUEISHA Inc.

Translation/John Werry
Touch-Up Art & Lettering/Steve Dutro
Design/Shawn Carrico
Editor/Mike Montesa

The stories, characters, and incidents mentioned in this publication are entirely fictional.

Printed in Canada

Published by VIZ Media, LLC
P.O. Box 77010
San Francisco, CA 94107

10 9 8 7 6 5 4 3 2 1
First printing, September 2022

VIZ SIGNATURE

MEDIA
viz.com

THIS IS THE LAST PAGE.

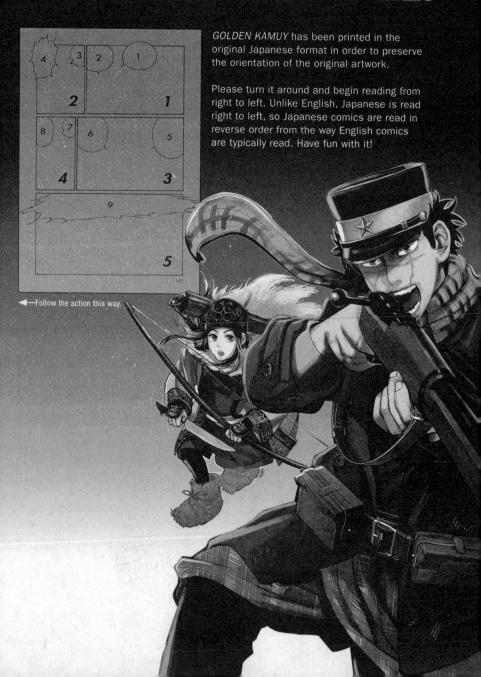

GOLDEN KAMUY has been printed in the original Japanese format in order to preserve the orientation of the original artwork.

Please turn it around and begin reading from right to left. Unlike English, Japanese is read right to left, so Japanese comics are read in reverse order from the way English comics are typically read. Have fun with it!

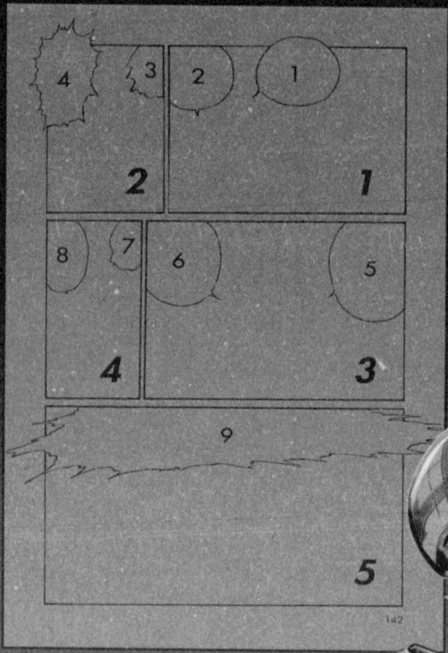
1
2
3
4
5
6
7
8
9
1
2
3
4
5
142

←Follow the action this way.

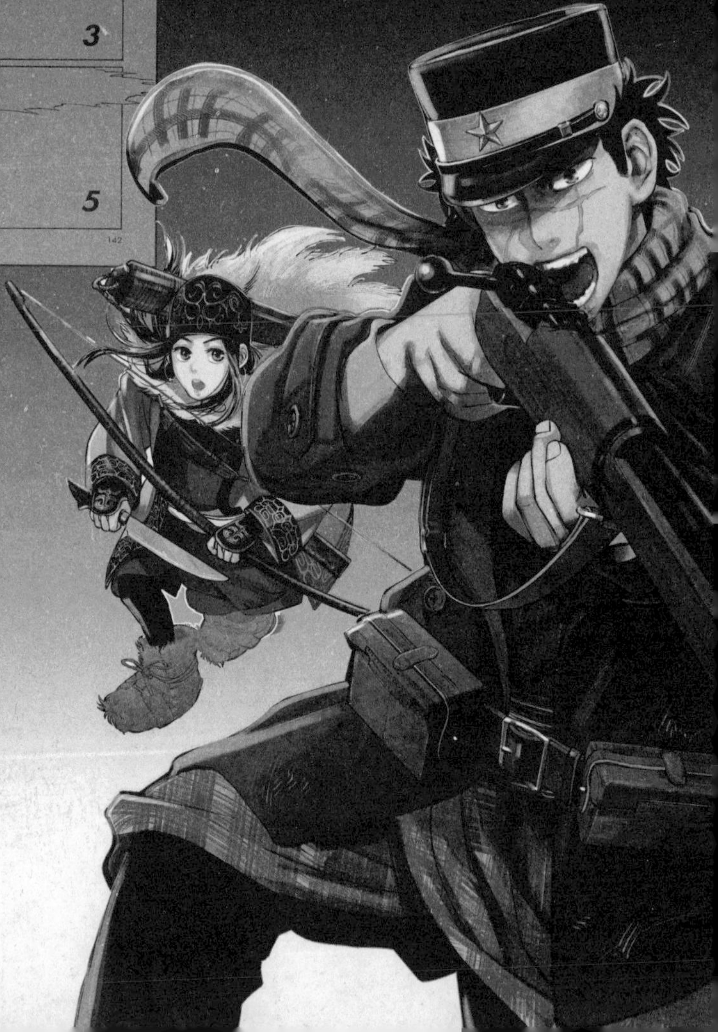